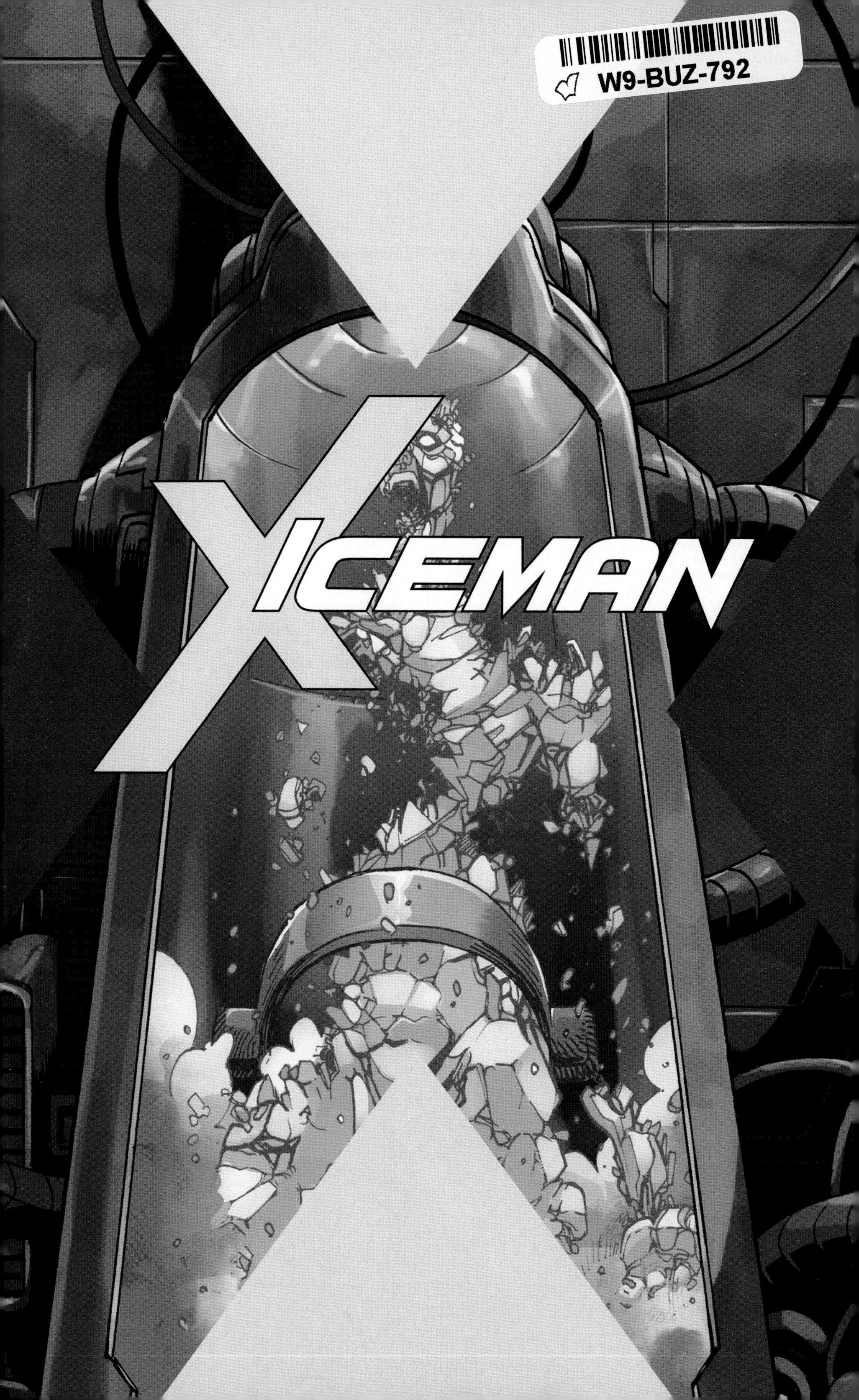
ICEMAN

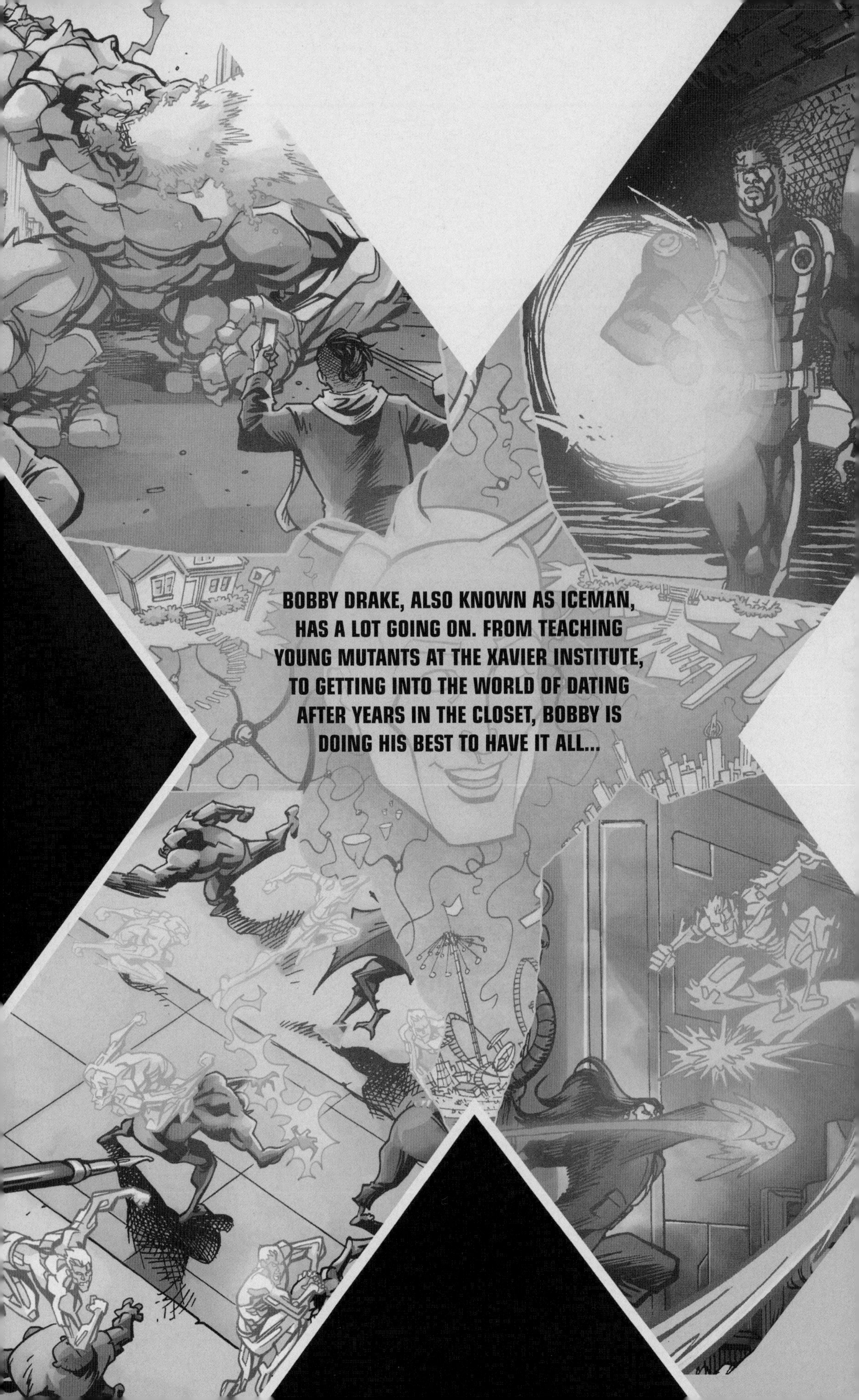
BOBBY DRAKE, ALSO KNOWN AS ICEMAN, HAS A LOT GOING ON. FROM TEACHING YOUNG MUTANTS AT THE XAVIER INSTITUTE, TO GETTING INTO THE WORLD OF DATING AFTER YEARS IN THE CLOSET, BOBBY IS DOING HIS BEST TO HAVE IT ALL...

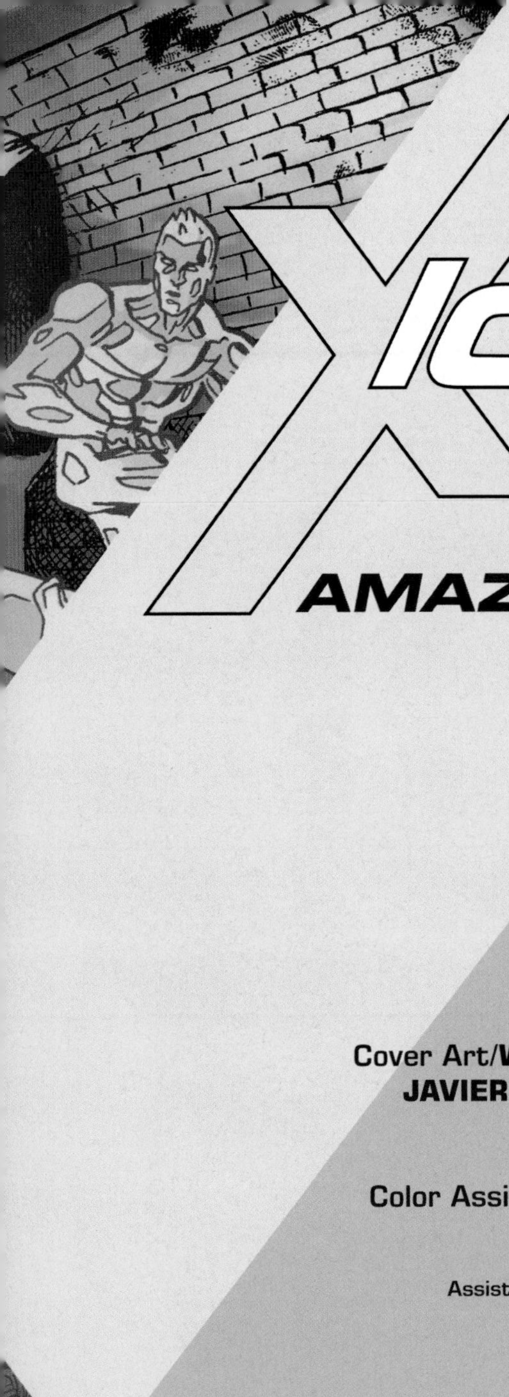

ICEMAN

AMAZING FRIENDS

Writer/**SINA GRACE**

Artist/**NATHAN STOCKMAN**

Color Artists/**FEDERICO BLEE**
& ANDRES MOSSA (Iceman #5)

Letterer/**VC's JOE SABINO**

Cover Art/**W. SCOTT FORBES** (Iceman #1-5) and
JAVIER GARRÓN & **ROMULO FAJARDO JR.**
(Uncanny X-Men: Winter's End)

Color Assistant/**ULISES ARREOLA** (Iceman #4)

Editor/**DARREN SHAN**
Assistant Editors/**ANNALISE BISSA** & **DANNY KHAZEM**
X-Men Group Editor/**JORDAN D. WHITE**

ICEMAN CREATED BY **STAN LEE** & **JACK KIRBY**

Collection Editor/**KATERI WOODY** • Assistant Editor/**CAITLIN O'CONNELL**
Editor, Special Projects/**MARK D. BEAZLEY** • Senior Editor, Special Projects/ **JENNIFER GRÜNWALD**
VP Production & Special Projects/**JEFF YOUNGQUIST** • SVP Print, Sales & Marketing/**DAVID GABRIEL**
Book Designer/**STACIE ZUCKER** WITH **JAY BOWEN**

Editor in Chief/**C.B. CEBULSKI** • Chief Creative Officer/**JOE QUESADA**
President/**DAN BUCKLEY** • Executive Producer/**ALAN FINE**

ICEMAN VOL. 3: AMAZING FRIENDS. Contains material originally published in magazine form as ICEMAN #1-5 and UNCANNY X-MEN: WINTER'S END #1. First printing 2019. ISBN 978-1-302-91483-7. Published by MARVEL WORLDWIDE, INC., a subsidiary of MARVEL ENTERTAINMENT, LLC. OFFICE OF PUBLICATION: 135 West 50th Street, New York, NY 10020. **Printed in the U.S.A.** DAN BUCKLEY, President, Marvel Entertainment; JOHN NEE, Publisher; JOE QUESADA, Chief Creative Officer; TOM BREVOORT, SVP of Publishing; DAVID BOGART, SVP of Business Affairs & Operations, Publishing & Partnership; DAVID GABRIEL, SVP of Sales & Marketing, Publishing; JEFF YOUNGQUIST, VP of Production & Special Projects; DAN CARR, Executive Director of Publishing Technology; ALEX MORALES, Director of Publishing Operations; DAN EDINGTON, Managing Editor; SUSAN CRESPI, Production Manager; STAN LEE, Chairman Emeritus. For information regarding advertising in Marvel Comics or on Marvel.com, please contact Vit DeBellis, Custom Solutions & Integrated Advertising Manager, at vdebellis@marvel.com. For Marvel subscription inquiries, please call 888-511-5480. **Manufactured between 2/15/2019 and 3/19/2019 by LSC COMMUNICATIONS INC., KENDALLVILLE, IN, USA.**

10 9 8 7 6 5 4 3 2 1

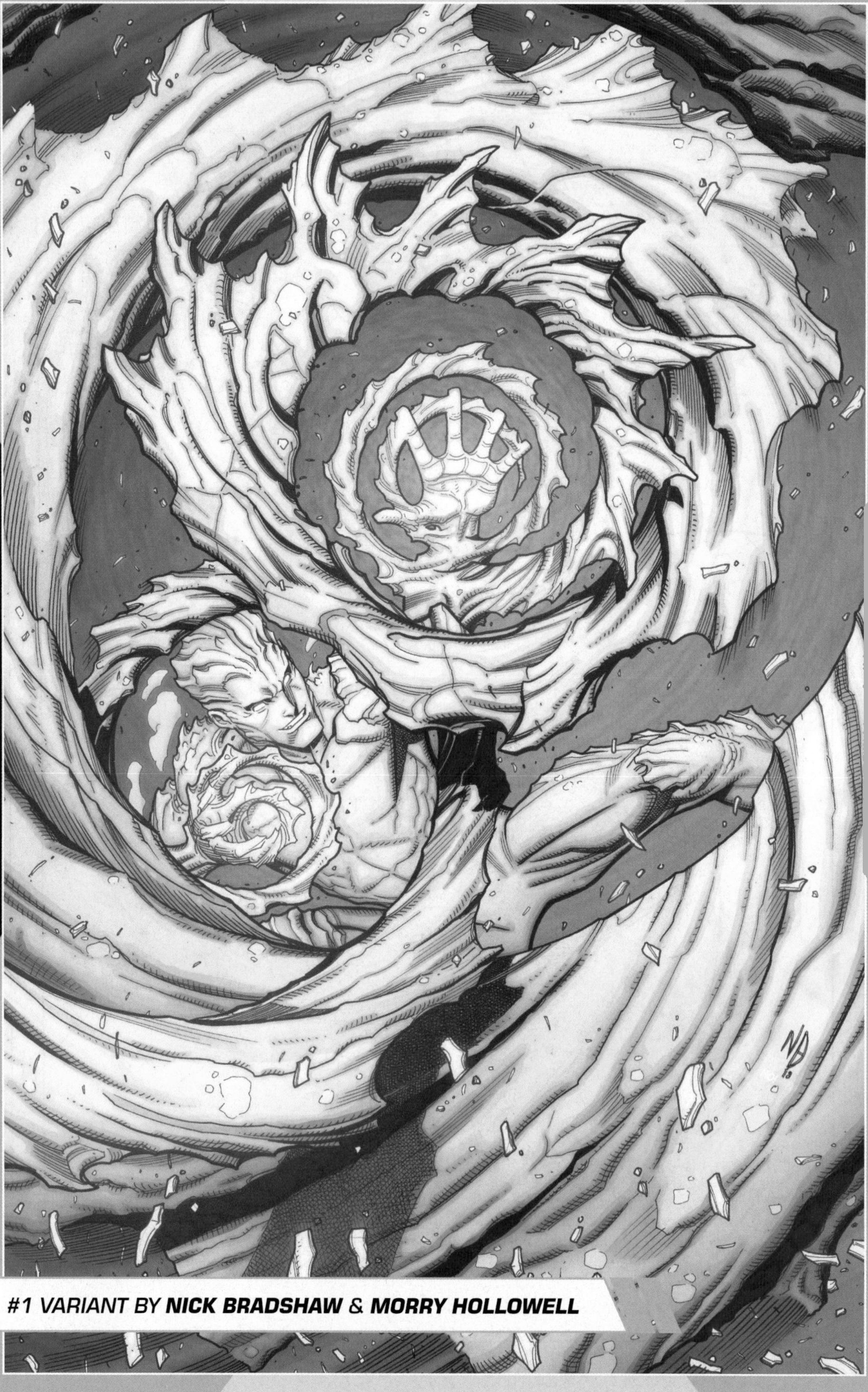

#1 VARIANT BY **NICK BRADSHAW** & **MORRY HOLLOWELL**

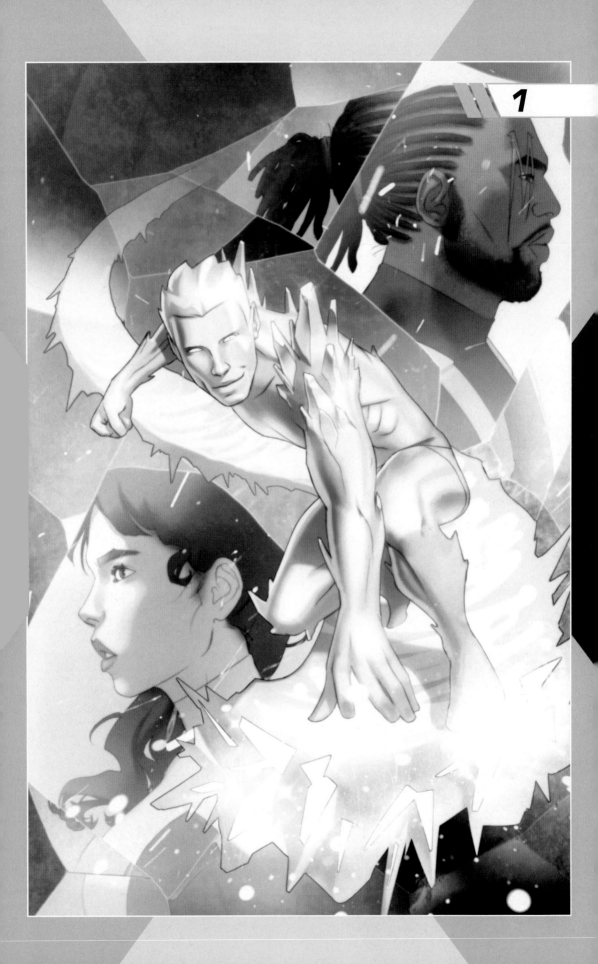

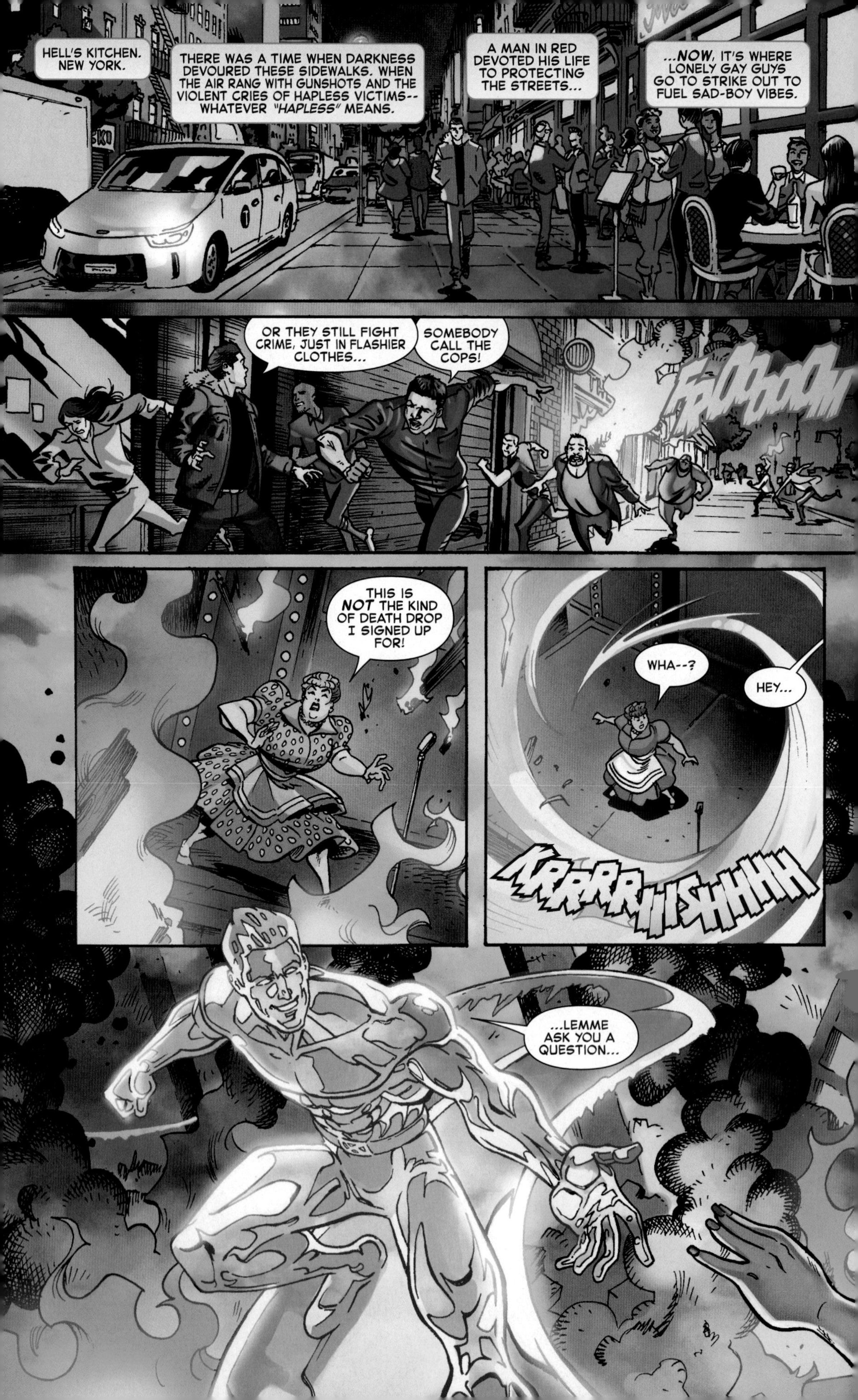
HELL'S KITCHEN. NEW YORK.
THERE WAS A TIME WHEN DARKNESS DEVOURED THESE SIDEWALKS. WHEN THE AIR RANG WITH GUNSHOTS AND THE VIOLENT CRIES OF HAPLESS VICTIMS-- WHATEVER "HAPLESS" MEANS.
A MAN IN RED DEVOTED HIS LIFE TO PROTECTING THE STREETS...
...NOW, IT'S WHERE LONELY GAY GUYS GO TO STRIKE OUT TO FUEL SAD-BOY VIBES.
OR THEY STILL FIGHT CRIME, JUST IN FLASHIER CLOTHES...
SOMEBODY CALL THE COPS!
FBLOOOOOOM
THIS IS NOT THE KIND OF DEATH DROP I SIGNED UP FOR!
WHA--?
HEY...
KRRRRIIISHHHH
...LEMME ASK YOU A QUESTION...

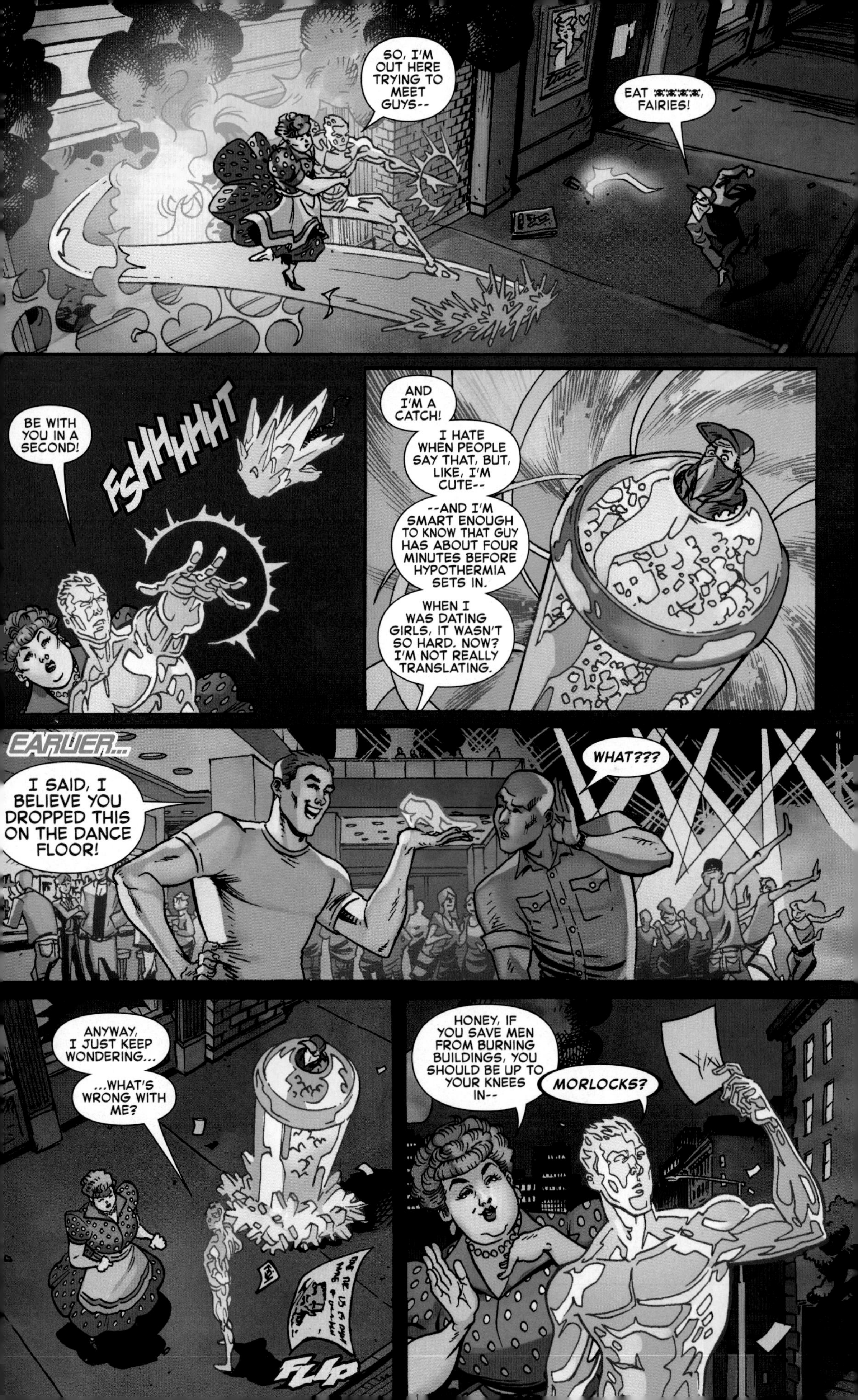
SO, I'M OUT HERE TRYING TO MEET GUYS--
EAT ☠✱☠✱, FAIRIES!
BE WITH YOU IN A SECOND!
FSHHHHHT
AND I'M A CATCH!
I HATE WHEN PEOPLE SAY THAT, BUT, LIKE, I'M CUTE--
--AND I'M SMART ENOUGH TO KNOW THAT GUY HAS ABOUT FOUR MINUTES BEFORE HYPOTHERMIA SETS IN.
WHEN I WAS DATING GIRLS, IT WASN'T SO HARD. NOW? I'M NOT REALLY TRANSLATING.
EARLIER...
I SAID, I BELIEVE YOU DROPPED THIS ON THE DANCE FLOOR!
WHAT???
ANYWAY, I JUST KEEP WONDERING...
...WHAT'S WRONG WITH ME?
FLIP
HONEY, IF YOU SAVE MEN FROM BURNING BUILDINGS, YOU SHOULD BE UP TO YOUR KNEES IN--
MORLOCKS?

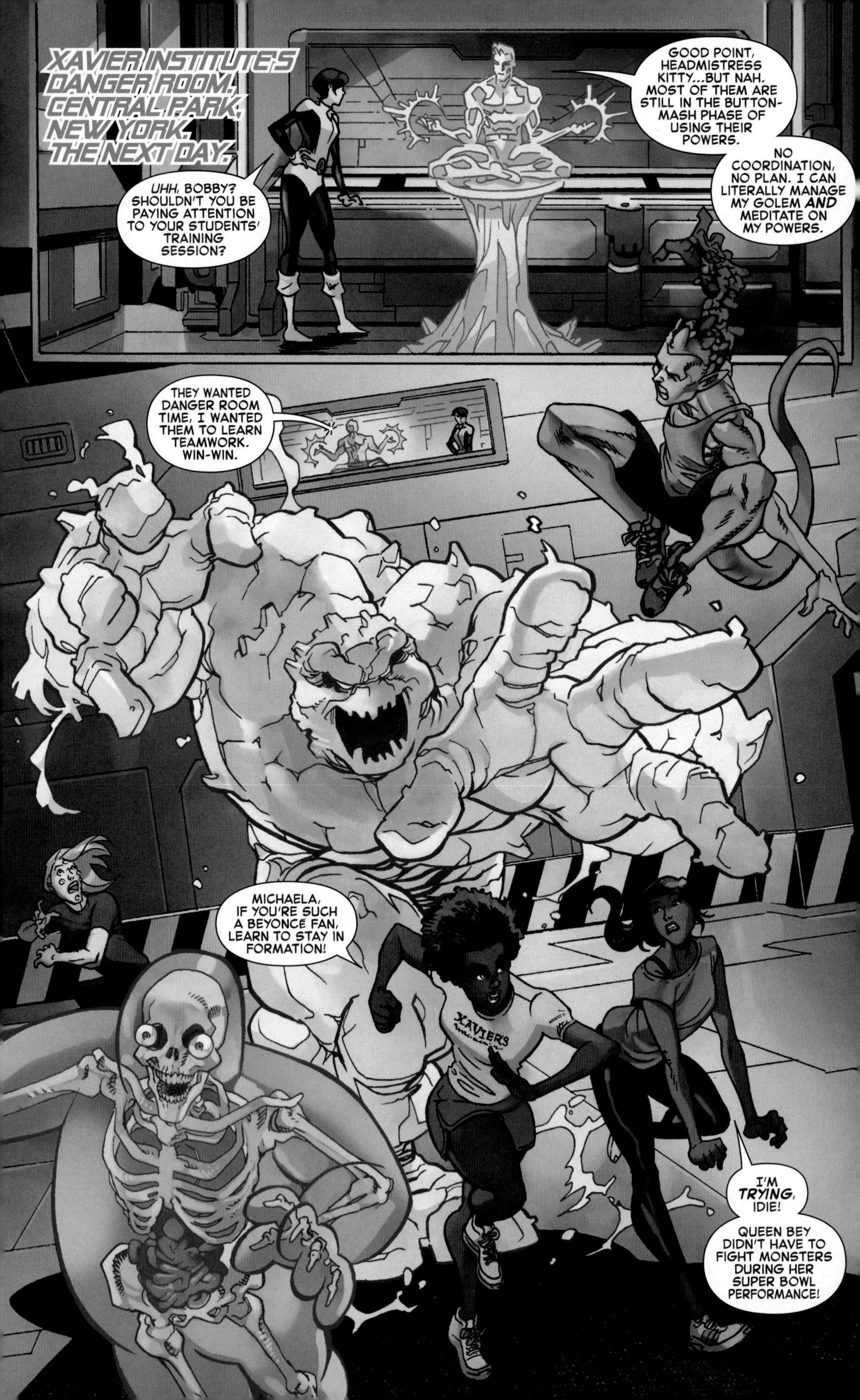
XAVIER INSTITUTE'S DANGER ROOM. CENTRAL PARK, NEW YORK. THE NEXT DAY.
UHH, BOBBY? SHOULDN'T YOU BE PAYING ATTENTION TO YOUR STUDENTS' TRAINING SESSION?
GOOD POINT, HEADMISTRESS KITTY...BUT NAH. MOST OF THEM ARE STILL IN THE BUTTON-MASH PHASE OF USING THEIR POWERS.
NO COORDINATION, NO PLAN. I CAN LITERALLY MANAGE MY GOLEM AND MEDITATE ON MY POWERS.
THEY WANTED DANGER ROOM TIME, I WANTED THEM TO LEARN TEAMWORK. WIN-WIN.
XAVIER'S
MICHAELA, IF YOU'RE SUCH A BEYONCE FAN, LEARN TO STAY IN FORMATION!
I'M TRYING, IDIE!
QUEEN BEY DIDN'T HAVE TO FIGHT MONSTERS DURING HER SUPER BOWL PERFORMANCE!

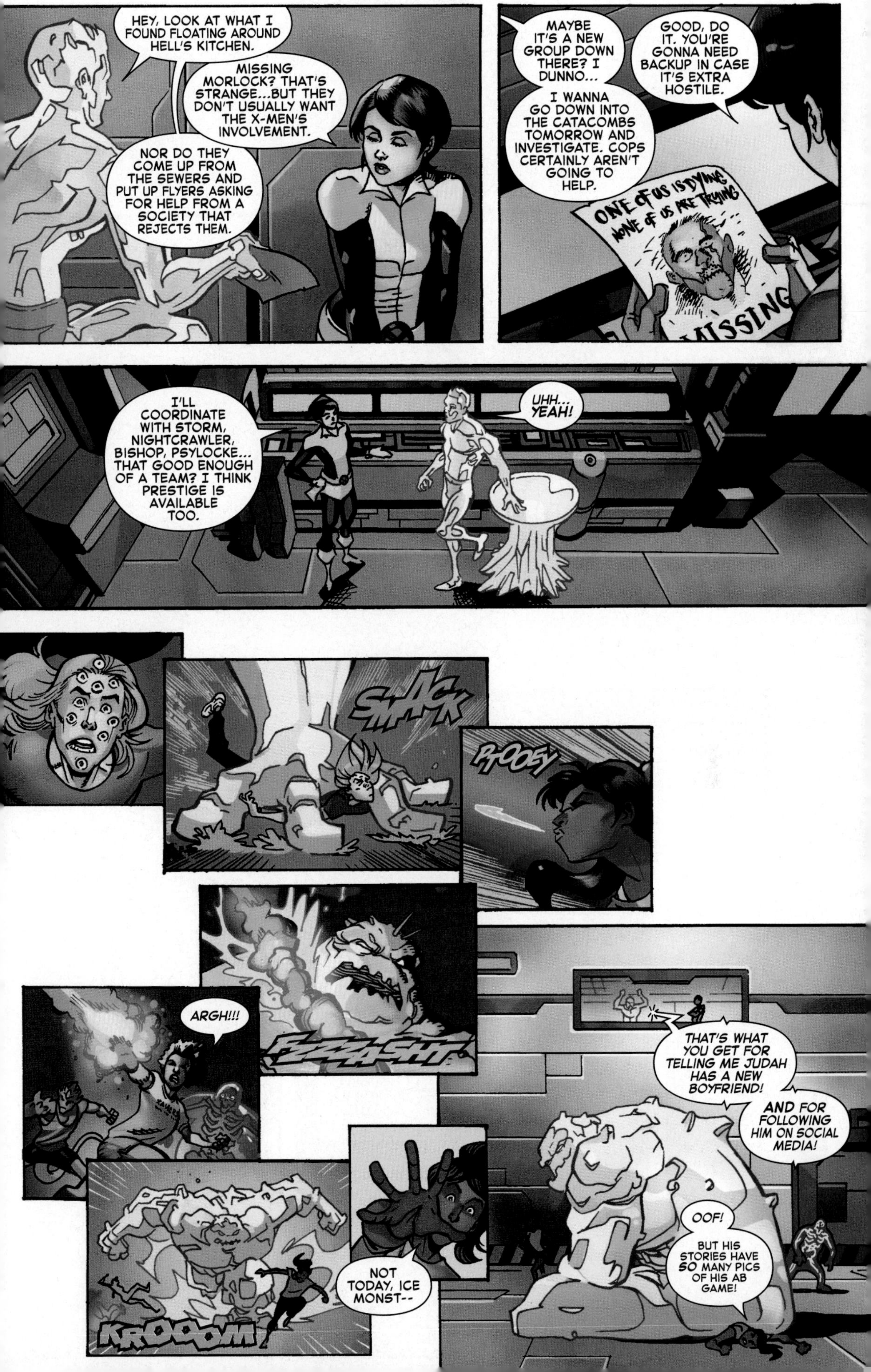
HEY, LOOK AT WHAT I FOUND FLOATING AROUND HELL'S KITCHEN.
MISSING MORLOCK? THAT'S STRANGE...BUT THEY DON'T USUALLY WANT THE X-MEN'S INVOLVEMENT.
NOR DO THEY COME UP FROM THE SEWERS AND PUT UP FLYERS ASKING FOR HELP FROM A SOCIETY THAT REJECTS THEM.
MAYBE IT'S A NEW GROUP DOWN THERE? I DUNNO...
I WANNA GO DOWN INTO THE CATACOMBS TOMORROW AND INVESTIGATE. COPS CERTAINLY AREN'T GOING TO HELP.
GOOD, DO IT. YOU'RE GONNA NEED BACKUP IN CASE IT'S EXTRA HOSTILE.
ONE OF US IS DYING
NONE OF US ARE TRYING
MISSING
I'LL COORDINATE WITH STORM, NIGHTCRAWLER, BISHOP, PSYLOCKE... THAT GOOD ENOUGH OF A TEAM? I THINK PRESTIGE IS AVAILABLE TOO.
UHH... YEAH!
SMACK
PTOOEY
FZZZZASHT
ARGH!!!
KROOOM
NOT TODAY, ICE MONST--
THAT'S WHAT YOU GET FOR TELLING ME JUDAH HAS A NEW BOYFRIEND!
AND FOR FOLLOWING HIM ON SOCIAL MEDIA!
OOF!
BUT HIS STORIES HAVE SO MANY PICS OF HIS AB GAME!

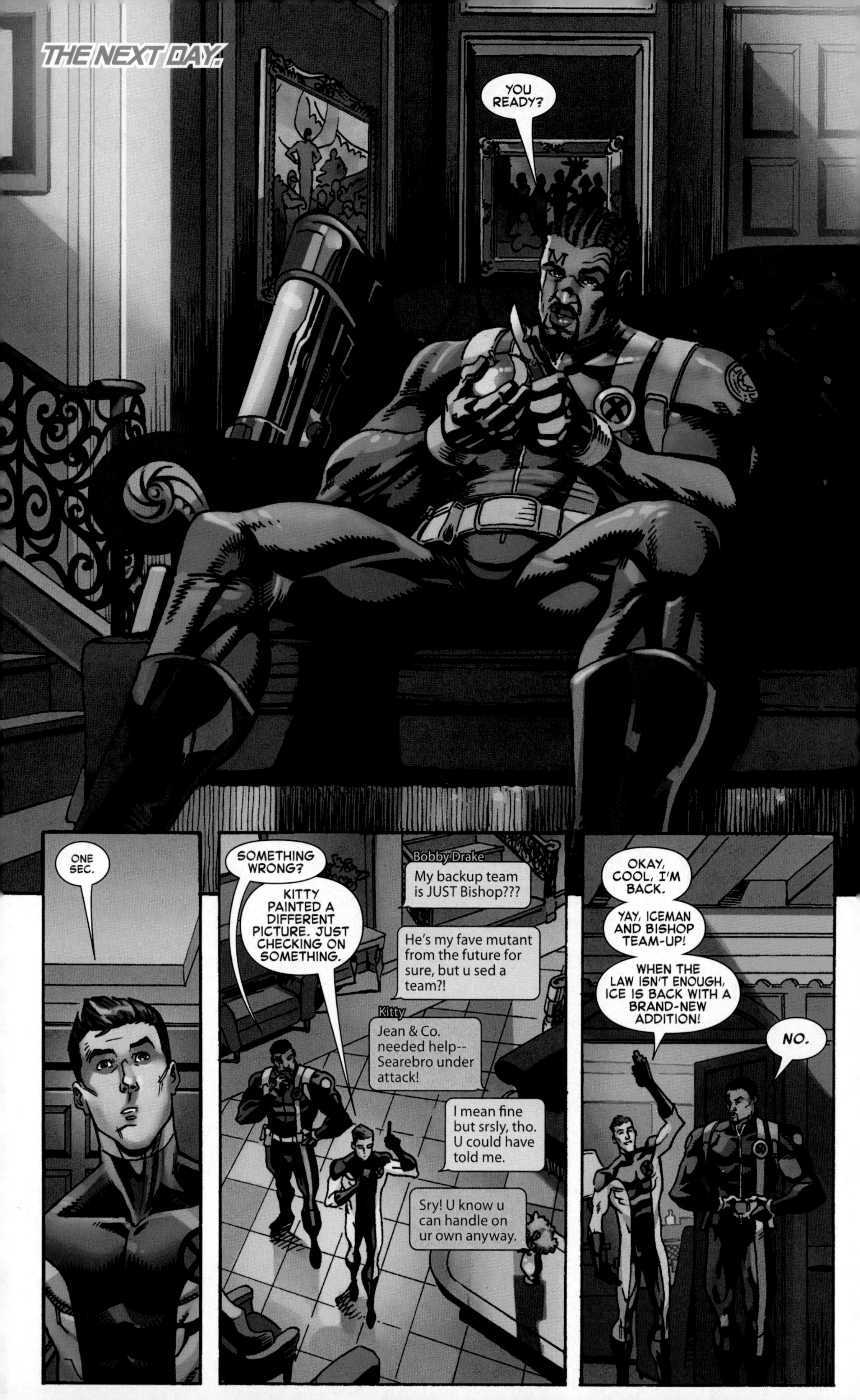
THE NEXT DAY.
YOU READY?
ONE SEC.
SOMETHING WRONG?
KITTY PAINTED A DIFFERENT PICTURE. JUST CHECKING ON SOMETHING.
Bobby Drake
My backup team is JUST Bishop???
He's my fave mutant from the future for sure, but u sed a team?!
Kitty
Jean & Co. needed help-- Searebro under attack!
I mean fine but srsly, tho. U could have told me.
Sry! U know u can handle on ur own anyway.
OKAY, COOL, I'M BACK.
YAY, ICEMAN AND BISHOP TEAM-UP!
WHEN THE LAW ISN'T ENOUGH, ICE IS BACK WITH A BRAND-NEW ADDITION!
NO.

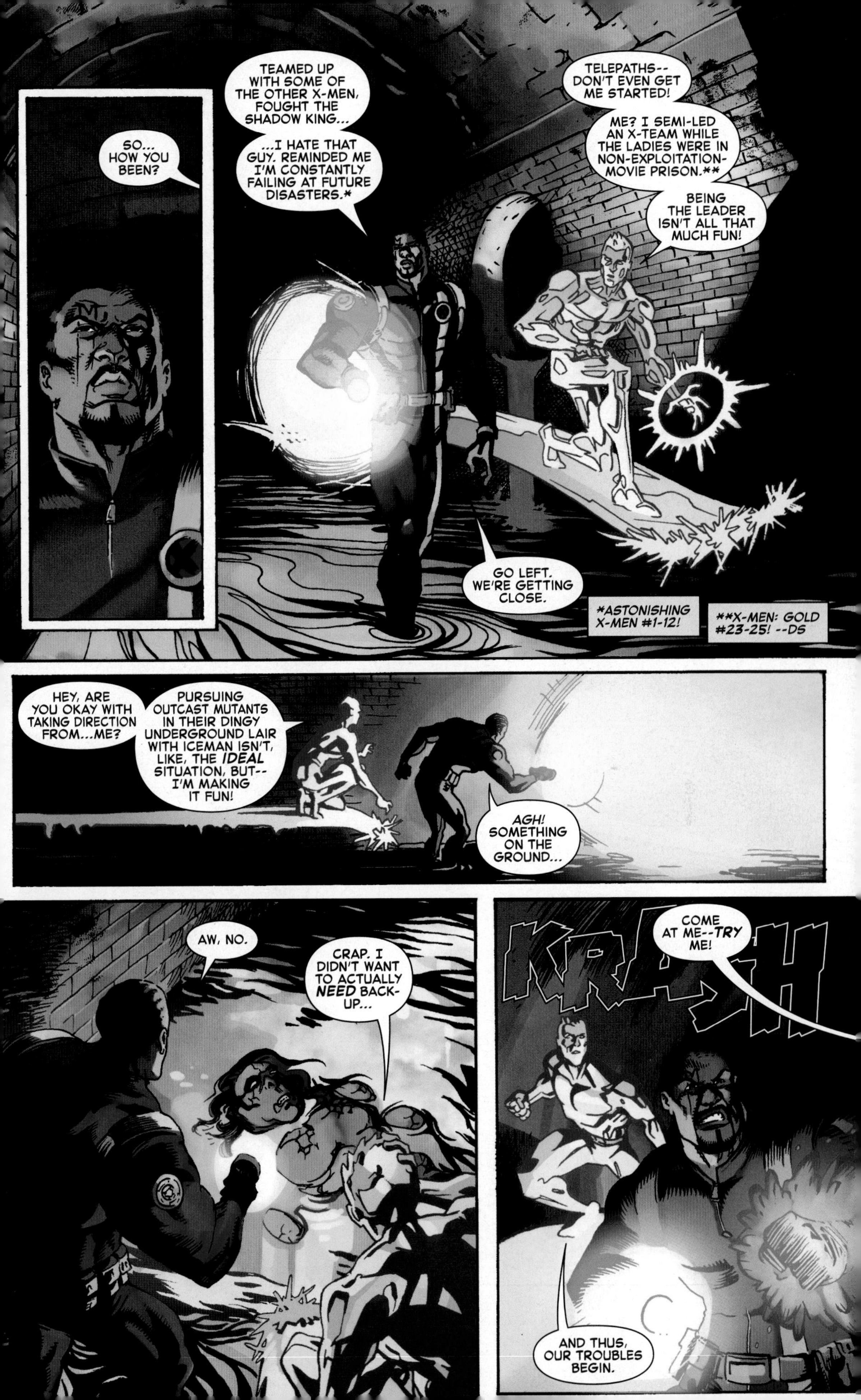
SO... HOW YOU BEEN?
TEAMED UP WITH SOME OF THE OTHER X-MEN, FOUGHT THE SHADOW KING...
...I HATE THAT GUY. REMINDED ME I'M CONSTANTLY FAILING AT FUTURE DISASTERS.*
TELEPATHS--DON'T EVEN GET ME STARTED!
ME? I SEMI-LED AN X-TEAM WHILE THE LADIES WERE IN NON-EXPLOITATION-MOVIE PRISON.**
BEING THE LEADER ISN'T ALL THAT MUCH FUN!
GO LEFT. WE'RE GETTING CLOSE.
*ASTONISHING X-MEN #1-12!
**X-MEN: GOLD #23-25! --DS
HEY, ARE YOU OKAY WITH TAKING DIRECTION FROM...ME?
PURSUING OUTCAST MUTANTS IN THEIR DINGY UNDERGROUND LAIR WITH ICEMAN ISN'T, LIKE, THE IDEAL SITUATION, BUT--I'M MAKING IT FUN!
AGH! SOMETHING ON THE GROUND...
AW, NO.
CRAP. I DIDN'T WANT TO ACTUALLY NEED BACK-UP...
KRASH
COME AT ME--TRY ME!
AND THUS, OUR TROUBLES BEGIN.

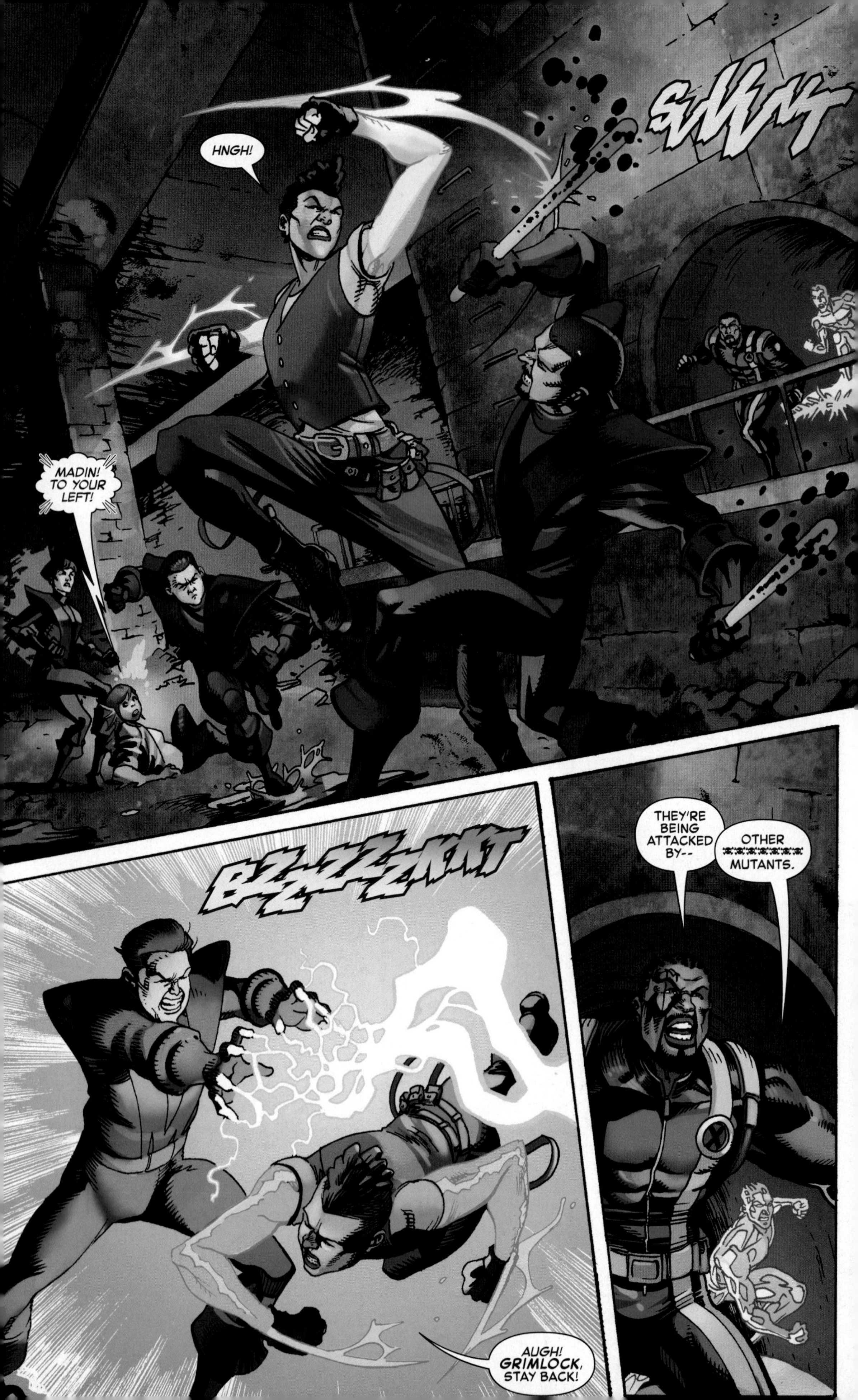
HNGH!
SSNIKT
MADIN! TO YOUR LEFT!
BZZZZZZKKKT
THEY'RE BEING ATTACKED BY--
OTHER ☠☠☠☠☠☠☠ MUTANTS.
AUGH! GRIMLOCK, STAY BACK!

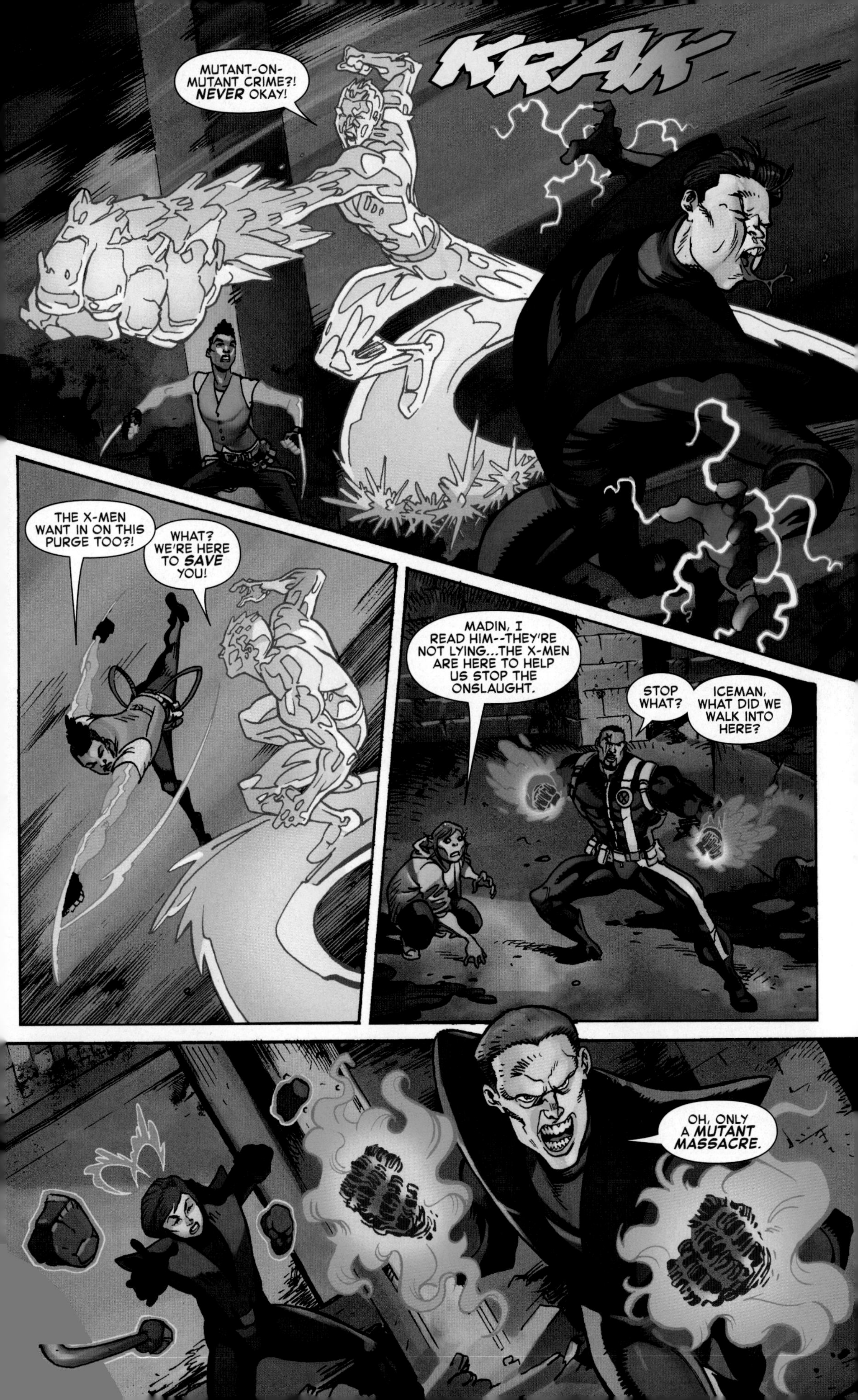
KRAK
MUTANT-ON-MUTANT CRIME?! NEVER OKAY!
THE X-MEN WANT IN ON THIS PURGE TOO?!
WHAT? WE'RE HERE TO SAVE YOU!
MADIN, I READ HIM--THEY'RE NOT LYING...THE X-MEN ARE HERE TO HELP US STOP THE ONSLAUGHT.
STOP WHAT?
ICEMAN, WHAT DID WE WALK INTO HERE?
OH, ONLY A MUTANT MASSACRE.

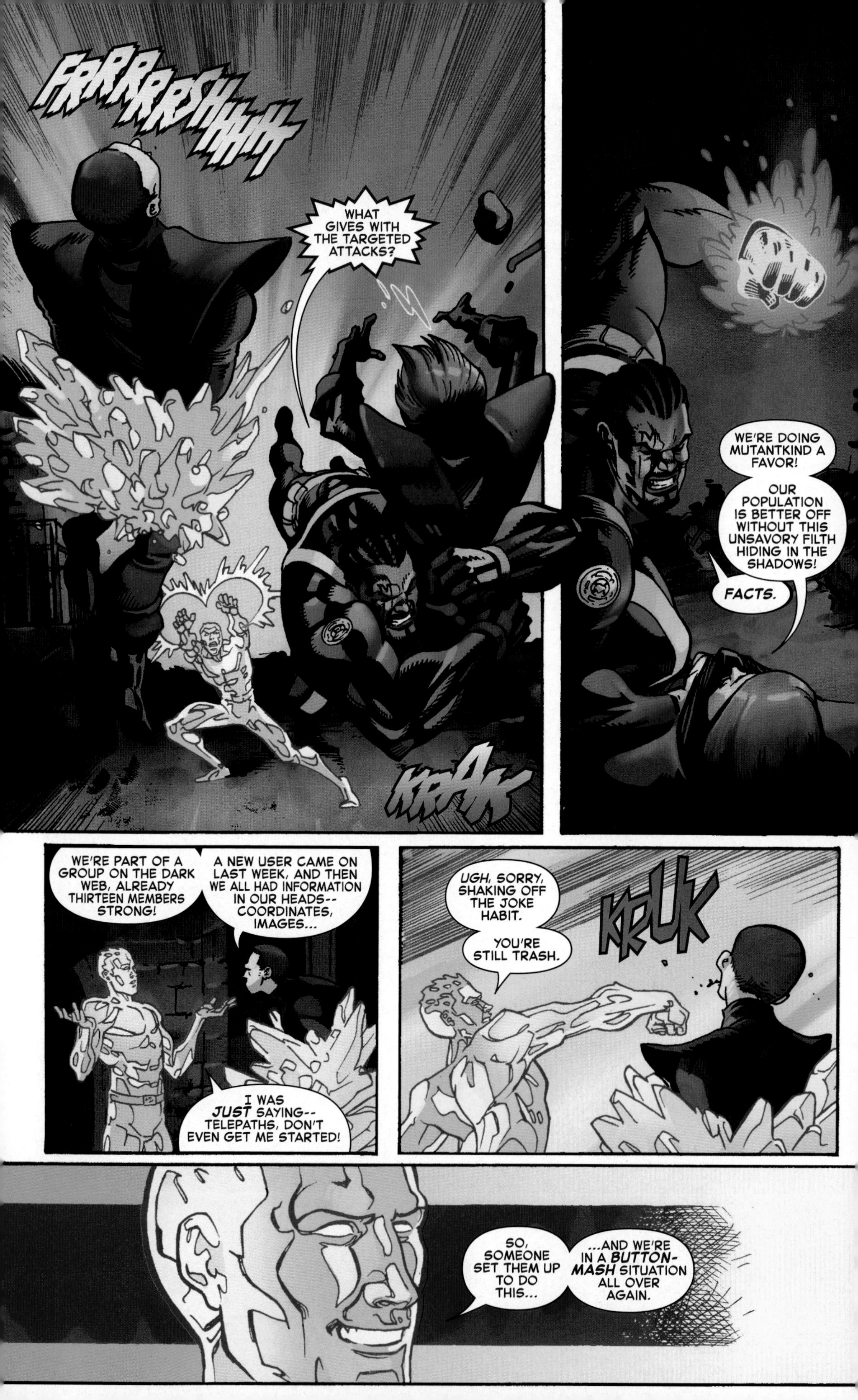
FRRRRRSHHHH
WHAT GIVES WITH THE TARGETED ATTACKS?
KRAK
WE'RE DOING MUTANTKIND A FAVOR!
OUR POPULATION IS BETTER OFF WITHOUT THIS UNSAVORY FILTH HIDING IN THE SHADOWS!
FACTS.
WE'RE PART OF A GROUP ON THE DARK WEB, ALREADY THIRTEEN MEMBERS STRONG!
A NEW USER CAME ON LAST WEEK, AND THEN WE ALL HAD INFORMATION IN OUR HEADS-- COORDINATES, IMAGES...
I WAS JUST SAYING-- TELEPATHS, DON'T EVEN GET ME STARTED!
UGH, SORRY, SHAKING OFF THE JOKE HABIT.
YOU'RE STILL TRASH.
KRUK
SO, SOMEONE SET THEM UP TO DO THIS...
...AND WE'RE IN A BUTTON-MASH SITUATION ALL OVER AGAIN.

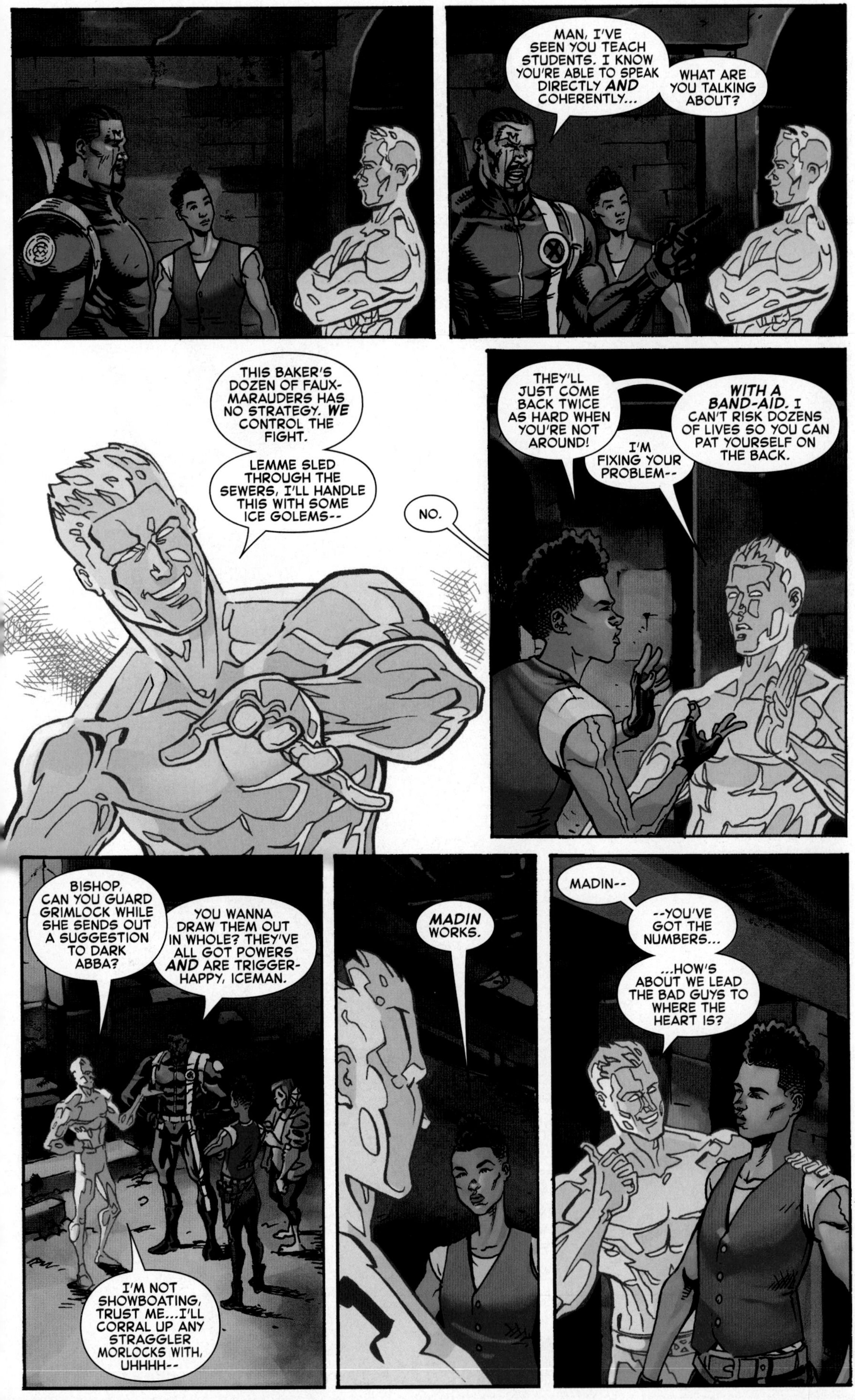
MAN, I'VE SEEN YOU TEACH STUDENTS. I KNOW YOU'RE ABLE TO SPEAK DIRECTLY AND COHERENTLY...
WHAT ARE YOU TALKING ABOUT?
THIS BAKER'S DOZEN OF FAUX-MARAUDERS HAS NO STRATEGY. WE CONTROL THE FIGHT.
LEMME SLED THROUGH THE SEWERS, I'LL HANDLE THIS WITH SOME ICE GOLEMS--
NO.
THEY'LL JUST COME BACK TWICE AS HARD WHEN YOU'RE NOT AROUND!
I'M FIXING YOUR PROBLEM--
WITH A BAND-AID. I CAN'T RISK DOZENS OF LIVES SO YOU CAN PAT YOURSELF ON THE BACK.
BISHOP, CAN YOU GUARD GRIMLOCK WHILE SHE SENDS OUT A SUGGESTION TO DARK ABBA?
YOU WANNA DRAW THEM OUT IN WHOLE? THEY'VE ALL GOT POWERS AND ARE TRIGGER-HAPPY, ICEMAN.
I'M NOT SHOWBOATING, TRUST ME...I'LL CORRAL UP ANY STRAGGLER MORLOCKS WITH, UHHHH--
MADIN WORKS.
MADIN--
--YOU'VE GOT THE NUMBERS...
...HOW'S ABOUT WE LEAD THE BAD GUYS TO WHERE THE HEART IS?

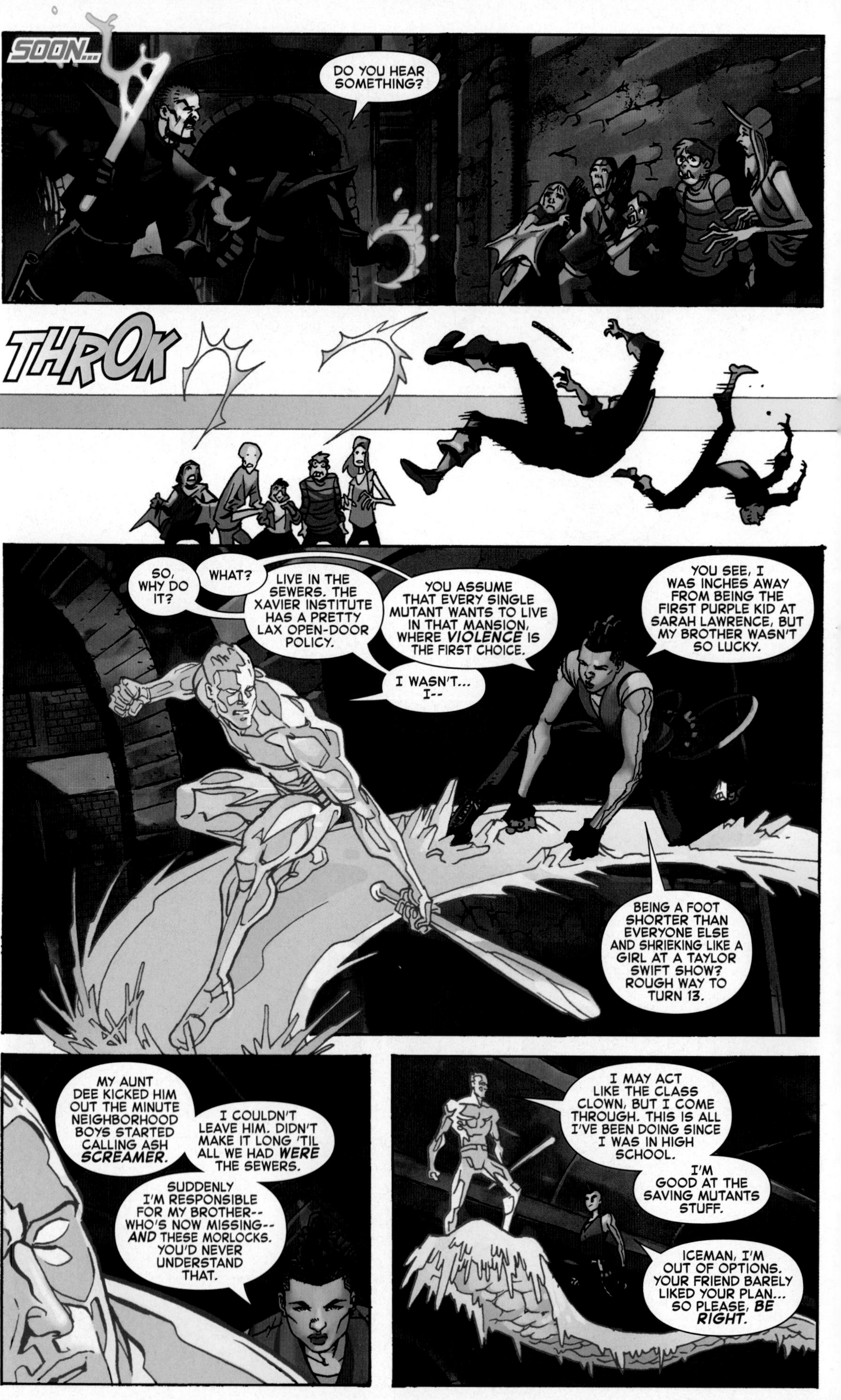
SOON...
DO YOU HEAR SOMETHING?
THROK
SO, WHY DO IT?
WHAT?
LIVE IN THE SEWERS. THE XAVIER INSTITUTE HAS A PRETTY LAX OPEN-DOOR POLICY.
YOU ASSUME THAT EVERY SINGLE MUTANT WANTS TO LIVE IN THAT MANSION, WHERE VIOLENCE IS THE FIRST CHOICE.
I WASN'T... I--
YOU SEE, I WAS INCHES AWAY FROM BEING THE FIRST PURPLE KID AT SARAH LAWRENCE, BUT MY BROTHER WASN'T SO LUCKY.
BEING A FOOT SHORTER THAN EVERYONE ELSE AND SHRIEKING LIKE A GIRL AT A TAYLOR SWIFT SHOW? ROUGH WAY TO TURN 13.
MY AUNT DEE KICKED HIM OUT THE MINUTE NEIGHBORHOOD BOYS STARTED CALLING ASH SCREAMER.
I COULDN'T LEAVE HIM. DIDN'T MAKE IT LONG 'TIL ALL WE HAD WERE THE SEWERS.
SUDDENLY I'M RESPONSIBLE FOR MY BROTHER-- WHO'S NOW MISSING-- AND THESE MORLOCKS. YOU'D NEVER UNDERSTAND THAT.
I MAY ACT LIKE THE CLASS CLOWN, BUT I COME THROUGH. THIS IS ALL I'VE BEEN DOING SINCE I WAS IN HIGH SCHOOL.
I'M GOOD AT THE SAVING MUTANTS STUFF.
ICEMAN, I'M OUT OF OPTIONS. YOUR FRIEND BARELY LIKED YOUR PLAN... SO PLEASE, BE RIGHT.

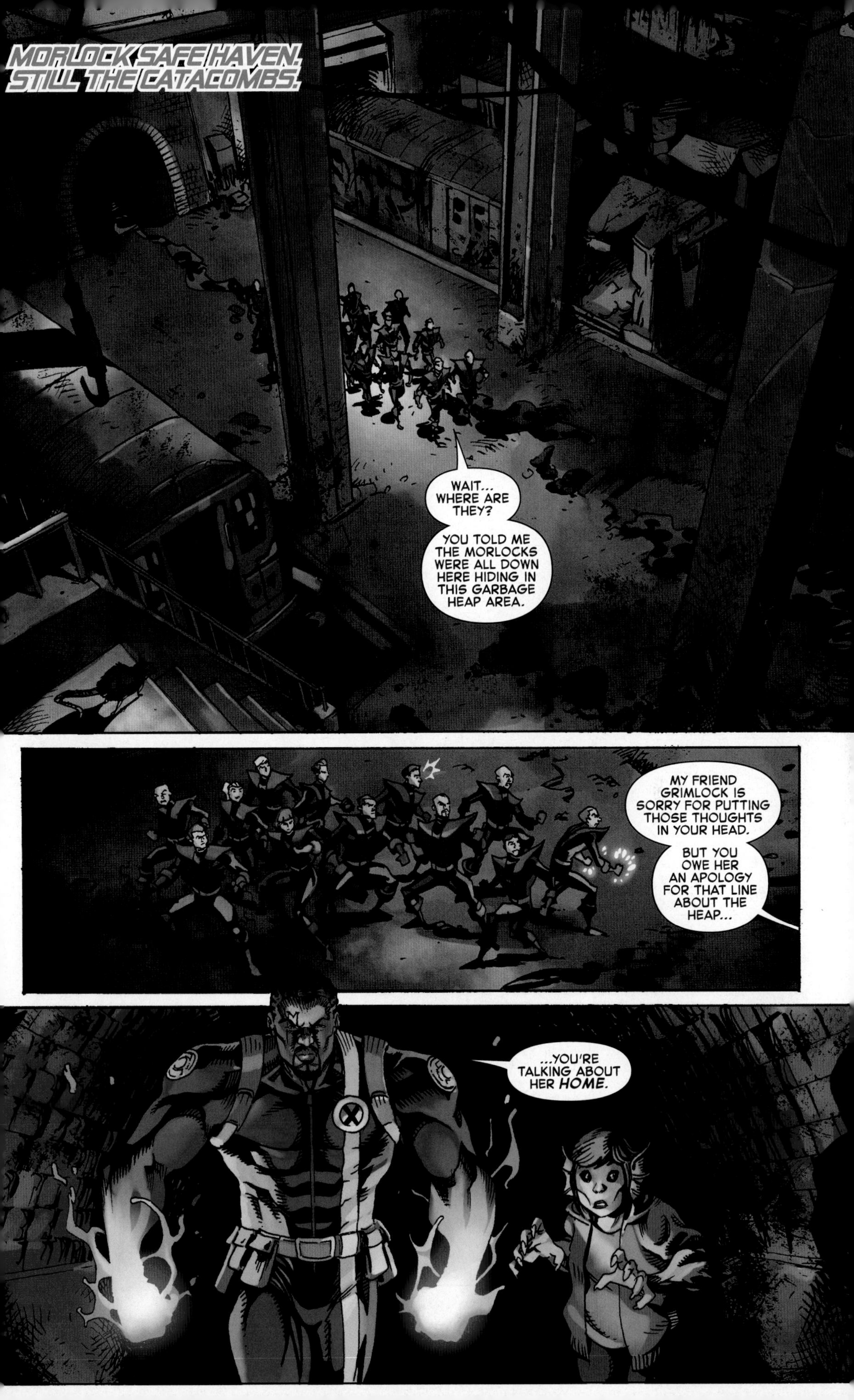
MORLOCK SAFE HAVEN. STILL THE CATACOMBS.
WAIT... WHERE ARE THEY?
YOU TOLD ME THE MORLOCKS WERE ALL DOWN HERE HIDING IN THIS GARBAGE HEAP AREA.
MY FRIEND GRIMLOCK IS SORRY FOR PUTTING THOSE THOUGHTS IN YOUR HEAD.
BUT YOU OWE HER AN APOLOGY FOR THAT LINE ABOUT THE HEAP...
...YOU'RE TALKING ABOUT HER HOME.

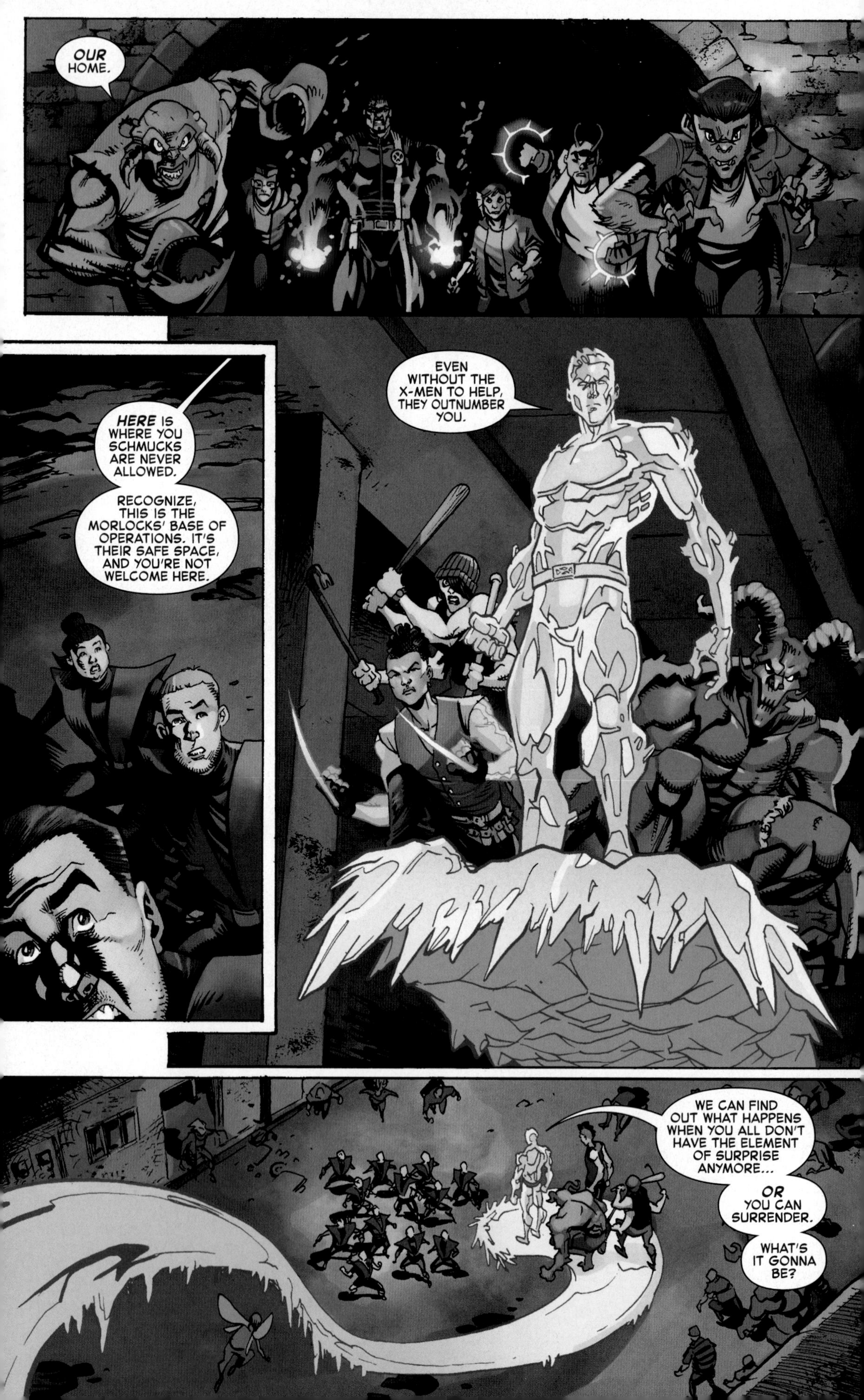
OUR HOME.
HERE IS WHERE YOU SCHMUCKS ARE NEVER ALLOWED.
RECOGNIZE, THIS IS THE MORLOCKS' BASE OF OPERATIONS. IT'S THEIR SAFE SPACE, AND YOU'RE NOT WELCOME HERE.
EVEN WITHOUT THE X-MEN TO HELP, THEY OUTNUMBER YOU.
WE CAN FIND OUT WHAT HAPPENS WHEN YOU ALL DON'T HAVE THE ELEMENT OF SURPRISE ANYMORE...
OR YOU CAN SURRENDER.
WHAT'S IT GONNA BE?

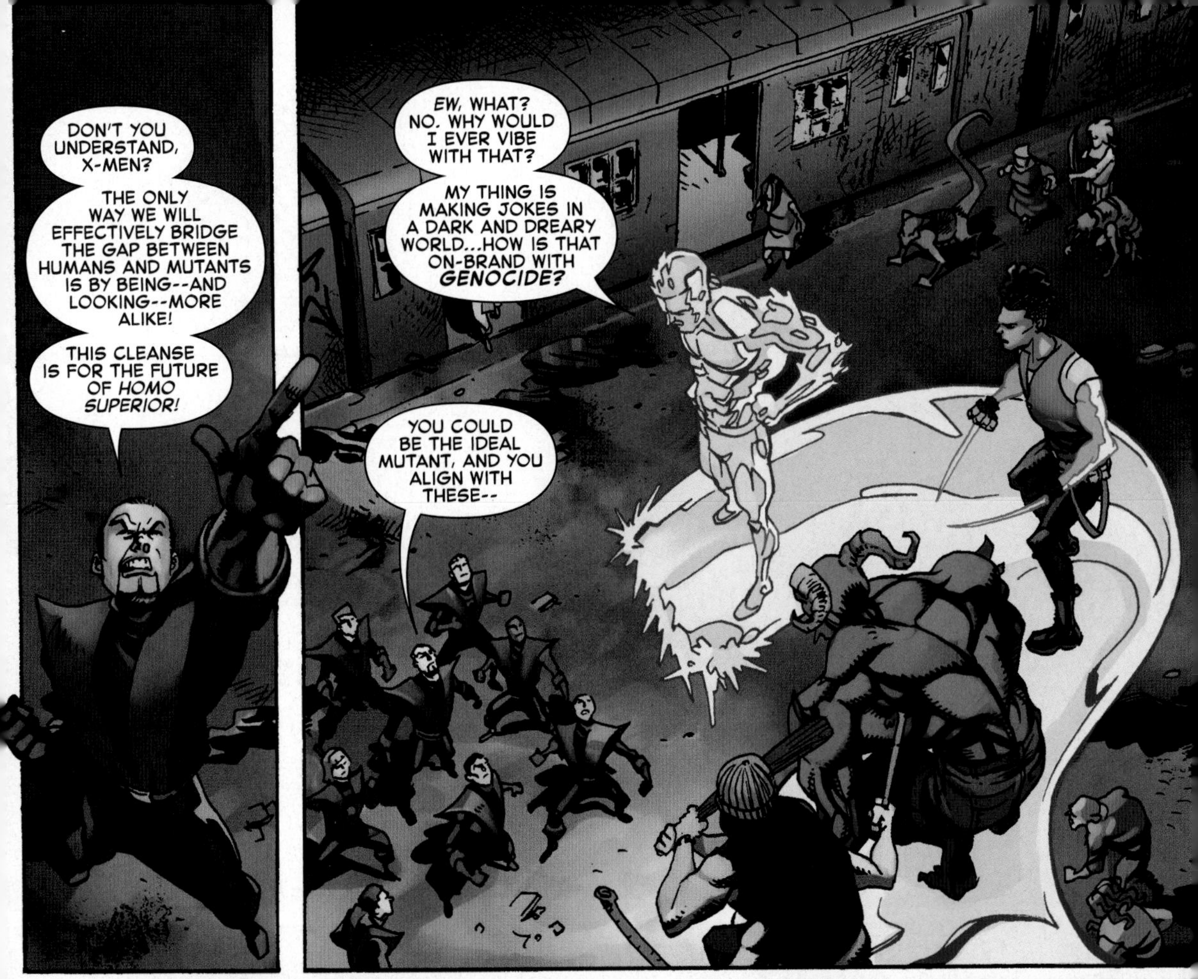
DON'T YOU UNDERSTAND, X-MEN?
THE ONLY WAY WE WILL EFFECTIVELY BRIDGE THE GAP BETWEEN HUMANS AND MUTANTS IS BY BEING--AND LOOKING--MORE ALIKE!
THIS CLEANSE IS FOR THE FUTURE OF *HOMO SUPERIOR!*
EW, WHAT? NO. WHY WOULD I EVER VIBE WITH THAT?
MY THING IS MAKING JOKES IN A DARK AND DREARY WORLD...HOW IS THAT ON-BRAND WITH ***GENOCIDE?***
YOU COULD BE THE IDEAL MUTANT, AND YOU ALIGN WITH THESE--

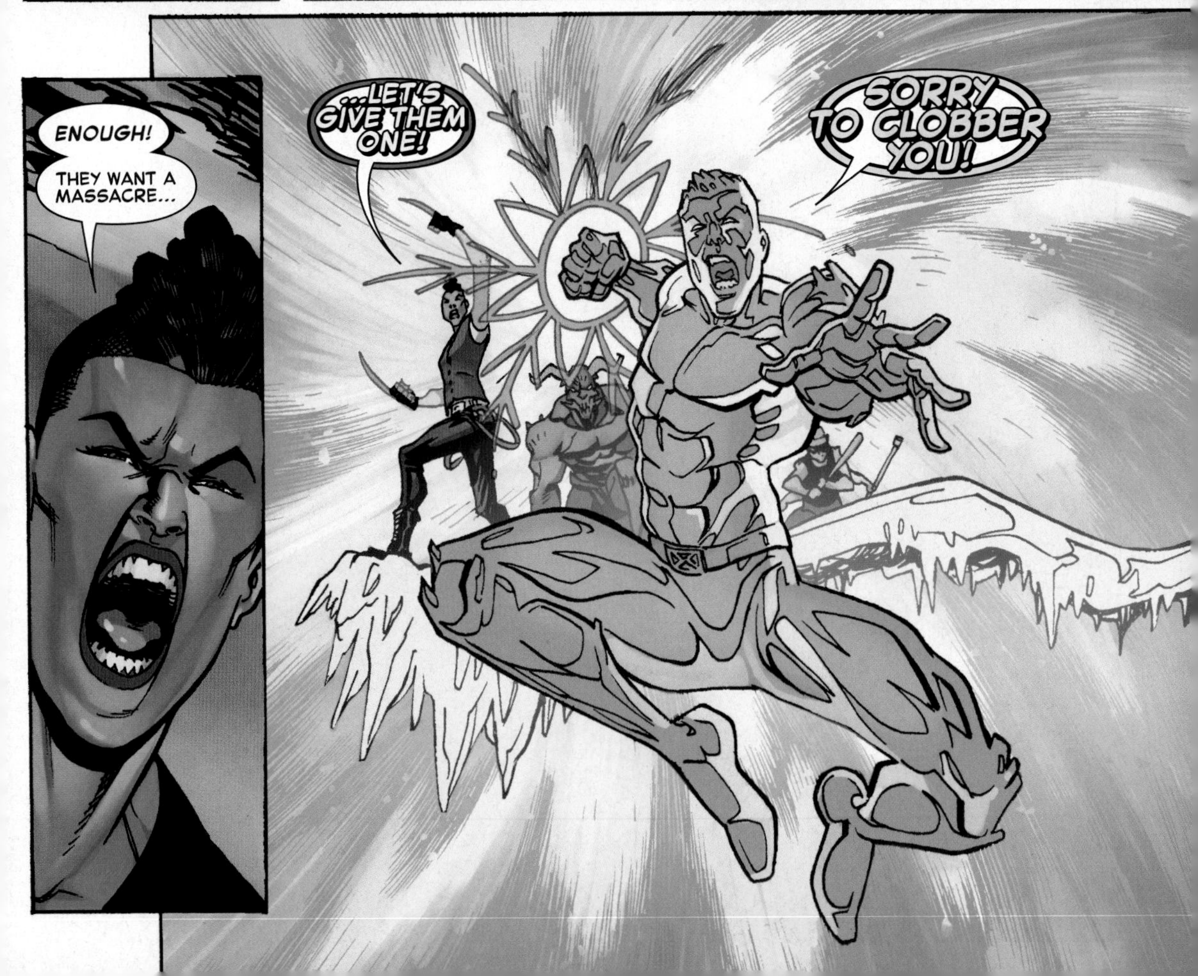
ENOUGH!
THEY WANT A MASSACRE...
...LET'S GIVE THEM ONE!
SORRY TO CLOBBER YOU!

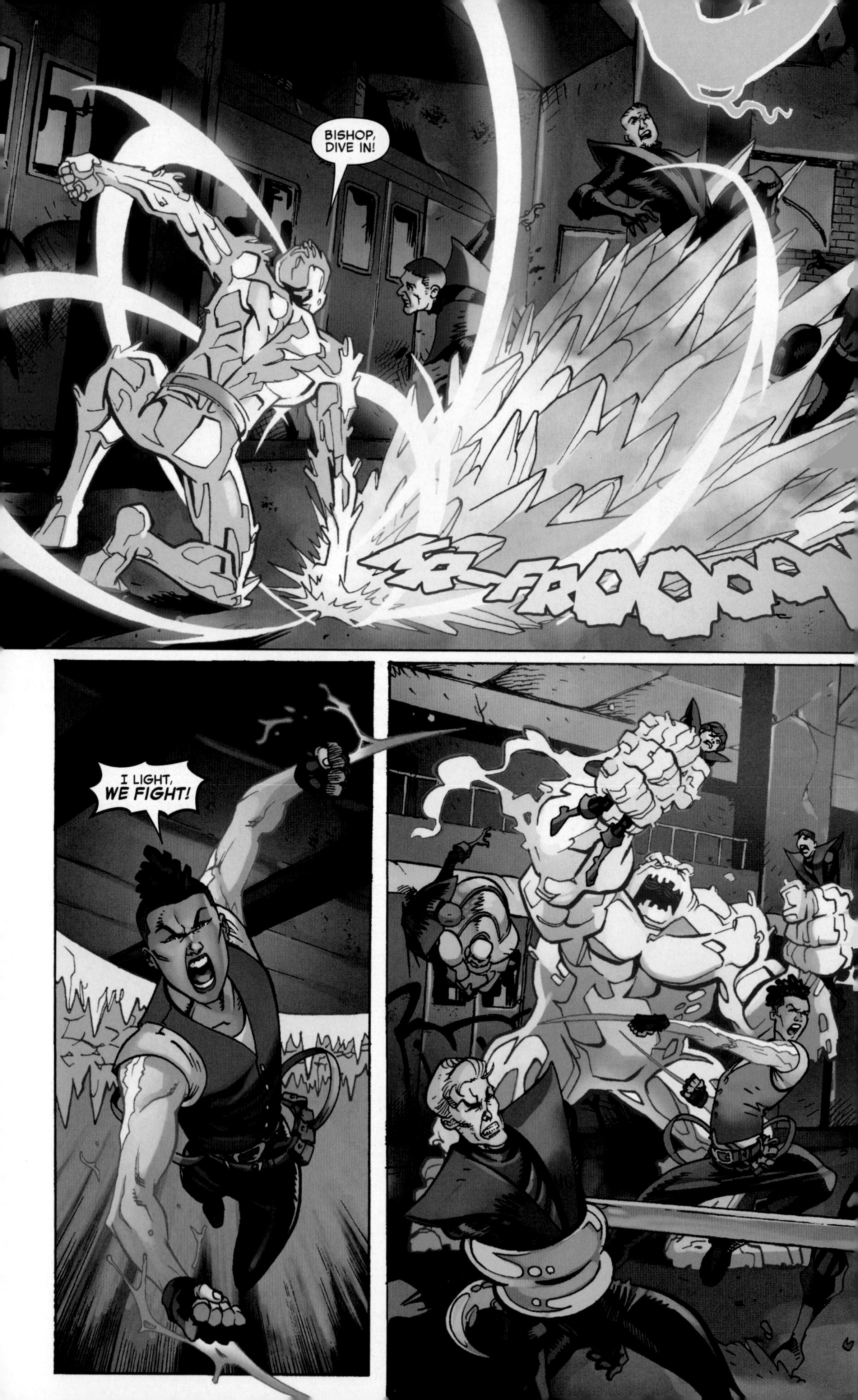
BISHOP, DIVE IN!
I LIGHT, WE FIGHT!

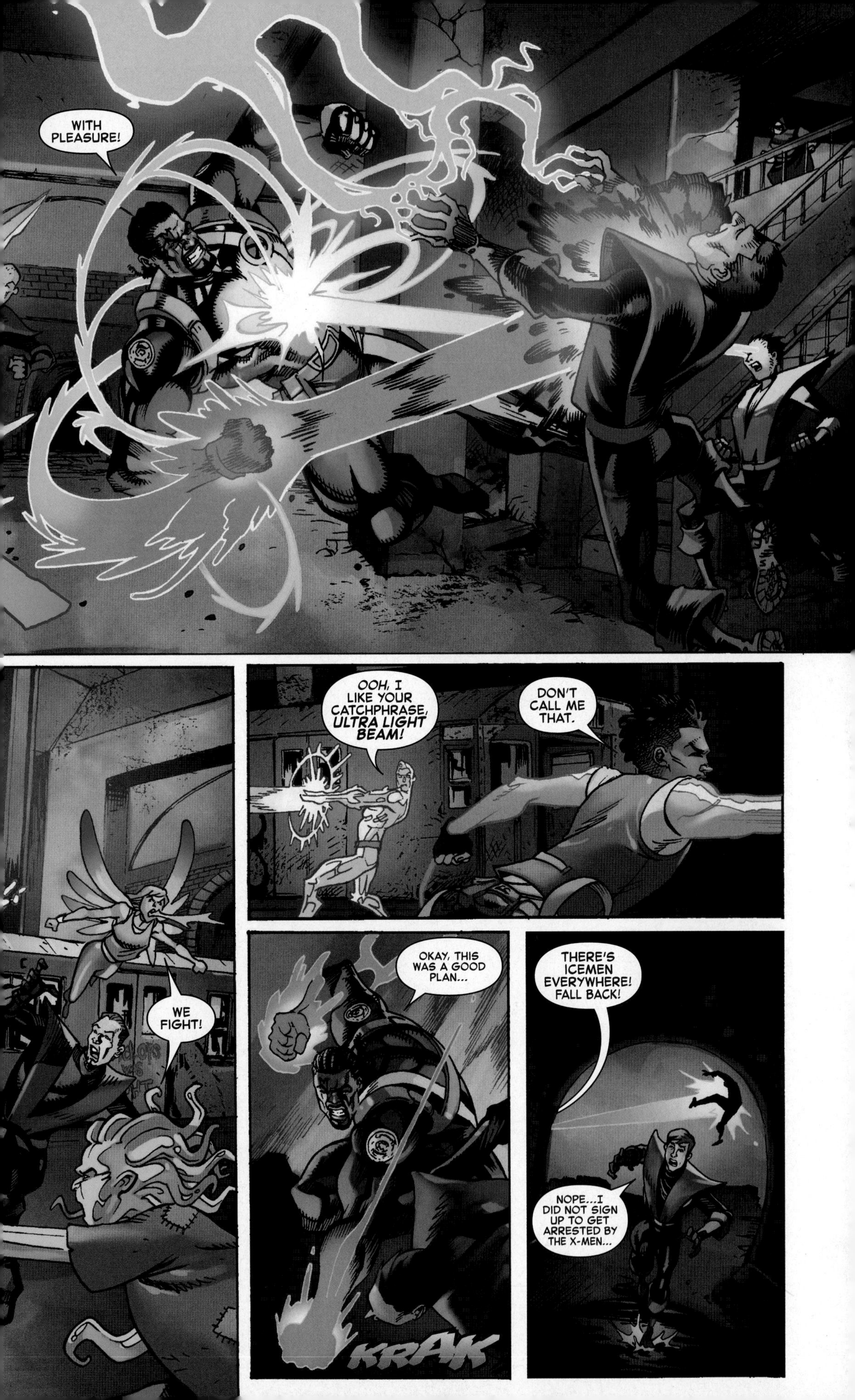
WITH PLEASURE!
WE FIGHT!
OOH, I LIKE YOUR CATCHPHRASE, *ULTRA LIGHT BEAM!*
DON'T CALL ME THAT.
OKAY, THIS WAS A GOOD PLAN...
KRAK
THERE'S ICEMEN EVERYWHERE! FALL BACK!
NOPE...I DID NOT SIGN UP TO GET ARRESTED BY THE X-MEN...

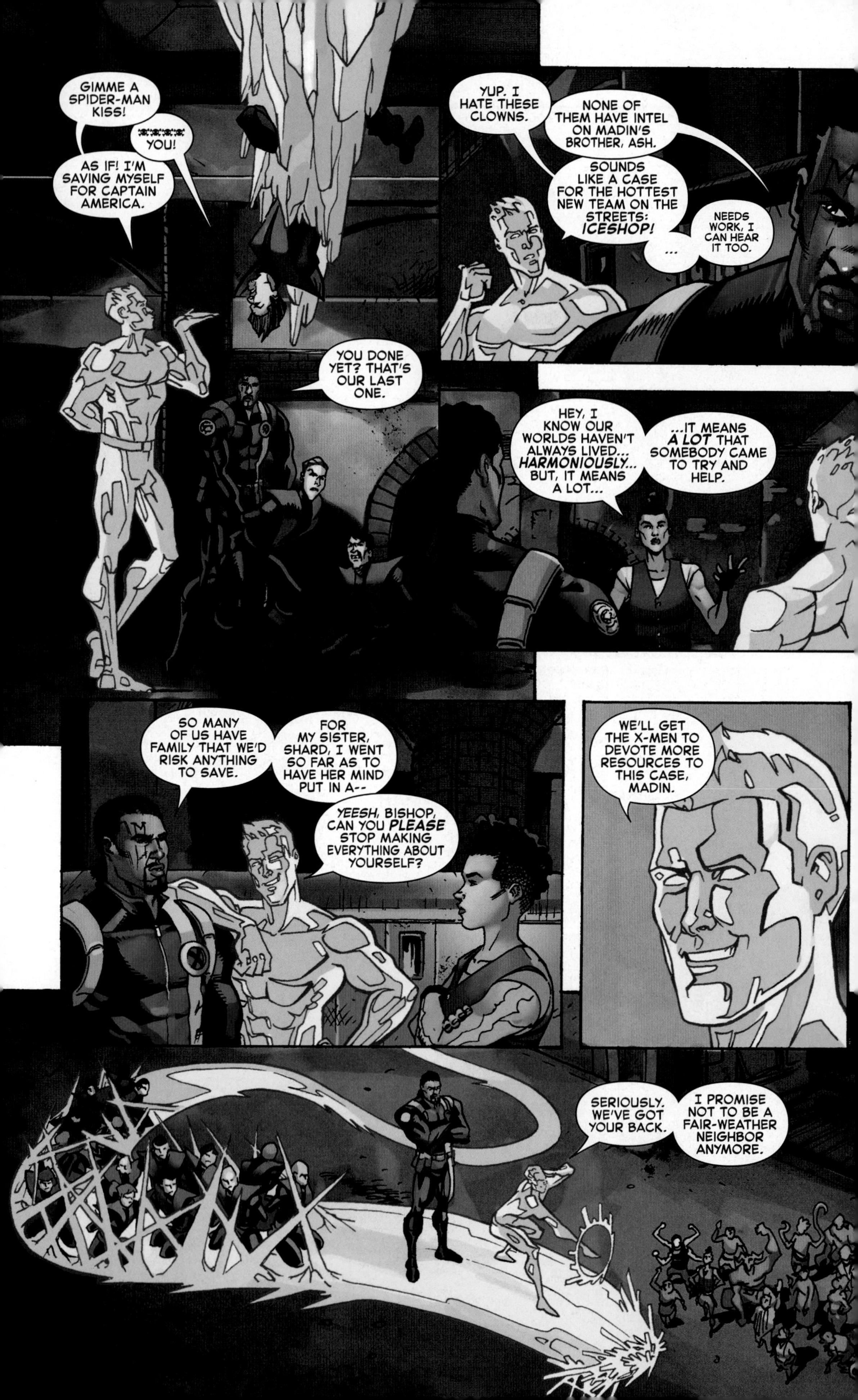
GIMME A SPIDER-MAN KISS!
YOU!
AS IF! I'M SAVING MYSELF FOR CAPTAIN AMERICA.
YOU DONE YET? THAT'S OUR LAST ONE.
YUP. I HATE THESE CLOWNS.
NONE OF THEM HAVE INTEL ON MADIN'S BROTHER, ASH.
SOUNDS LIKE A CASE FOR THE HOTTEST NEW TEAM ON THE STREETS: *ICESHOP!*
...
NEEDS WORK, I CAN HEAR IT TOO.
HEY, I KNOW OUR WORLDS HAVEN'T ALWAYS LIVED... *HARMONIOUSLY...* BUT, IT MEANS A LOT...
...IT MEANS *A LOT* THAT SOMEBODY CAME TO TRY AND HELP.
SO MANY OF US HAVE FAMILY THAT WE'D RISK ANYTHING TO SAVE.
FOR MY SISTER, SHARD, I WENT SO FAR AS TO HAVE HER MIND PUT IN A--
YEESH, BISHOP, CAN YOU *PLEASE* STOP MAKING EVERYTHING ABOUT YOURSELF?
WE'LL GET THE X-MEN TO DEVOTE MORE RESOURCES TO THIS CASE, MADIN.
SERIOUSLY. WE'VE GOT YOUR BACK.
I PROMISE NOT TO BE A FAIR-WEATHER NEIGHBOR ANYMORE.

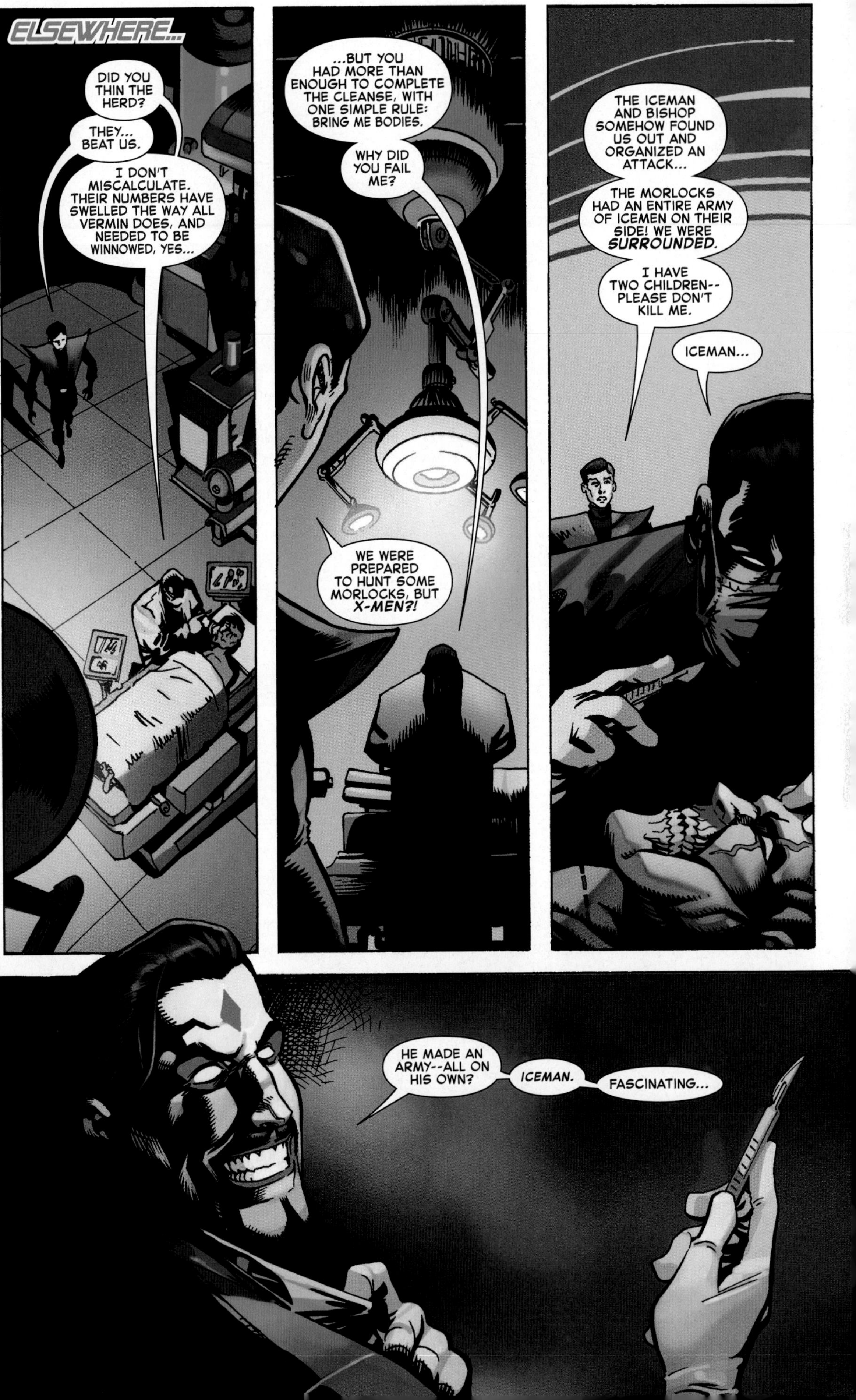
ELSEWHERE...
DID YOU THIN THE HERD?
THEY... BEAT US.
I DON'T MISCALCULATE. THEIR NUMBERS HAVE SWELLED THE WAY ALL VERMIN DOES, AND NEEDED TO BE WINNOWED, YES...
...BUT YOU HAD MORE THAN ENOUGH TO COMPLETE THE CLEANSE, WITH ONE SIMPLE RULE: BRING ME BODIES.
WHY DID YOU FAIL ME?
WE WERE PREPARED TO HUNT SOME MORLOCKS, BUT X-MEN?!
THE ICEMAN AND BISHOP SOMEHOW FOUND US OUT AND ORGANIZED AN ATTACK...
THE MORLOCKS HAD AN ENTIRE ARMY OF ICEMEN ON THEIR SIDE! WE WERE SURROUNDED.
I HAVE TWO CHILDREN-- PLEASE DON'T KILL ME.
ICEMAN...
HE MADE AN ARMY--ALL ON HIS OWN?
ICEMAN.
FASCINATING...

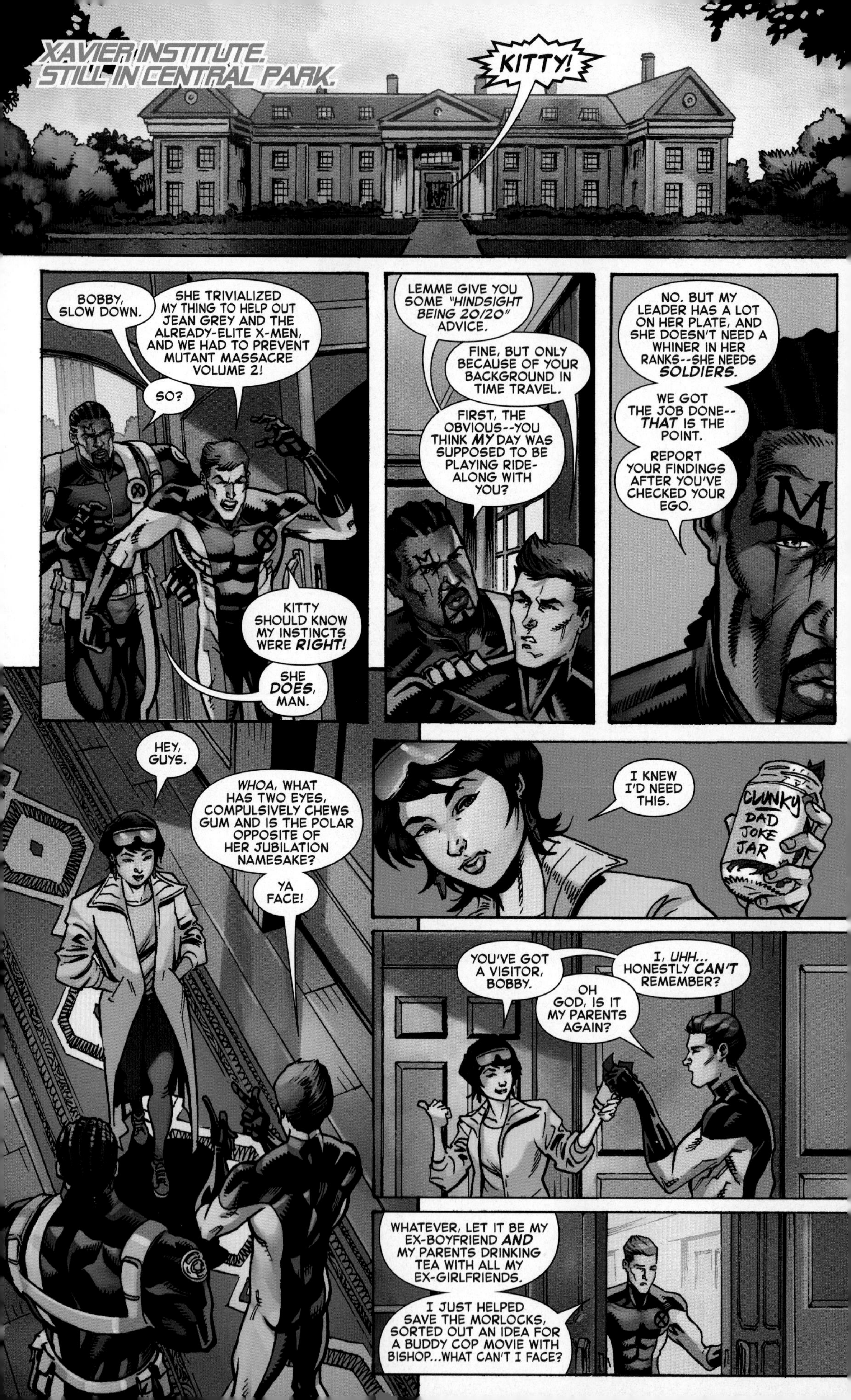
XAVIER INSTITUTE. STILL IN CENTRAL PARK.
KITTY!
BOBBY, SLOW DOWN.
SHE TRIVIALIZED MY THING TO HELP OUT JEAN GREY AND THE ALREADY-ELITE X-MEN, AND WE HAD TO PREVENT MUTANT MASSACRE VOLUME 2!
SO?
KITTY SHOULD KNOW MY INSTINCTS WERE RIGHT!
SHE DOES, MAN.
LEMME GIVE YOU SOME "HINDSIGHT BEING 20/20" ADVICE.
FINE, BUT ONLY BECAUSE OF YOUR BACKGROUND IN TIME TRAVEL.
FIRST, THE OBVIOUS--YOU THINK MY DAY WAS SUPPOSED TO BE PLAYING RIDE-ALONG WITH YOU?
NO. BUT MY LEADER HAS A LOT ON HER PLATE, AND SHE DOESN'T NEED A WHINER IN HER RANKS--SHE NEEDS SOLDIERS.
WE GOT THE JOB DONE--THAT IS THE POINT.
REPORT YOUR FINDINGS AFTER YOU'VE CHECKED YOUR EGO.
HEY, GUYS.
WHOA, WHAT HAS TWO EYES, COMPULSIVELY CHEWS GUM AND IS THE POLAR OPPOSITE OF HER JUBILATION NAMESAKE?
YA FACE!
I KNEW I'D NEED THIS.
CLUNKY DAD JOKE JAR
YOU'VE GOT A VISITOR, BOBBY.
I, UHH... HONESTLY CAN'T REMEMBER?
OH GOD, IS IT MY PARENTS AGAIN?
WHATEVER, LET IT BE MY EX-BOYFRIEND AND MY PARENTS DRINKING TEA WITH ALL MY EX-GIRLFRIENDS.
I JUST HELPED SAVE THE MORLOCKS, SORTED OUT AN IDEA FOR A BUDDY COP MOVIE WITH BISHOP...WHAT CAN'T I FACE?

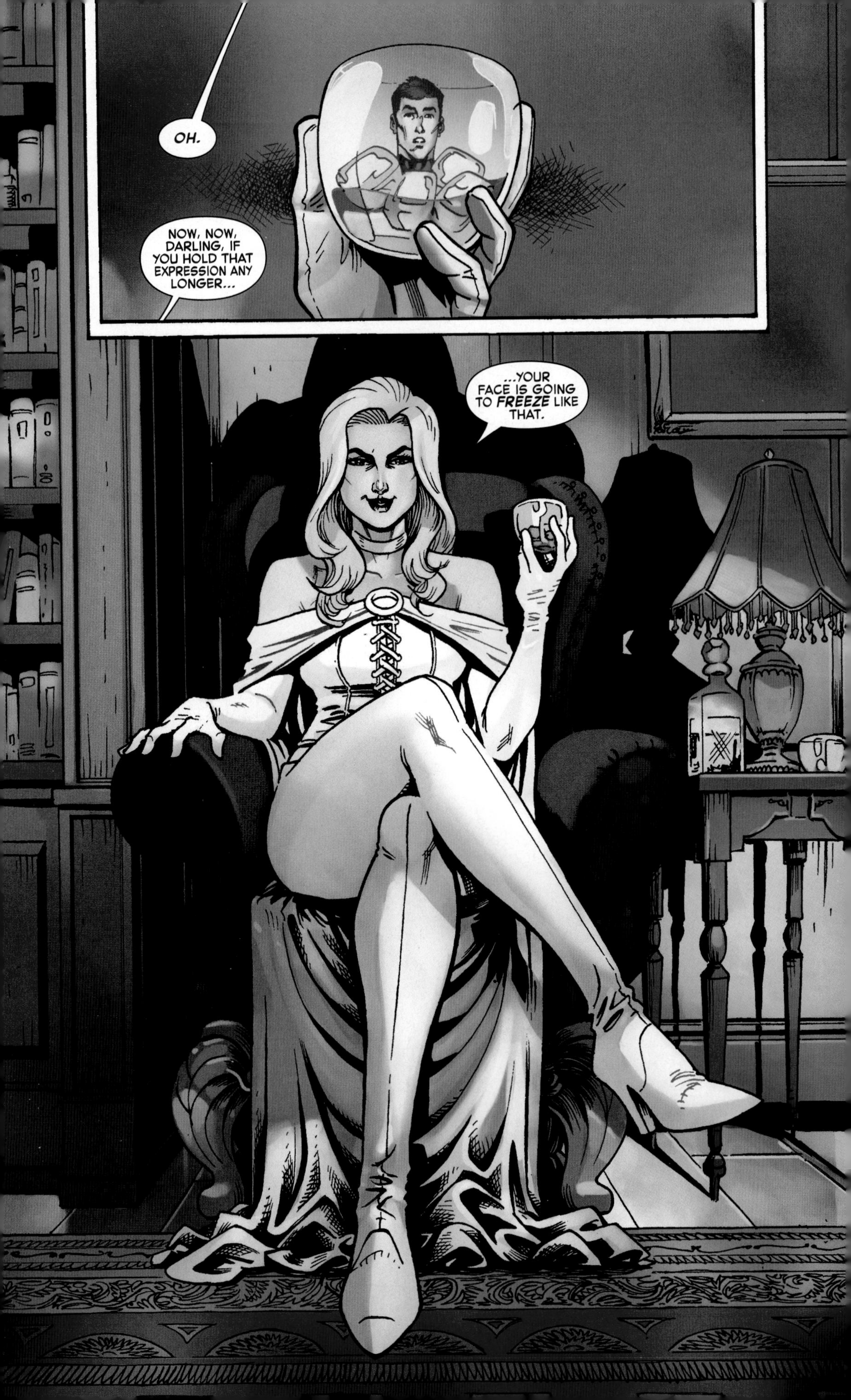
OH.
NOW, NOW, DARLING, IF YOU HOLD THAT EXPRESSION ANY LONGER...
...YOUR FACE IS GOING TO FREEZE LIKE THAT.

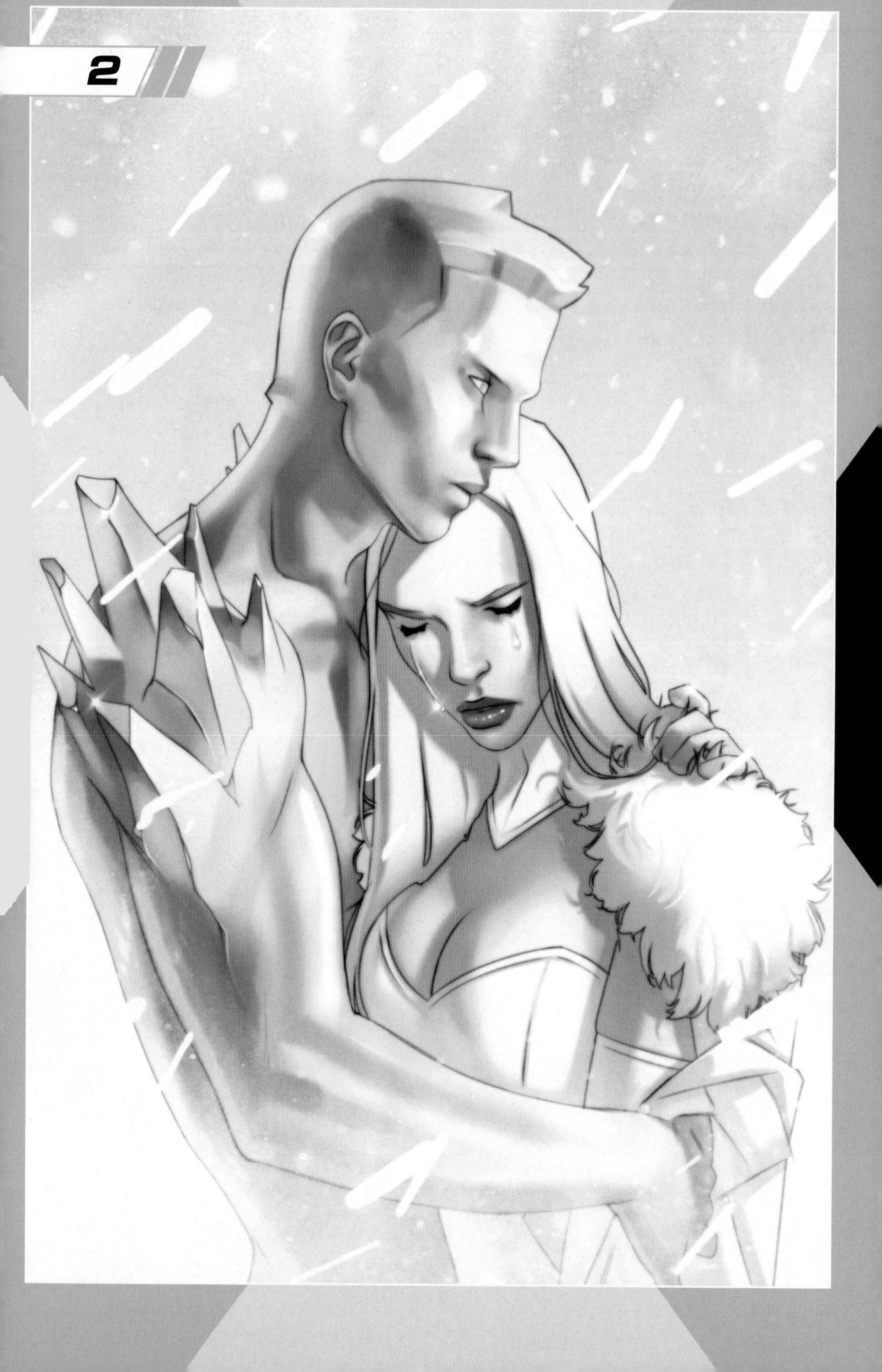
2

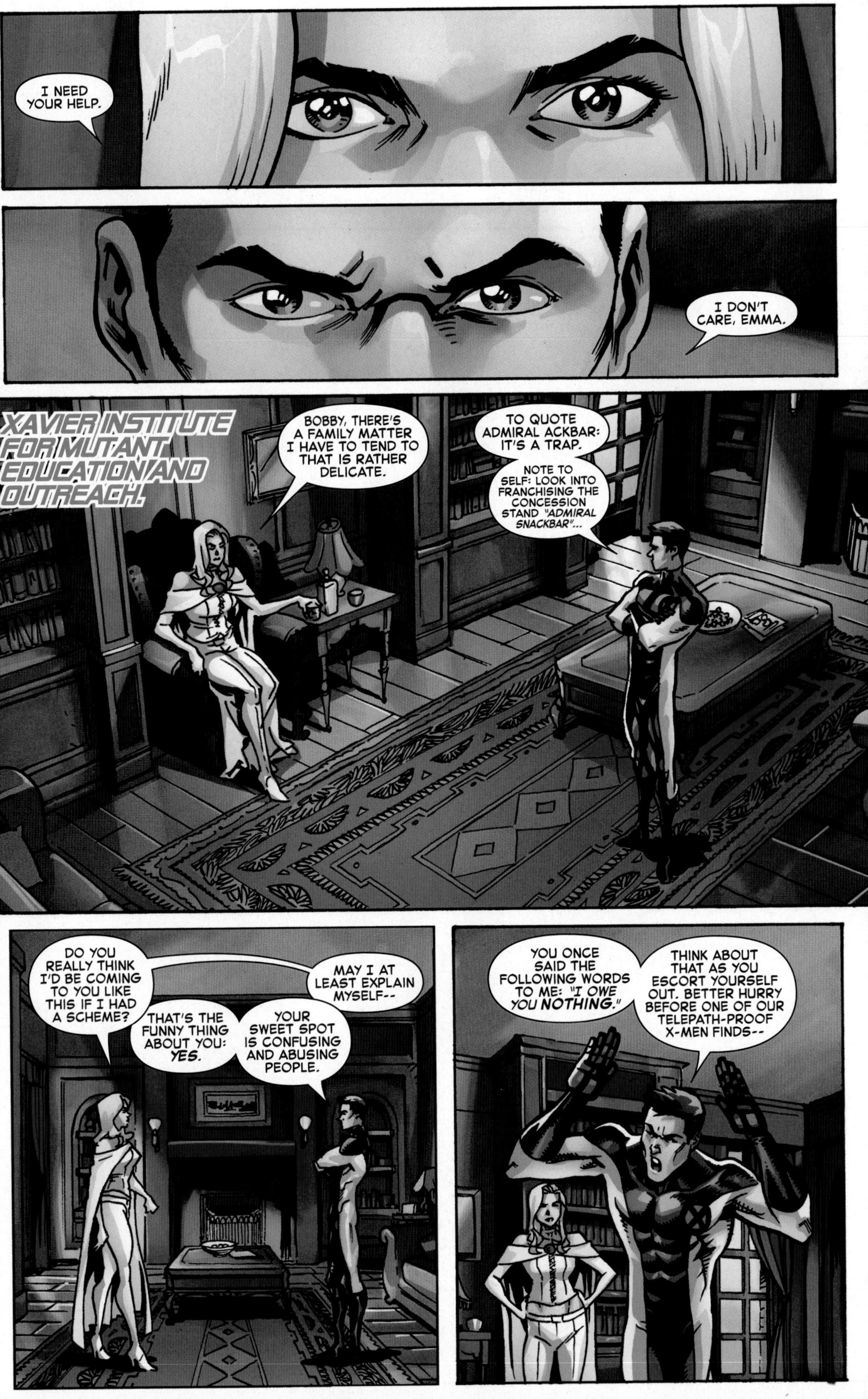
I NEED YOUR HELP.
I DON'T CARE, EMMA.
XAVIER INSTITUTE FOR MUTANT EDUCATION AND OUTREACH.
BOBBY, THERE'S A FAMILY MATTER I HAVE TO TEND TO THAT IS RATHER DELICATE.
TO QUOTE ADMIRAL ACKBAR: IT'S A TRAP.
NOTE TO SELF: LOOK INTO FRANCHISING THE CONCESSION STAND "ADMIRAL SNACKBAR"...
DO YOU REALLY THINK I'D BE COMING TO YOU LIKE THIS IF I HAD A SCHEME?
THAT'S THE FUNNY THING ABOUT YOU: YES.
YOUR SWEET SPOT IS CONFUSING AND ABUSING PEOPLE.
MAY I AT LEAST EXPLAIN MYSELF--
YOU ONCE SAID THE FOLLOWING WORDS TO ME: "I OWE YOU NOTHING."
THINK ABOUT THAT AS YOU ESCORT YOURSELF OUT. BETTER HURRY BEFORE ONE OF OUR TELEPATH-PROOF X-MEN FINDS--

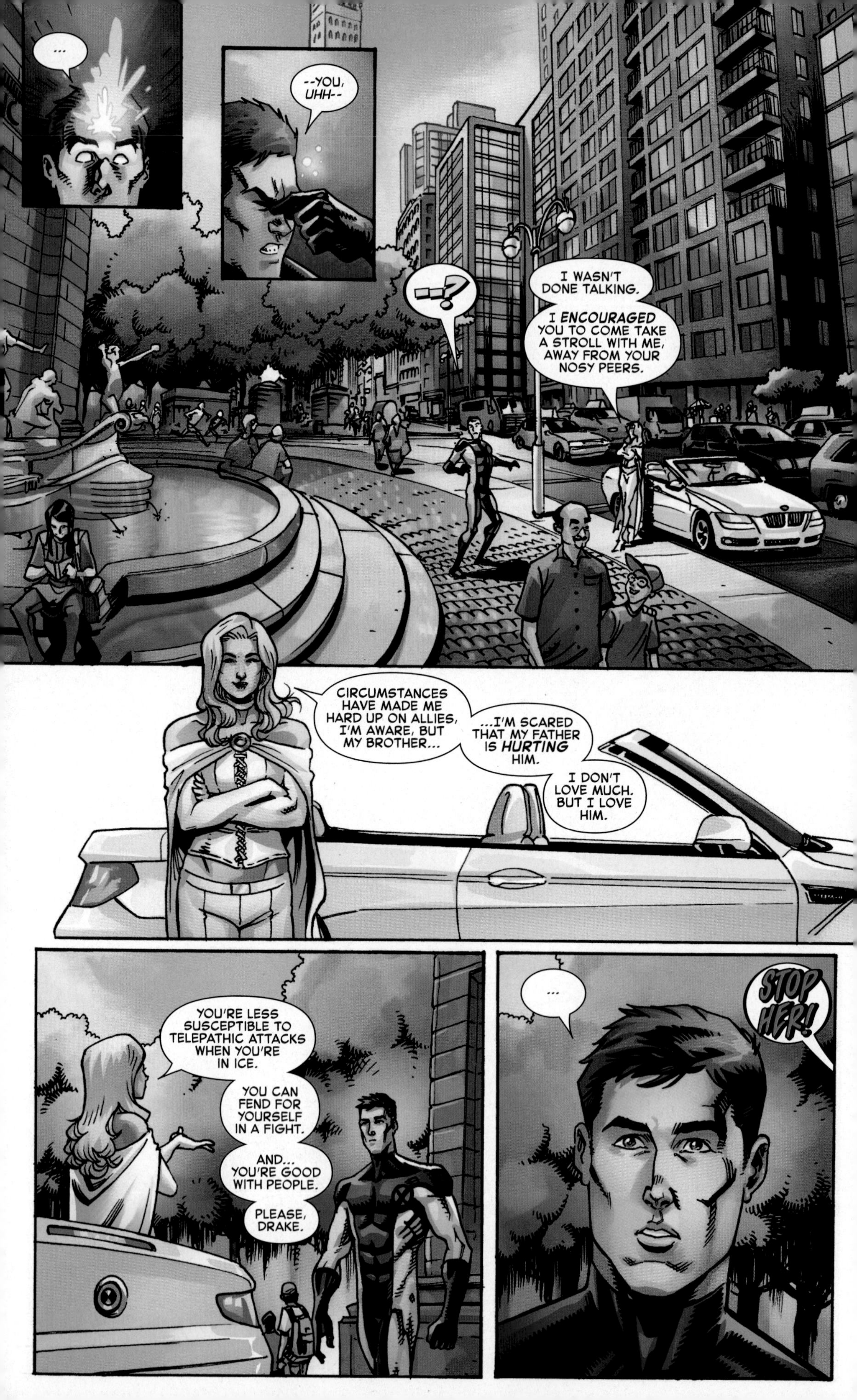
...
--YOU, UHH--
?
I WASN'T DONE TALKING.
I ENCOURAGED YOU TO COME TAKE A STROLL WITH ME, AWAY FROM YOUR NOSY PEERS.
CIRCUMSTANCES HAVE MADE ME HARD UP ON ALLIES, I'M AWARE, BUT MY BROTHER...
...I'M SCARED THAT MY FATHER IS HURTING HIM.
I DON'T LOVE MUCH. BUT I LOVE HIM.
YOU'RE LESS SUSCEPTIBLE TO TELEPATHIC ATTACKS WHEN YOU'RE IN ICE.
YOU CAN FEND FOR YOURSELF IN A FIGHT.
AND... YOU'RE GOOD WITH PEOPLE.
PLEASE, DRAKE.
...
STOP HER!

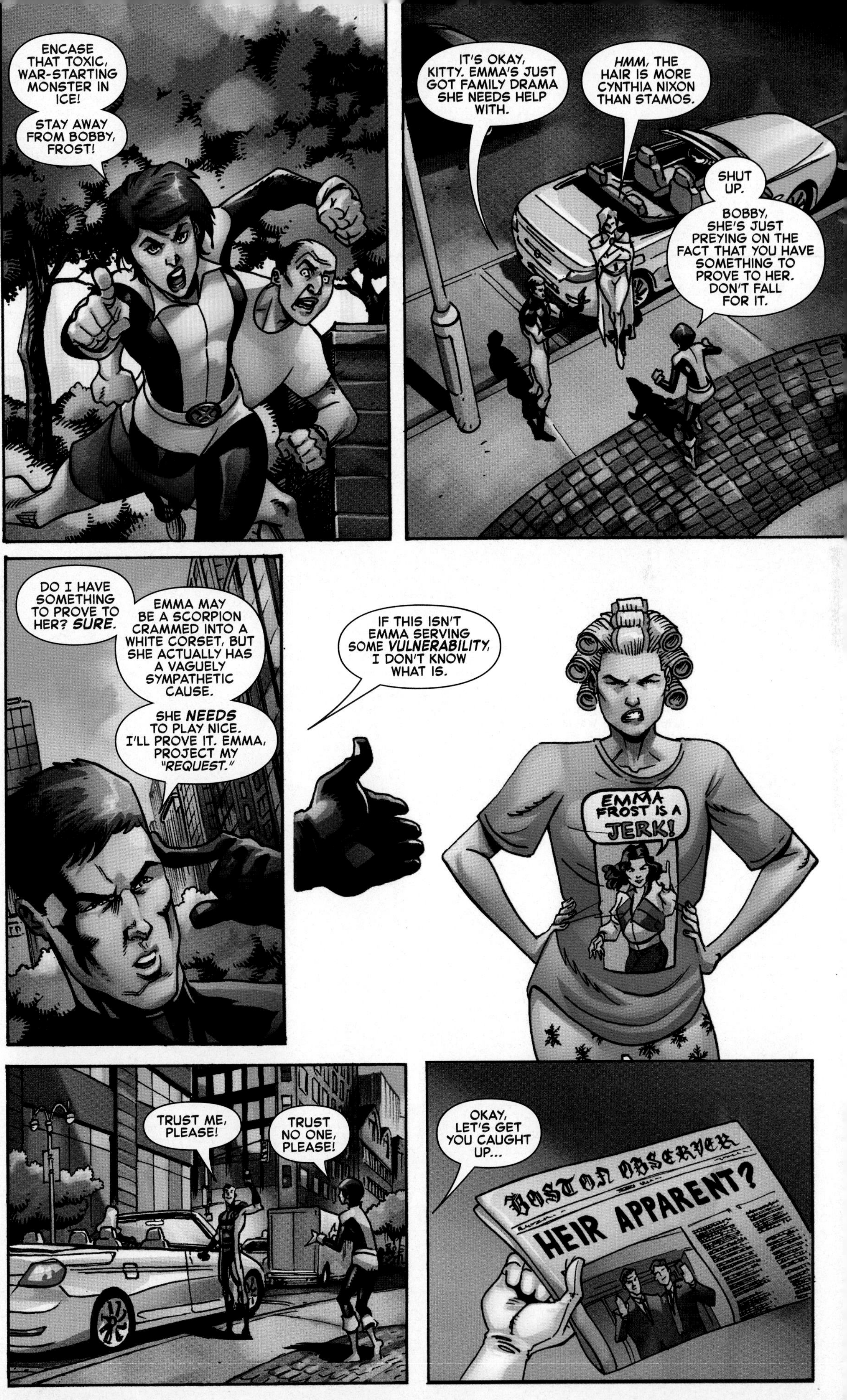
ENCASE THAT TOXIC, WAR-STARTING MONSTER IN ICE!
STAY AWAY FROM BOBBY, FROST!
IT'S OKAY, KITTY. EMMA'S JUST GOT FAMILY DRAMA SHE NEEDS HELP WITH.
HMM, THE HAIR IS MORE CYNTHIA NIXON THAN STAMOS.
SHUT UP.
BOBBY, SHE'S JUST PREYING ON THE FACT THAT YOU HAVE SOMETHING TO PROVE TO HER. DON'T FALL FOR IT.
DO I HAVE SOMETHING TO PROVE TO HER? ***SURE.***
EMMA MAY BE A SCORPION CRAMMED INTO A WHITE CORSET, BUT SHE ACTUALLY HAS A VAGUELY SYMPATHETIC CAUSE.
SHE ***NEEDS*** TO PLAY NICE. I'LL PROVE IT. EMMA, PROJECT MY *"REQUEST."*
IF THIS ISN'T EMMA SERVING SOME ***VULNERABILITY***, I DON'T KNOW WHAT IS.
EMMA FROST IS A JERK!
TRUST ME, PLEASE!
TRUST NO ONE, PLEASE!
OKAY, LET'S GET YOU CAUGHT UP...
BOSTON OBSERVER
HEIR APPARENT?

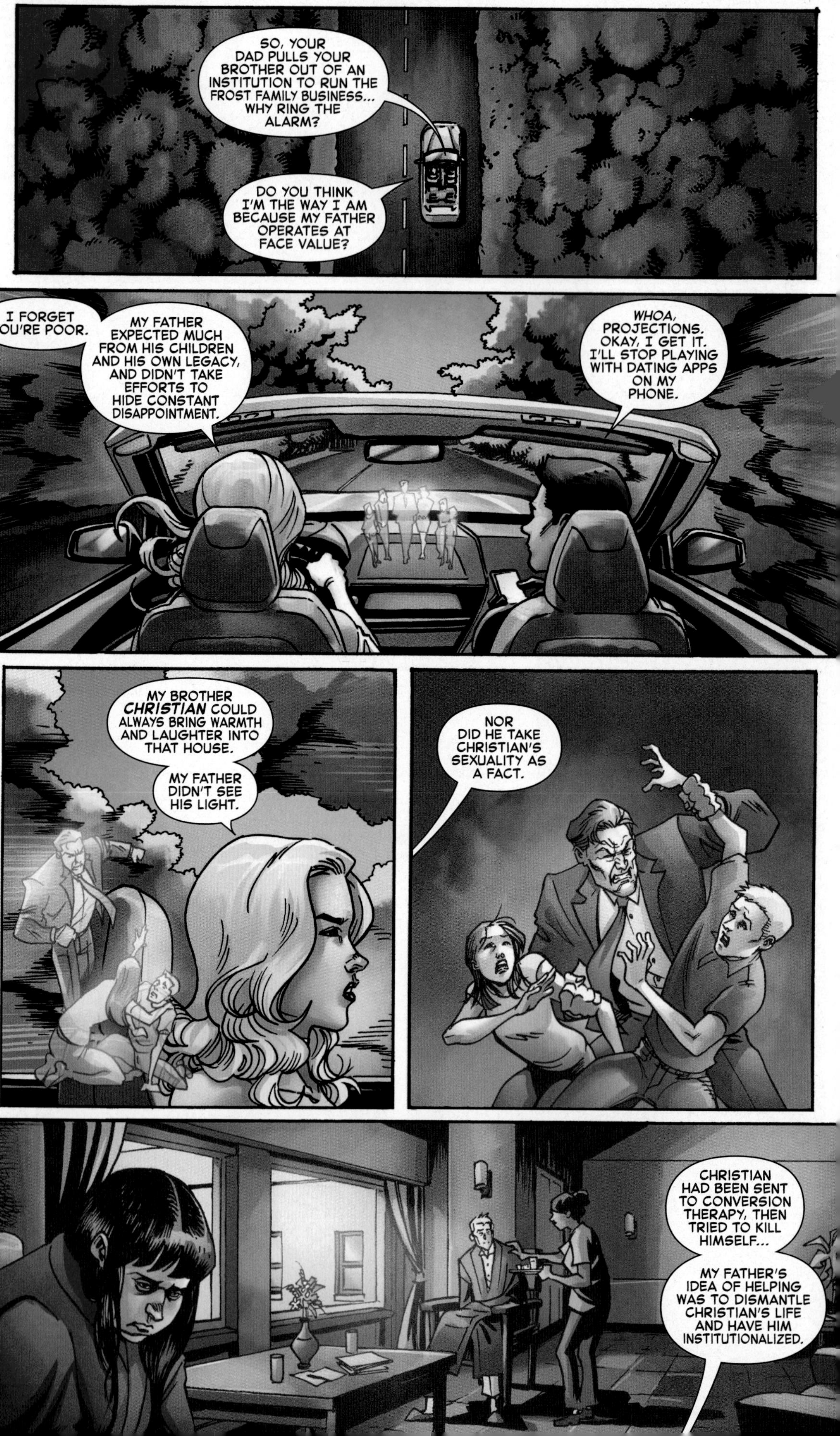
SO, YOUR DAD PULLS YOUR BROTHER OUT OF AN INSTITUTION TO RUN THE FROST FAMILY BUSINESS... WHY RING THE ALARM?
DO YOU THINK I'M THE WAY I AM BECAUSE MY FATHER OPERATES AT FACE VALUE?
I FORGET YOU'RE POOR.
MY FATHER EXPECTED MUCH FROM HIS CHILDREN AND HIS OWN LEGACY, AND DIDN'T TAKE EFFORTS TO HIDE CONSTANT DISAPPOINTMENT.
WHOA, PROJECTIONS. OKAY, I GET IT. I'LL STOP PLAYING WITH DATING APPS ON MY PHONE.
MY BROTHER CHRISTIAN COULD ALWAYS BRING WARMTH AND LAUGHTER INTO THAT HOUSE.
MY FATHER DIDN'T SEE HIS LIGHT.
NOR DID HE TAKE CHRISTIAN'S SEXUALITY AS A FACT.
CHRISTIAN HAD BEEN SENT TO CONVERSION THERAPY, THEN TRIED TO KILL HIMSELF...
MY FATHER'S IDEA OF HELPING WAS TO DISMANTLE CHRISTIAN'S LIFE AND HAVE HIM INSTITUTIONALIZED.

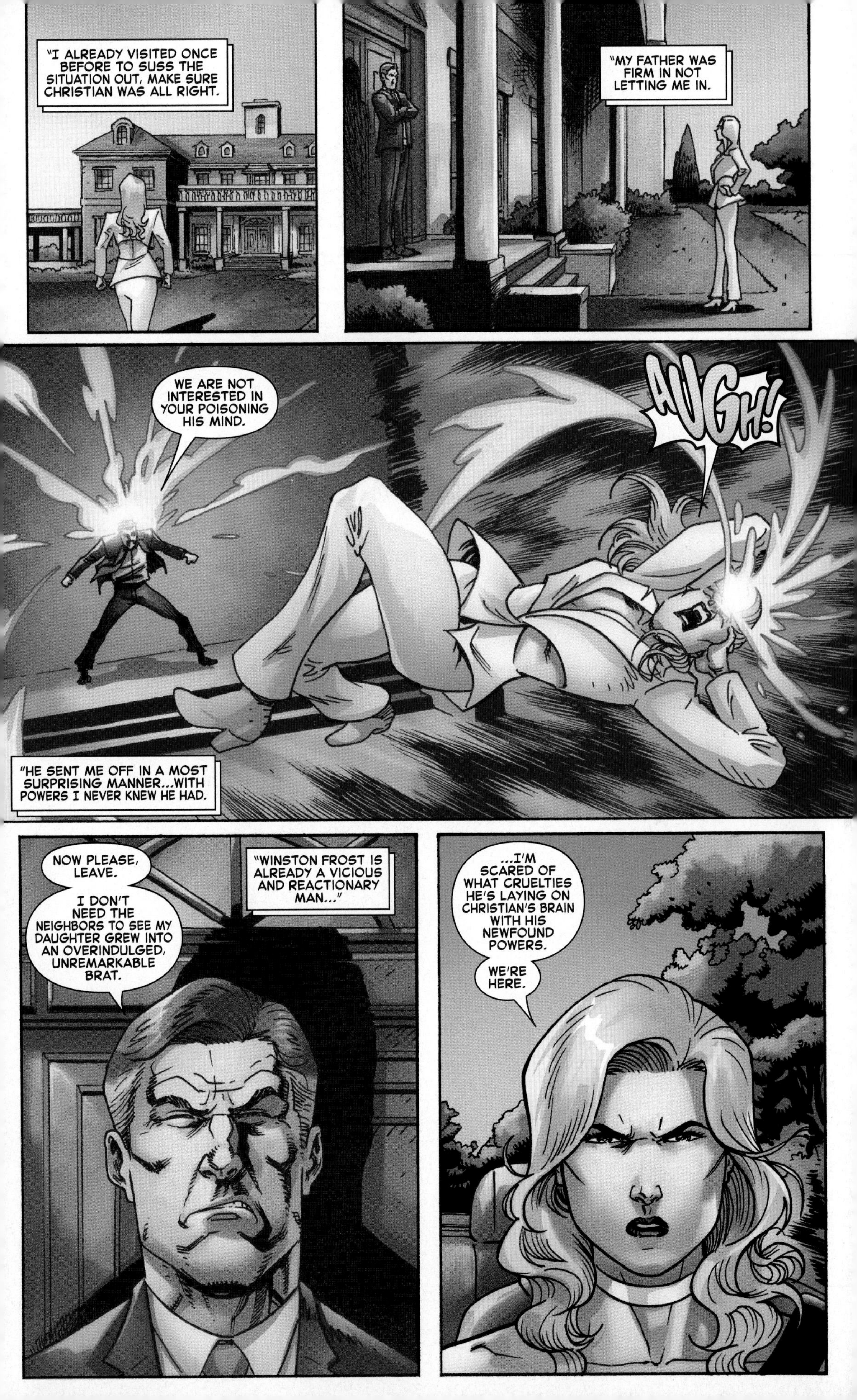

"I ALREADY VISITED ONCE BEFORE TO SUSS THE SITUATION OUT, MAKE SURE CHRISTIAN WAS ALL RIGHT.
"MY FATHER WAS FIRM IN NOT LETTING ME IN.
WE ARE NOT INTERESTED IN YOUR POISONING HIS MIND.
AUGH!
"HE SENT ME OFF IN A MOST SURPRISING MANNER...WITH POWERS I NEVER KNEW HE HAD.
NOW PLEASE, LEAVE.
I DON'T NEED THE NEIGHBORS TO SEE MY DAUGHTER GREW INTO AN OVERINDULGED, UNREMARKABLE BRAT.
"WINSTON FROST IS ALREADY A VICIOUS AND REACTIONARY MAN..."
...I'M SCARED OF WHAT CRUELTIES HE'S LAYING ON CHRISTIAN'S BRAIN WITH HIS NEWFOUND POWERS.
WE'RE HERE.

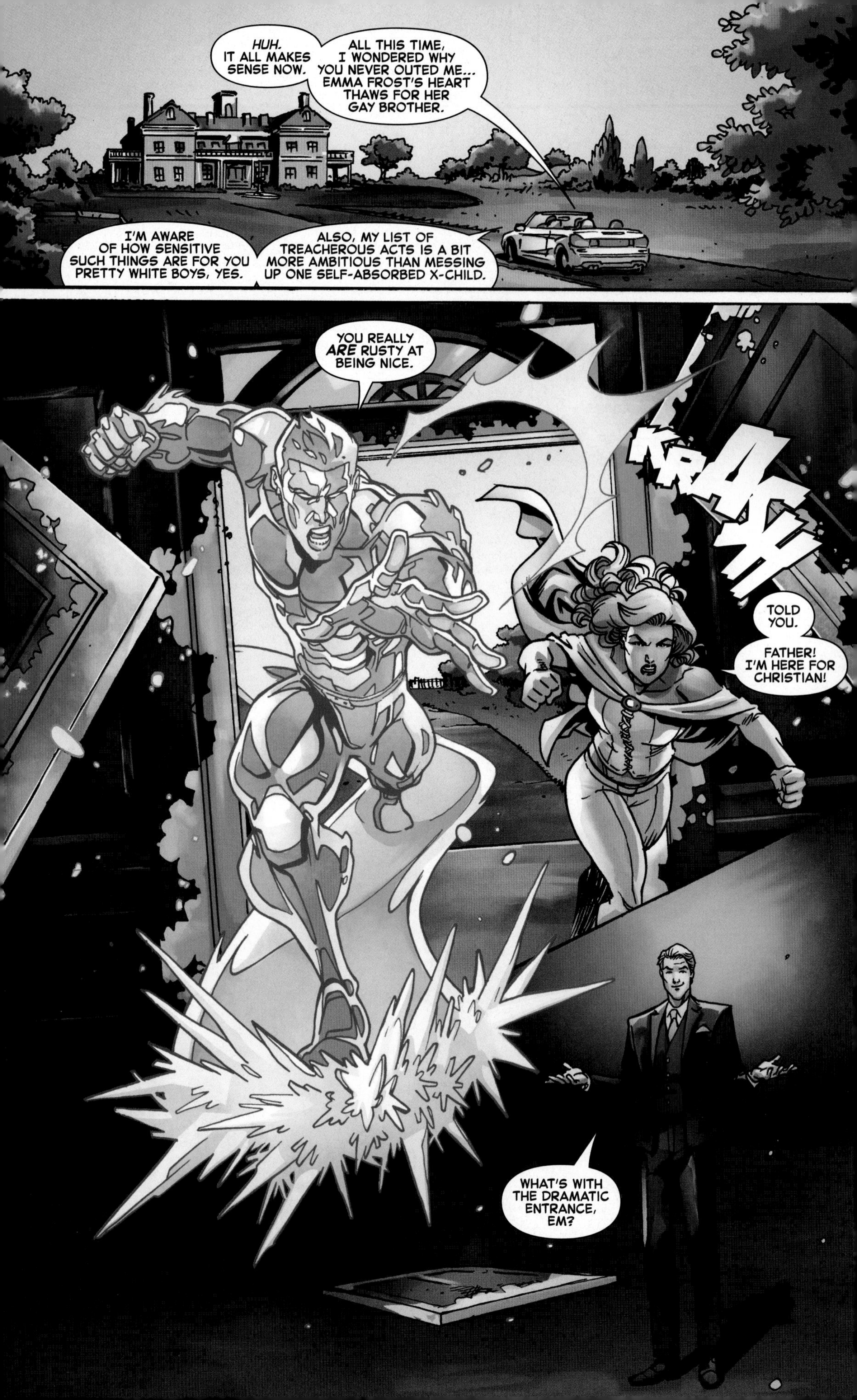
HUH. IT ALL MAKES SENSE NOW.
ALL THIS TIME, I WONDERED WHY YOU NEVER OUTED ME... EMMA FROST'S HEART THAWS FOR HER GAY BROTHER.
I'M AWARE OF HOW SENSITIVE SUCH THINGS ARE FOR YOU PRETTY WHITE BOYS, YES.
ALSO, MY LIST OF TREACHEROUS ACTS IS A BIT MORE AMBITIOUS THAN MESSING UP ONE SELF-ABSORBED X-CHILD.
YOU REALLY ARE RUSTY AT BEING NICE.
KRASH
TOLD YOU.
FATHER! I'M HERE FOR CHRISTIAN!
WHAT'S WITH THE DRAMATIC ENTRANCE, EM?

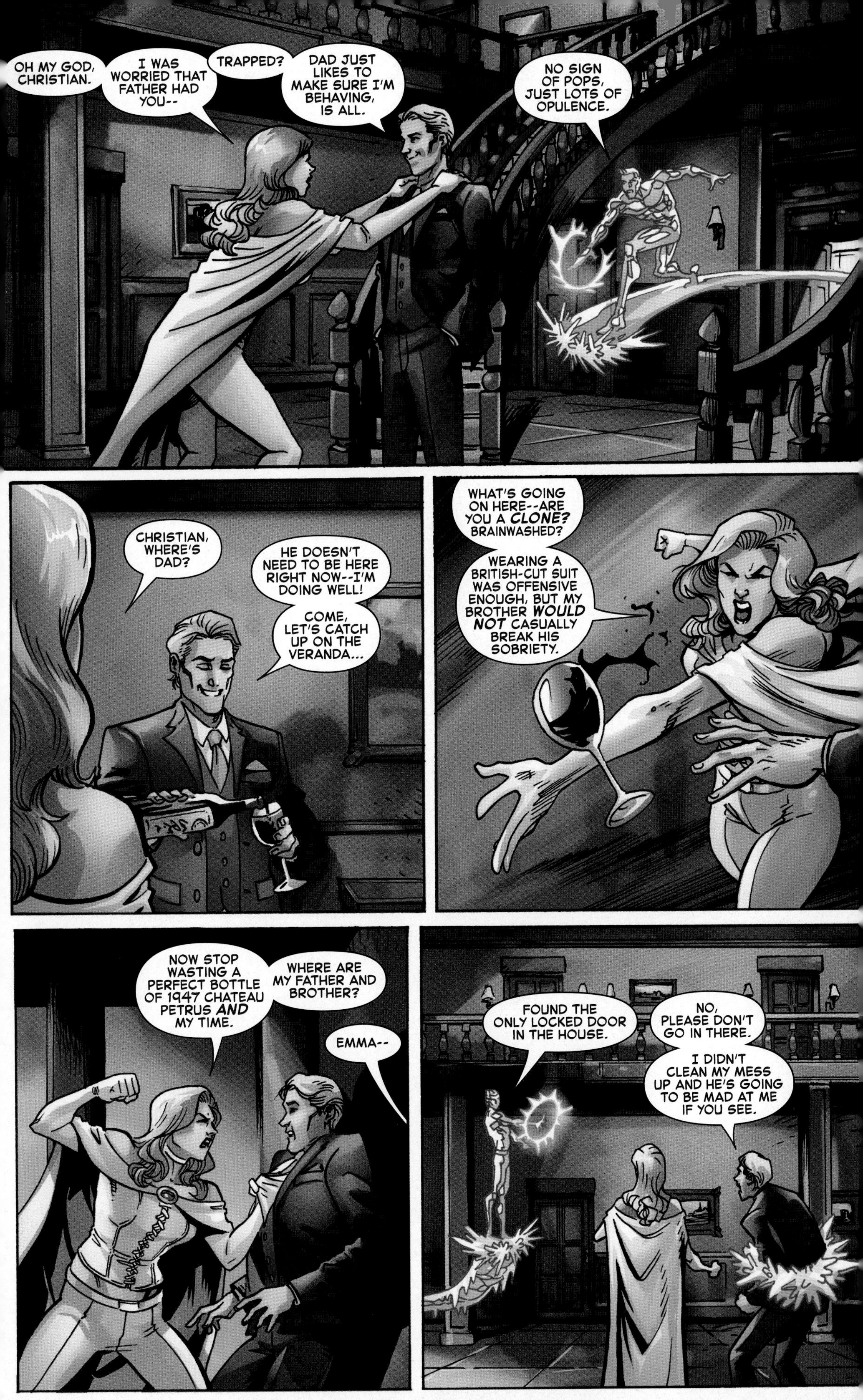

OH MY GOD, CHRISTIAN.
I WAS WORRIED THAT FATHER HAD YOU--
TRAPPED?
DAD JUST LIKES TO MAKE SURE I'M BEHAVING, IS ALL.
NO SIGN OF POPS, JUST LOTS OF OPULENCE.
CHRISTIAN, WHERE'S DAD?
HE DOESN'T NEED TO BE HERE RIGHT NOW--I'M DOING WELL!
COME, LET'S CATCH UP ON THE VERANDA...
WHAT'S GOING ON HERE--ARE YOU A CLONE? BRAINWASHED?
WEARING A BRITISH-CUT SUIT WAS OFFENSIVE ENOUGH, BUT MY BROTHER WOULD NOT CASUALLY BREAK HIS SOBRIETY.
NOW STOP WASTING A PERFECT BOTTLE OF 1947 CHATEAU PETRUS AND MY TIME.
WHERE ARE MY FATHER AND BROTHER?
EMMA--
FOUND THE ONLY LOCKED DOOR IN THE HOUSE.
NO, PLEASE DON'T GO IN THERE.
I DIDN'T CLEAN MY MESS UP AND HE'S GOING TO BE MAD AT ME IF YOU SEE.

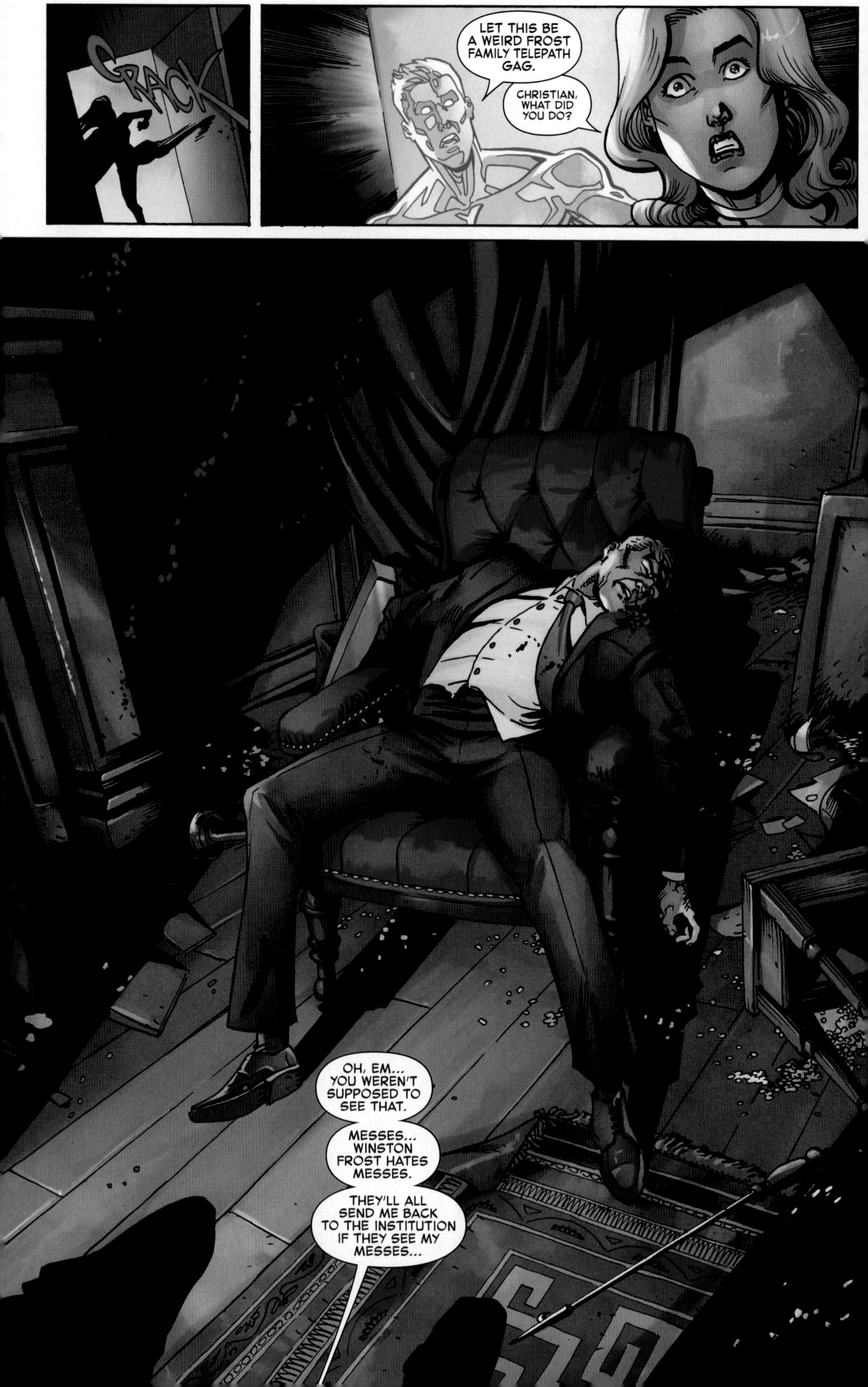
CRACK
LET THIS BE A WEIRD FROST FAMILY TELEPATH GAG.
CHRISTIAN, WHAT DID YOU DO?
OH, EM... YOU WEREN'T SUPPOSED TO SEE THAT.
MESSES... WINSTON FROST HATES MESSES.
THEY'LL ALL SEND ME BACK TO THE INSTITUTION IF THEY SEE MY MESSES...

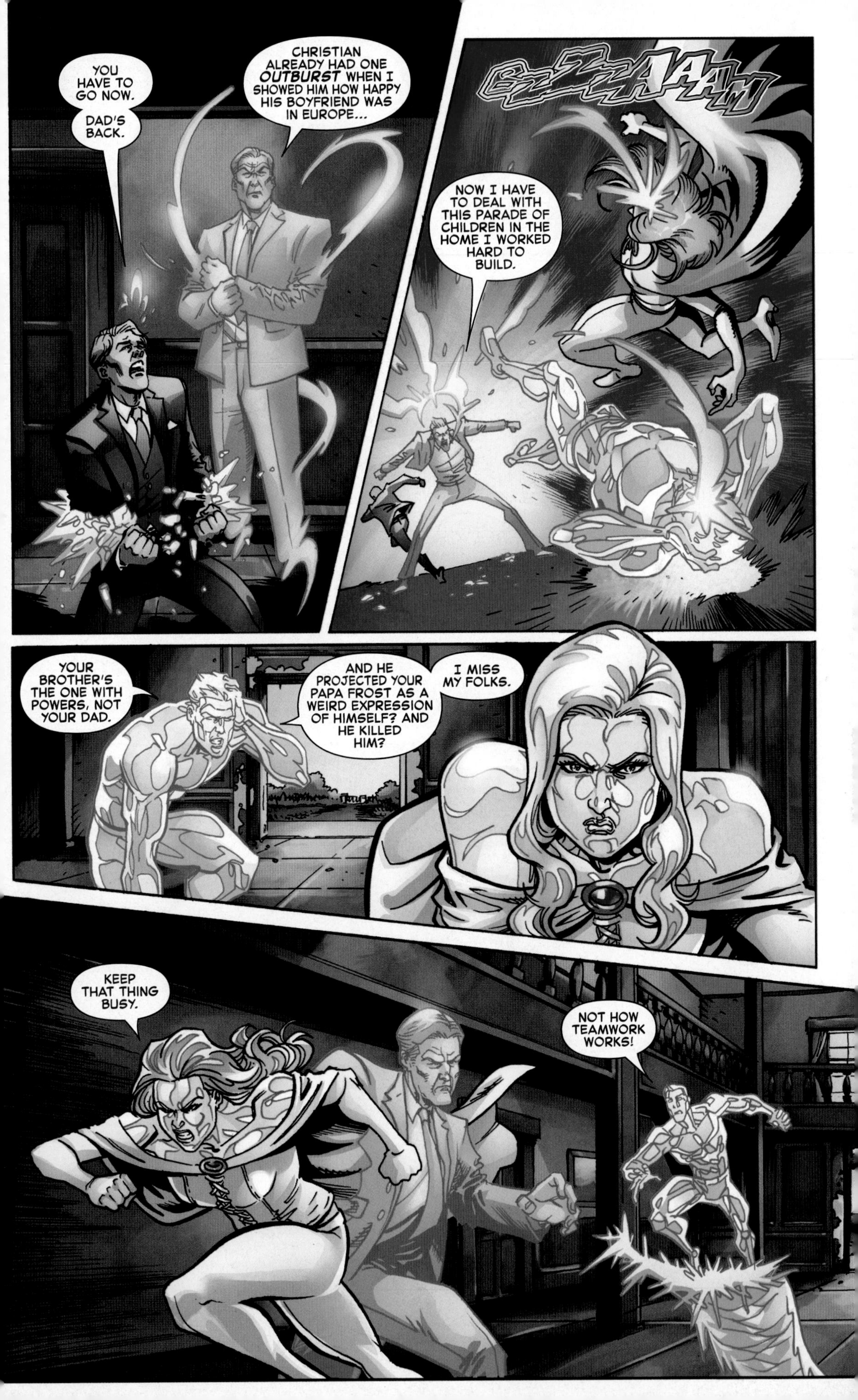
YOU HAVE TO GO NOW.
DAD'S BACK.
CHRISTIAN ALREADY HAD ONE OUTBURST WHEN I SHOWED HIM HOW HAPPY HIS BOYFRIEND WAS IN EUROPE...
NOW I HAVE TO DEAL WITH THIS PARADE OF CHILDREN IN THE HOME I WORKED HARD TO BUILD.
YOUR BROTHER'S THE ONE WITH POWERS, NOT YOUR DAD.
AND HE PROJECTED YOUR PAPA FROST AS A WEIRD EXPRESSION OF HIMSELF? AND HE KILLED HIM?
I MISS MY FOLKS.
KEEP THAT THING BUSY.
NOT HOW TEAMWORK WORKS!

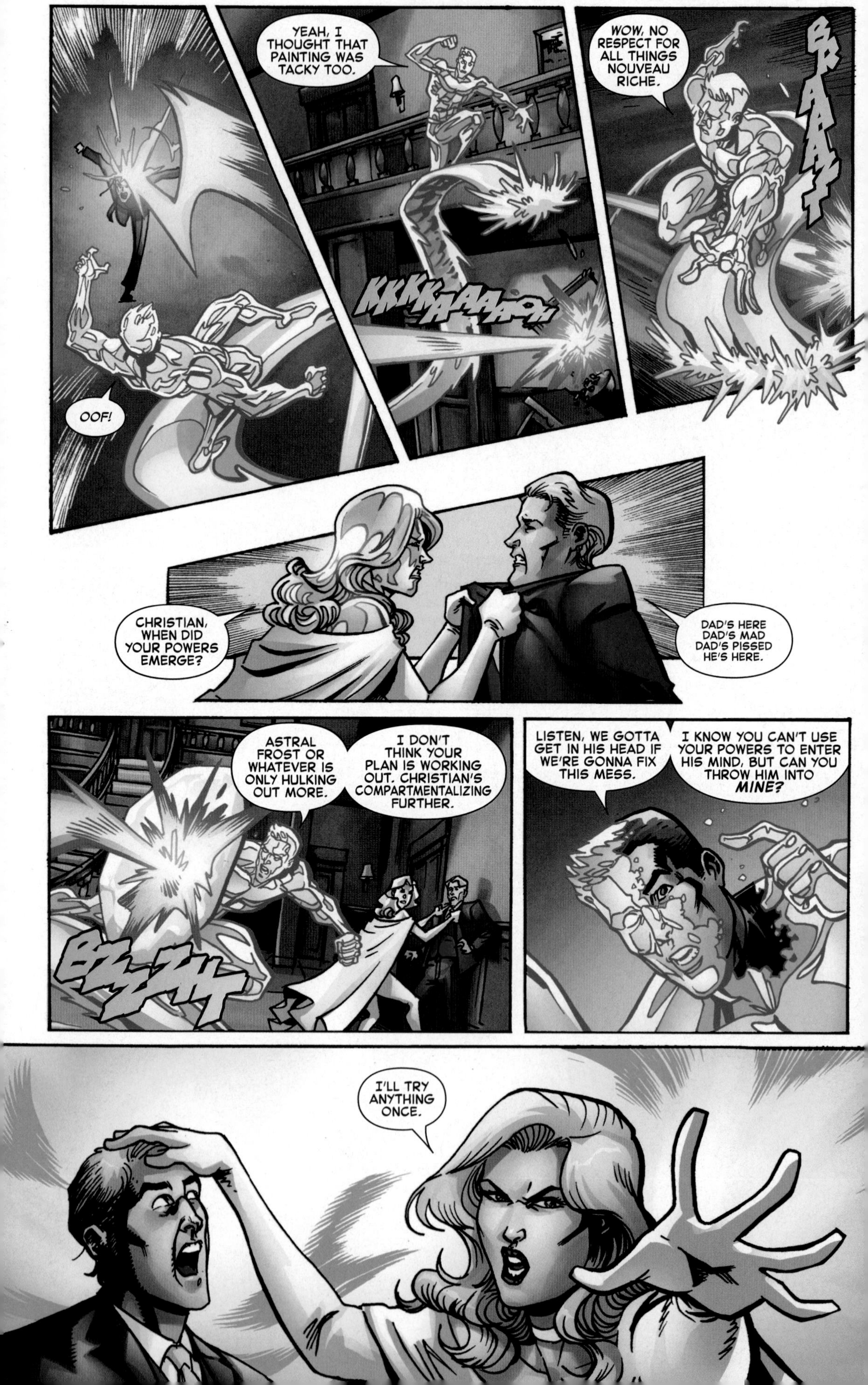
OOF!
YEAH, I THOUGHT THAT PAINTING WAS TACKY TOO.
KKKKAAAAAOH
WOW, NO RESPECT FOR ALL THINGS NOUVEAU RICHE.
BRAAKT
CHRISTIAN, WHEN DID YOUR POWERS EMERGE?
DAD'S HERE DAD'S MAD DAD'S PISSED HE'S HERE.
ASTRAL FROST OR WHATEVER IS ONLY HULKING OUT MORE.
I DON'T THINK YOUR PLAN IS WORKING OUT. CHRISTIAN'S COMPARTMENTALIZING FURTHER.
BZZZHT
LISTEN, WE GOTTA GET IN HIS HEAD IF WE'RE GONNA FIX THIS MESS.
I KNOW YOU CAN'T USE YOUR POWERS TO ENTER HIS MIND, BUT CAN YOU THROW HIM INTO *MINE?*
I'LL TRY ANYTHING ONCE.

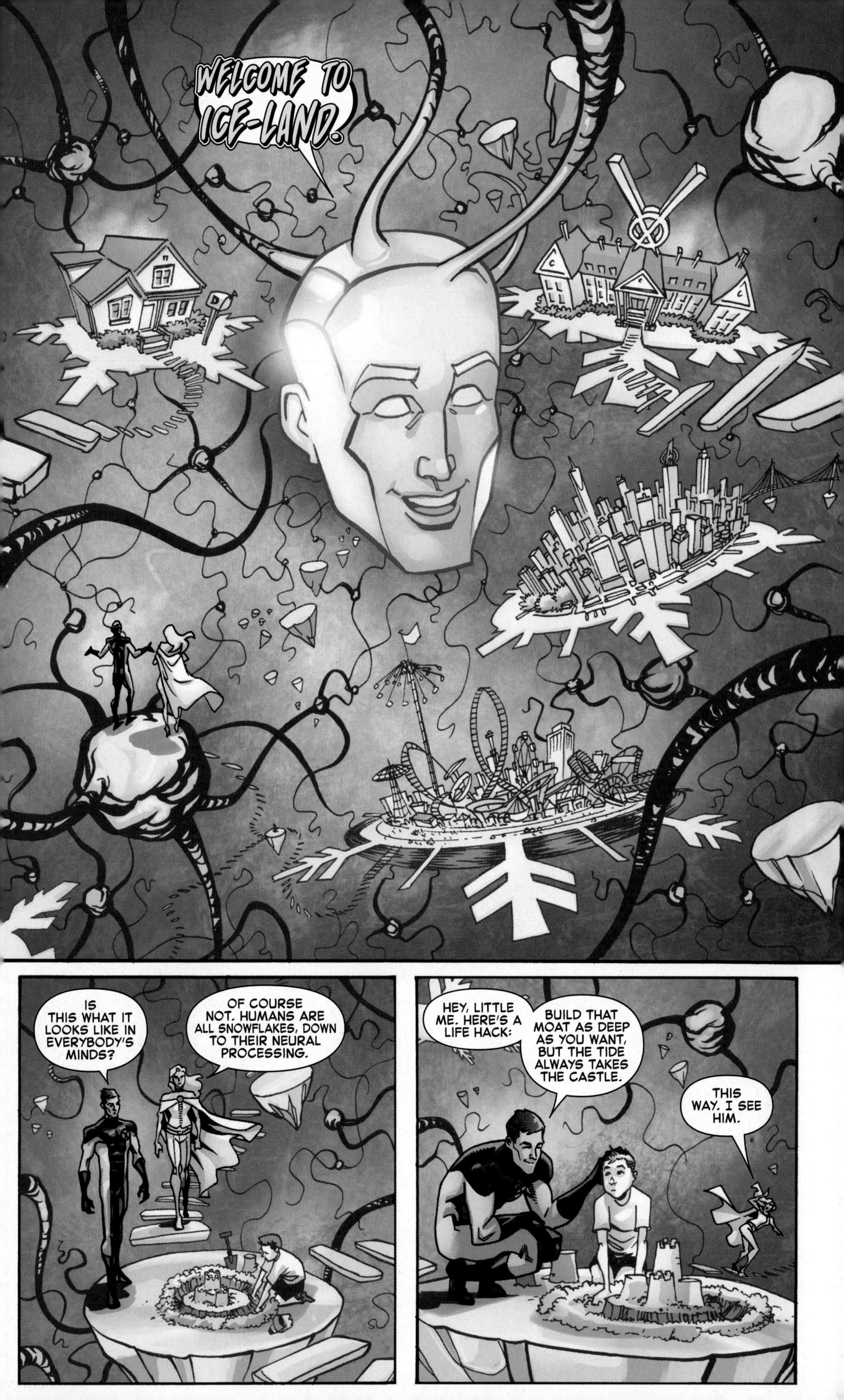
WELCOME TO ICE-LAND.
IS THIS WHAT IT LOOKS LIKE IN EVERYBODY'S MINDS?
OF COURSE NOT. HUMANS ARE ALL SNOWFLAKES, DOWN TO THEIR NEURAL PROCESSING.
HEY, LITTLE ME. HERE'S A LIFE HACK:
BUILD THAT MOAT AS DEEP AS YOU WANT, BUT THE TIDE ALWAYS TAKES THE CASTLE.
THIS WAY. I SEE HIM.

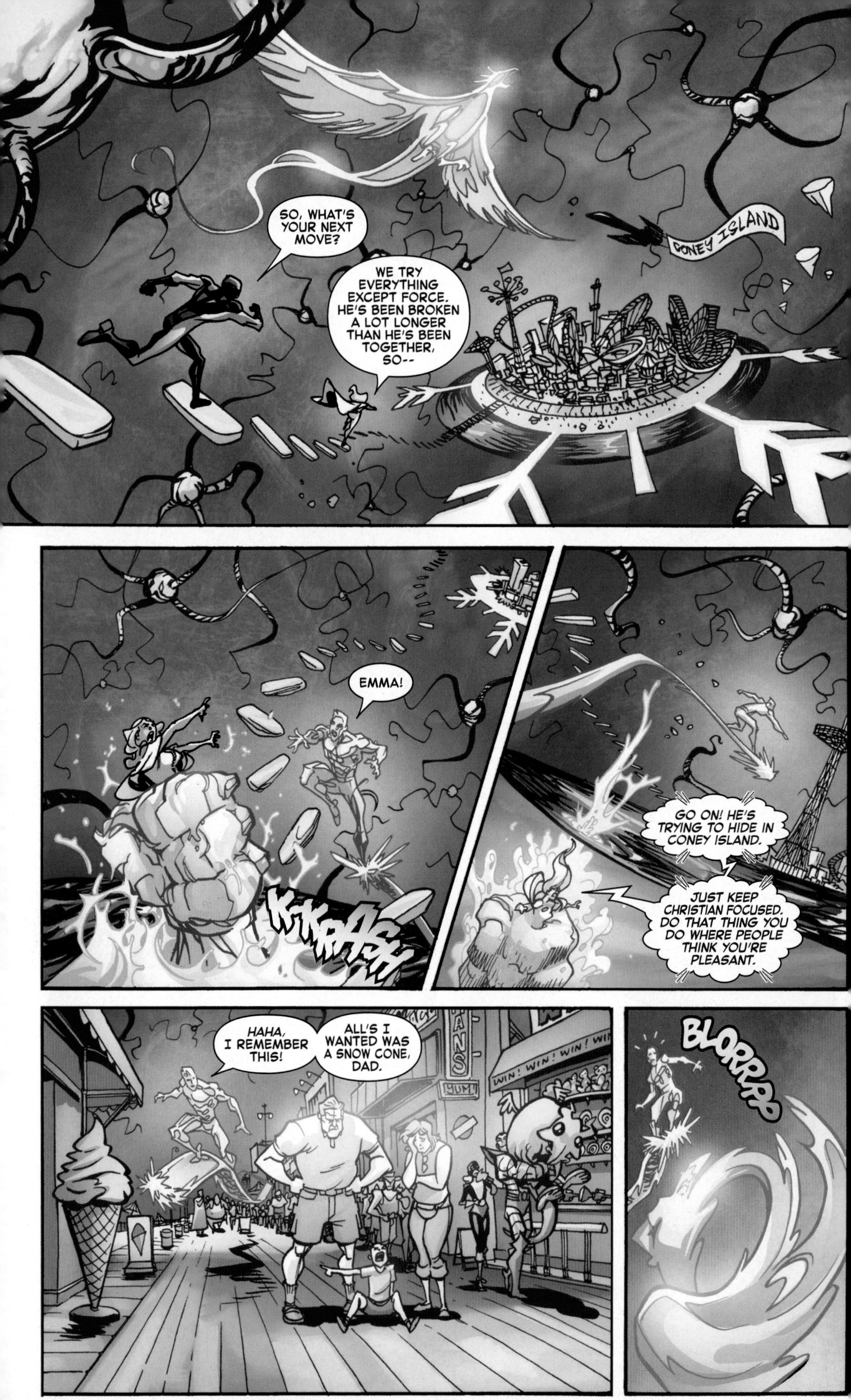
CONEY ISLAND
SO, WHAT'S YOUR NEXT MOVE?
WE TRY EVERYTHING EXCEPT FORCE. HE'S BEEN BROKEN A LOT LONGER THAN HE'S BEEN TOGETHER, SO--
EMMA!
K-KRASH
GO ON! HE'S TRYING TO HIDE IN CONEY ISLAND.
JUST KEEP CHRISTIAN FOCUSED. DO THAT THING YOU DO WHERE PEOPLE THINK YOU'RE PLEASANT.
HAHA, I REMEMBER THIS!
ALL'S I WANTED WAS A SNOW CONE, DAD.
WIN! WIN! WIN! WIN!
YUM!
BLORRRP

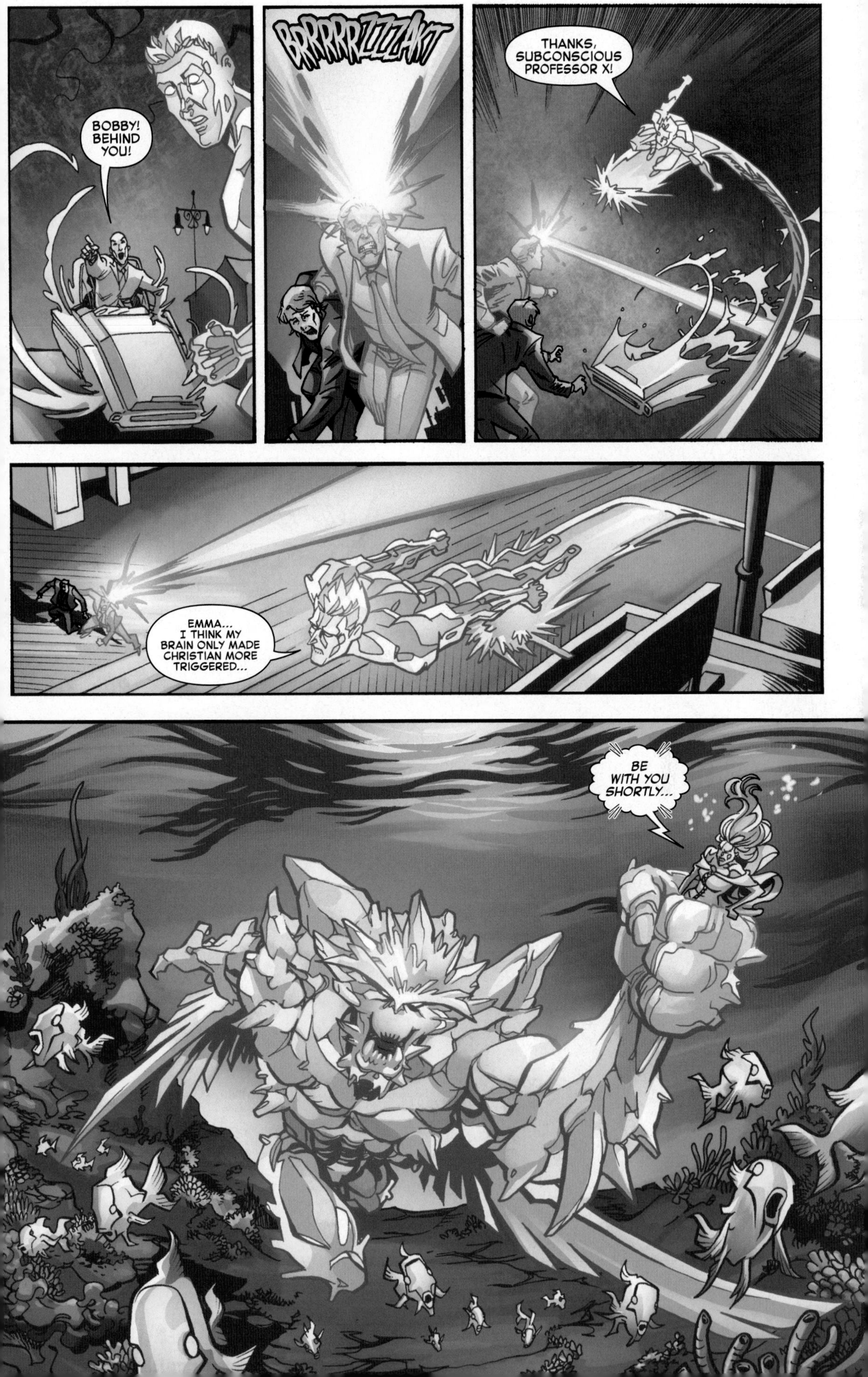

BOBBY! BEHIND YOU!
BRRRRRZZZZAKT
THANKS, SUBCONSCIOUS PROFESSOR X!
EMMA... I THINK MY BRAIN ONLY MADE CHRISTIAN MORE TRIGGERED...
BE WITH YOU SHORTLY...

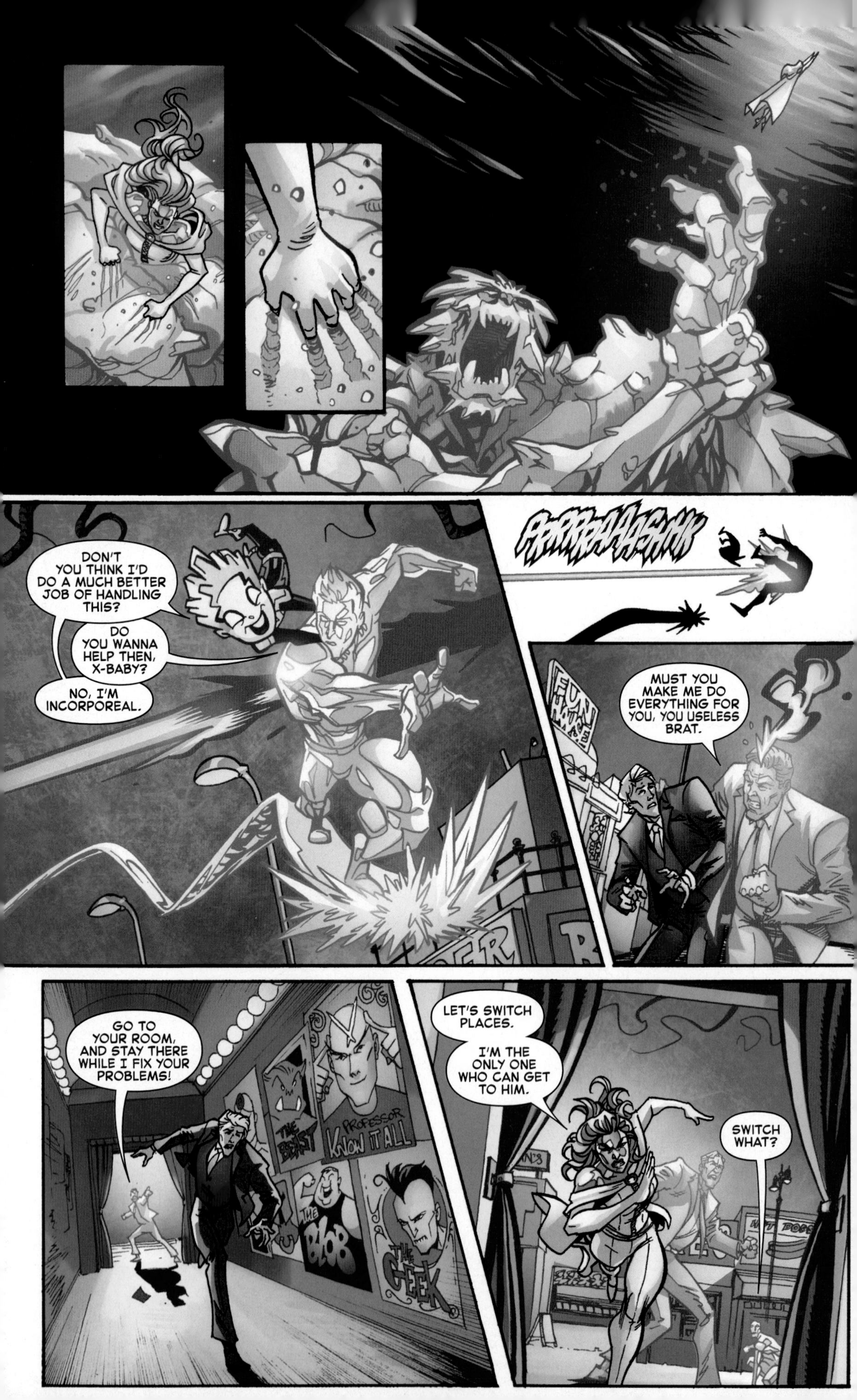

DON'T YOU THINK I'D DO A MUCH BETTER JOB OF HANDLING THIS?
DO YOU WANNA HELP THEN, X-BABY?
NO, I'M INCORPOREAL.
FUN
MUST YOU MAKE ME DO EVERYTHING FOR YOU, YOU USELESS BRAT.
GO TO YOUR ROOM, AND STAY THERE WHILE I FIX YOUR PROBLEMS!
THE BEAST
PROFESSOR KNOW IT ALL
THE BLOB
THE GEEK
LET'S SWITCH PLACES.
I'M THE ONLY ONE WHO CAN GET TO HIM.
SWITCH WHAT?

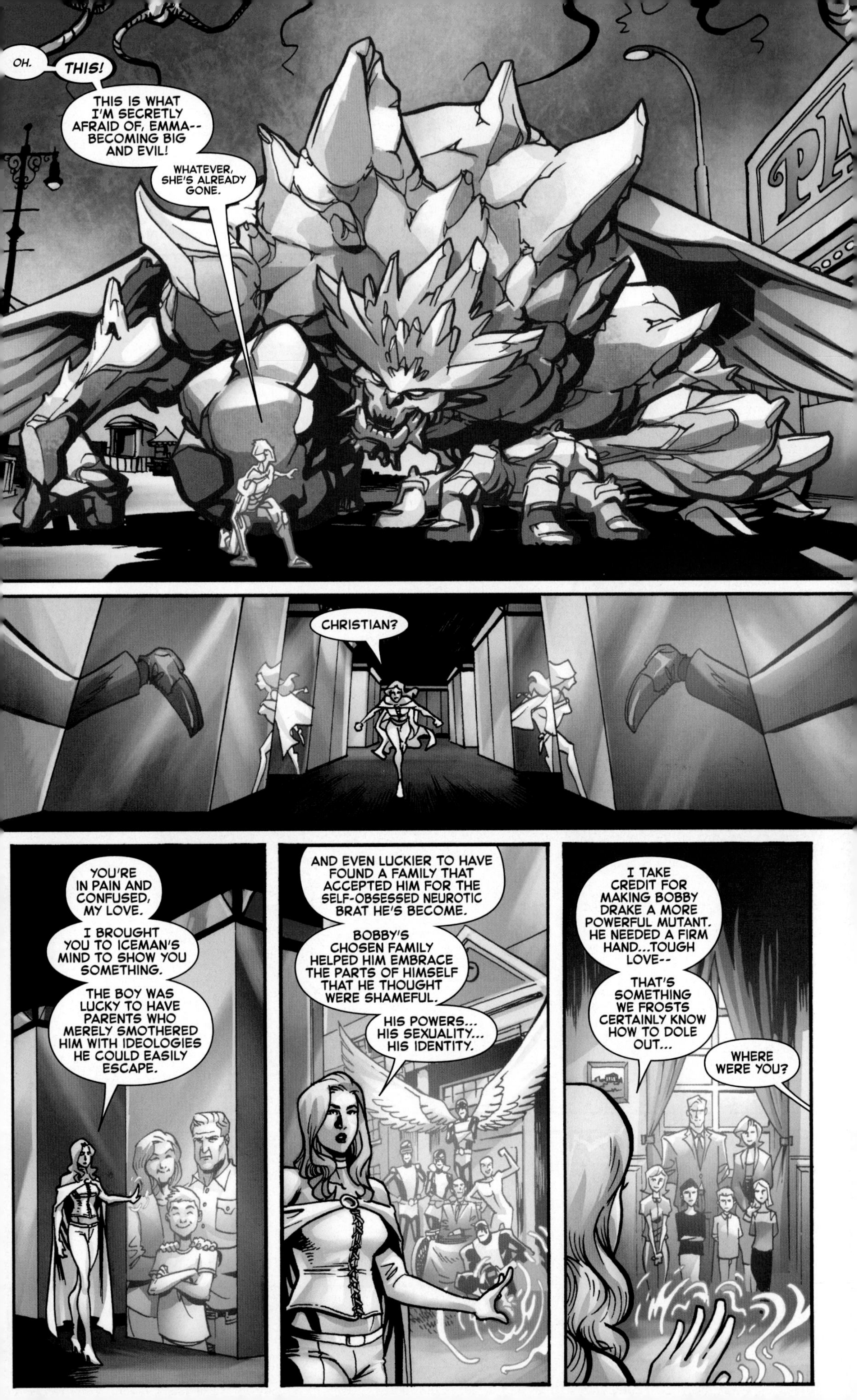
OH.
THIS!
THIS IS WHAT I'M SECRETLY AFRAID OF, EMMA-- BECOMING BIG AND EVIL!
WHATEVER, SHE'S ALREADY GONE.
CHRISTIAN?
YOU'RE IN PAIN AND CONFUSED, MY LOVE.
I BROUGHT YOU TO ICEMAN'S MIND TO SHOW YOU SOMETHING.
THE BOY WAS LUCKY TO HAVE PARENTS WHO MERELY SMOTHERED HIM WITH IDEOLOGIES HE COULD EASILY ESCAPE.
AND EVEN LUCKIER TO HAVE FOUND A FAMILY THAT ACCEPTED HIM FOR THE SELF-OBSESSED NEUROTIC BRAT HE'S BECOME.
BOBBY'S CHOSEN FAMILY HELPED HIM EMBRACE THE PARTS OF HIMSELF THAT HE THOUGHT WERE SHAMEFUL.
HIS POWERS... HIS SEXUALITY... HIS IDENTITY.
I TAKE CREDIT FOR MAKING BOBBY DRAKE A MORE POWERFUL MUTANT. HE NEEDED A FIRM HAND...TOUGH LOVE--
THAT'S SOMETHING WE FROSTS CERTAINLY KNOW HOW TO DOLE OUT...
WHERE WERE YOU?

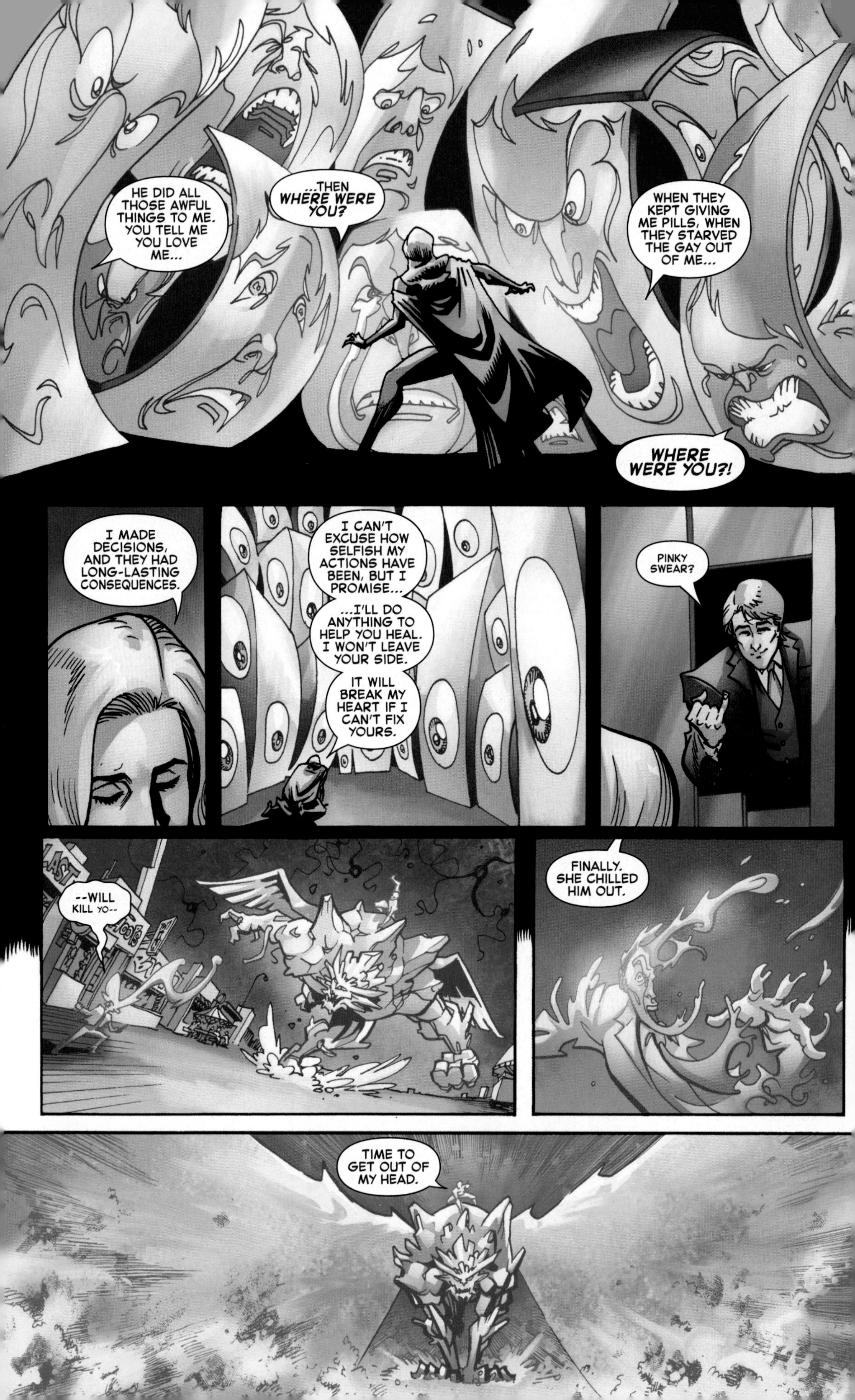
HE DID ALL THOSE AWFUL THINGS TO ME. YOU TELL ME YOU LOVE ME...
...THEN WHERE WERE YOU?
WHEN THEY KEPT GIVING ME PILLS, WHEN THEY STARVED THE GAY OUT OF ME...
WHERE WERE YOU?!
I MADE DECISIONS, AND THEY HAD LONG-LASTING CONSEQUENCES.
I CAN'T EXCUSE HOW SELFISH MY ACTIONS HAVE BEEN, BUT I PROMISE...
...I'LL DO ANYTHING TO HELP YOU HEAL. I WON'T LEAVE YOUR SIDE.
IT WILL BREAK MY HEART IF I CAN'T FIX YOURS.
PINKY SWEAR?
--WILL KILL YO--
FINALLY. SHE CHILLED HIM OUT.
TIME TO GET OUT OF MY HEAD.

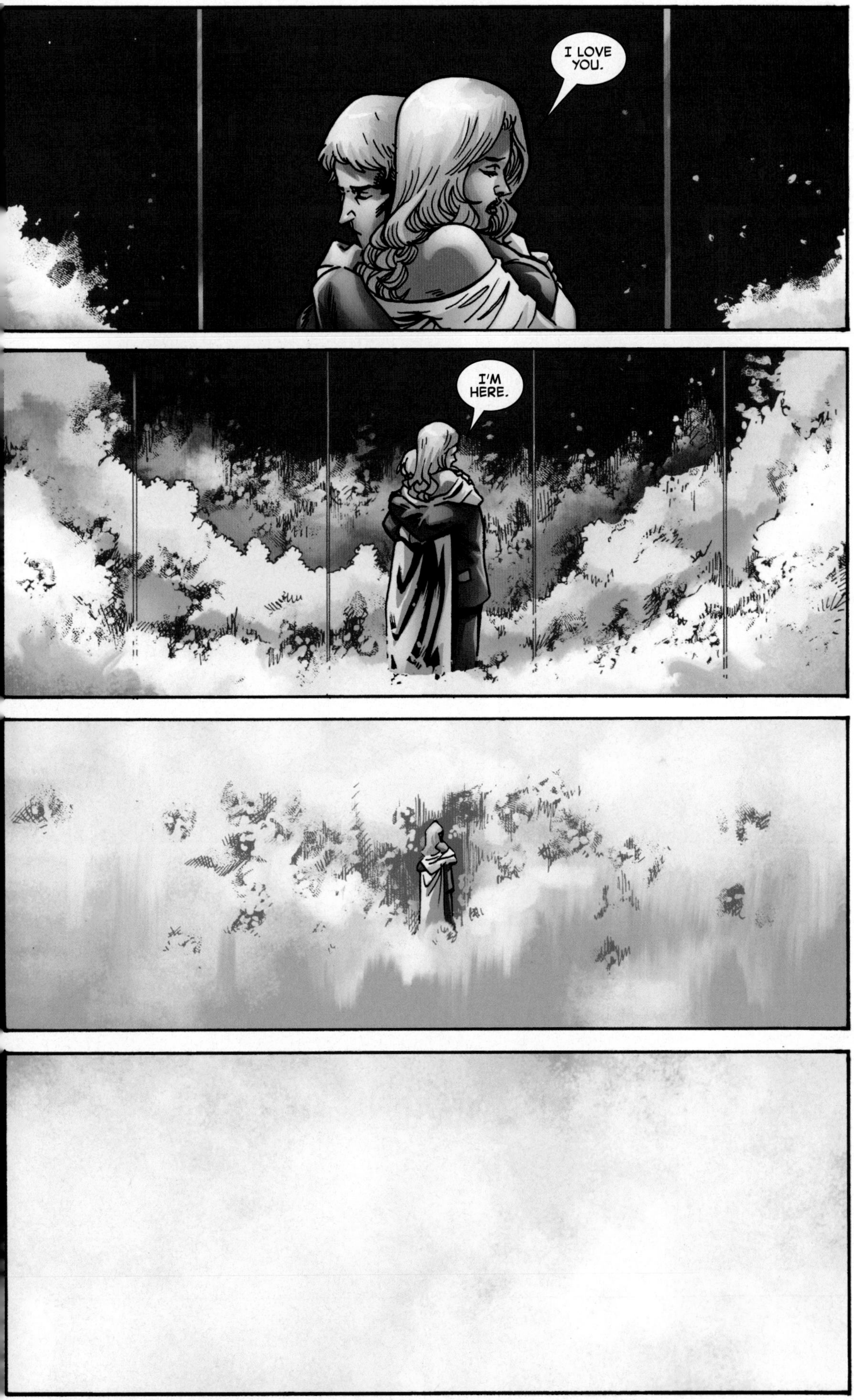
I LOVE YOU.
I'M HERE.

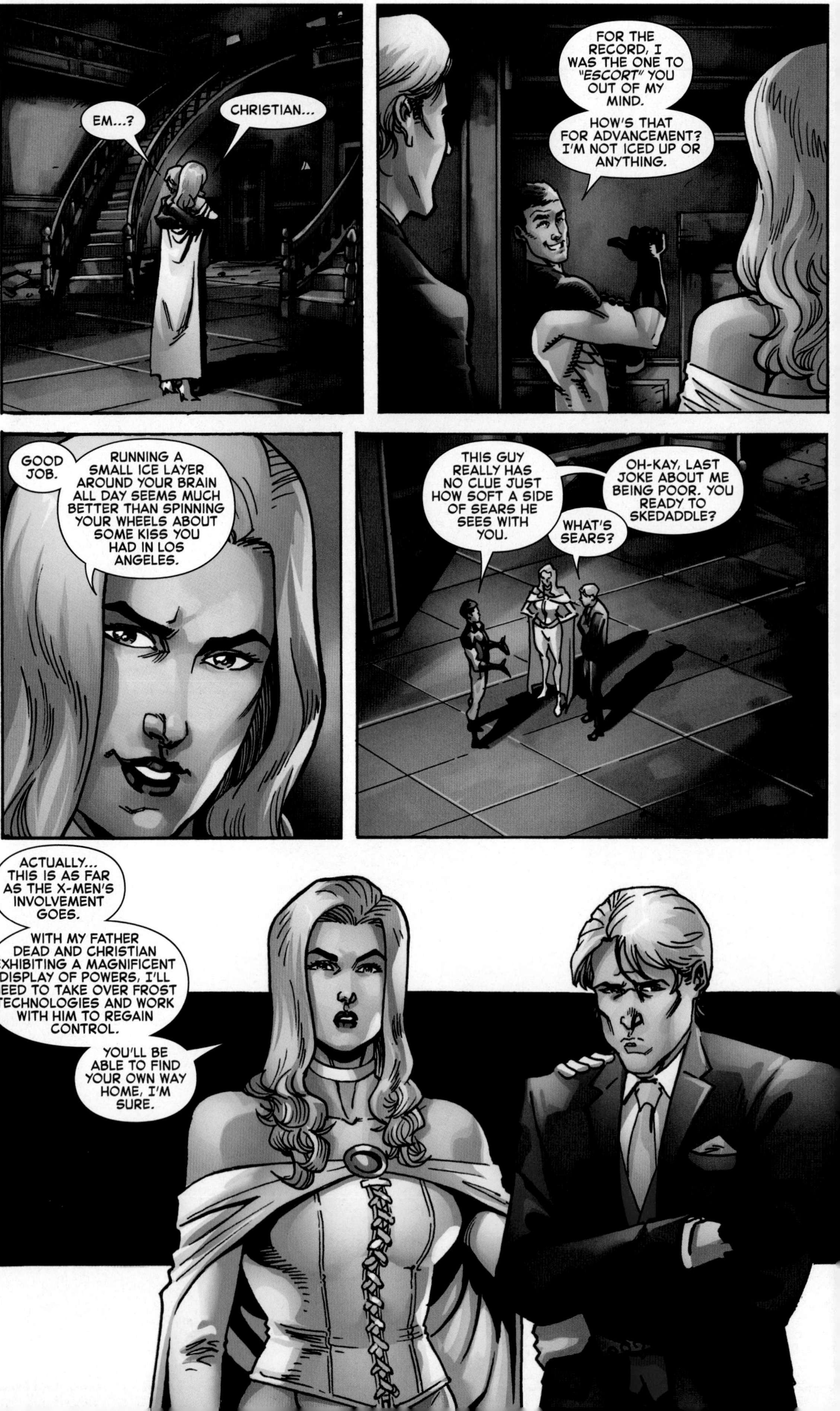
EM...?
CHRISTIAN...
FOR THE RECORD, I WAS THE ONE TO "ESCORT" YOU OUT OF MY MIND.
HOW'S THAT FOR ADVANCEMENT? I'M NOT ICED UP OR ANYTHING.
GOOD JOB.
RUNNING A SMALL ICE LAYER AROUND YOUR BRAIN ALL DAY SEEMS MUCH BETTER THAN SPINNING YOUR WHEELS ABOUT SOME KISS YOU HAD IN LOS ANGELES.
THIS GUY REALLY HAS NO CLUE JUST HOW SOFT A SIDE OF SEARS HE SEES WITH YOU.
WHAT'S SEARS?
OH-KAY, LAST JOKE ABOUT ME BEING POOR. YOU READY TO SKEDADDLE?
ACTUALLY... THIS IS AS FAR AS THE X-MEN'S INVOLVEMENT GOES.
WITH MY FATHER DEAD AND CHRISTIAN EXHIBITING A MAGNIFICENT DISPLAY OF POWERS, I'LL NEED TO TAKE OVER FROST TECHNOLOGIES AND WORK WITH HIM TO REGAIN CONTROL.
YOU'LL BE ABLE TO FIND YOUR OWN WAY HOME, I'M SURE.

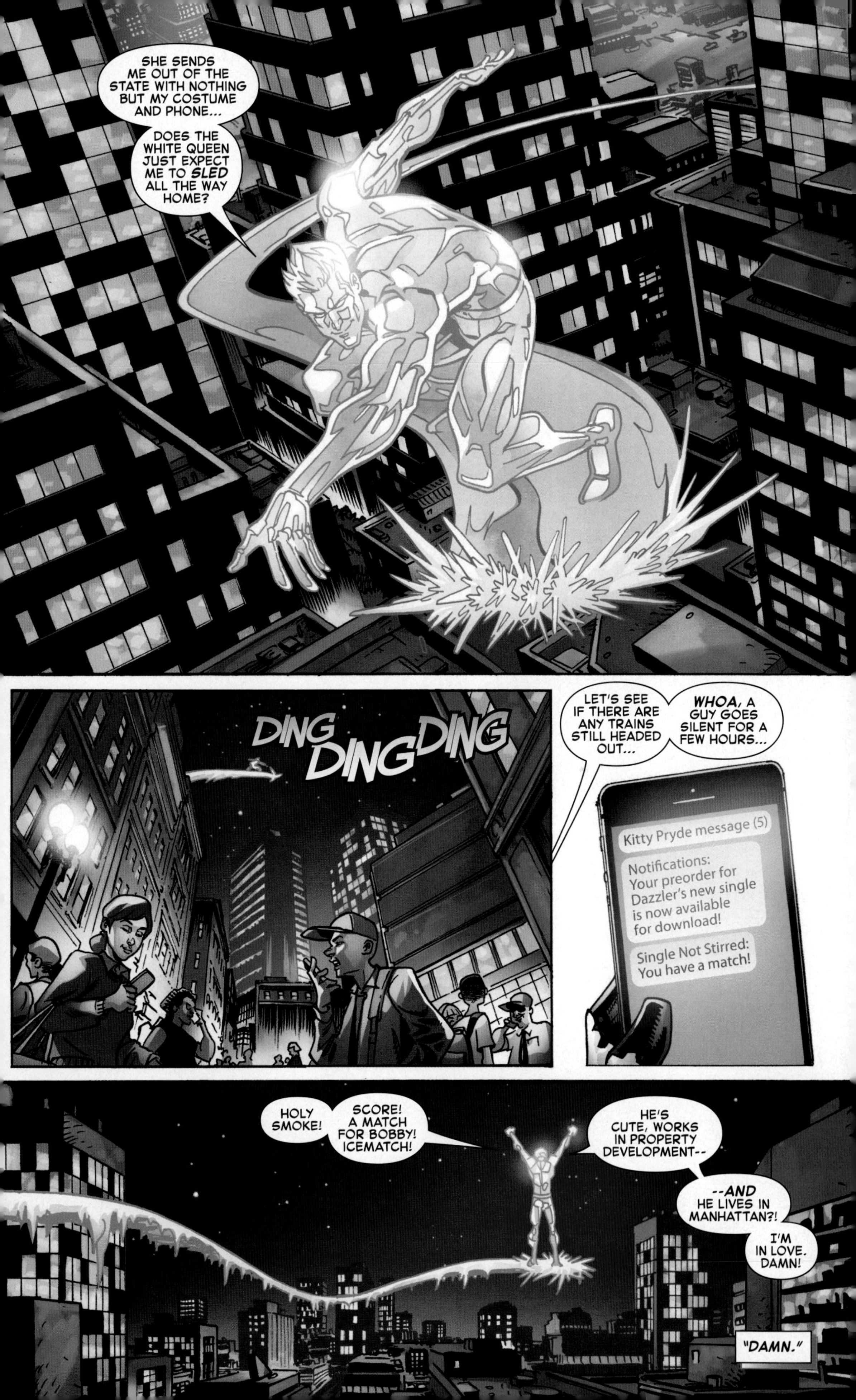
SHE SENDS ME OUT OF THE STATE WITH NOTHING BUT MY COSTUME AND PHONE...
DOES THE WHITE QUEEN JUST EXPECT ME TO SLED ALL THE WAY HOME?
DING DING DING
LET'S SEE IF THERE ARE ANY TRAINS STILL HEADED OUT...
WHOA, A GUY GOES SILENT FOR A FEW HOURS...
Kitty Pryde message (5)
Notifications: Your preorder for Dazzler's new single is now available for download!
Single Not Stirred: You have a match!
HOLY SMOKE!
SCORE! A MATCH FOR BOBBY! ICEMATCH!
HE'S CUTE, WORKS IN PROPERTY DEVELOPMENT--
--AND HE LIVES IN MANHATTAN?!
I'M IN LOVE. DAMN!
"DAMN."

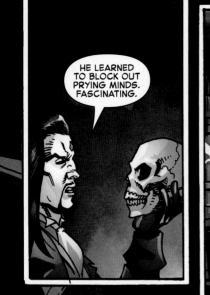

HE LEARNED TO BLOCK OUT PRYING MINDS. FASCINATING.

HMM. I'M NOT READY TO EXPOSE MYSELF TO THE X-MEN JUST YET...

...BUT I NEED ICEMAN PHYSICALLY HERE TO COMPLETE MY ANALYSIS FOR OUR LITTLE PROJECT.

ARE YOU EXCITED TO FIGHT YOUR FIRST X-MAN?

#1 VARIANT BY **SKOTTIE YOUNG**

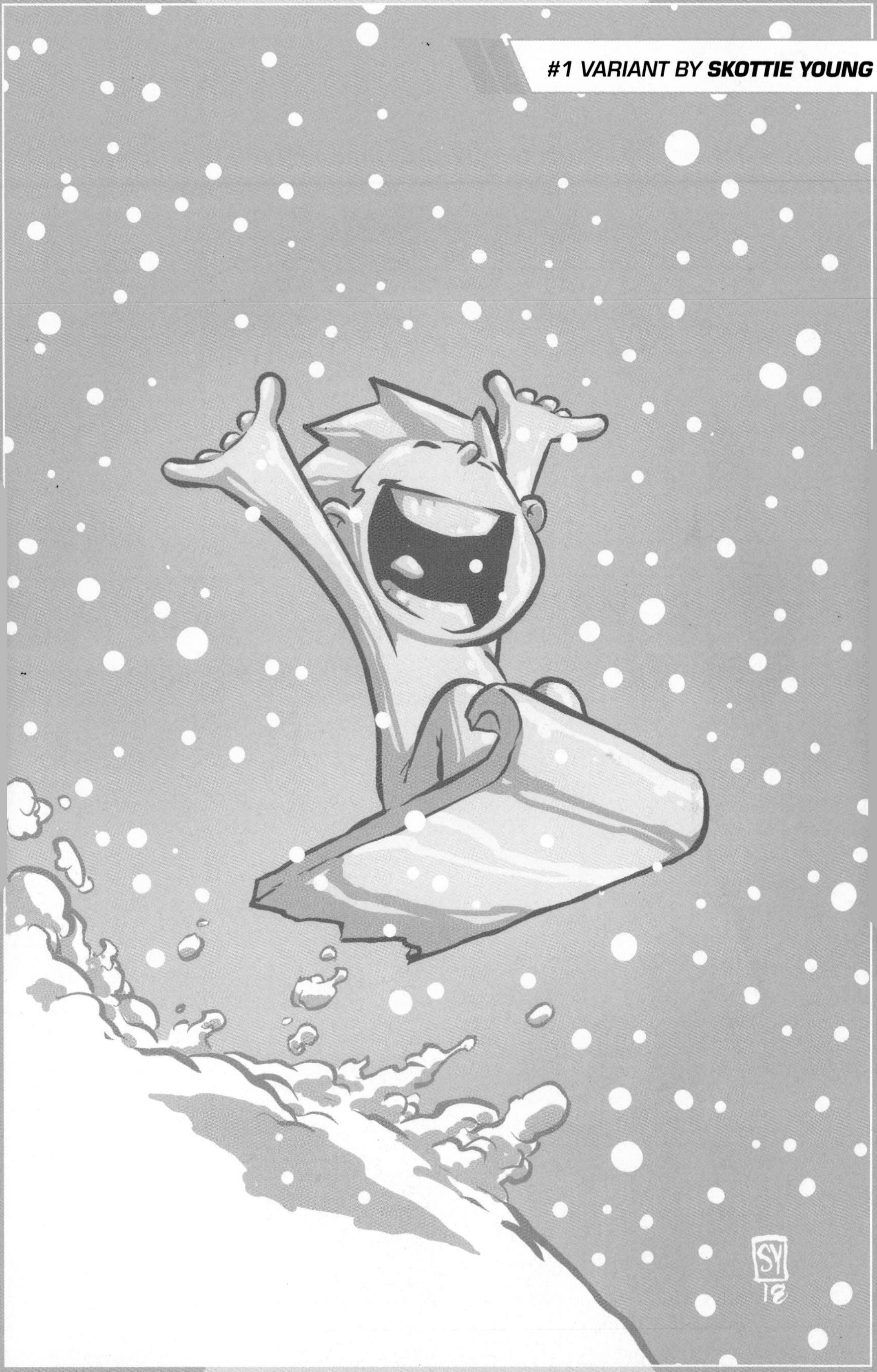
SY
18

3

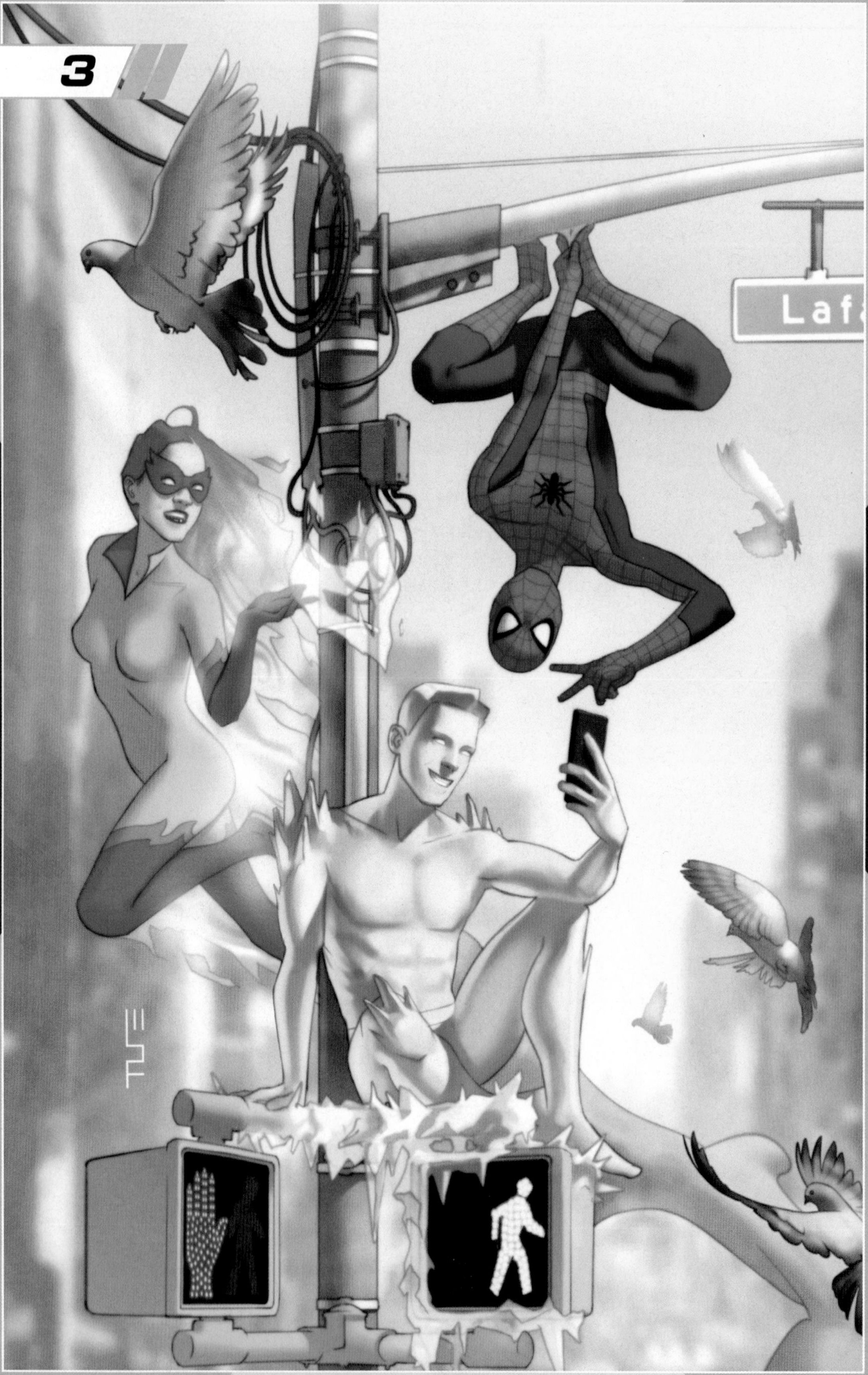
Lafa

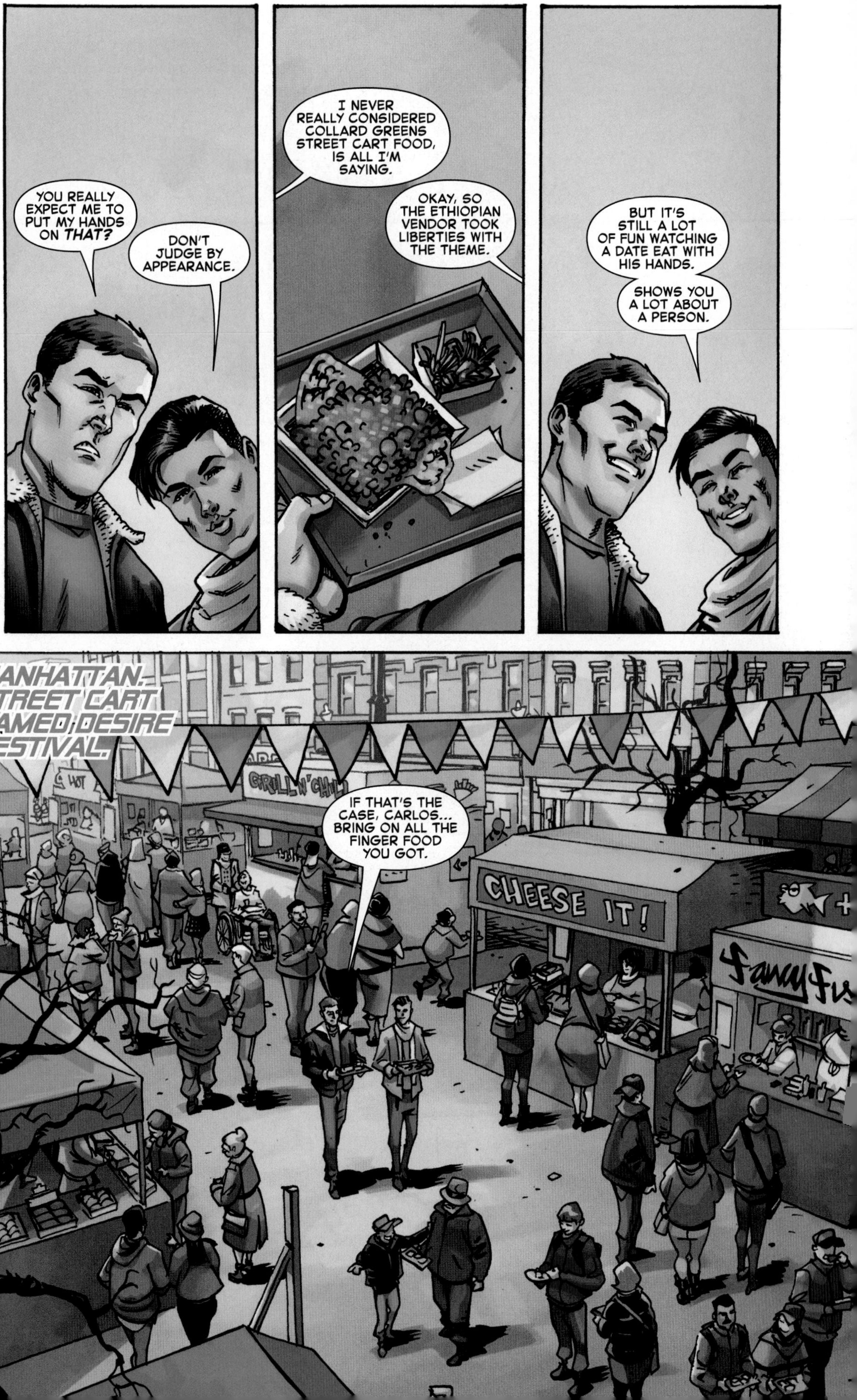
YOU REALLY EXPECT ME TO PUT MY HANDS ON *THAT?*
DON'T JUDGE BY APPEARANCE.
I NEVER REALLY CONSIDERED COLLARD GREENS STREET CART FOOD, IS ALL I'M SAYING.
OKAY, SO THE ETHIOPIAN VENDOR TOOK LIBERTIES WITH THE THEME.
BUT IT'S STILL A LOT OF FUN WATCHING A DATE EAT WITH HIS HANDS.
SHOWS YOU A LOT ABOUT A PERSON.
MANHATTAN. STREET CART NAMED DESIRE FESTIVAL.
IF THAT'S THE CASE, CARLOS... BRING ON ALL THE FINGER FOOD YOU GOT.
CHEESE IT!

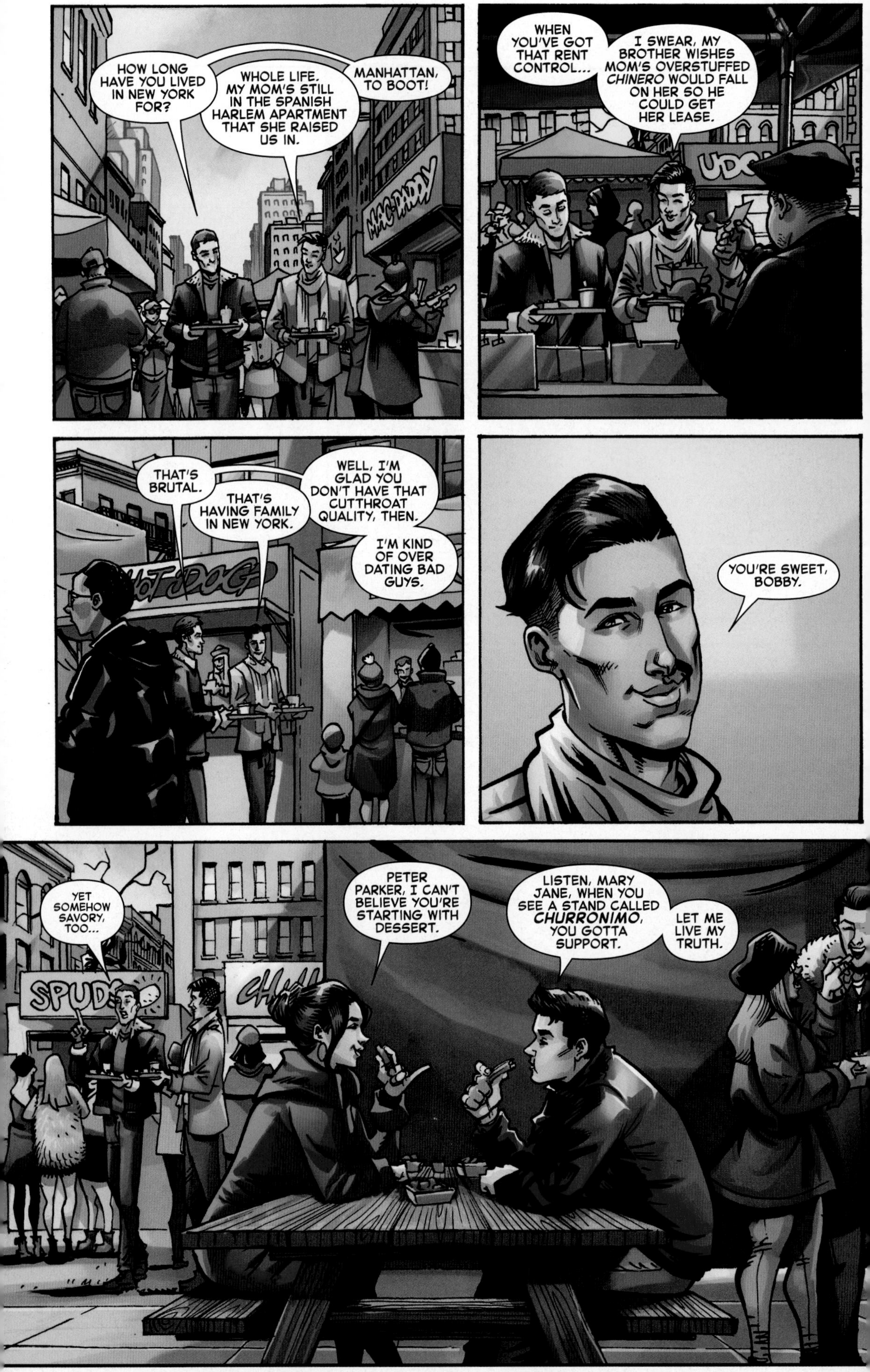

HOW LONG HAVE YOU LIVED IN NEW YORK FOR?
WHOLE LIFE. MY MOM'S STILL IN THE SPANISH HARLEM APARTMENT THAT SHE RAISED US IN.
MANHATTAN, TO BOOT!
MAC-DADDY
WHEN YOU'VE GOT THAT RENT CONTROL...
I SWEAR, MY BROTHER WISHES MOM'S OVERSTUFFED *CHINERO* WOULD FALL ON HER SO HE COULD GET HER LEASE.
THAT'S BRUTAL.
THAT'S HAVING FAMILY IN NEW YORK.
WELL, I'M GLAD YOU DON'T HAVE THAT CUTTHROAT QUALITY, THEN.
I'M KIND OF OVER DATING BAD GUYS.
HOT DOG
YOU'RE SWEET, BOBBY.
YET SOMEHOW SAVORY, TOO...
SPUDS
PETER PARKER, I CAN'T BELIEVE YOU'RE STARTING WITH DESSERT.
LISTEN, MARY JANE, WHEN YOU SEE A STAND CALLED **CHURRONIMO**, YOU GOTTA SUPPORT.
LET ME LIVE MY TRUTH.

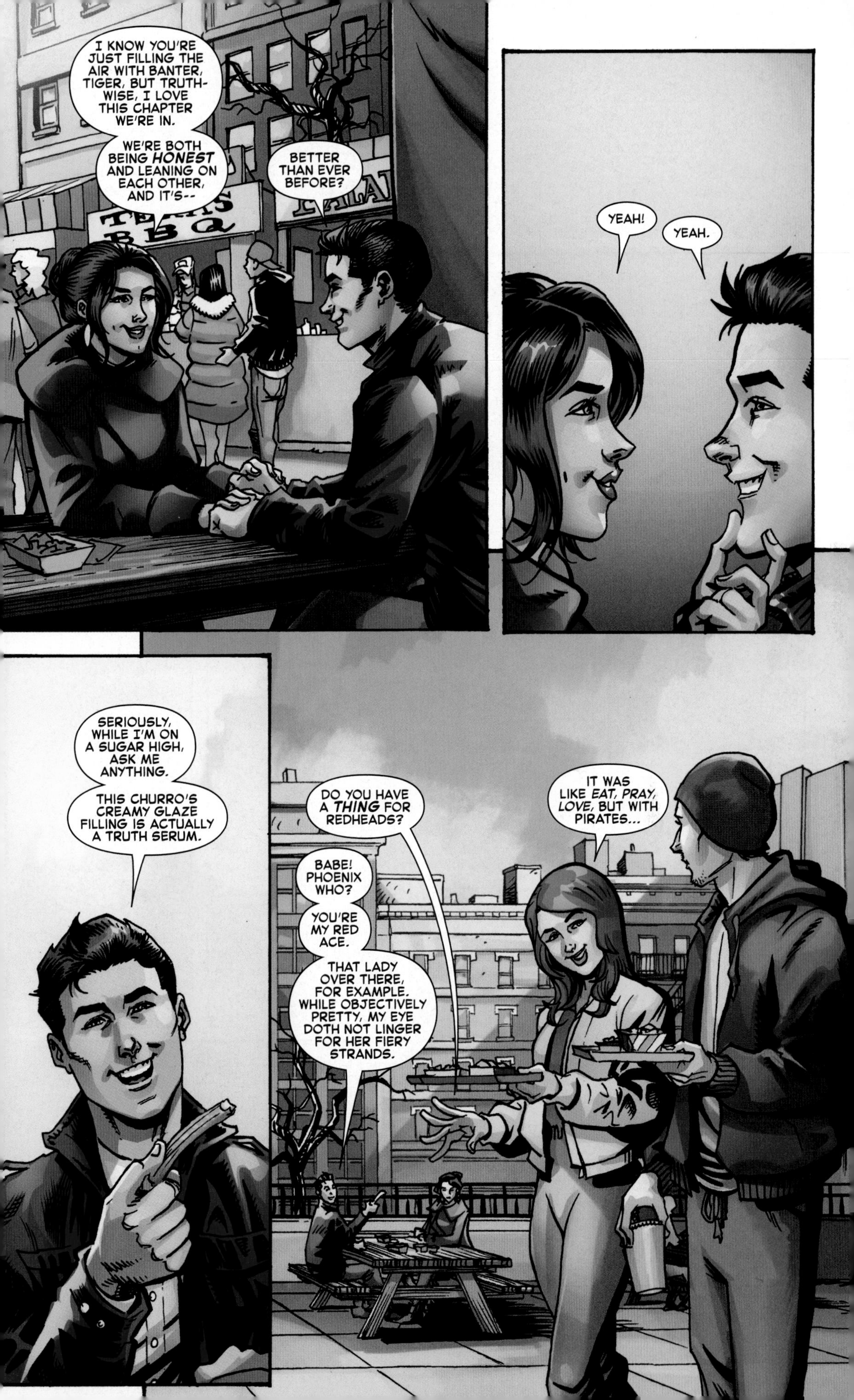
I KNOW YOU'RE JUST FILLING THE AIR WITH BANTER, TIGER, BUT TRUTH-WISE, I LOVE THIS CHAPTER WE'RE IN.
WE'RE BOTH BEING *HONEST* AND LEANING ON EACH OTHER, AND IT'S--
BETTER THAN EVER BEFORE?
YEAH!
YEAH.
SERIOUSLY, WHILE I'M ON A SUGAR HIGH, ASK ME ANYTHING.
THIS CHURRO'S CREAMY GLAZE FILLING IS ACTUALLY A TRUTH SERUM.
DO YOU HAVE A *THING* FOR REDHEADS?
BABE! PHOENIX WHO?
YOU'RE MY RED ACE.
THAT LADY OVER THERE, FOR EXAMPLE. WHILE OBJECTIVELY PRETTY, MY EYE DOTH NOT LINGER FOR HER FIERY STRANDS.
IT WAS LIKE *EAT, PRAY, LOVE,* BUT WITH PIRATES...

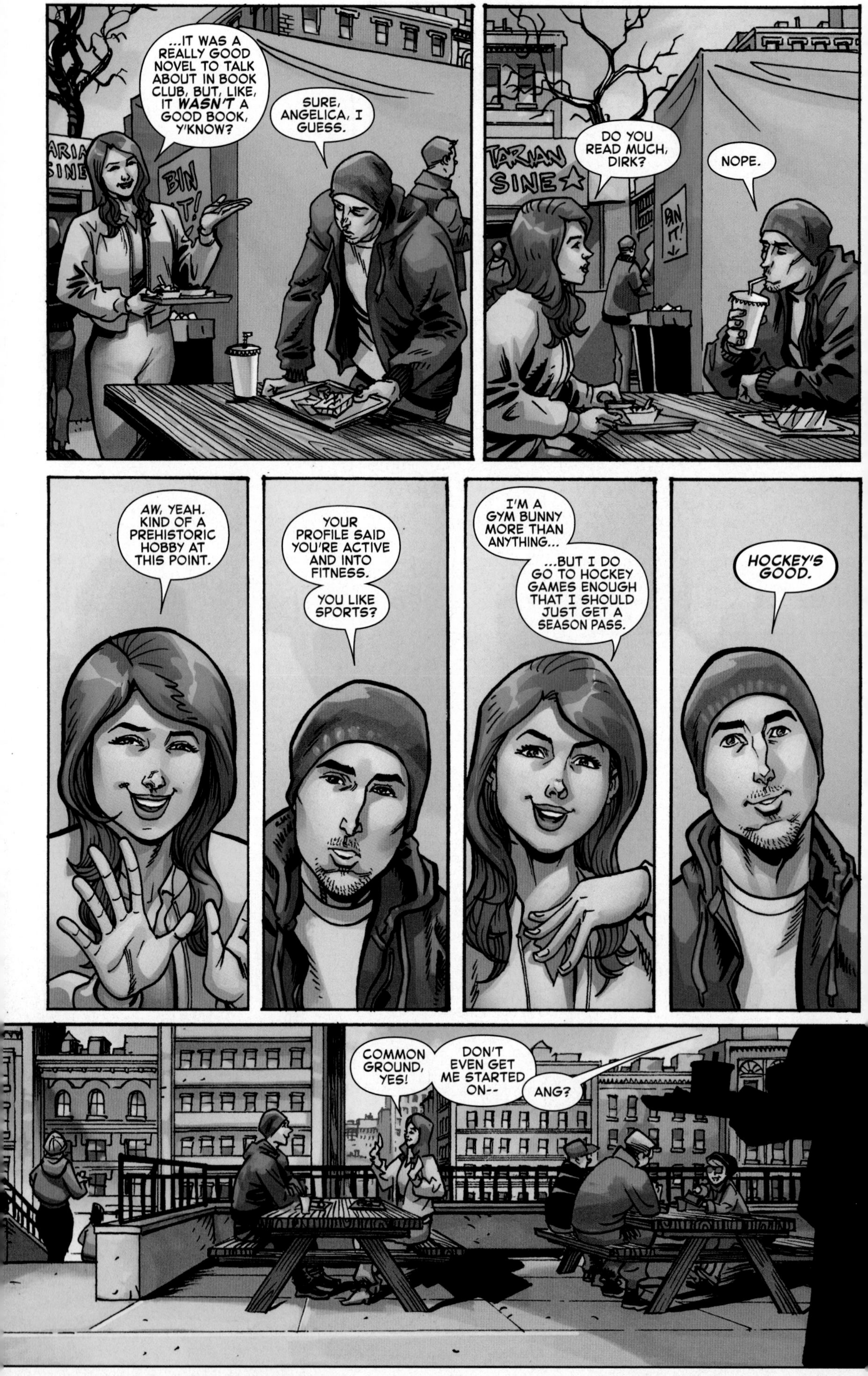

...IT WAS A REALLY GOOD NOVEL TO TALK ABOUT IN BOOK CLUB, BUT, LIKE, IT ***WASN'T*** A GOOD BOOK, Y'KNOW?
SURE, ANGELICA, I GUESS.
BIN IT!
DO YOU READ MUCH, DIRK?
NOPE.
AW, YEAH. KIND OF A PREHISTORIC HOBBY AT THIS POINT.
YOUR PROFILE SAID YOU'RE ACTIVE AND INTO FITNESS.
YOU LIKE SPORTS?
I'M A GYM BUNNY MORE THAN ANYTHING...
...BUT I DO GO TO HOCKEY GAMES ENOUGH THAT I SHOULD JUST GET A SEASON PASS.
HOCKEY'S GOOD.
COMMON GROUND, YES!
DON'T EVEN GET ME STARTED ON--
ANG?

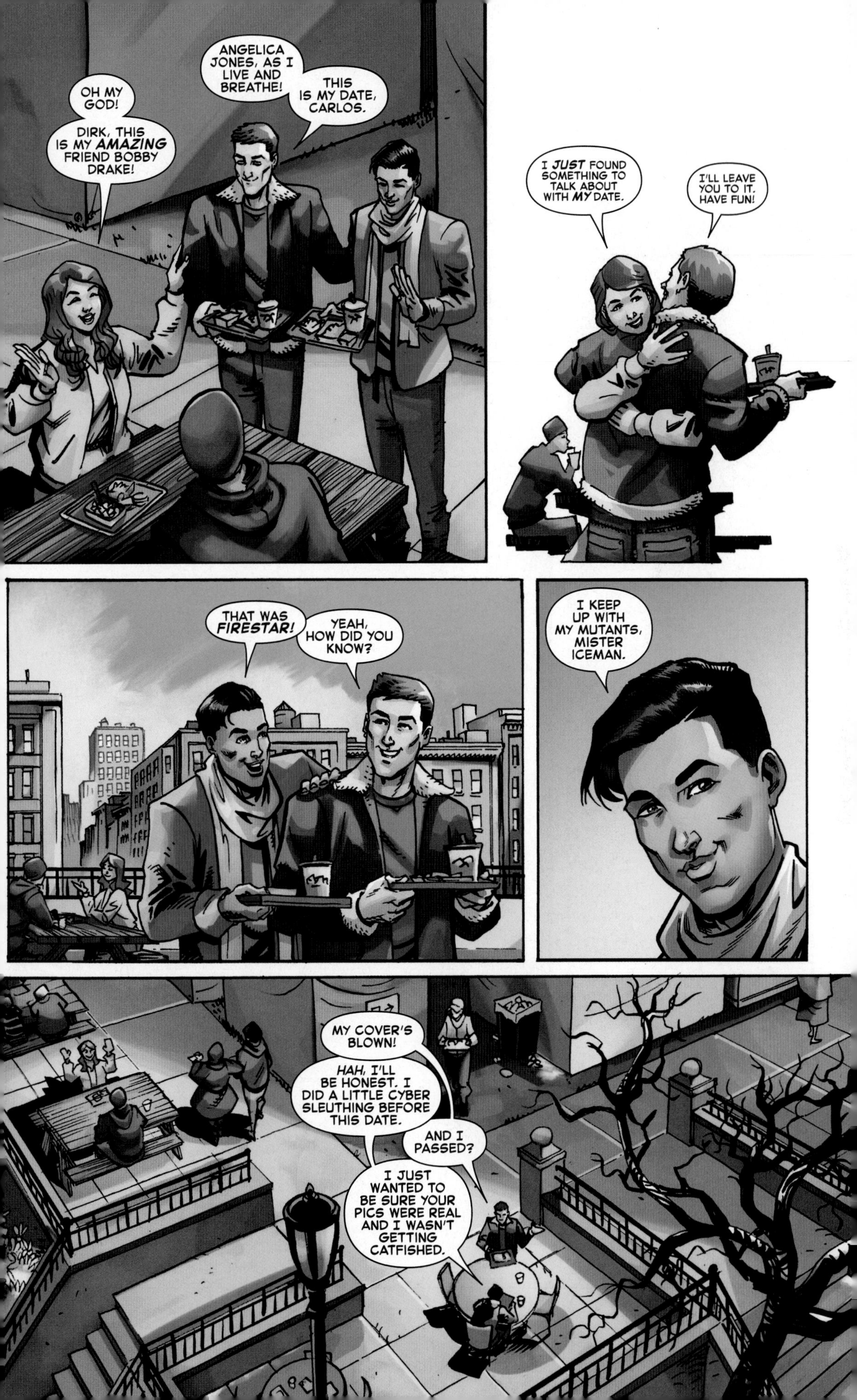
OH MY GOD!
DIRK, THIS IS MY AMAZING FRIEND BOBBY DRAKE!
ANGELICA JONES, AS I LIVE AND BREATHE!
THIS IS MY DATE, CARLOS.
I JUST FOUND SOMETHING TO TALK ABOUT WITH MY DATE.
I'LL LEAVE YOU TO IT. HAVE FUN!
THAT WAS FIRESTAR!
YEAH, HOW DID YOU KNOW?
I KEEP UP WITH MY MUTANTS, MISTER ICEMAN.
MY COVER'S BLOWN!
HAH, I'LL BE HONEST. I DID A LITTLE CYBER SLEUTHING BEFORE THIS DATE.
AND I PASSED?
I JUST WANTED TO BE SURE YOUR PICS WERE REAL AND I WASN'T GETTING CATFISHED.

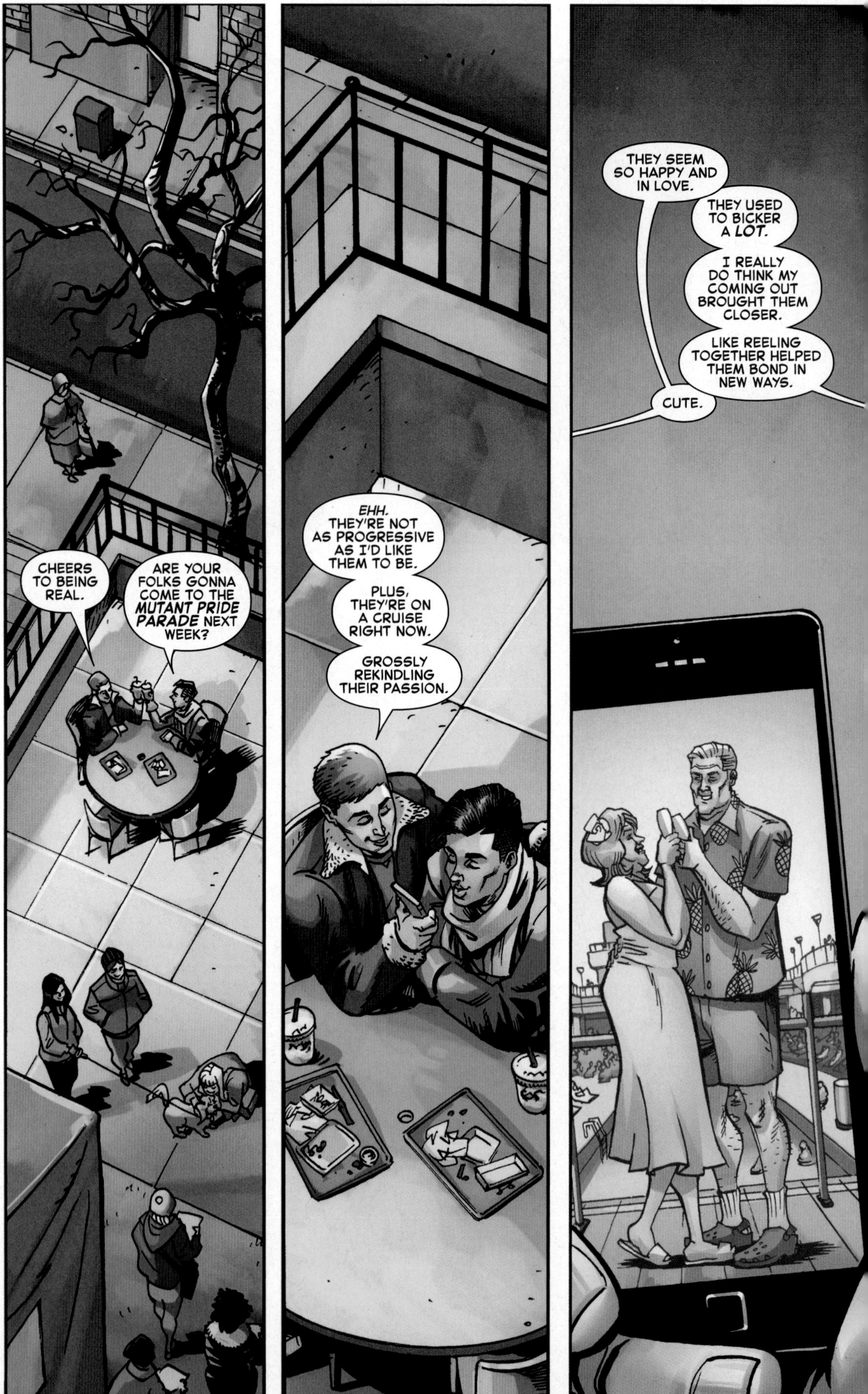
CHEERS TO BEING REAL.
ARE YOUR FOLKS GONNA COME TO THE MUTANT PRIDE PARADE NEXT WEEK?
EHH. THEY'RE NOT AS PROGRESSIVE AS I'D LIKE THEM TO BE.
PLUS, THEY'RE ON A CRUISE RIGHT NOW.
GROSSLY REKINDLING THEIR PASSION.
THEY SEEM SO HAPPY AND IN LOVE.
THEY USED TO BICKER A LOT.
I REALLY DO THINK MY COMING OUT BROUGHT THEM CLOSER.
LIKE REELING TOGETHER HELPED THEM BOND IN NEW WAYS.
CUTE.

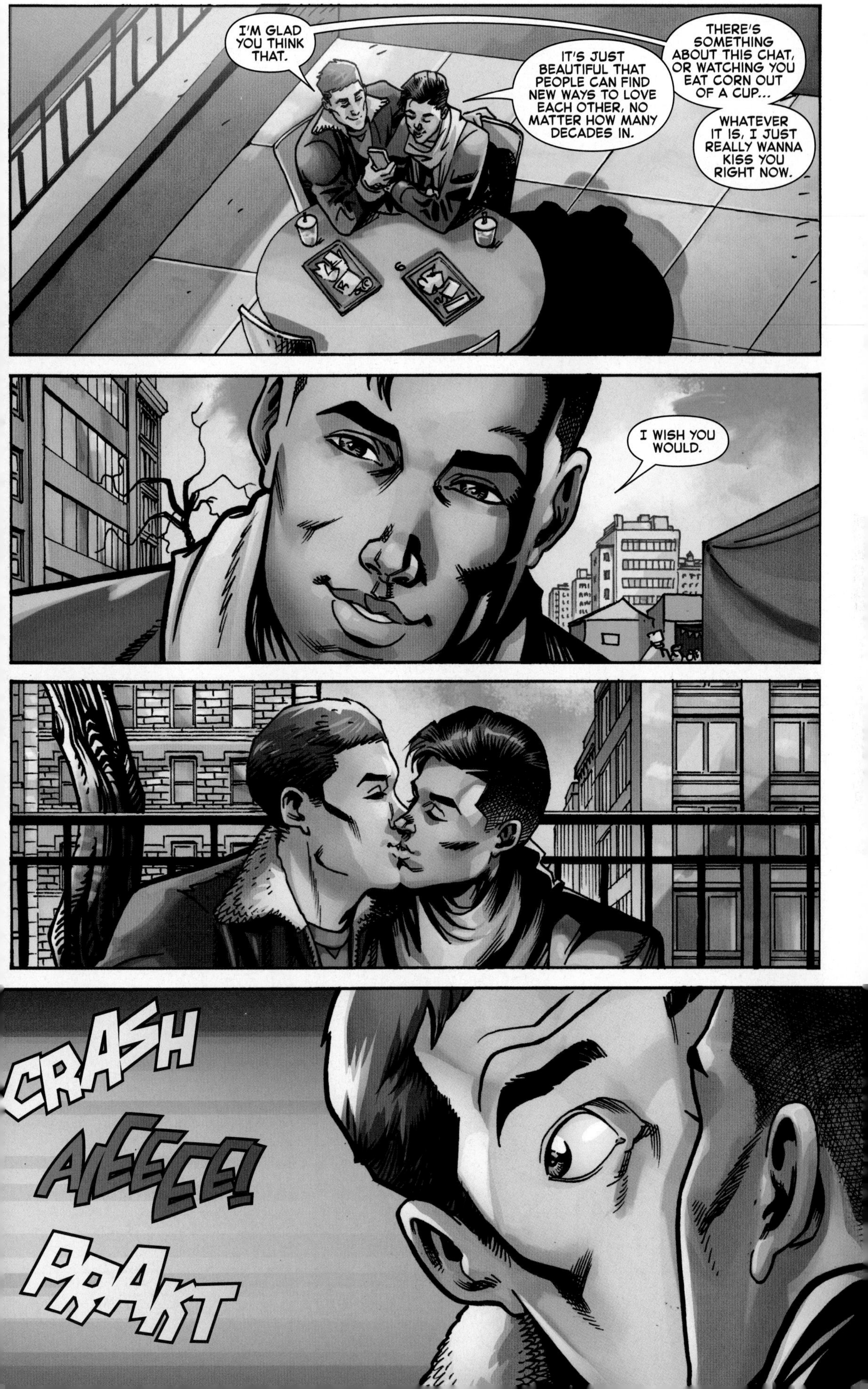
I'M GLAD YOU THINK THAT.
IT'S JUST BEAUTIFUL THAT PEOPLE CAN FIND NEW WAYS TO LOVE EACH OTHER, NO MATTER HOW MANY DECADES IN.
THERE'S SOMETHING ABOUT THIS CHAT, OR WATCHING YOU EAT CORN OUT OF A CUP...
WHATEVER IT IS, I JUST REALLY WANNA KISS YOU RIGHT NOW.
I WISH YOU WOULD.
CRASH
AIEEEE!
PRAKT

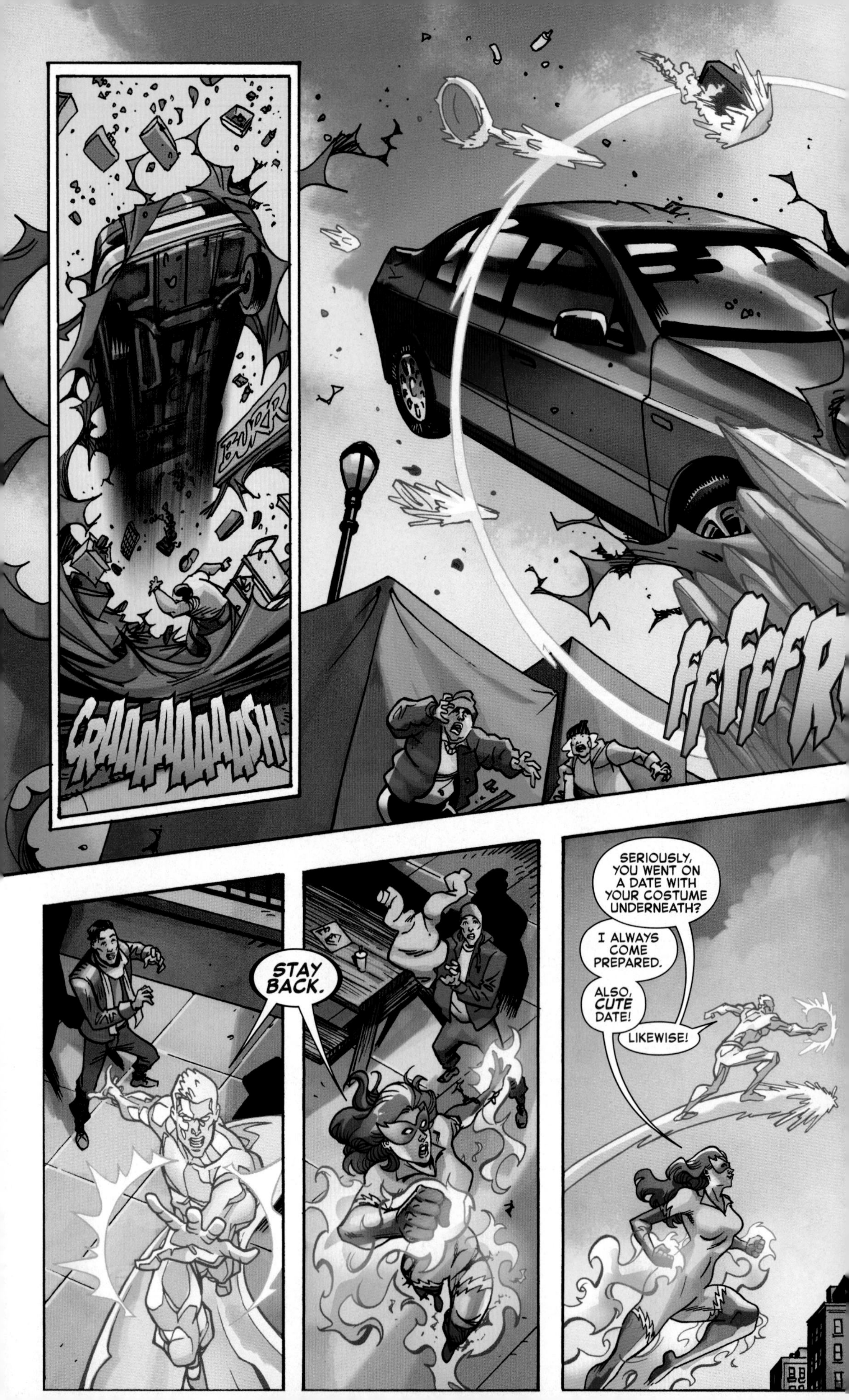

CRAAAAAAAASH
FFFFR
STAY BACK.
SERIOUSLY, YOU WENT ON A DATE WITH YOUR COSTUME UNDERNEATH?
I ALWAYS COME PREPARED.
ALSO, CUTE DATE!
LIKEWISE!

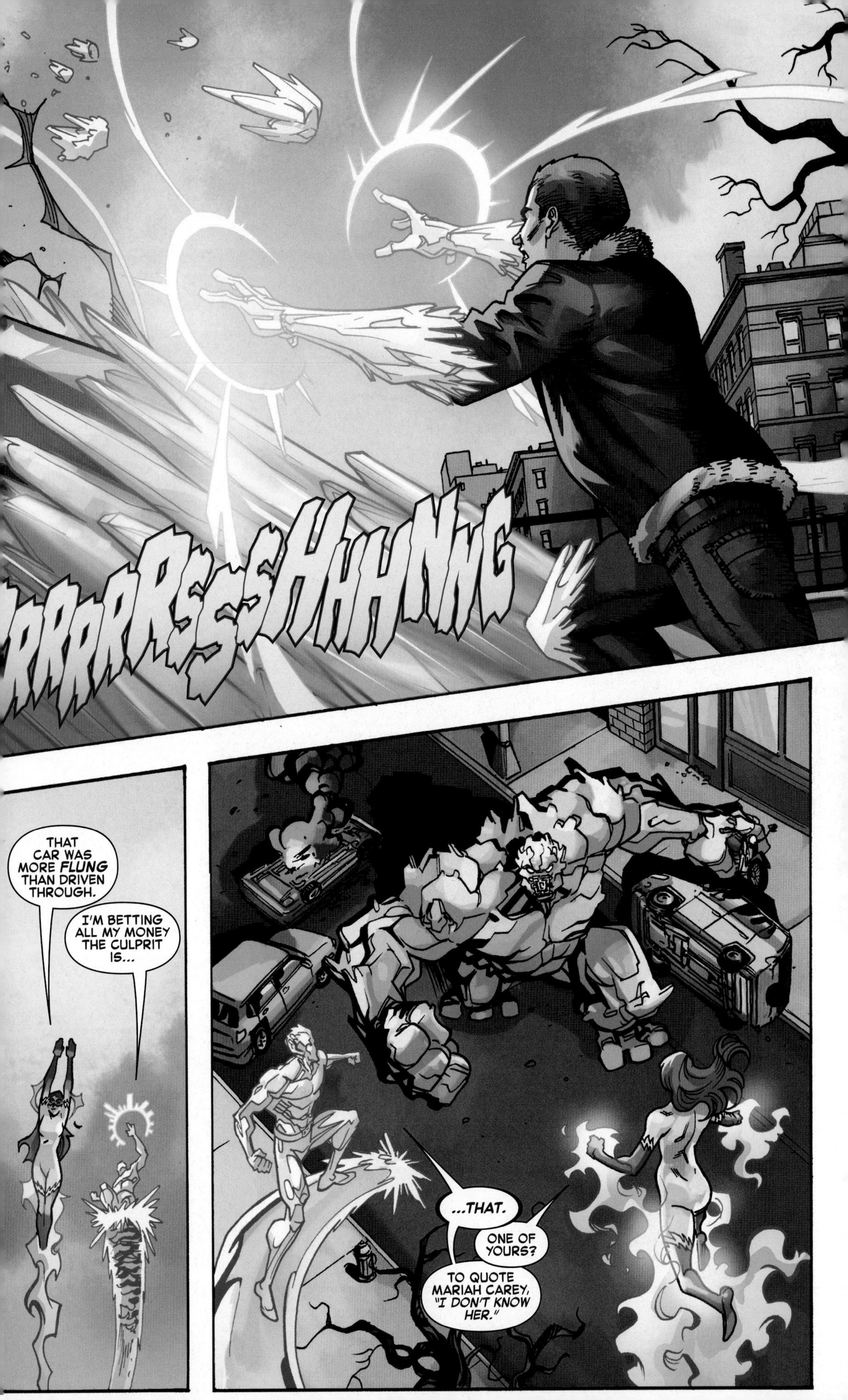
KRRRRRRSSHHHNNG
THAT CAR WAS MORE *FLUNG* THAN DRIVEN THROUGH.
I'M BETTING ALL MY MONEY THE CULPRIT IS...
...THAT.
ONE OF YOURS?
TO QUOTE MARIAH CAREY, *"I DON'T KNOW HER."*

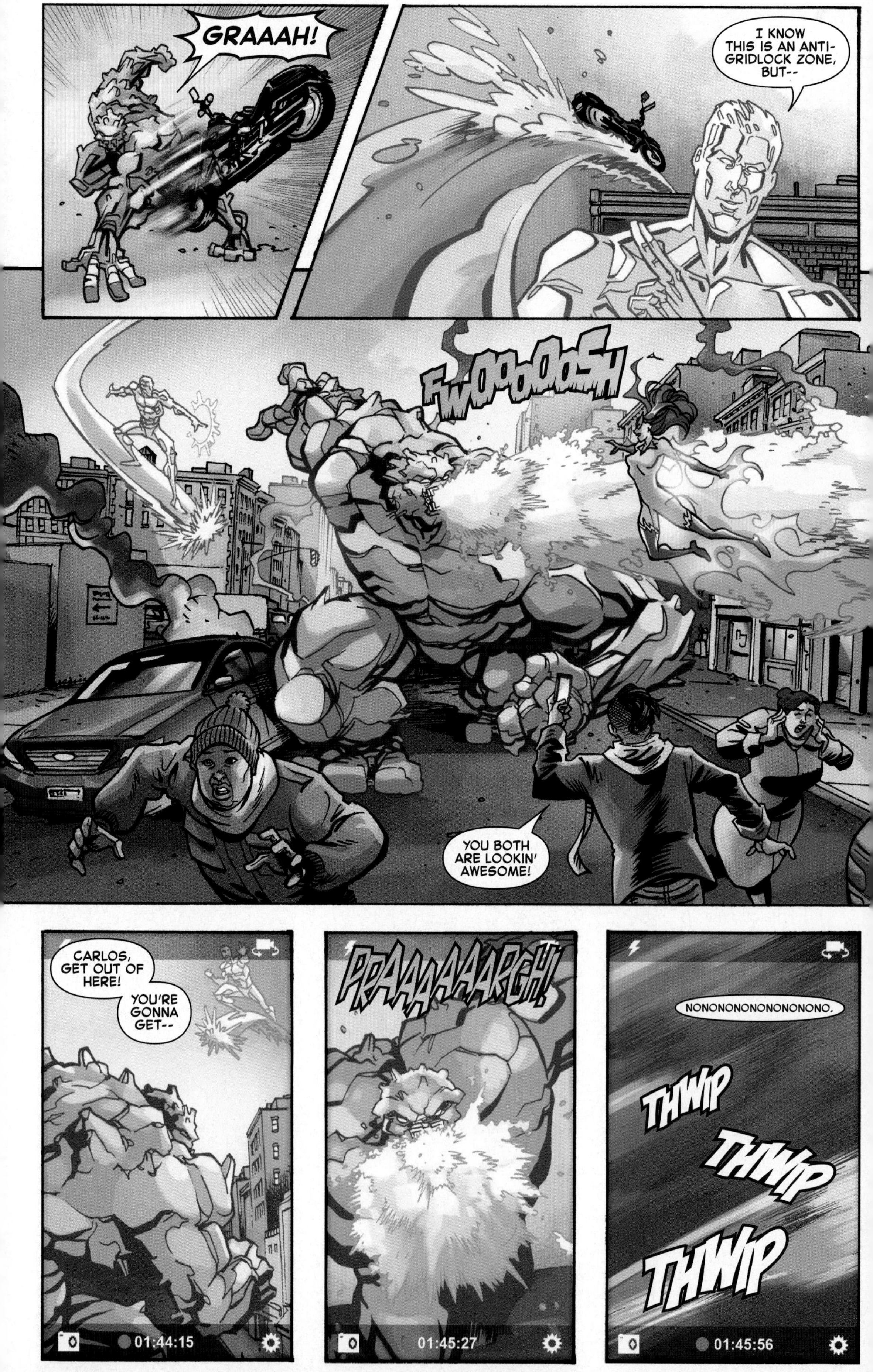
GRAAAH!
I KNOW THIS IS AN ANTI-GRIDLOCK ZONE, BUT--
FWOOOOOSH
YOU BOTH ARE LOOKIN' AWESOME!
CARLOS, GET OUT OF HERE!
YOU'RE GONNA GET--
01:44:15
PRAAAAAAARGH!
01:45:27
NONONONONONONONONO.
THWIP
THWIP
THWIP
01:45:56

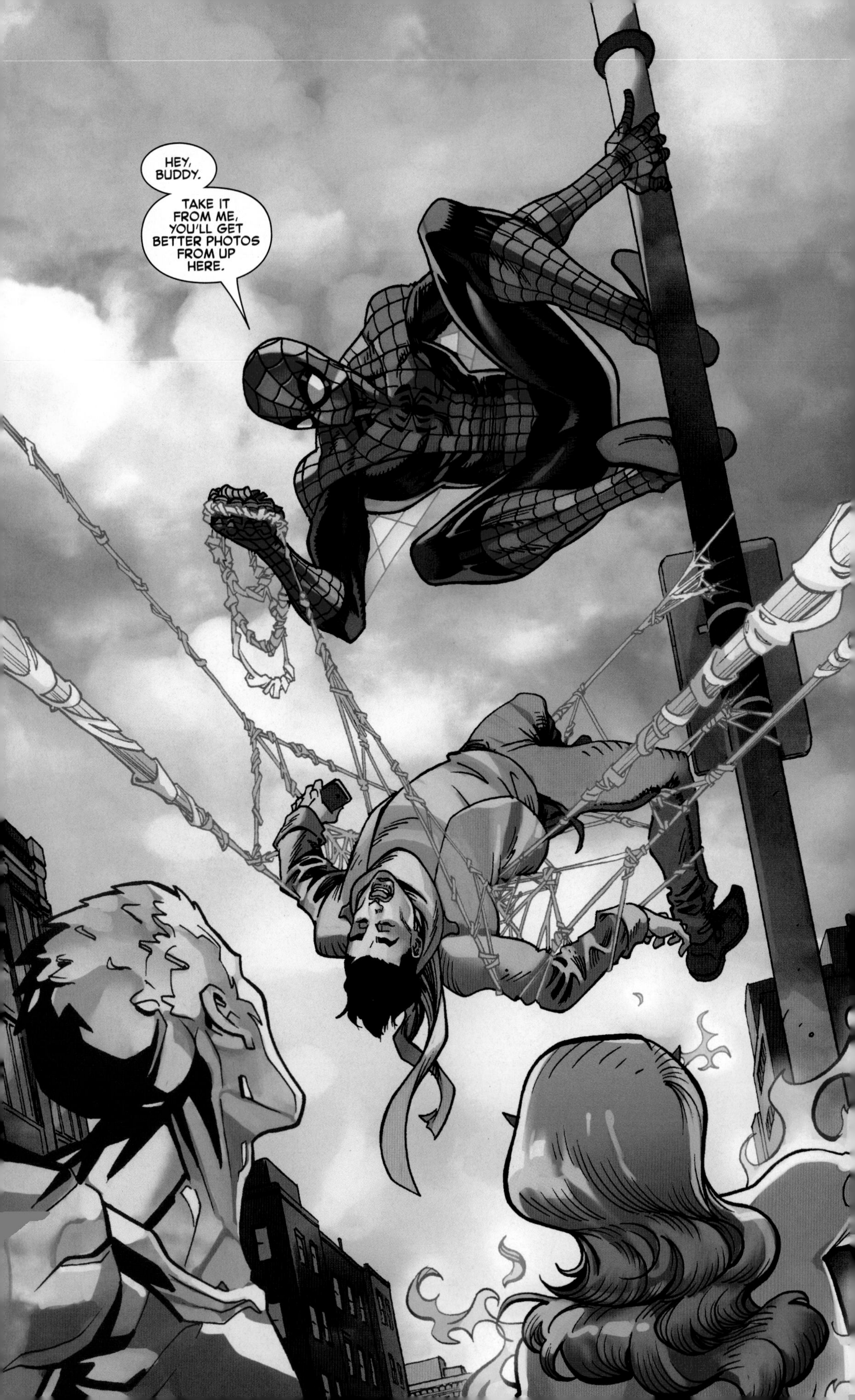
HEY, BUDDY.
TAKE IT FROM ME, YOU'LL GET BETTER PHOTOS FROM UP HERE.

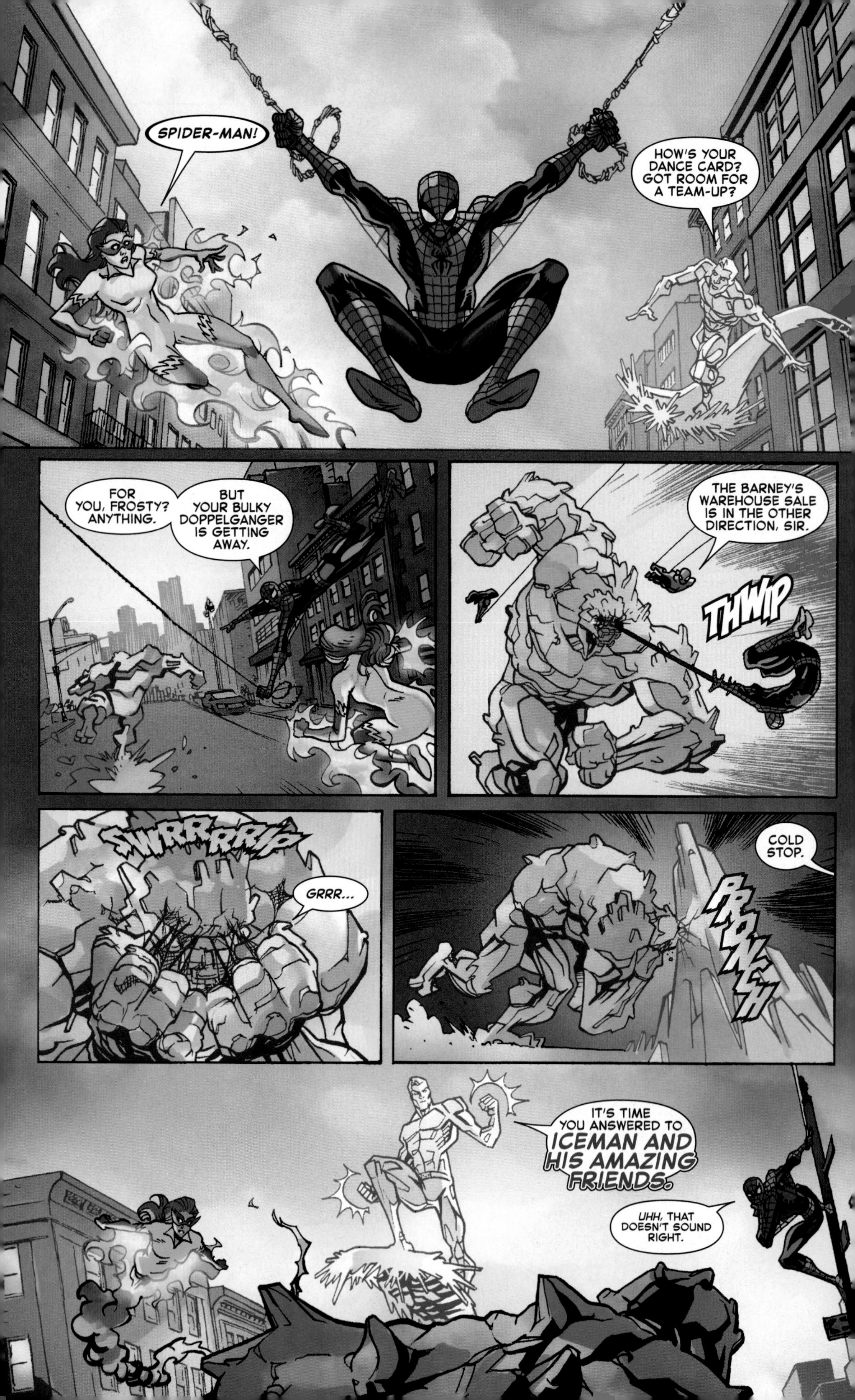
SPIDER-MAN!
HOW'S YOUR DANCE CARD? GOT ROOM FOR A TEAM-UP?
FOR YOU, FROSTY? ANYTHING.
BUT YOUR BULKY DOPPELGANGER IS GETTING AWAY.
THE BARNEY'S WAREHOUSE SALE IS IN THE OTHER DIRECTION, SIR.
THWIP
SWRRRRIP
GRRR...
COLD STOP.
KRONCH
IT'S TIME YOU ANSWERED TO ICEMAN AND HIS AMAZING FRIENDS.
UHH, THAT DOESN'T SOUND RIGHT.

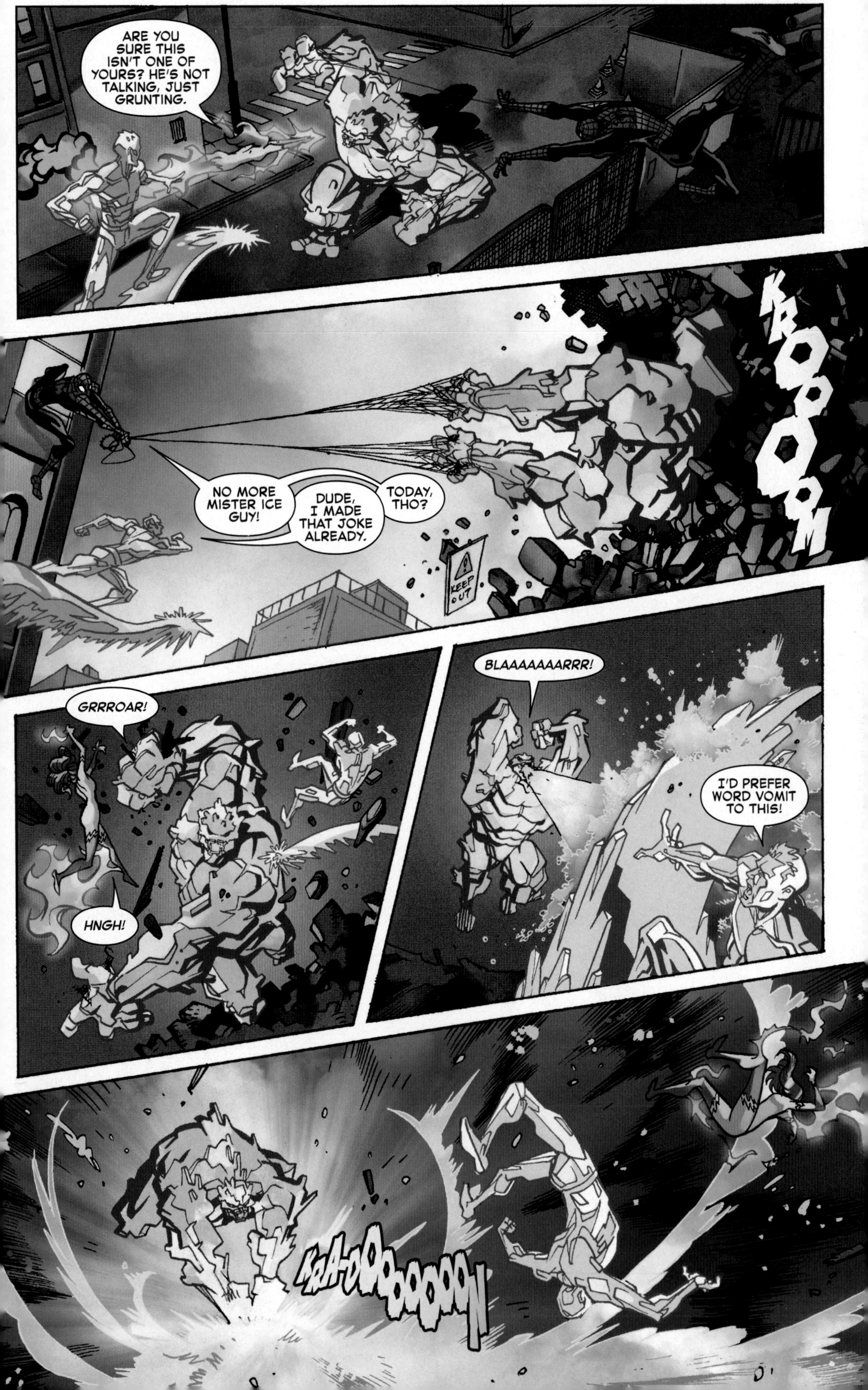
ARE YOU SURE THIS ISN'T ONE OF YOURS? HE'S NOT TALKING, JUST GRUNTING.
KROOOOOM
NO MORE MISTER ICE GUY!
DUDE, I MADE THAT JOKE ALREADY.
TODAY, THO?
KEEP OUT
GRRROAR!
HNGH!
BLAAAAAAARRR!
I'D PREFER WORD VOMIT TO THIS!
KRA-DOOOOOOON

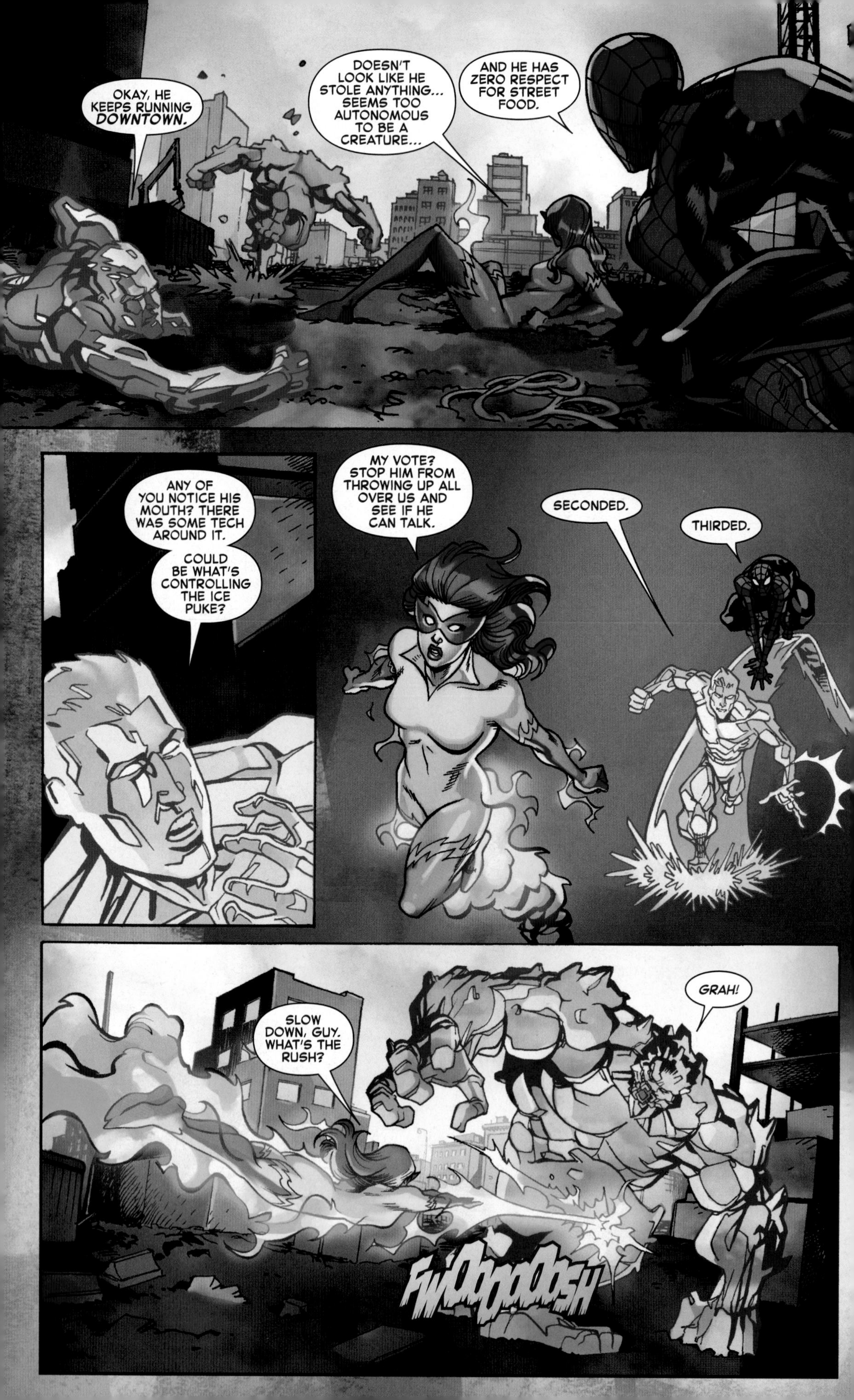
OKAY, HE KEEPS RUNNING *DOWNTOWN.*
DOESN'T LOOK LIKE HE STOLE ANYTHING... SEEMS TOO AUTONOMOUS TO BE A CREATURE...
AND HE HAS ZERO RESPECT FOR STREET FOOD.
ANY OF YOU NOTICE HIS MOUTH? THERE WAS SOME TECH AROUND IT.
COULD BE WHAT'S CONTROLLING THE ICE PUKE?
MY VOTE? STOP HIM FROM THROWING UP ALL OVER US AND SEE IF HE CAN TALK.
SECONDED.
THIRDED.
SLOW DOWN, GUY. WHAT'S THE RUSH?
GRAH!
FWOOOOOOSH

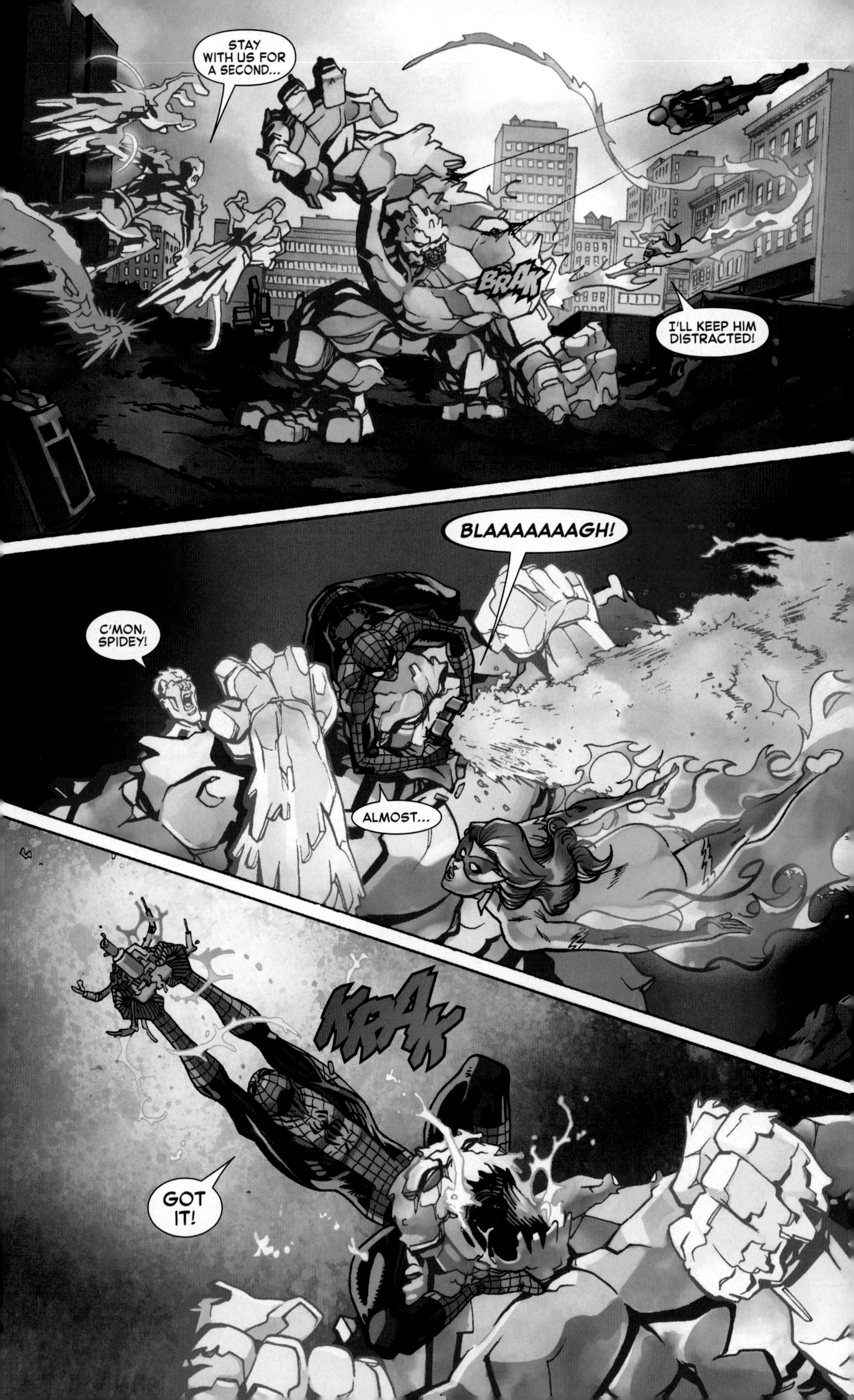
STAY WITH US FOR A SECOND...
BRAK
I'LL KEEP HIM DISTRACTED!
BLAAAAAAAGH!
C'MON, SPIDEY!
ALMOST...
KRAK
GOT IT!

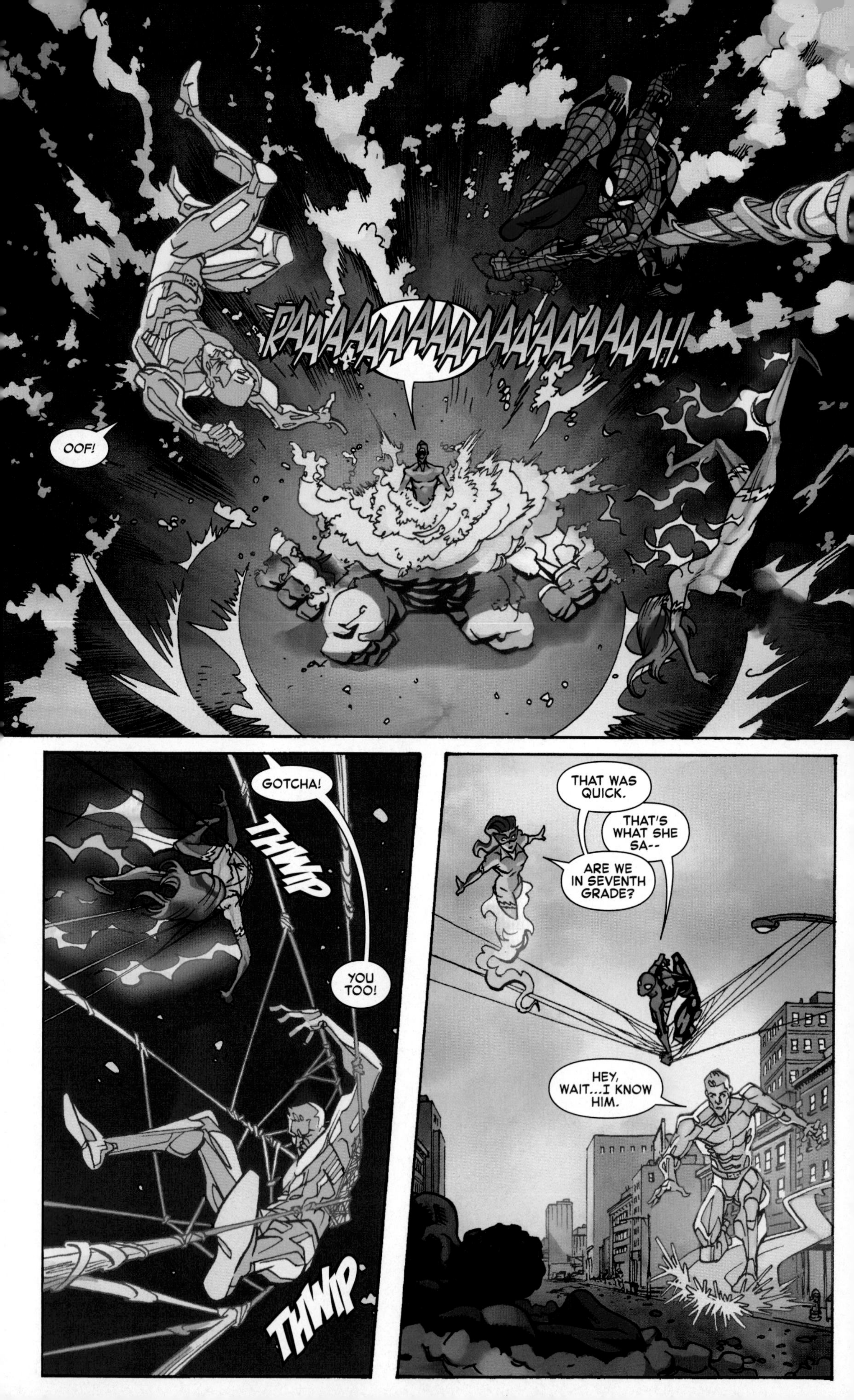
RAAAAAAAAAAAAAAAAAAAAH!
OOF!
GOTCHA!
THWIP
YOU TOO!
THWIP
THAT WAS QUICK.
THAT'S WHAT SHE SA--
ARE WE IN SEVENTH GRADE?
HEY, WAIT...I KNOW HIM.

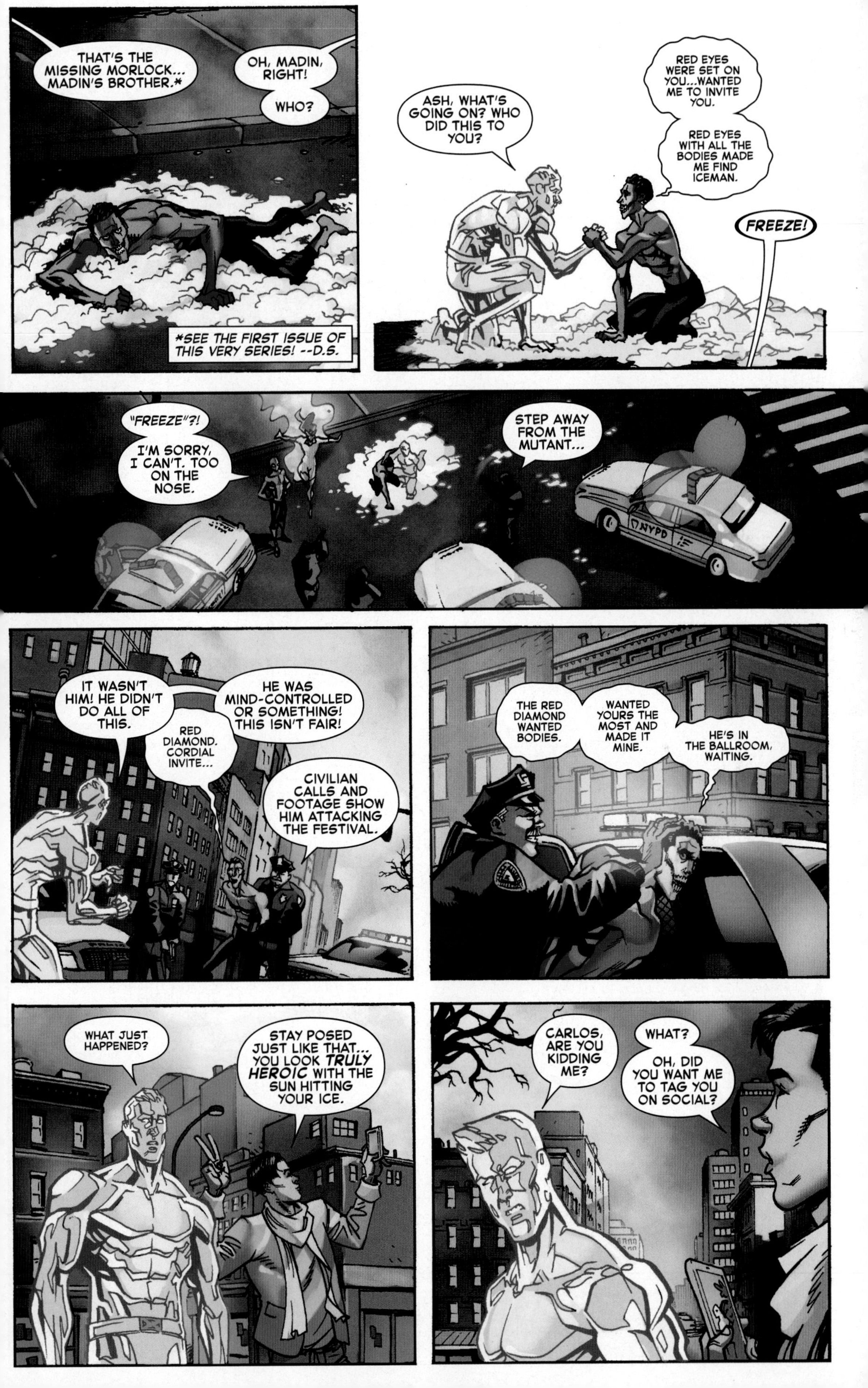
THAT'S THE MISSING MORLOCK... MADIN'S BROTHER.*
OH, MADIN, RIGHT!
WHO?
*SEE THE FIRST ISSUE OF THIS VERY SERIES! --D.S.
ASH, WHAT'S GOING ON? WHO DID THIS TO YOU?
RED EYES WERE SET ON YOU...WANTED ME TO INVITE YOU.
RED EYES WITH ALL THE BODIES MADE ME FIND ICEMAN.
FREEZE!
"FREEZE"?!
I'M SORRY, I CAN'T. TOO ON THE NOSE.
STEP AWAY FROM THE MUTANT...
IT WASN'T HIM! HE DIDN'T DO ALL OF THIS.
HE WAS MIND-CONTROLLED OR SOMETHING! THIS ISN'T FAIR!
RED DIAMOND. CORDIAL INVITE...
CIVILIAN CALLS AND FOOTAGE SHOW HIM ATTACKING THE FESTIVAL.
THE RED DIAMOND WANTED BODIES.
WANTED YOURS THE MOST AND MADE IT MINE.
HE'S IN THE BALLROOM, WAITING.
WHAT JUST HAPPENED?
STAY POSED JUST LIKE THAT... YOU LOOK TRULY HEROIC WITH THE SUN HITTING YOUR ICE.
CARLOS, ARE YOU KIDDING ME?
WHAT?
OH, DID YOU WANT ME TO TAG YOU ON SOCIAL?

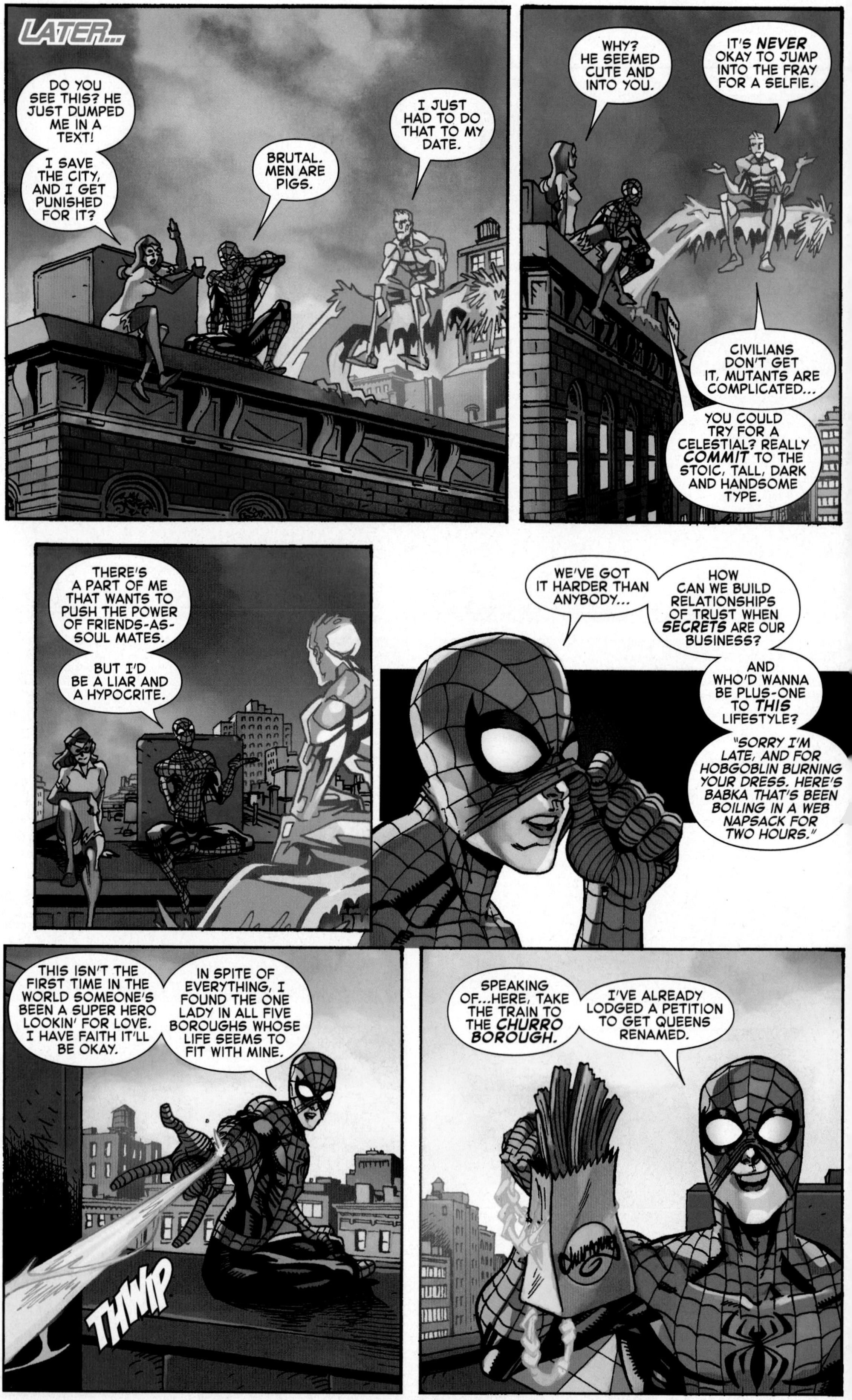
LATER...
DO YOU SEE THIS? HE JUST DUMPED ME IN A TEXT!
I SAVE THE CITY, AND I GET PUNISHED FOR IT?
BRUTAL. MEN ARE PIGS.
I JUST HAD TO DO THAT TO MY DATE.
WHY? HE SEEMED CUTE AND INTO YOU.
IT'S NEVER OKAY TO JUMP INTO THE FRAY FOR A SELFIE.
CIVILIANS DON'T GET IT, MUTANTS ARE COMPLICATED...
YOU COULD TRY FOR A CELESTIAL? REALLY COMMIT TO THE STOIC, TALL, DARK AND HANDSOME TYPE.
THERE'S A PART OF ME THAT WANTS TO PUSH THE POWER OF FRIENDS-AS-SOUL MATES.
BUT I'D BE A LIAR AND A HYPOCRITE.
WE'VE GOT IT HARDER THAN ANYBODY...
HOW CAN WE BUILD RELATIONSHIPS OF TRUST WHEN SECRETS ARE OUR BUSINESS?
AND WHO'D WANNA BE PLUS-ONE TO THIS LIFESTYLE?
"SORRY I'M LATE, AND FOR HOBGOBLIN BURNING YOUR DRESS. HERE'S BABKA THAT'S BEEN BOILING IN A WEB NAPSACK FOR TWO HOURS."
THIS ISN'T THE FIRST TIME IN THE WORLD SOMEONE'S BEEN A SUPER HERO LOOKIN' FOR LOVE. I HAVE FAITH IT'LL BE OKAY.
IN SPITE OF EVERYTHING, I FOUND THE ONE LADY IN ALL FIVE BOROUGHS WHOSE LIFE SEEMS TO FIT WITH MINE.
THWIP
SPEAKING OF...HERE, TAKE THE TRAIN TO THE CHURRO BOROUGH.
I'VE ALREADY LODGED A PETITION TO GET QUEENS RENAMED.

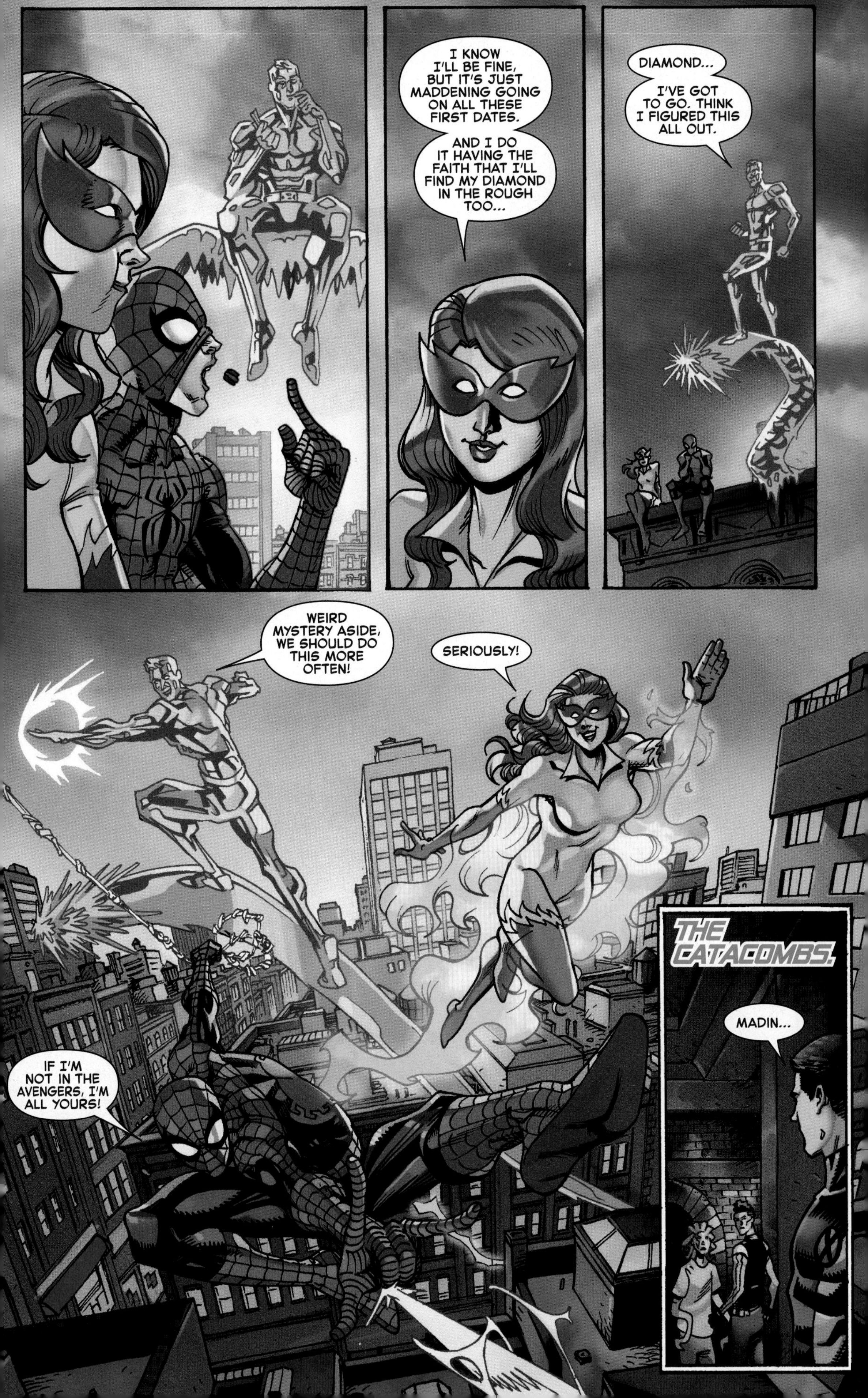
I KNOW I'LL BE FINE, BUT IT'S JUST MADDENING GOING ON ALL THESE FIRST DATES.
AND I DO IT HAVING THE FAITH THAT I'LL FIND MY DIAMOND IN THE ROUGH TOO...
DIAMOND...
I'VE GOT TO GO. THINK I FIGURED THIS ALL OUT.
WEIRD MYSTERY ASIDE, WE SHOULD DO THIS MORE OFTEN!
SERIOUSLY!
IF I'M NOT IN THE AVENGERS, I'M ALL YOURS!
THE CATACOMBS.
MADIN...

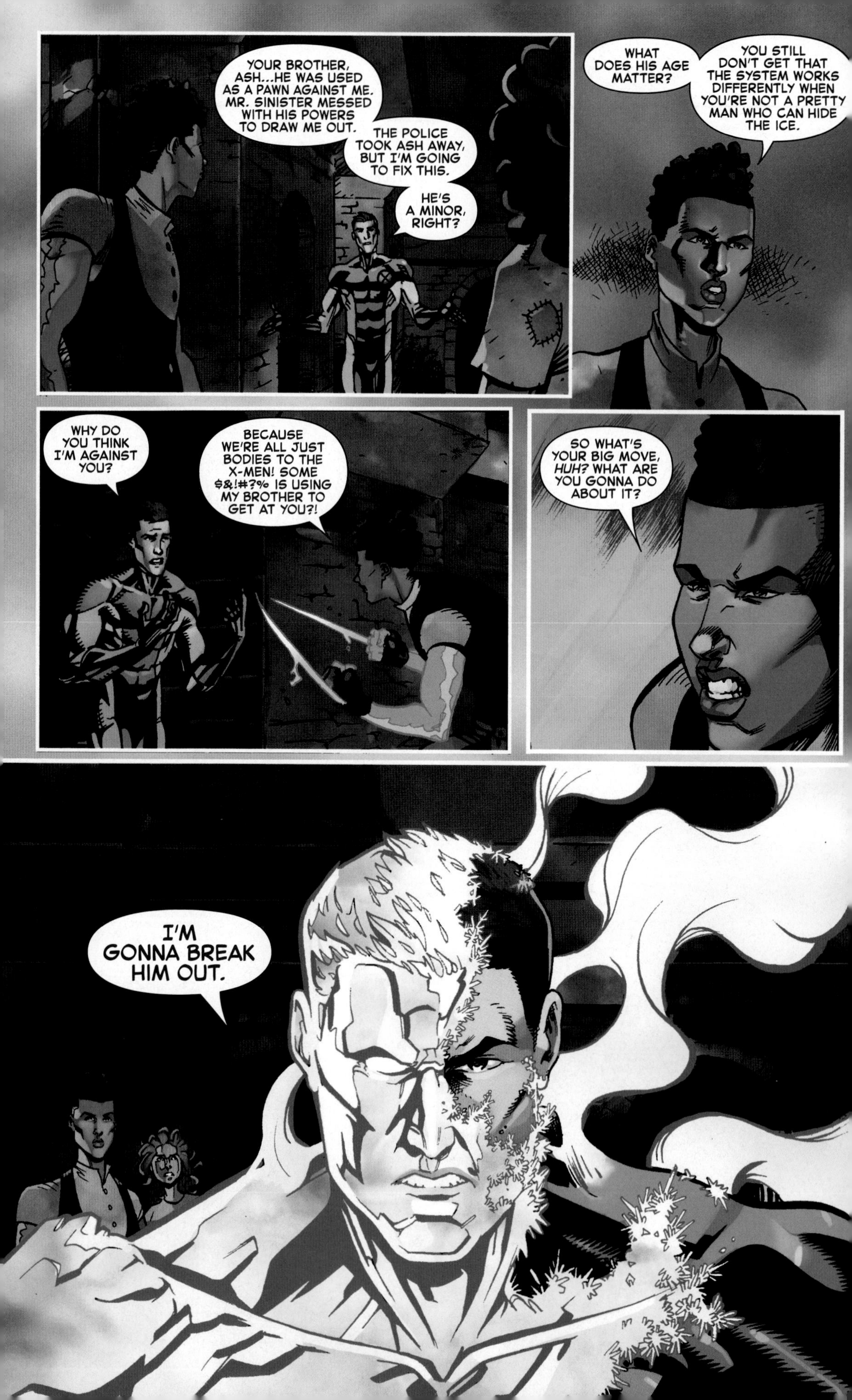
YOUR BROTHER, ASH...HE WAS USED AS A PAWN AGAINST ME. MR. SINISTER MESSED WITH HIS POWERS TO DRAW ME OUT.
THE POLICE TOOK ASH AWAY, BUT I'M GOING TO FIX THIS.
HE'S A MINOR, RIGHT?
WHAT DOES HIS AGE MATTER?
YOU STILL DON'T GET THAT THE SYSTEM WORKS DIFFERENTLY WHEN YOU'RE NOT A PRETTY MAN WHO CAN HIDE THE ICE.
WHY DO YOU THINK I'M AGAINST YOU?
BECAUSE WE'RE ALL JUST BODIES TO THE X-MEN! SOME $&!#?% IS USING MY BROTHER TO GET AT YOU?!
SO WHAT'S YOUR BIG MOVE, *HUH?* WHAT ARE YOU GONNA DO ABOUT IT?
I'M GONNA BREAK HIM OUT.

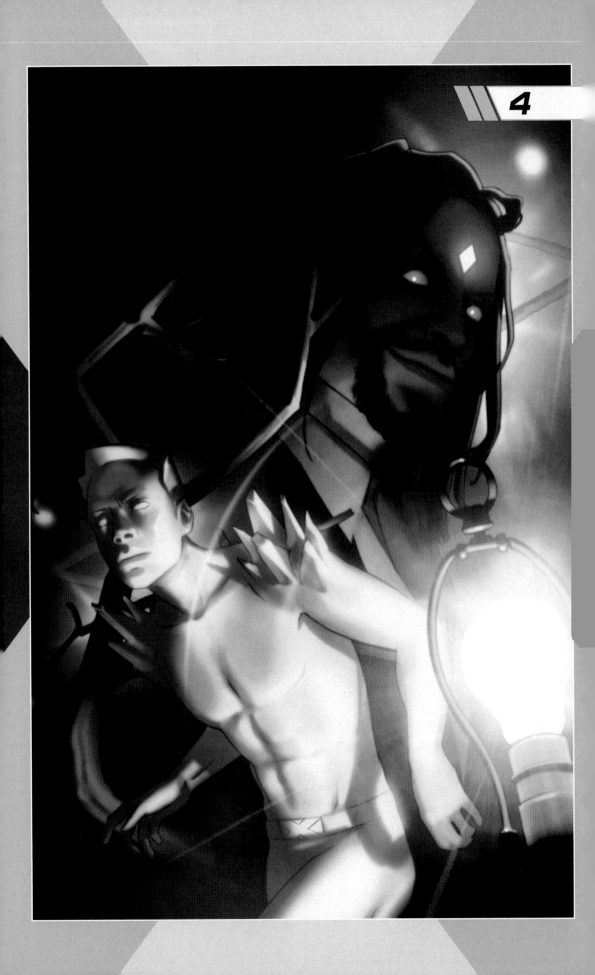

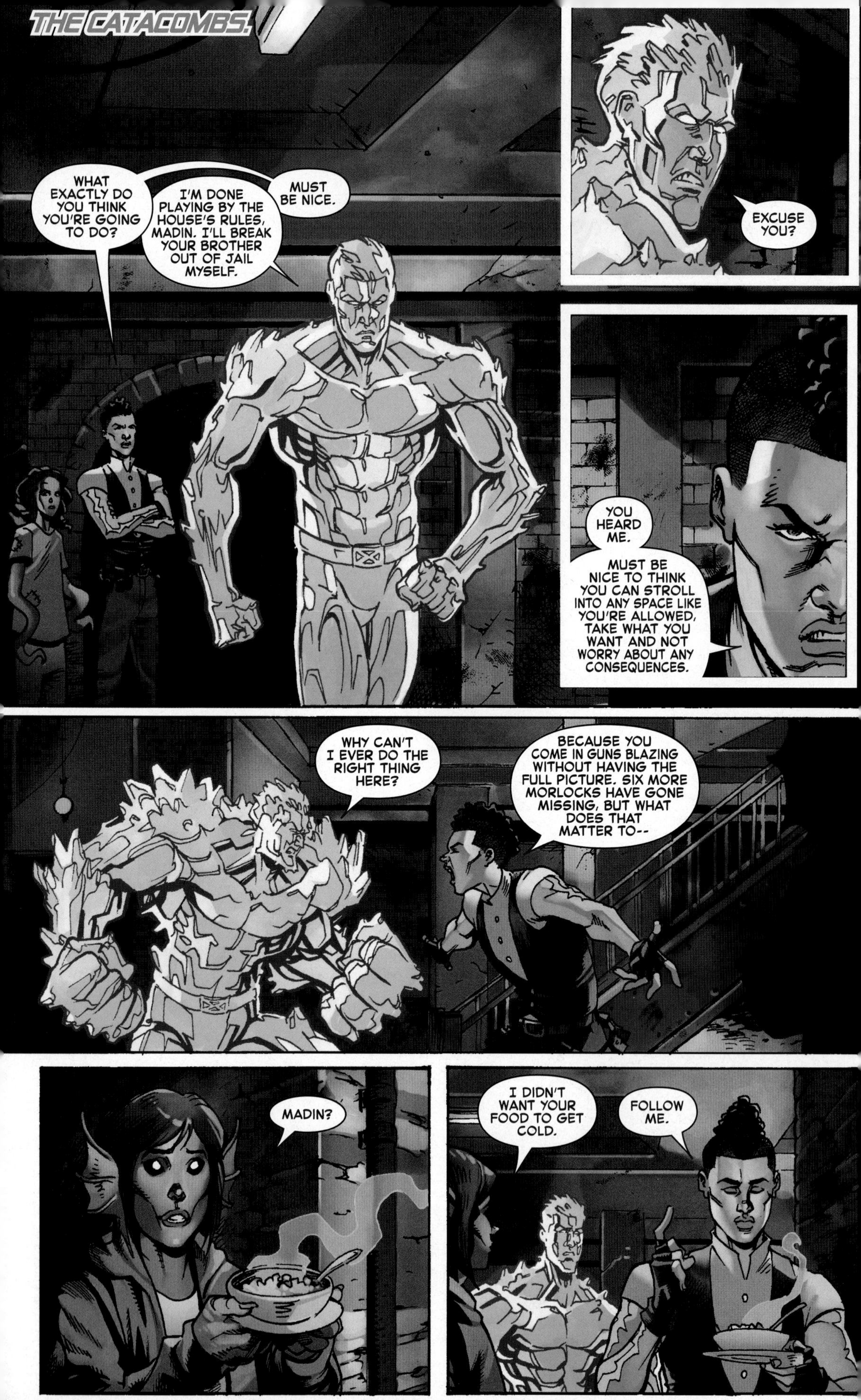
THE CATACOMBS.
WHAT EXACTLY DO YOU THINK YOU'RE GOING TO DO?
I'M DONE PLAYING BY THE HOUSE'S RULES, MADIN. I'LL BREAK YOUR BROTHER OUT OF JAIL MYSELF.
MUST BE NICE.
EXCUSE YOU?
YOU HEARD ME.
MUST BE NICE TO THINK YOU CAN STROLL INTO ANY SPACE LIKE YOU'RE ALLOWED, TAKE WHAT YOU WANT AND NOT WORRY ABOUT ANY CONSEQUENCES.
WHY CAN'T I EVER DO THE RIGHT THING HERE?
BECAUSE YOU COME IN GUNS BLAZING WITHOUT HAVING THE FULL PICTURE. SIX MORE MORLOCKS HAVE GONE MISSING, BUT WHAT DOES THAT MATTER TO--
MADIN?
I DIDN'T WANT YOUR FOOD TO GET COLD.
FOLLOW ME.

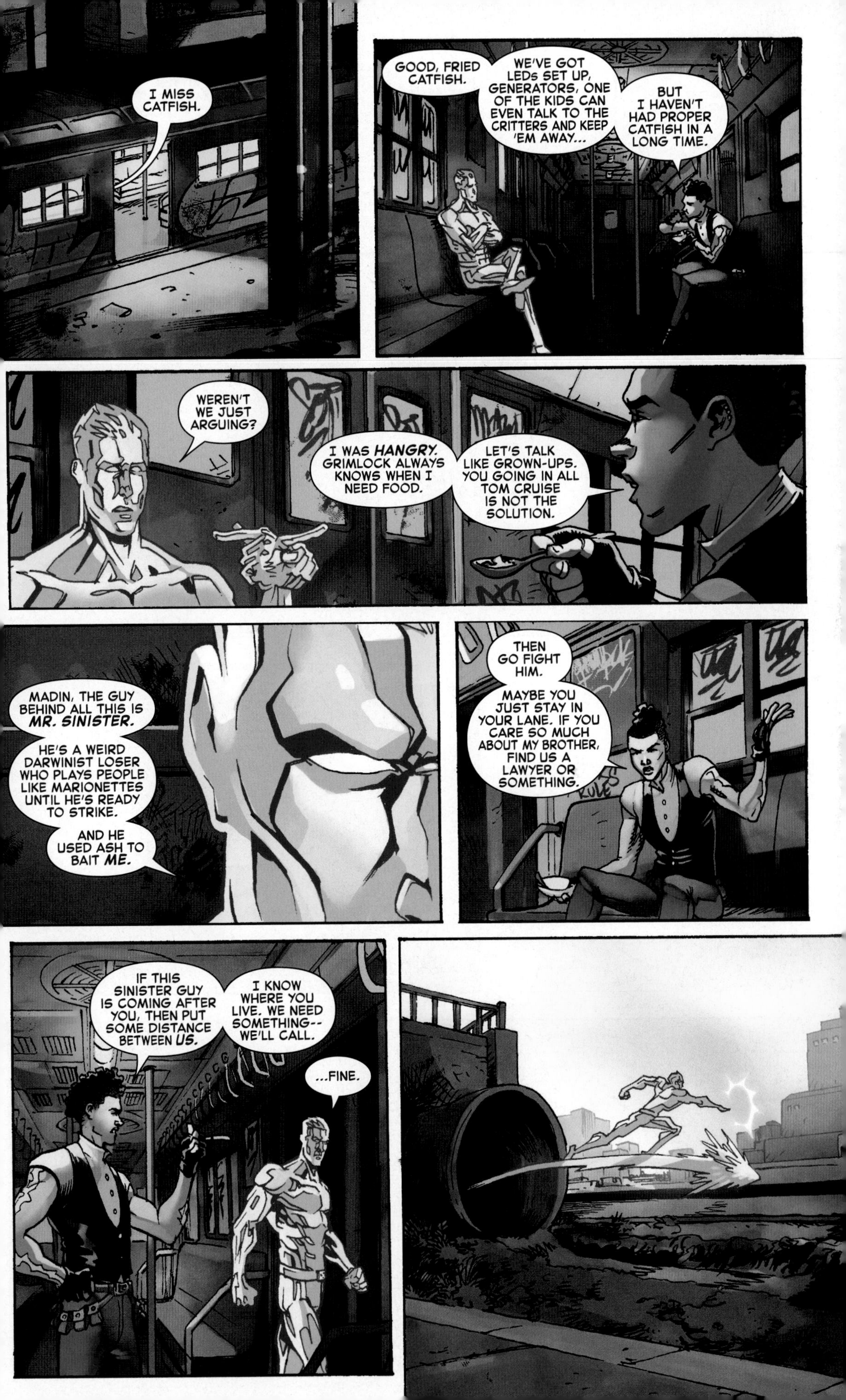
I MISS CATFISH.
GOOD, FRIED CATFISH.
WE'VE GOT LEDs SET UP, GENERATORS, ONE OF THE KIDS CAN EVEN TALK TO THE CRITTERS AND KEEP 'EM AWAY...
BUT I HAVEN'T HAD PROPER CATFISH IN A LONG TIME.
WEREN'T WE JUST ARGUING?
I WAS HANGRY. GRIMLOCK ALWAYS KNOWS WHEN I NEED FOOD.
LET'S TALK LIKE GROWN-UPS. YOU GOING IN ALL TOM CRUISE IS NOT THE SOLUTION.
MADIN, THE GUY BEHIND ALL THIS IS MR. SINISTER.
HE'S A WEIRD DARWINIST LOSER WHO PLAYS PEOPLE LIKE MARIONETTES UNTIL HE'S READY TO STRIKE.
AND HE USED ASH TO BAIT ME.
THEN GO FIGHT HIM.
MAYBE YOU JUST STAY IN YOUR LANE. IF YOU CARE SO MUCH ABOUT MY BROTHER, FIND US A LAWYER OR SOMETHING.
IF THIS SINISTER GUY IS COMING AFTER YOU, THEN PUT SOME DISTANCE BETWEEN US.
I KNOW WHERE YOU LIVE. WE NEED SOMETHING-- WE'LL CALL.
...FINE.

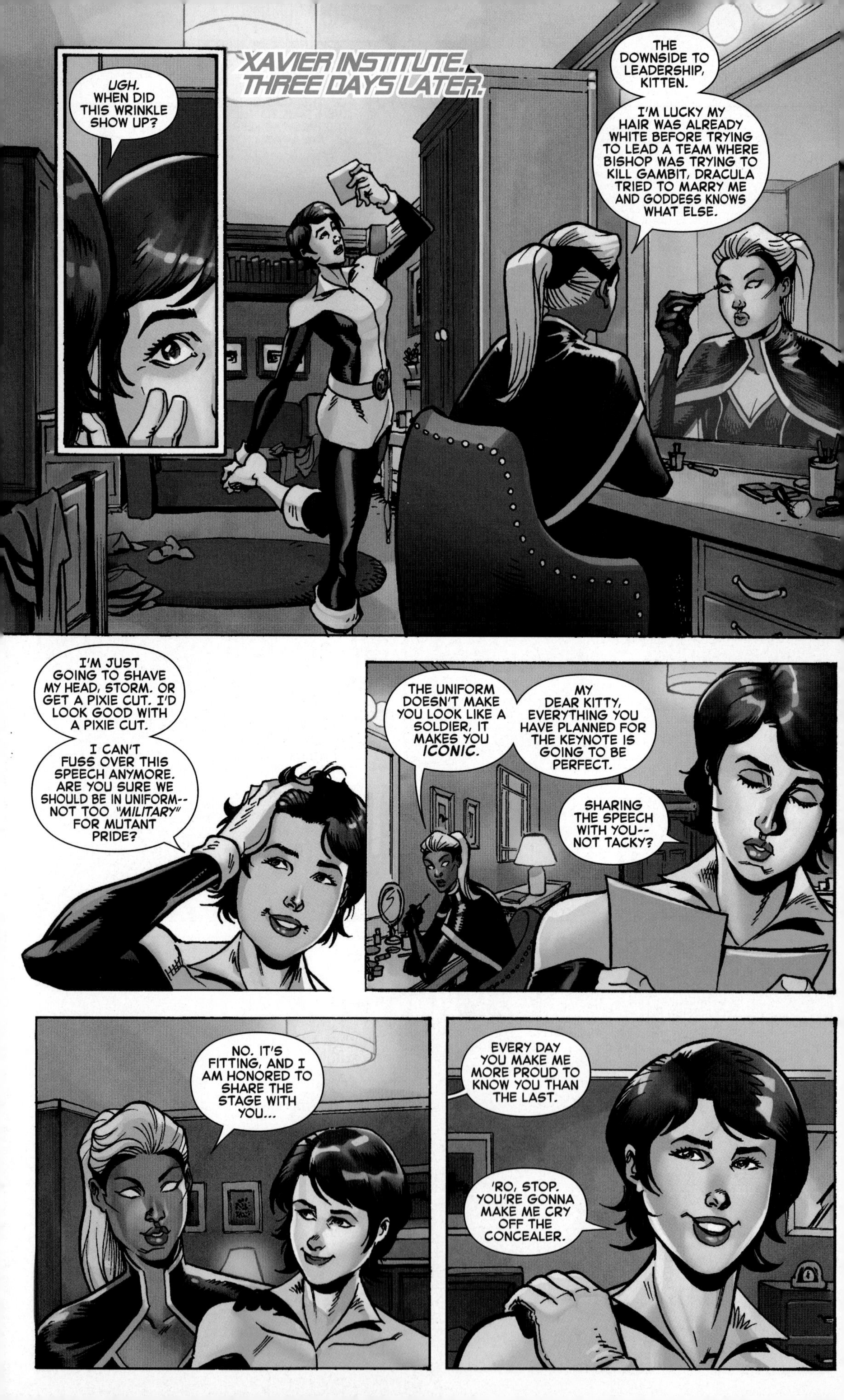
XAVIER INSTITUTE. THREE DAYS LATER.
UGH. WHEN DID THIS WRINKLE SHOW UP?
THE DOWNSIDE TO LEADERSHIP, KITTEN.
I'M LUCKY MY HAIR WAS ALREADY WHITE BEFORE TRYING TO LEAD A TEAM WHERE BISHOP WAS TRYING TO KILL GAMBIT, DRACULA TRIED TO MARRY ME AND GODDESS KNOWS WHAT ELSE.
I'M JUST GOING TO SHAVE MY HEAD, STORM. OR GET A PIXIE CUT. I'D LOOK GOOD WITH A PIXIE CUT.
I CAN'T FUSS OVER THIS SPEECH ANYMORE. ARE YOU SURE WE SHOULD BE IN UNIFORM-- NOT TOO "MILITARY" FOR MUTANT PRIDE?
THE UNIFORM DOESN'T MAKE YOU LOOK LIKE A SOLDIER, IT MAKES YOU ICONIC.
MY DEAR KITTY, EVERYTHING YOU HAVE PLANNED FOR THE KEYNOTE IS GOING TO BE PERFECT.
SHARING THE SPEECH WITH YOU-- NOT TACKY?
NO. IT'S FITTING, AND I AM HONORED TO SHARE THE STAGE WITH YOU...
EVERY DAY YOU MAKE ME MORE PROUD TO KNOW YOU THAN THE LAST.
'RO, STOP. YOU'RE GONNA MAKE ME CRY OFF THE CONCEALER.

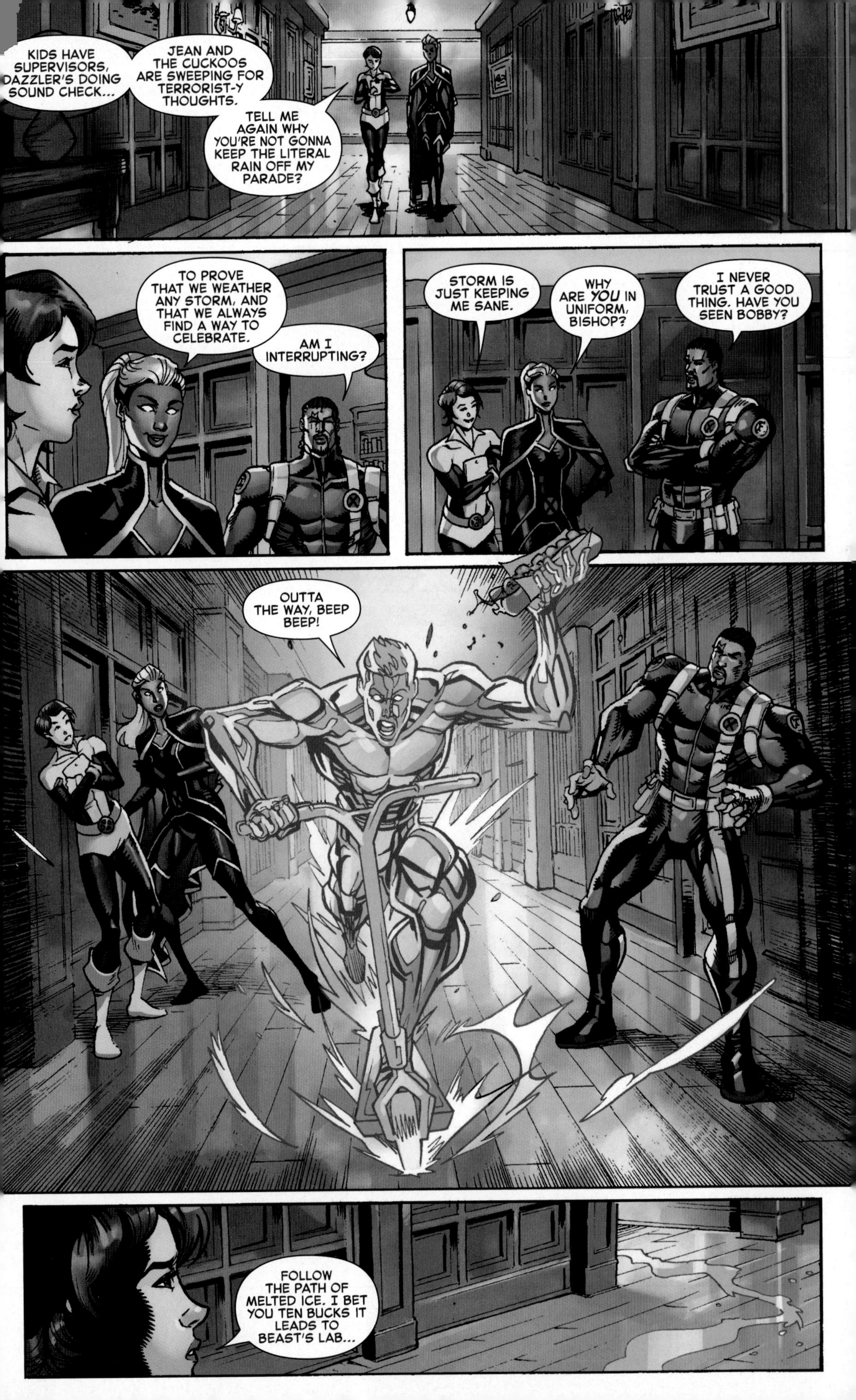
KIDS HAVE SUPERVISORS, DAZZLER'S DOING SOUND CHECK...
JEAN AND THE CUCKOOS ARE SWEEPING FOR TERRORIST-Y THOUGHTS.
TELL ME AGAIN WHY YOU'RE NOT GONNA KEEP THE LITERAL RAIN OFF MY PARADE?
TO PROVE THAT WE WEATHER ANY STORM, AND THAT WE ALWAYS FIND A WAY TO CELEBRATE.
AM I INTERRUPTING?
STORM IS JUST KEEPING ME SANE.
WHY ARE YOU IN UNIFORM, BISHOP?
I NEVER TRUST A GOOD THING. HAVE YOU SEEN BOBBY?
OUTTA THE WAY, BEEP BEEP!
FOLLOW THE PATH OF MELTED ICE. I BET YOU TEN BUCKS IT LEADS TO BEAST'S LAB...

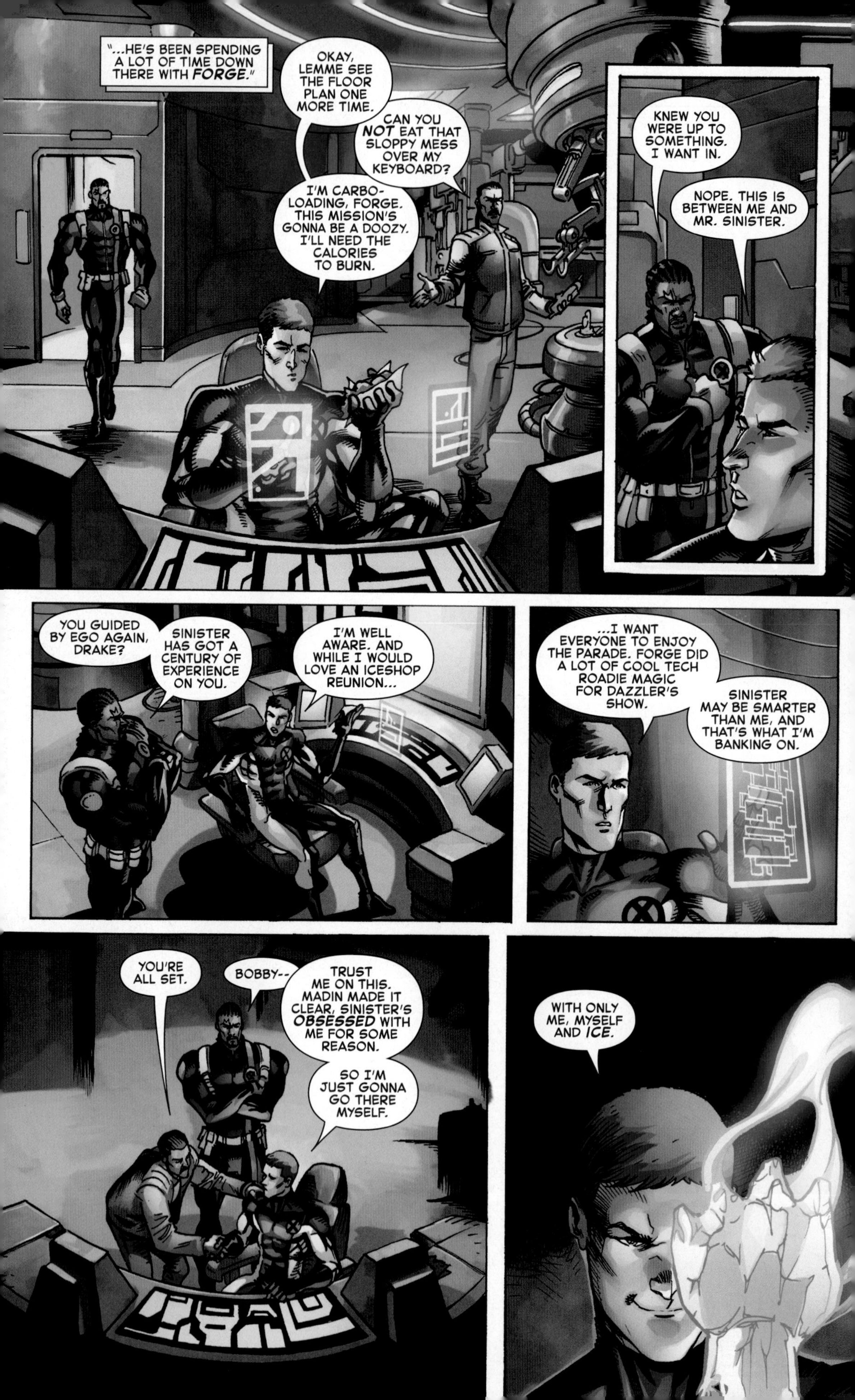
"...HE'S BEEN SPENDING A LOT OF TIME DOWN THERE WITH *FORGE*."
OKAY, LEMME SEE THE FLOOR PLAN ONE MORE TIME.
CAN YOU *NOT* EAT THAT SLOPPY MESS OVER MY KEYBOARD?
I'M CARBO-LOADING, FORGE. THIS MISSION'S GONNA BE A DOOZY. I'LL NEED THE CALORIES TO BURN.
KNEW YOU WERE UP TO SOMETHING. I WANT IN.
NOPE. THIS IS BETWEEN ME AND MR. SINISTER.
YOU GUIDED BY EGO AGAIN, DRAKE?
SINISTER HAS GOT A CENTURY OF EXPERIENCE ON YOU.
I'M WELL AWARE. AND WHILE I WOULD LOVE AN ICESHOP REUNION...
...I WANT EVERYONE TO ENJOY THE PARADE. FORGE DID A LOT OF COOL TECH ROADIE MAGIC FOR DAZZLER'S SHOW.
SINISTER MAY BE SMARTER THAN ME, AND THAT'S WHAT I'M BANKING ON.
YOU'RE ALL SET.
BOBBY--
TRUST ME ON THIS. MADIN MADE IT CLEAR, SINISTER'S *OBSESSED* WITH ME FOR SOME REASON.
SO I'M JUST GONNA GO THERE MYSELF.
WITH ONLY ME, MYSELF AND *ICE*.

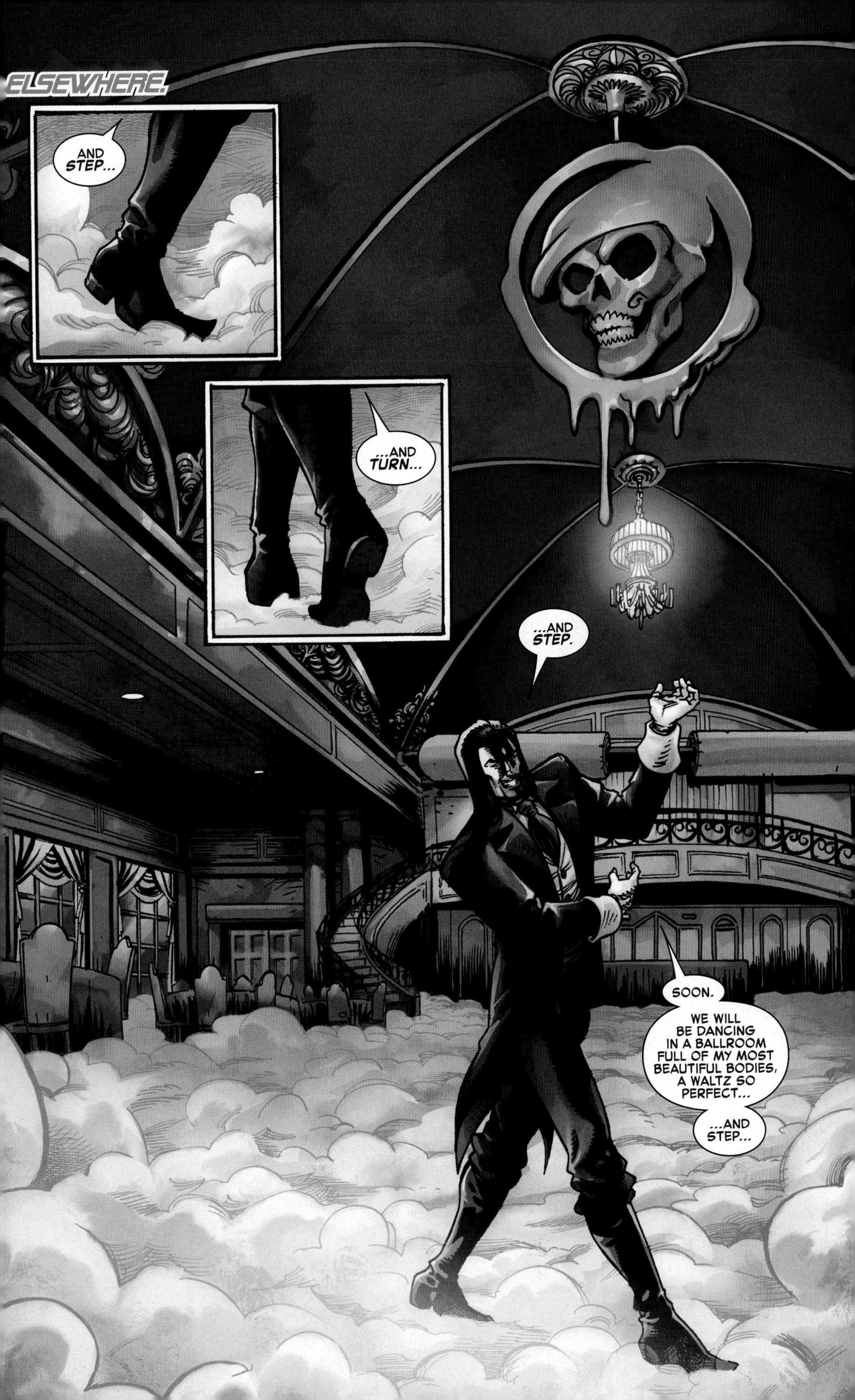
ELSEWHERE.
AND STEP...
...AND TURN...
...AND STEP.
SOON.
WE WILL BE DANCING IN A BALLROOM FULL OF MY MOST BEAUTIFUL BODIES, A WALTZ SO PERFECT...
...AND STEP...

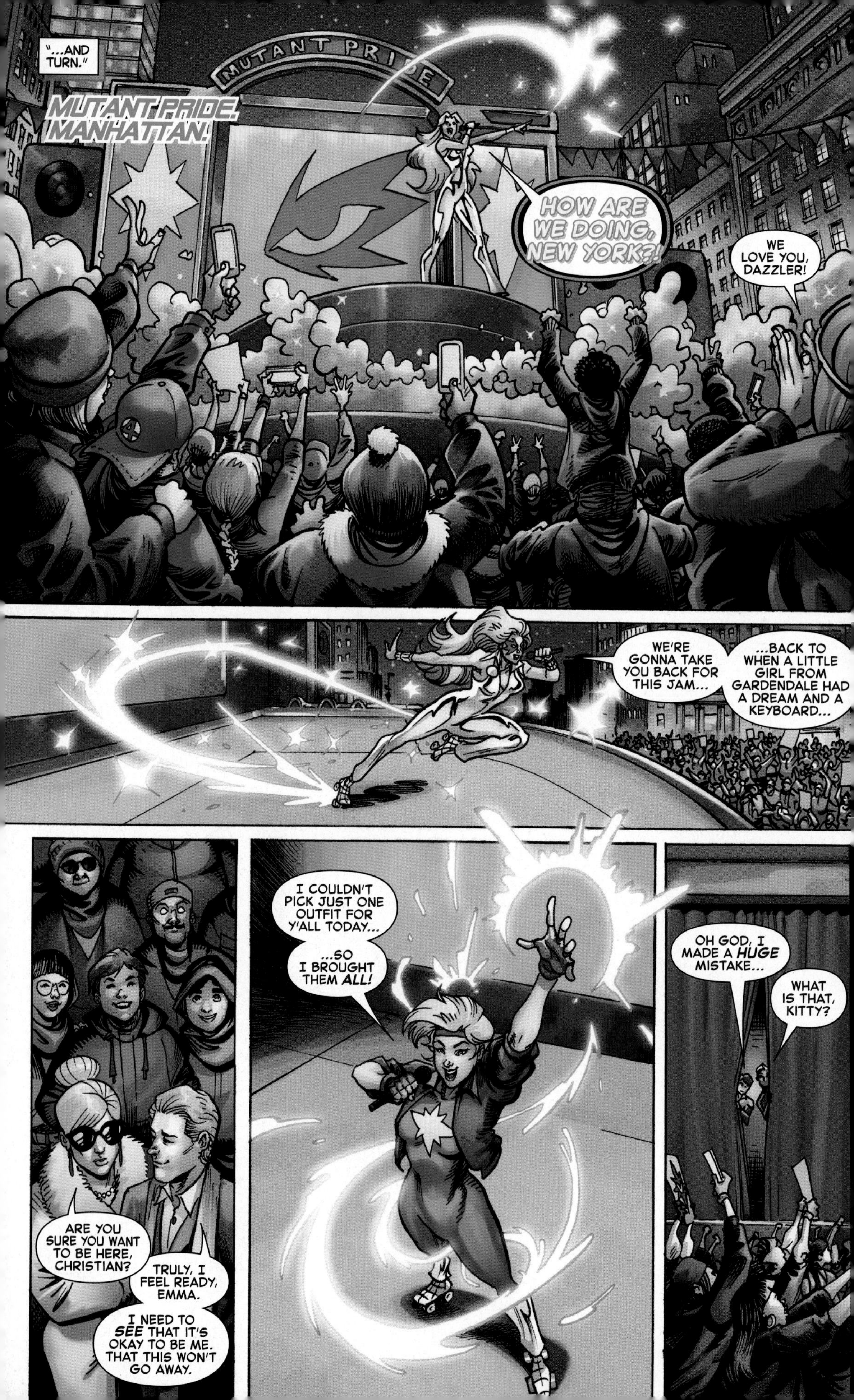
"...AND TURN."
MUTANT PRIDE
MUTANT PRIDE. MANHATTAN!
HOW ARE WE DOING, NEW YORK?!
WE LOVE YOU, DAZZLER!
WE'RE GONNA TAKE YOU BACK FOR THIS JAM...
...BACK TO WHEN A LITTLE GIRL FROM GARDENDALE HAD A DREAM AND A KEYBOARD...
ARE YOU SURE YOU WANT TO BE HERE, CHRISTIAN?
TRULY, I FEEL READY, EMMA.
I NEED TO SEE THAT IT'S OKAY TO BE ME. THAT THIS WON'T GO AWAY.
I COULDN'T PICK JUST ONE OUTFIT FOR Y'ALL TODAY...
...SO I BROUGHT THEM ALL!
OH GOD, I MADE A HUGE MISTAKE...
WHAT IS THAT, KITTY?

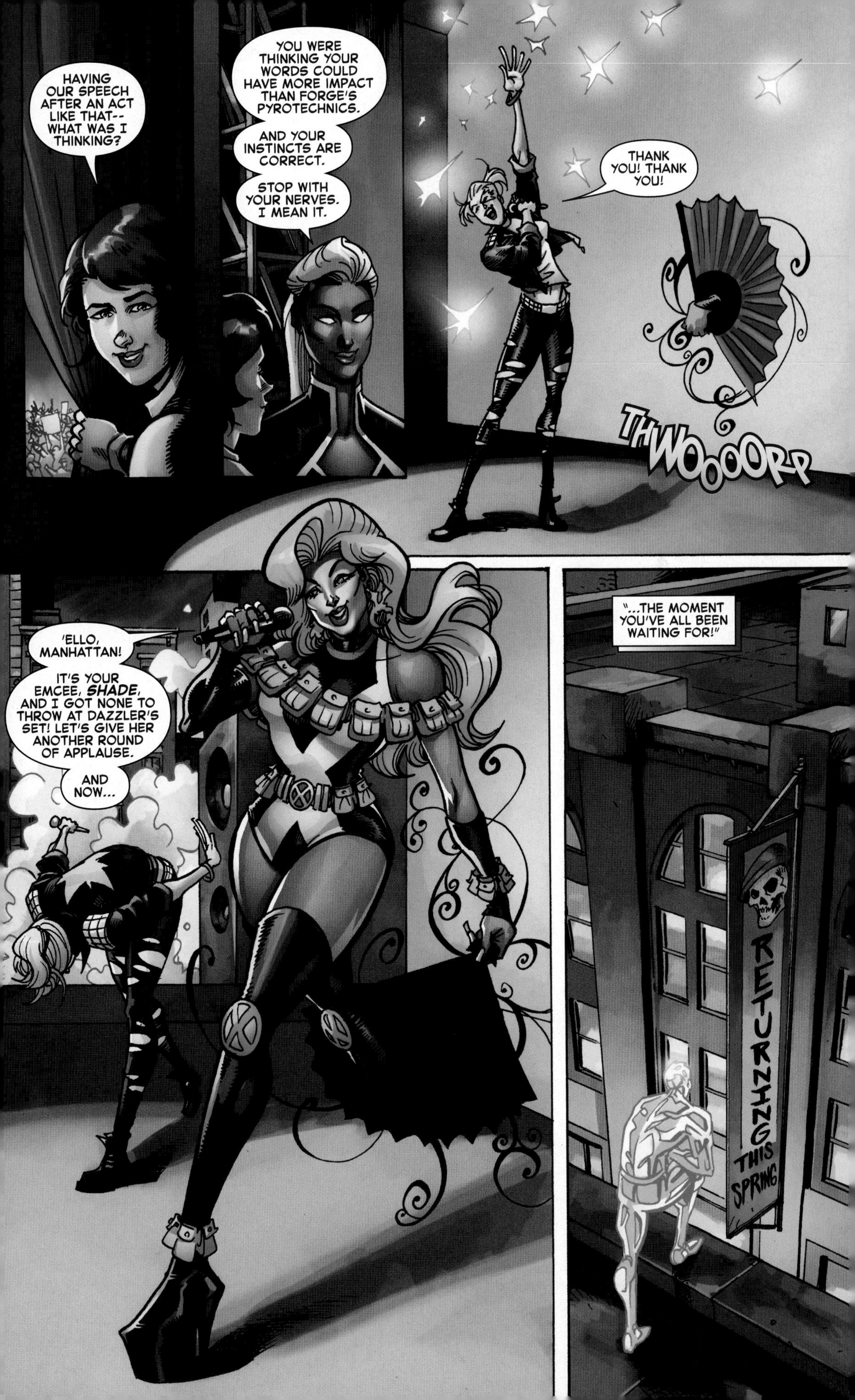
HAVING OUR SPEECH AFTER AN ACT LIKE THAT-- WHAT WAS I THINKING?
YOU WERE THINKING YOUR WORDS COULD HAVE MORE IMPACT THAN FORGE'S PYROTECHNICS.
AND YOUR INSTINCTS ARE CORRECT.
STOP WITH YOUR NERVES. I MEAN IT.
THANK YOU! THANK YOU!
THWOOOORP
'ELLO, MANHATTAN!
IT'S YOUR EMCEE, SHADE, AND I GOT NONE TO THROW AT DAZZLER'S SET! LET'S GIVE HER ANOTHER ROUND OF APPLAUSE.
AND NOW...
"...THE MOMENT YOU'VE ALL BEEN WAITING FOR!"
RETURNING THIS SPRING

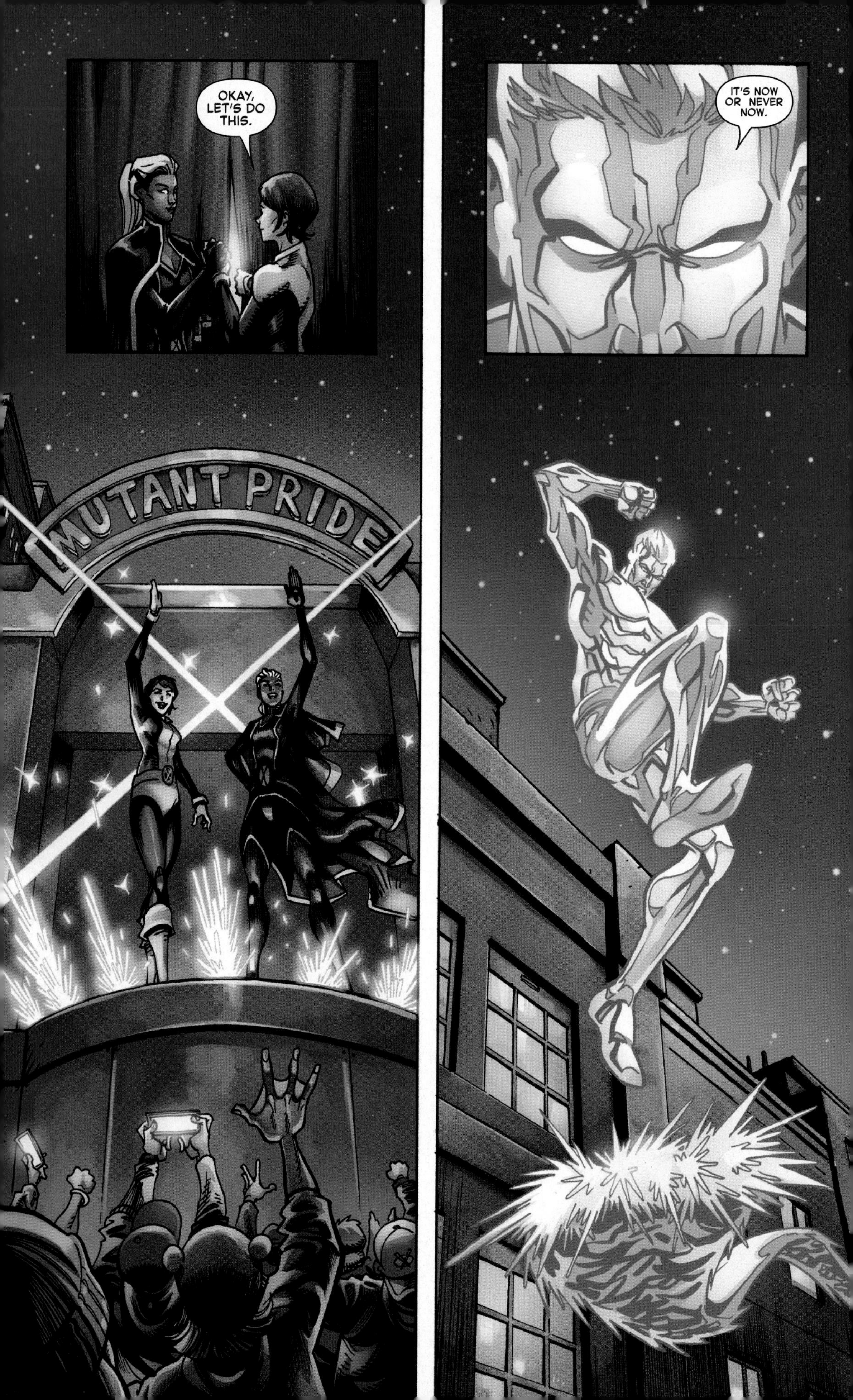
OKAY, LET'S DO THIS.
MUTANT PRIDE
IT'S NOW OR NEVER NOW.

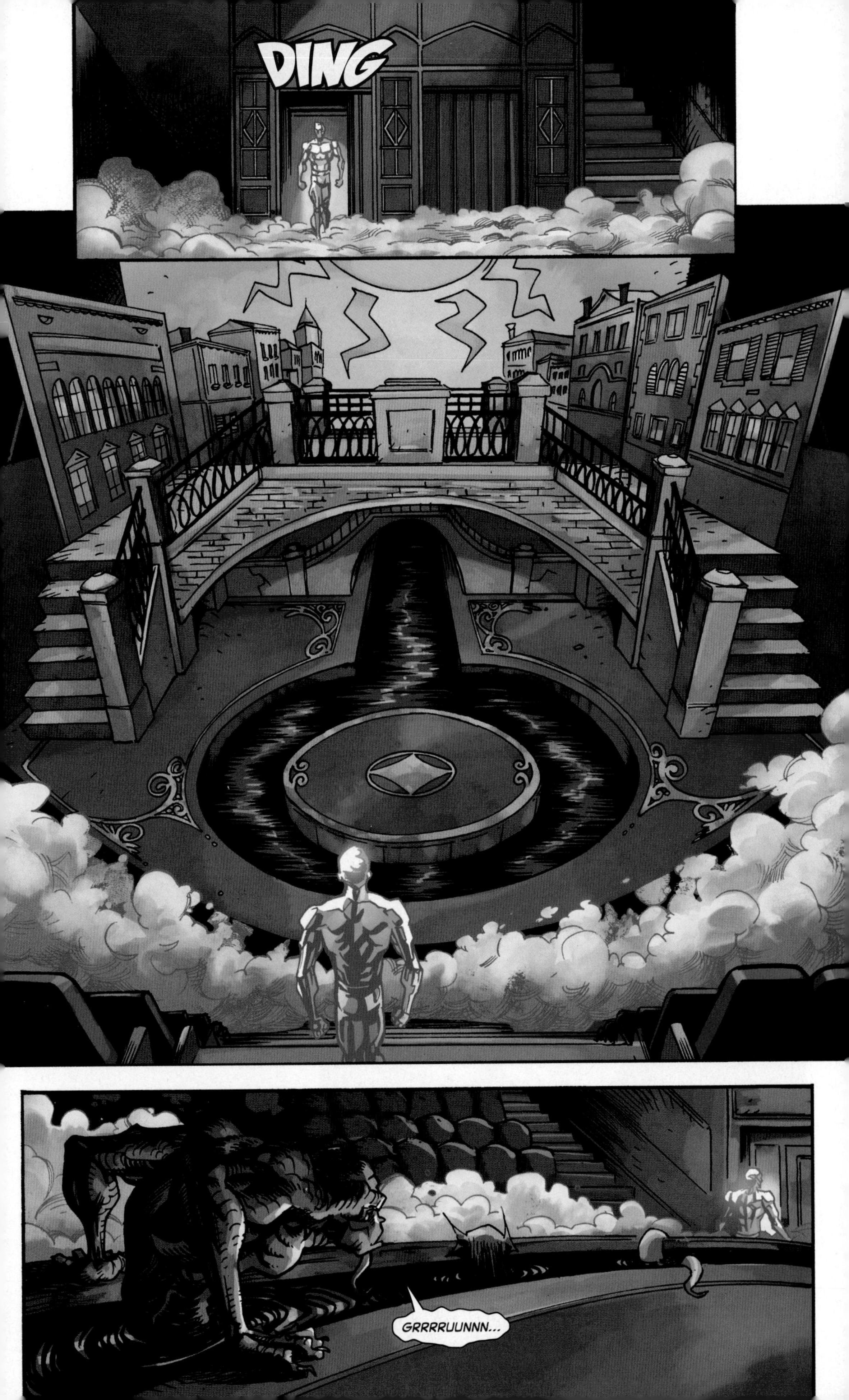
DING
GRRRRUUNNN...

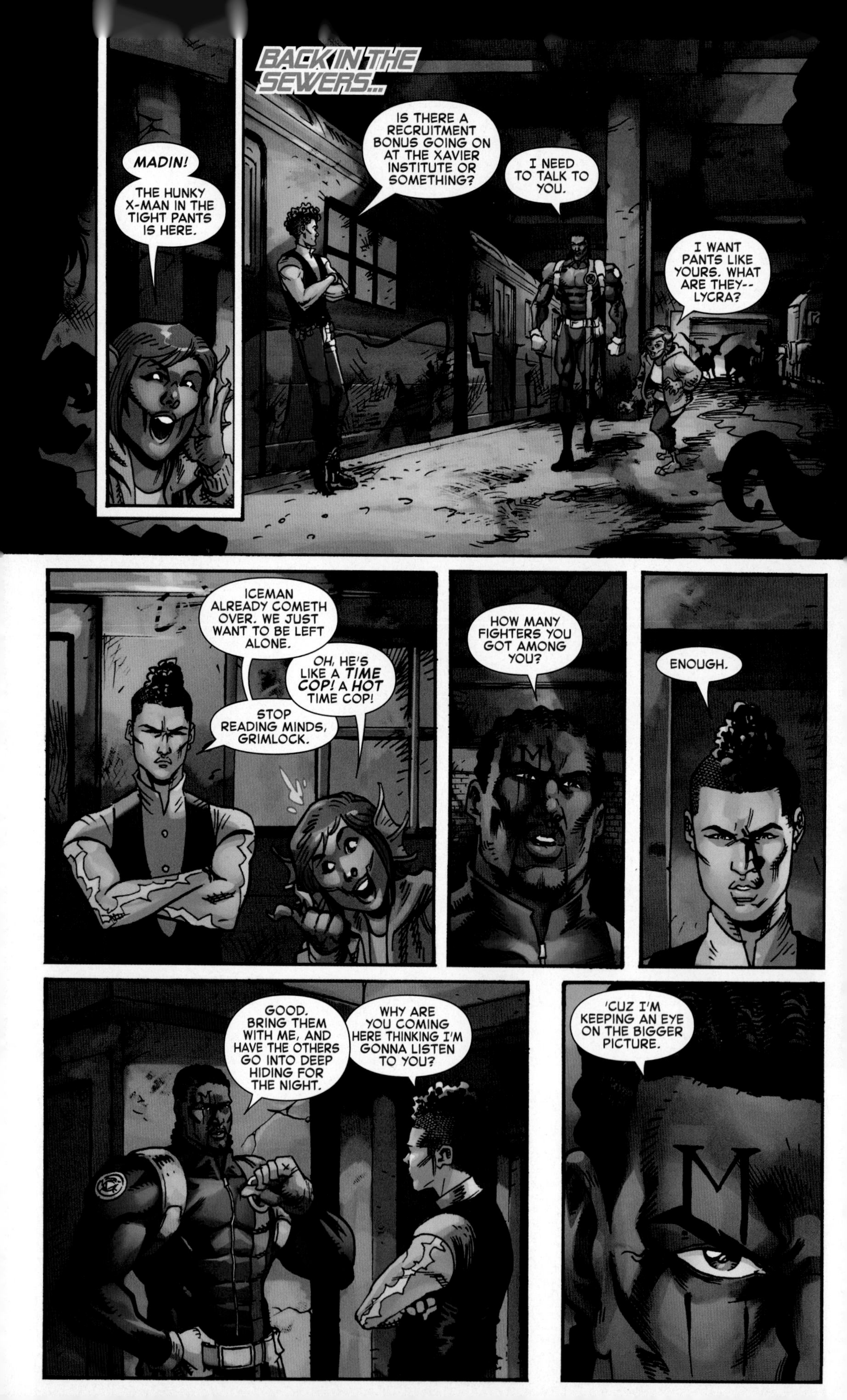
BACK IN THE SEWERS...
MADIN!
THE HUNKY X-MAN IN THE TIGHT PANTS IS HERE.
IS THERE A RECRUITMENT BONUS GOING ON AT THE XAVIER INSTITUTE OR SOMETHING?
I NEED TO TALK TO YOU.
I WANT PANTS LIKE YOURS. WHAT ARE THEY--LYCRA?
ICEMAN ALREADY COMETH OVER. WE JUST WANT TO BE LEFT ALONE.
OH, HE'S LIKE A TIME COP! A HOT TIME COP!
STOP READING MINDS, GRIMLOCK.
HOW MANY FIGHTERS YOU GOT AMONG YOU?
ENOUGH.
GOOD. BRING THEM WITH ME, AND HAVE THE OTHERS GO INTO DEEP HIDING FOR THE NIGHT.
WHY ARE YOU COMING HERE THINKING I'M GONNA LISTEN TO YOU?
'CUZ I'M KEEPING AN EYE ON THE BIGGER PICTURE.

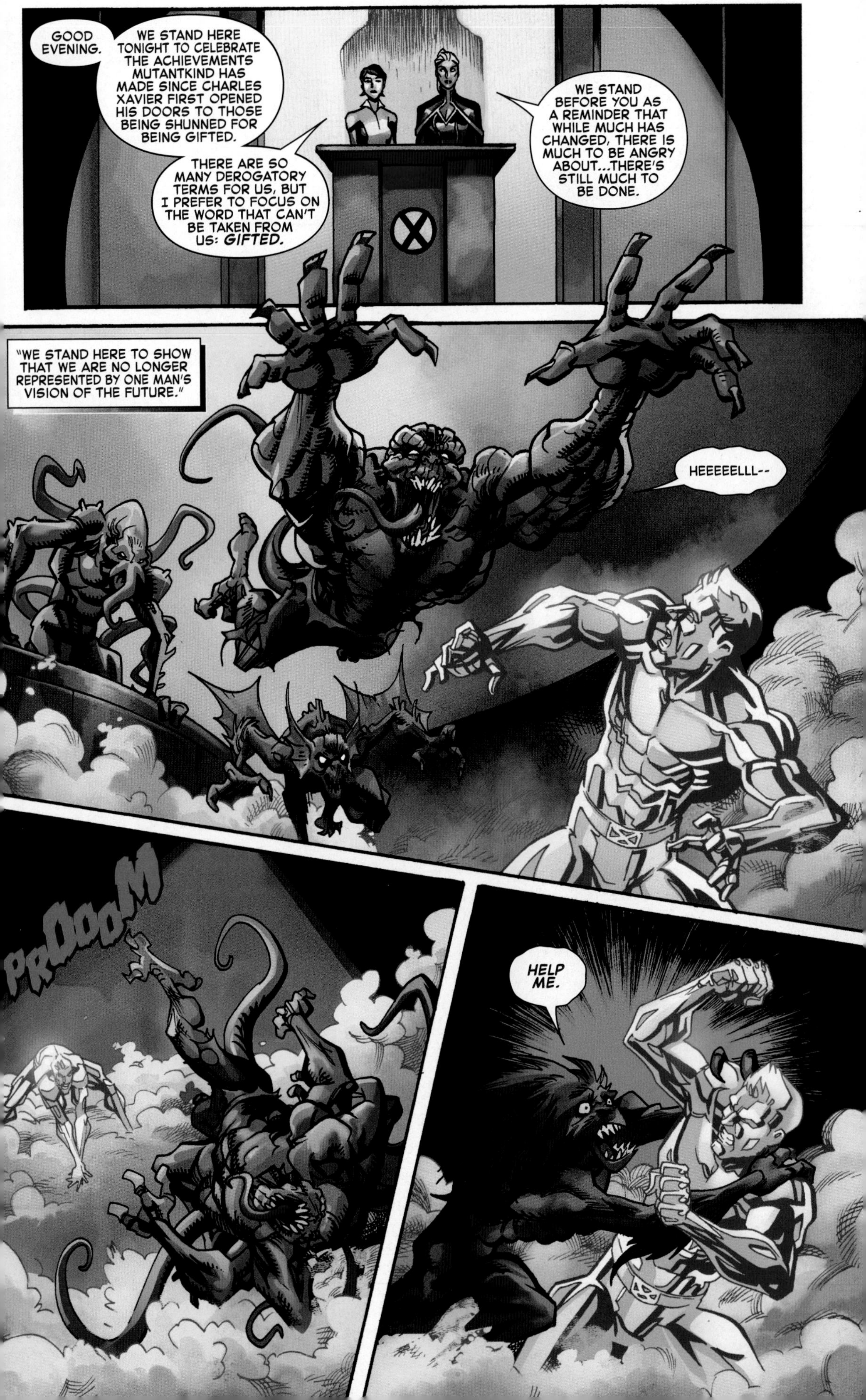
GOOD EVENING.
WE STAND HERE TONIGHT TO CELEBRATE THE ACHIEVEMENTS MUTANTKIND HAS MADE SINCE CHARLES XAVIER FIRST OPENED HIS DOORS TO THOSE BEING SHUNNED FOR BEING GIFTED.
THERE ARE SO MANY DEROGATORY TERMS FOR US, BUT I PREFER TO FOCUS ON THE WORD THAT CAN'T BE TAKEN FROM US: GIFTED.
WE STAND BEFORE YOU AS A REMINDER THAT WHILE MUCH HAS CHANGED, THERE IS MUCH TO BE ANGRY ABOUT...THERE'S STILL MUCH TO BE DONE.
"WE STAND HERE TO SHOW THAT WE ARE NO LONGER REPRESENTED BY ONE MAN'S VISION OF THE FUTURE."
HEEEEELLL--
PROOOM
HELP ME.

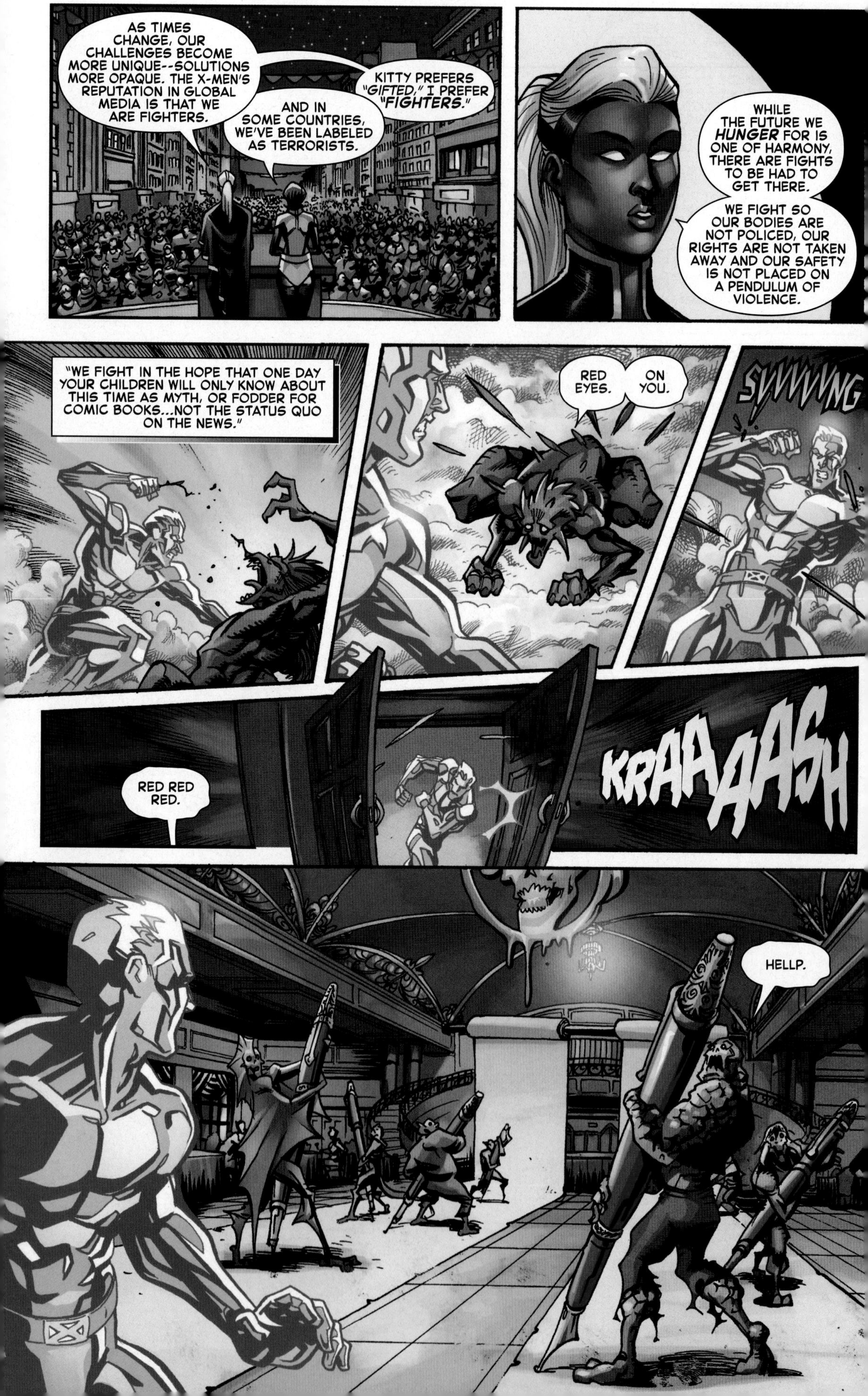
AS TIMES CHANGE, OUR CHALLENGES BECOME MORE UNIQUE--SOLUTIONS MORE OPAQUE. THE X-MEN'S REPUTATION IN GLOBAL MEDIA IS THAT WE ARE FIGHTERS.
KITTY PREFERS "GIFTED," I PREFER "FIGHTERS."
AND IN SOME COUNTRIES, WE'VE BEEN LABELED AS TERRORISTS.
WHILE THE FUTURE WE HUNGER FOR IS ONE OF HARMONY, THERE ARE FIGHTS TO BE HAD TO GET THERE.
WE FIGHT SO OUR BODIES ARE NOT POLICED, OUR RIGHTS ARE NOT TAKEN AWAY AND OUR SAFETY IS NOT PLACED ON A PENDULUM OF VIOLENCE.
"WE FIGHT IN THE HOPE THAT ONE DAY YOUR CHILDREN WILL ONLY KNOW ABOUT THIS TIME AS MYTH, OR FODDER FOR COMIC BOOKS...NOT THE STATUS QUO ON THE NEWS."
RED EYES.
ON YOU.
SVVVVNG
RED RED RED.
KRAAAASH
HELLP.

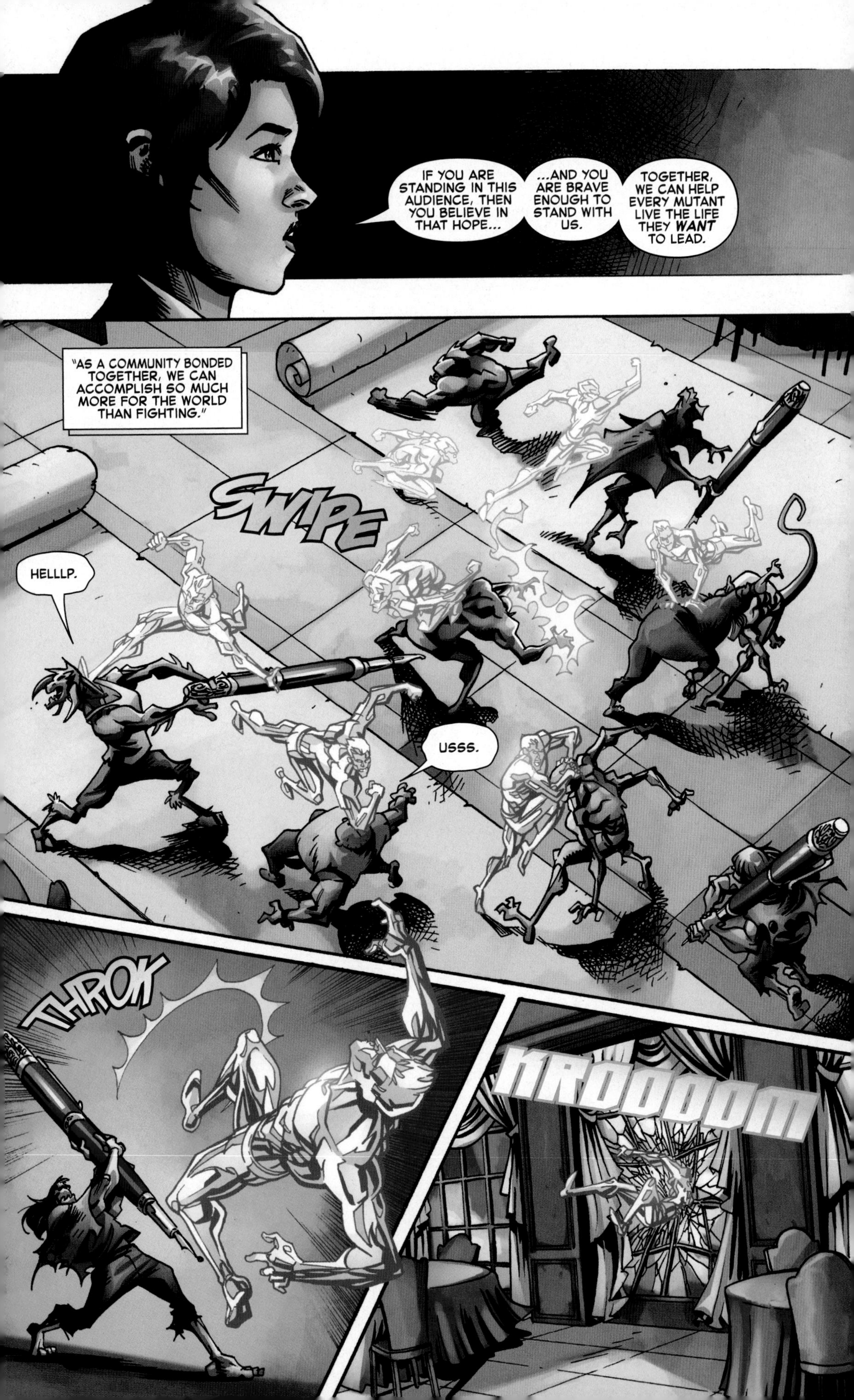

IF YOU ARE STANDING IN THIS AUDIENCE, THEN YOU BELIEVE IN THAT HOPE...
...AND YOU ARE BRAVE ENOUGH TO STAND WITH US.
TOGETHER, WE CAN HELP EVERY MUTANT LIVE THE LIFE THEY *WANT* TO LEAD.
"AS A COMMUNITY BONDED TOGETHER, WE CAN ACCOMPLISH SO MUCH MORE FOR THE WORLD THAN FIGHTING."
SWIPE
HELLLP.
USSS.
THROK
KROOOOOM

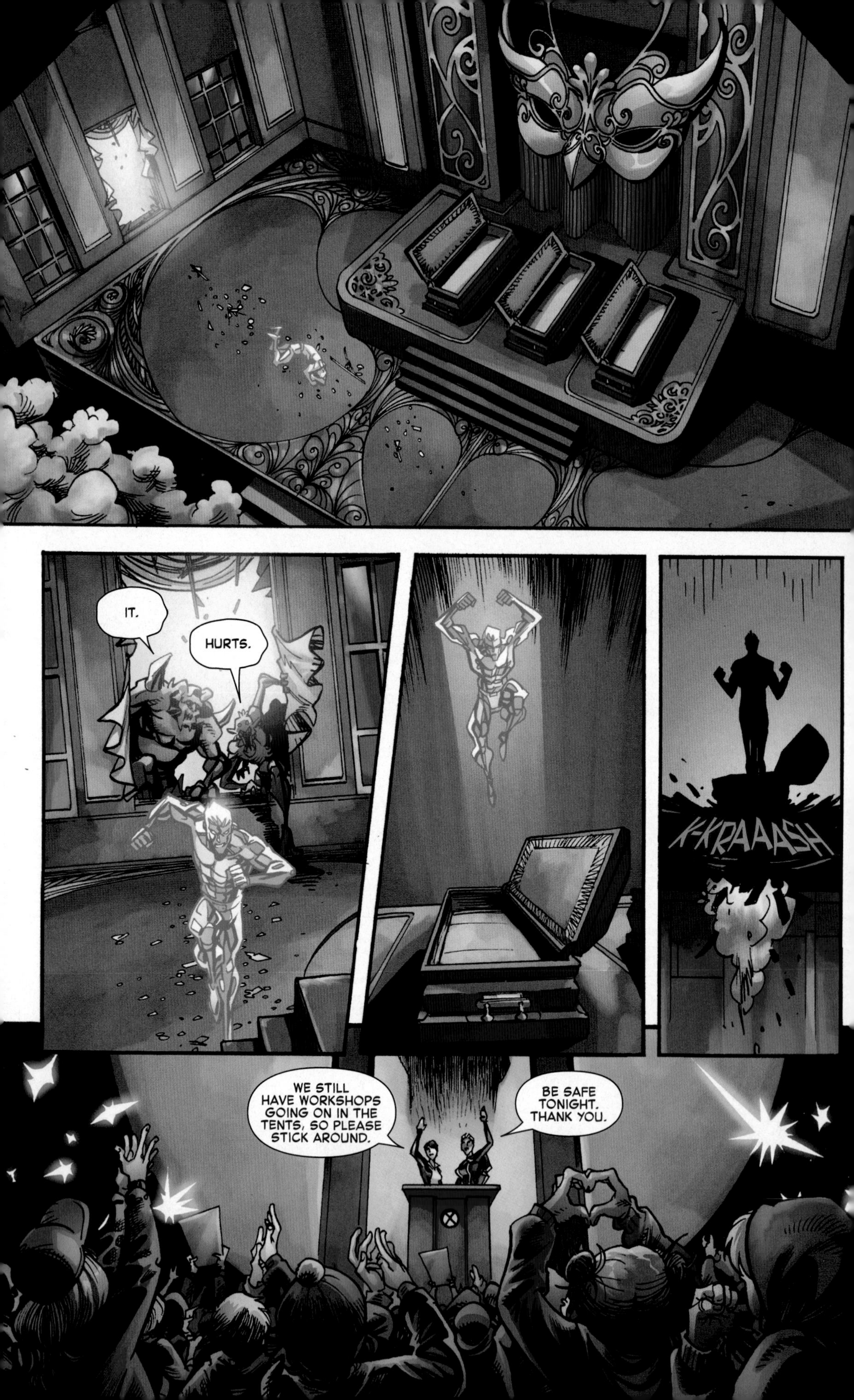
IT.
HURTS.
K-KRAAASH
WE STILL HAVE WORKSHOPS GOING ON IN THE TENTS, SO PLEASE STICK AROUND.
BE SAFE TONIGHT. THANK YOU.

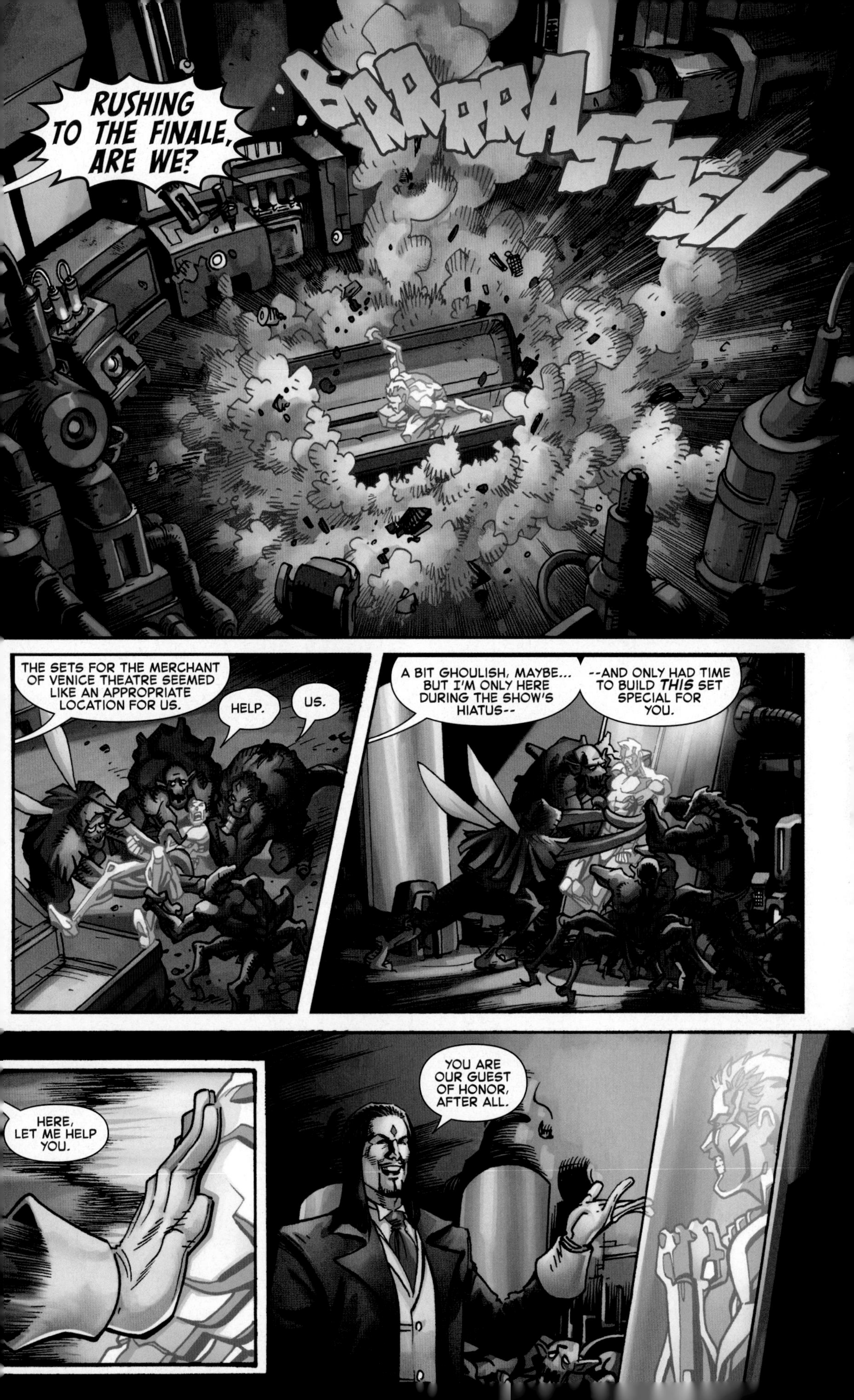
RUSHING TO THE FINALE, ARE WE?
BRRRRASSSSH
THE SETS FOR THE MERCHANT OF VENICE THEATRE SEEMED LIKE AN APPROPRIATE LOCATION FOR US.
HELP.
US.
A BIT GHOULISH, MAYBE... BUT I'M ONLY HERE DURING THE SHOW'S HIATUS--
--AND ONLY HAD TIME TO BUILD THIS SET SPECIAL FOR YOU.
HERE, LET ME HELP YOU.
YOU ARE OUR GUEST OF HONOR, AFTER ALL.

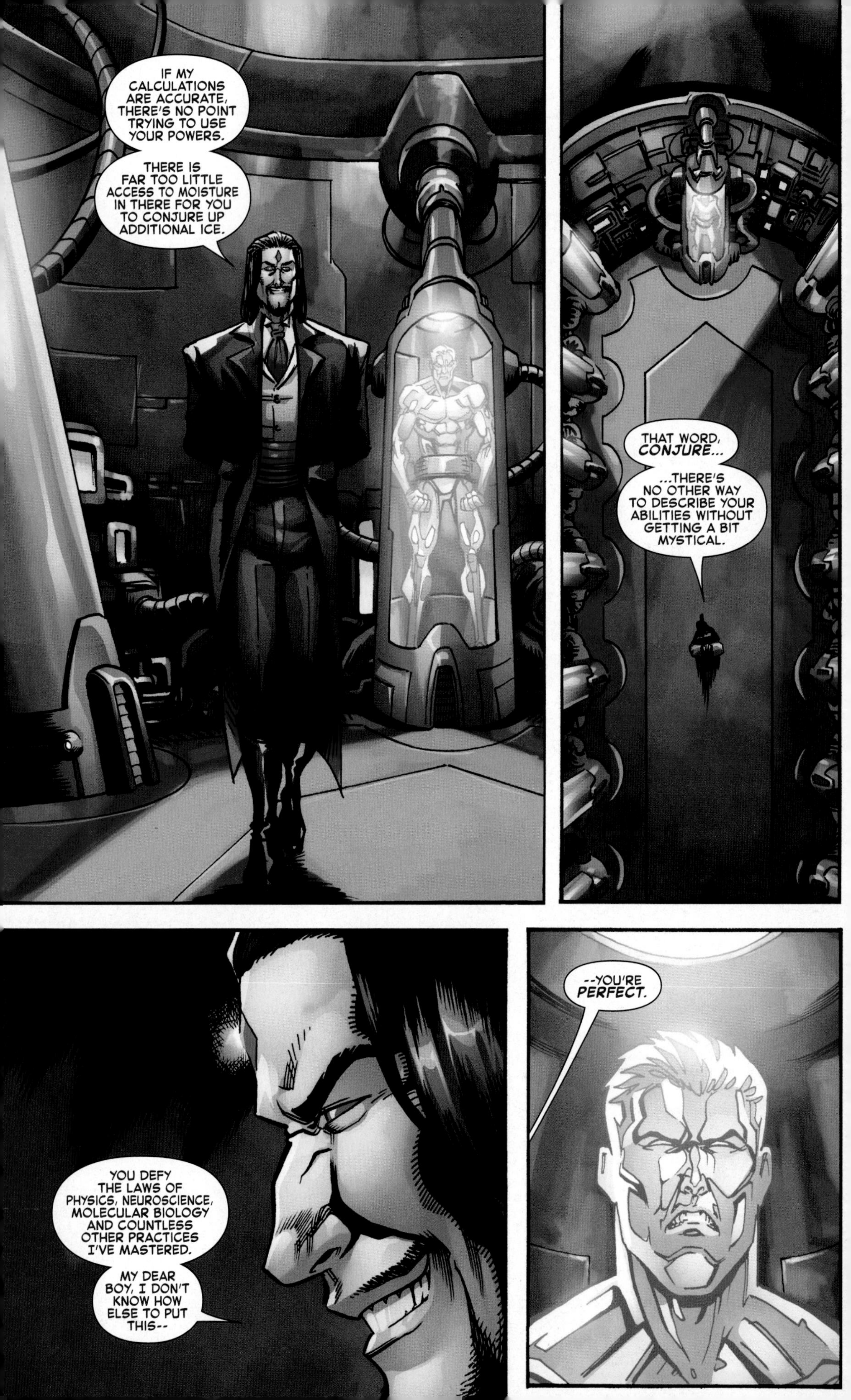
IF MY CALCULATIONS ARE ACCURATE, THERE'S NO POINT TRYING TO USE YOUR POWERS.
THERE IS FAR TOO LITTLE ACCESS TO MOISTURE IN THERE FOR YOU TO CONJURE UP ADDITIONAL ICE.
THAT WORD, *CONJURE*...
...THERE'S NO OTHER WAY TO DESCRIBE YOUR ABILITIES WITHOUT GETTING A BIT MYSTICAL.
YOU DEFY THE LAWS OF PHYSICS, NEUROSCIENCE, MOLECULAR BIOLOGY AND COUNTLESS OTHER PRACTICES I'VE MASTERED.
MY DEAR BOY, I DON'T KNOW HOW ELSE TO PUT THIS--
--YOU'RE *PERFECT*.

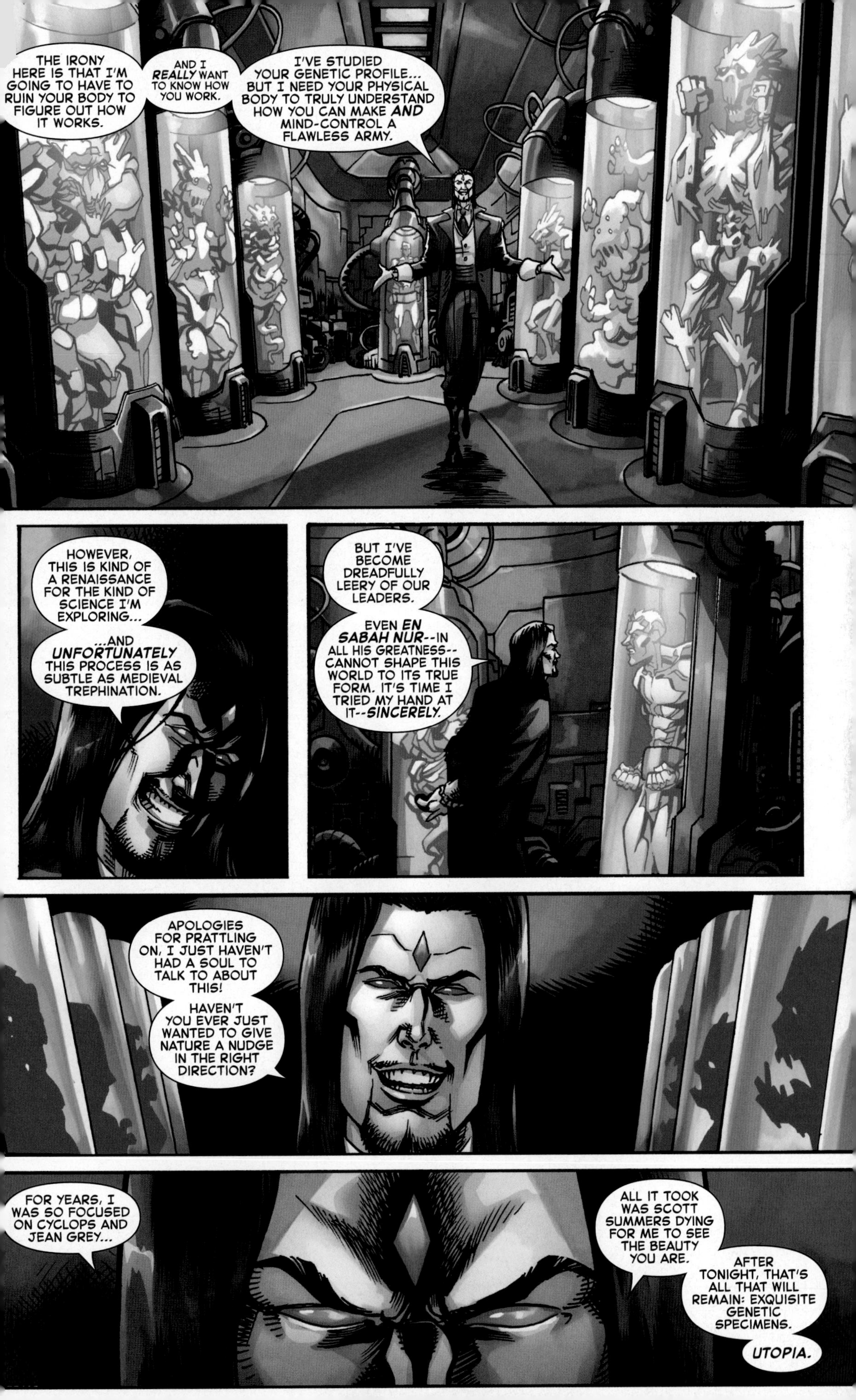
THE IRONY HERE IS THAT I'M GOING TO HAVE TO RUIN YOUR BODY TO FIGURE OUT HOW IT WORKS.
AND I REALLY WANT TO KNOW HOW YOU WORK.
I'VE STUDIED YOUR GENETIC PROFILE... BUT I NEED YOUR PHYSICAL BODY TO TRULY UNDERSTAND HOW YOU CAN MAKE AND MIND-CONTROL A FLAWLESS ARMY.
HOWEVER, THIS IS KIND OF A RENAISSANCE FOR THE KIND OF SCIENCE I'M EXPLORING...
...AND UNFORTUNATELY THIS PROCESS IS AS SUBTLE AS MEDIEVAL TREPHINATION.
BUT I'VE BECOME DREADFULLY LEERY OF OUR LEADERS.
EVEN EN SABAH NUR--IN ALL HIS GREATNESS--CANNOT SHAPE THIS WORLD TO ITS TRUE FORM. IT'S TIME I TRIED MY HAND AT IT--SINCERELY.
APOLOGIES FOR PRATTLING ON, I JUST HAVEN'T HAD A SOUL TO TALK TO ABOUT THIS!
HAVEN'T YOU EVER JUST WANTED TO GIVE NATURE A NUDGE IN THE RIGHT DIRECTION?
FOR YEARS, I WAS SO FOCUSED ON CYCLOPS AND JEAN GREY...
ALL IT TOOK WAS SCOTT SUMMERS DYING FOR ME TO SEE THE BEAUTY YOU ARE.
AFTER TONIGHT, THAT'S ALL THAT WILL REMAIN: EXQUISITE GENETIC SPECIMENS.
UTOPIA.

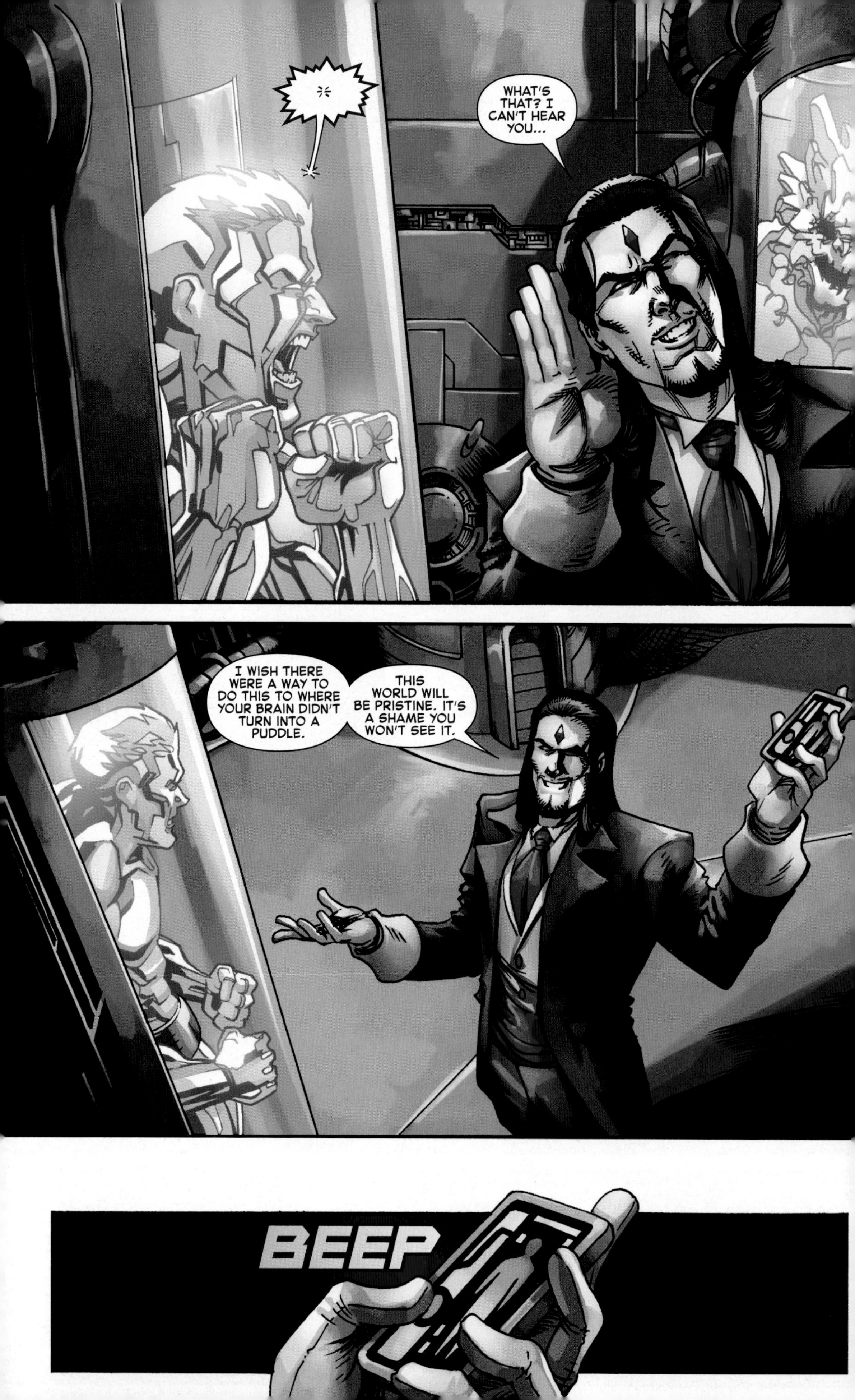

WHAT'S THAT? I CAN'T HEAR YOU...
I WISH THERE WERE A WAY TO DO THIS TO WHERE YOUR BRAIN DIDN'T TURN INTO A PUDDLE.
THIS WORLD WILL BE PRISTINE. IT'S A SHAME YOU WON'T SEE IT.
BEEP

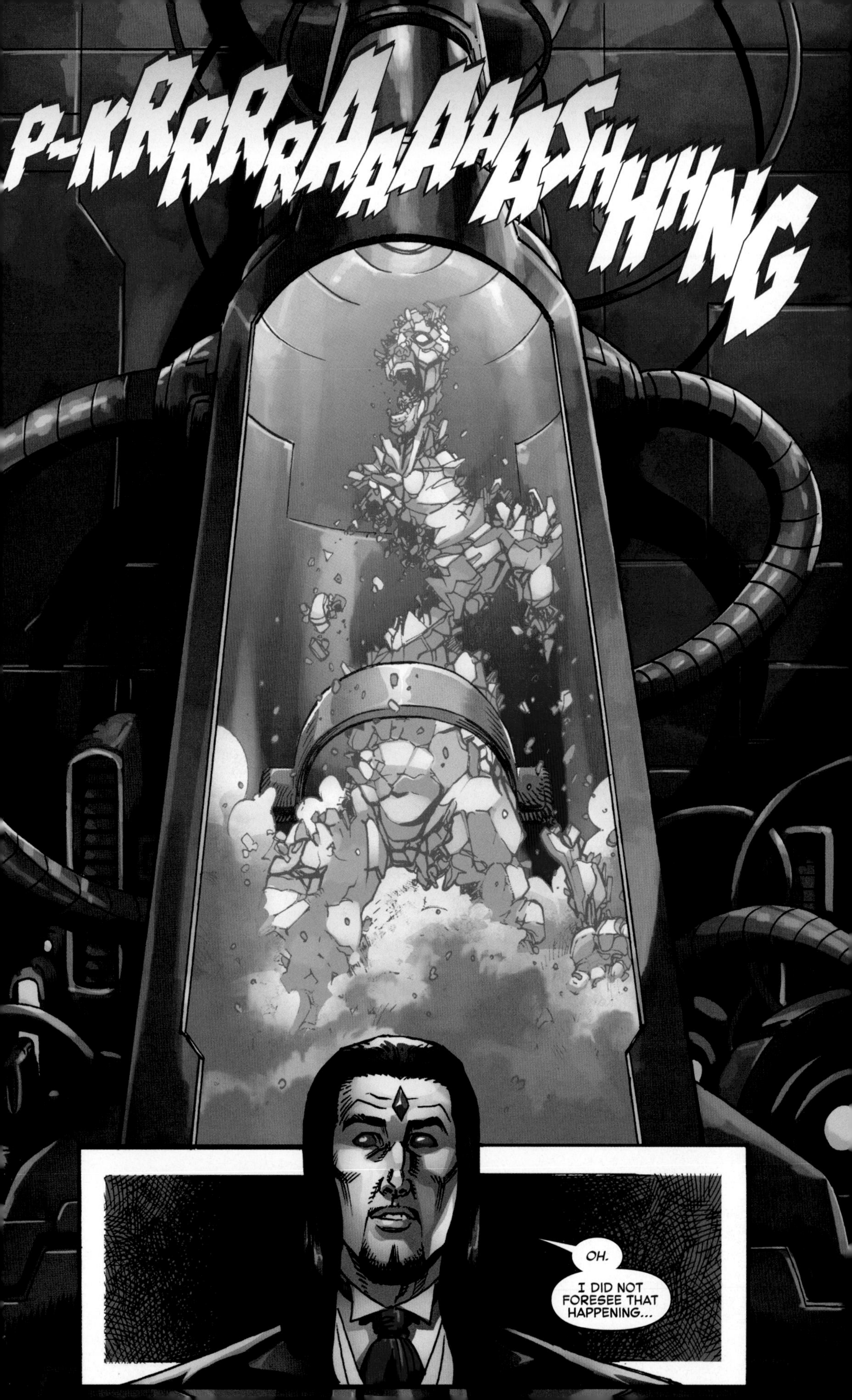
P-KRRRRAAAAASHHHNG
OH.
I DID NOT FORESEE THAT HAPPENING...

5

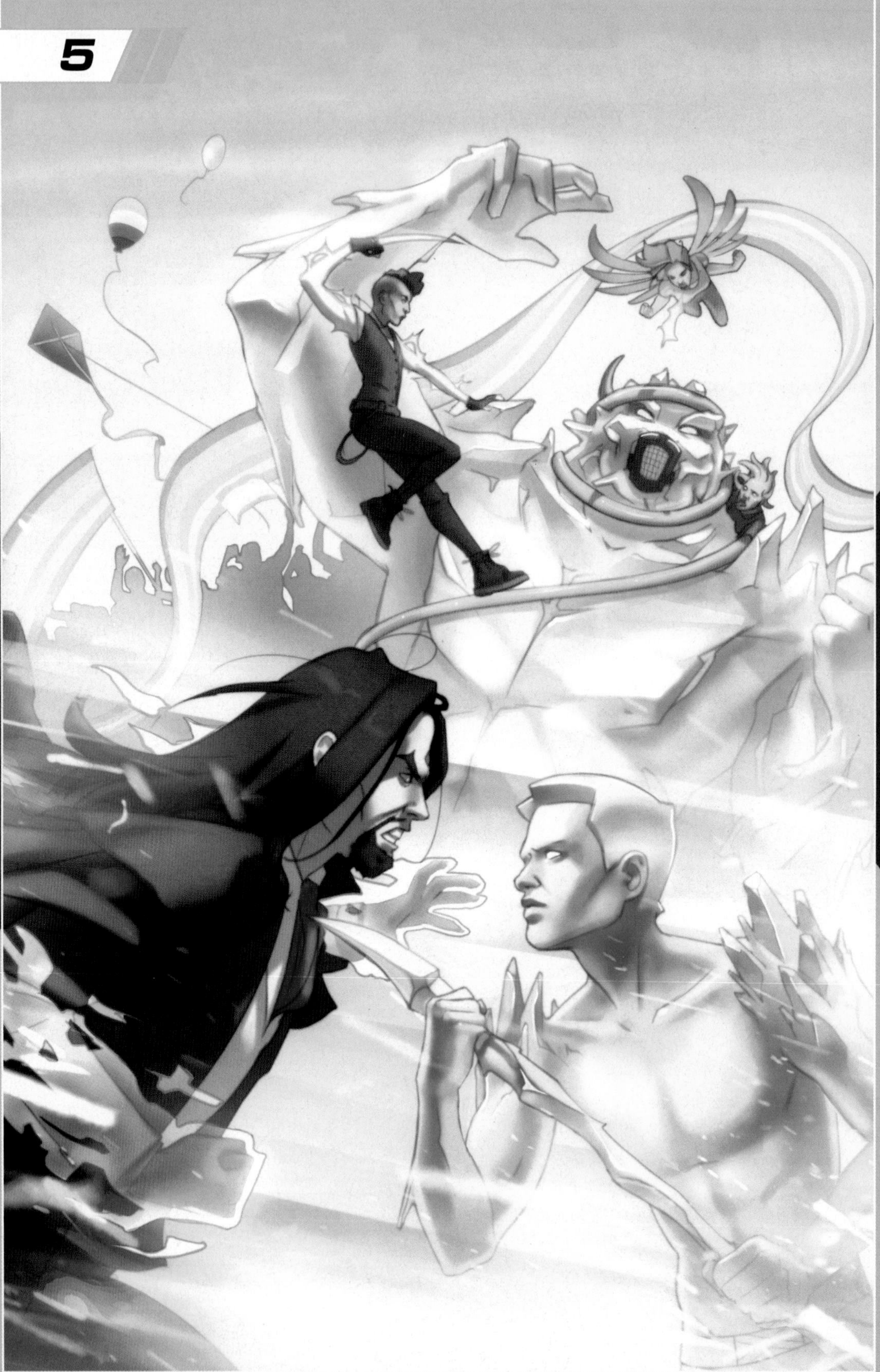

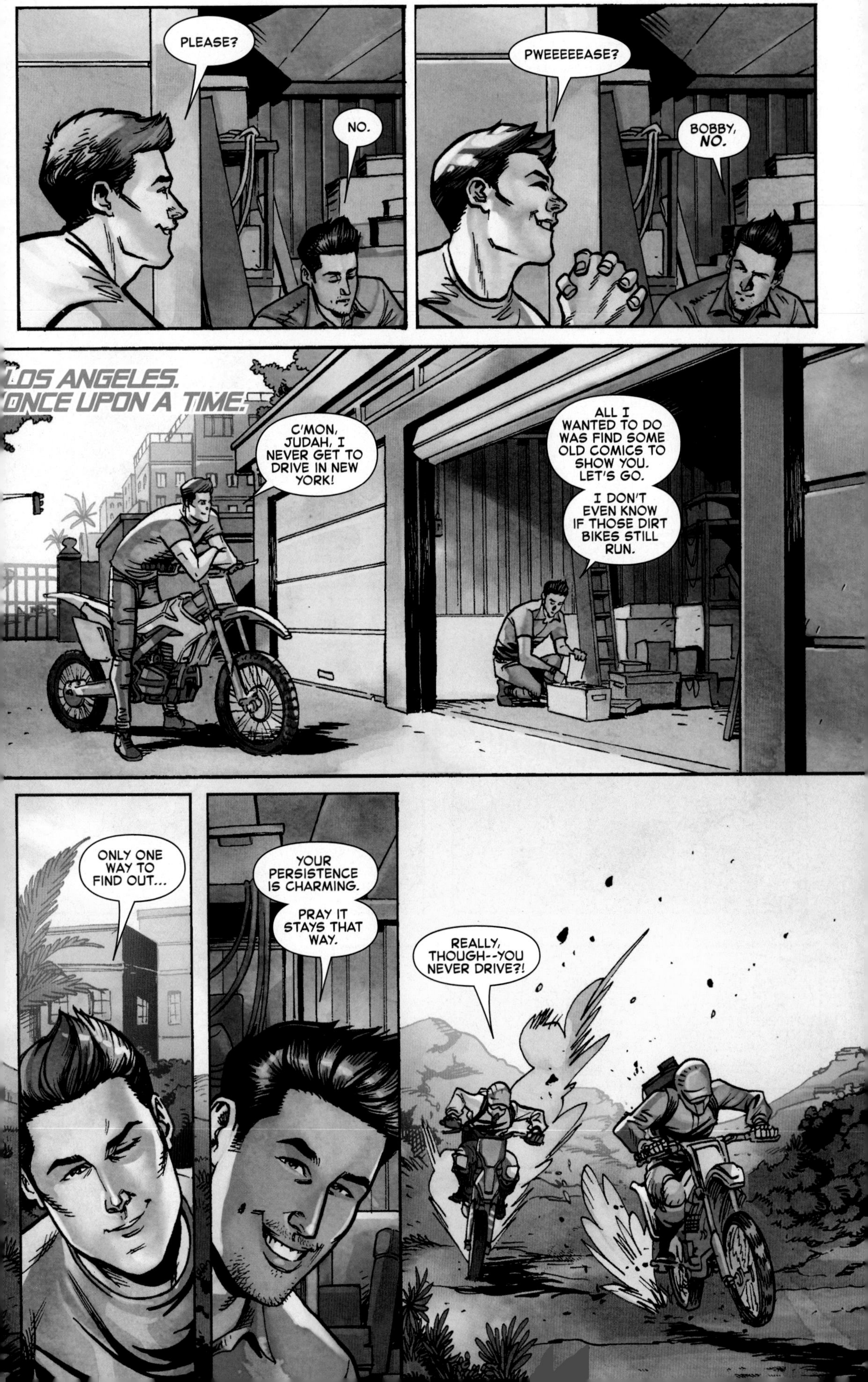
PLEASE?
NO.
PWEEEEEEASE?
BOBBY, NO.
LOS ANGELES. ONCE UPON A TIME.
C'MON, JUDAH, I NEVER GET TO DRIVE IN NEW YORK!
ALL I WANTED TO DO WAS FIND SOME OLD COMICS TO SHOW YOU. LET'S GO.
I DON'T EVEN KNOW IF THOSE DIRT BIKES STILL RUN.
ONLY ONE WAY TO FIND OUT...
YOUR PERSISTENCE IS CHARMING.
PRAY IT STAYS THAT WAY.
REALLY, THOUGH--YOU NEVER DRIVE?!

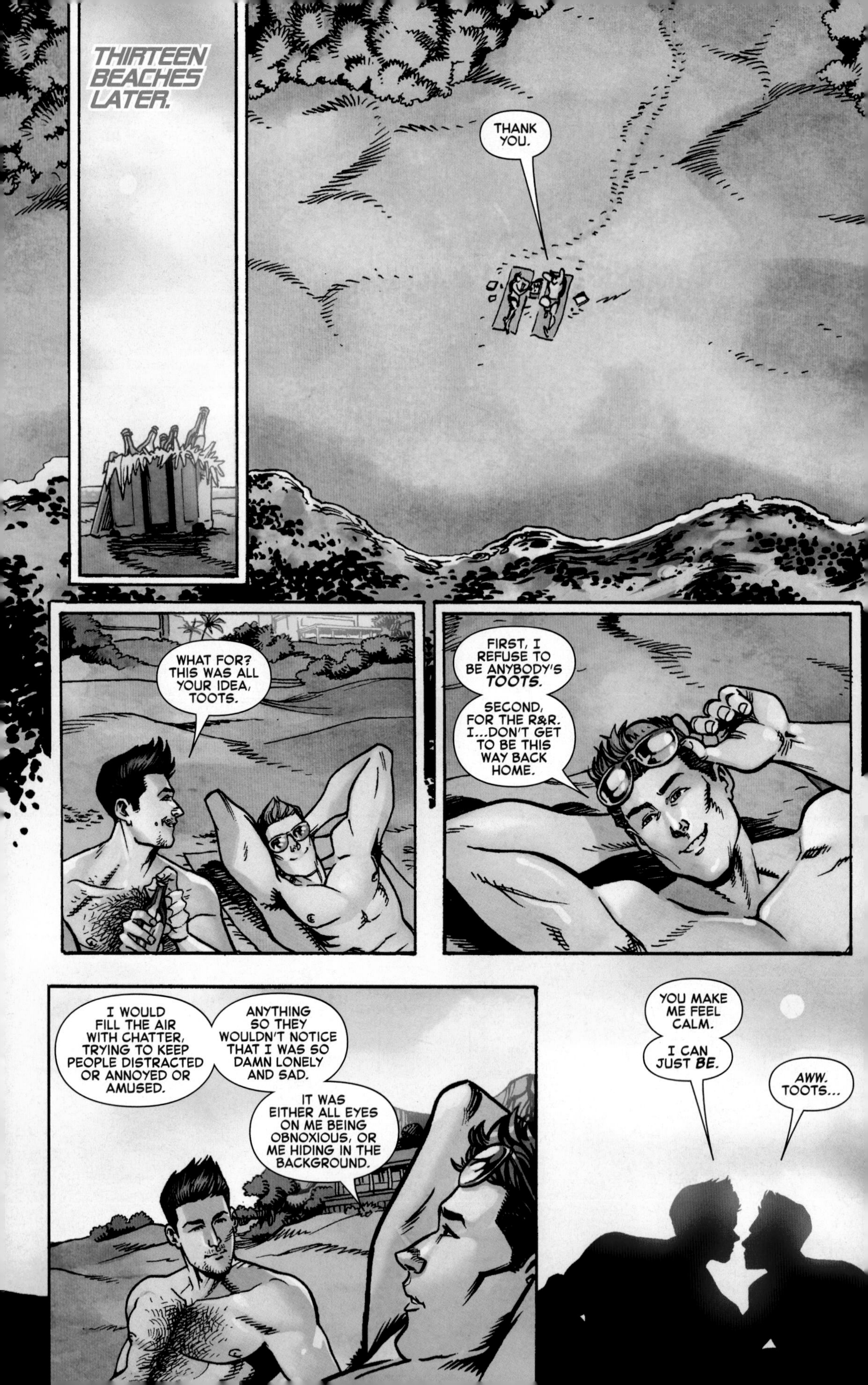
THIRTEEN BEACHES LATER.
THANK YOU.
WHAT FOR? THIS WAS ALL YOUR IDEA, TOOTS.
FIRST, I REFUSE TO BE ANYBODY'S TOOTS.
SECOND, FOR THE R&R. I...DON'T GET TO BE THIS WAY BACK HOME.
I WOULD FILL THE AIR WITH CHATTER, TRYING TO KEEP PEOPLE DISTRACTED OR ANNOYED OR AMUSED.
ANYTHING SO THEY WOULDN'T NOTICE THAT I WAS SO DAMN LONELY AND SAD.
IT WAS EITHER ALL EYES ON ME BEING OBNOXIOUS, OR ME HIDING IN THE BACKGROUND.
YOU MAKE ME FEEL CALM.
I CAN JUST BE.
AWW. TOOTS...

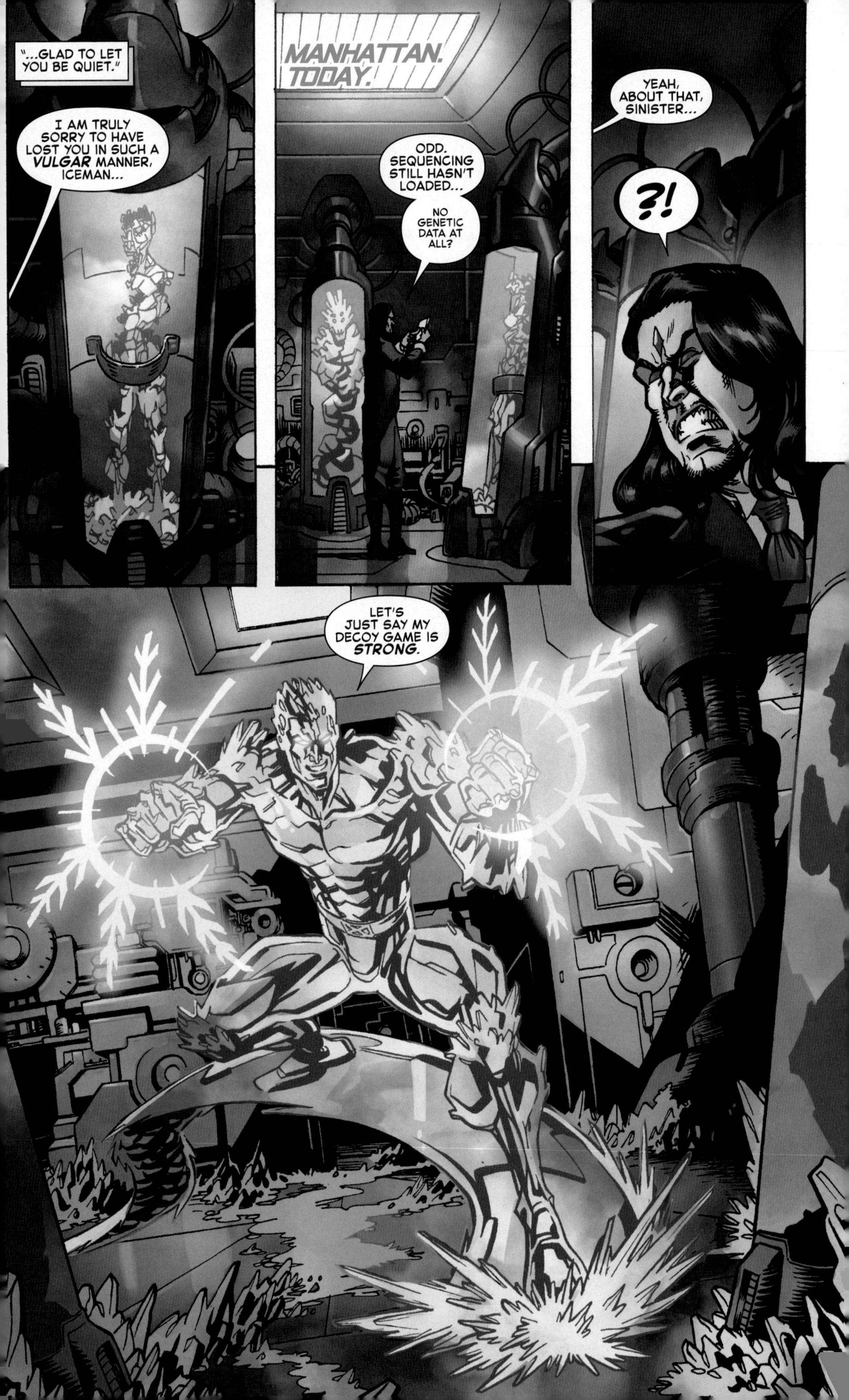
"...GLAD TO LET YOU BE QUIET."
I AM TRULY SORRY TO HAVE LOST YOU IN SUCH A VULGAR MANNER, ICEMAN...
MANHATTAN. TODAY.
ODD. SEQUENCING STILL HASN'T LOADED...
NO GENETIC DATA AT ALL?
YEAH, ABOUT THAT, SINISTER...
?!
LET'S JUST SAY MY DECOY GAME IS STRONG.

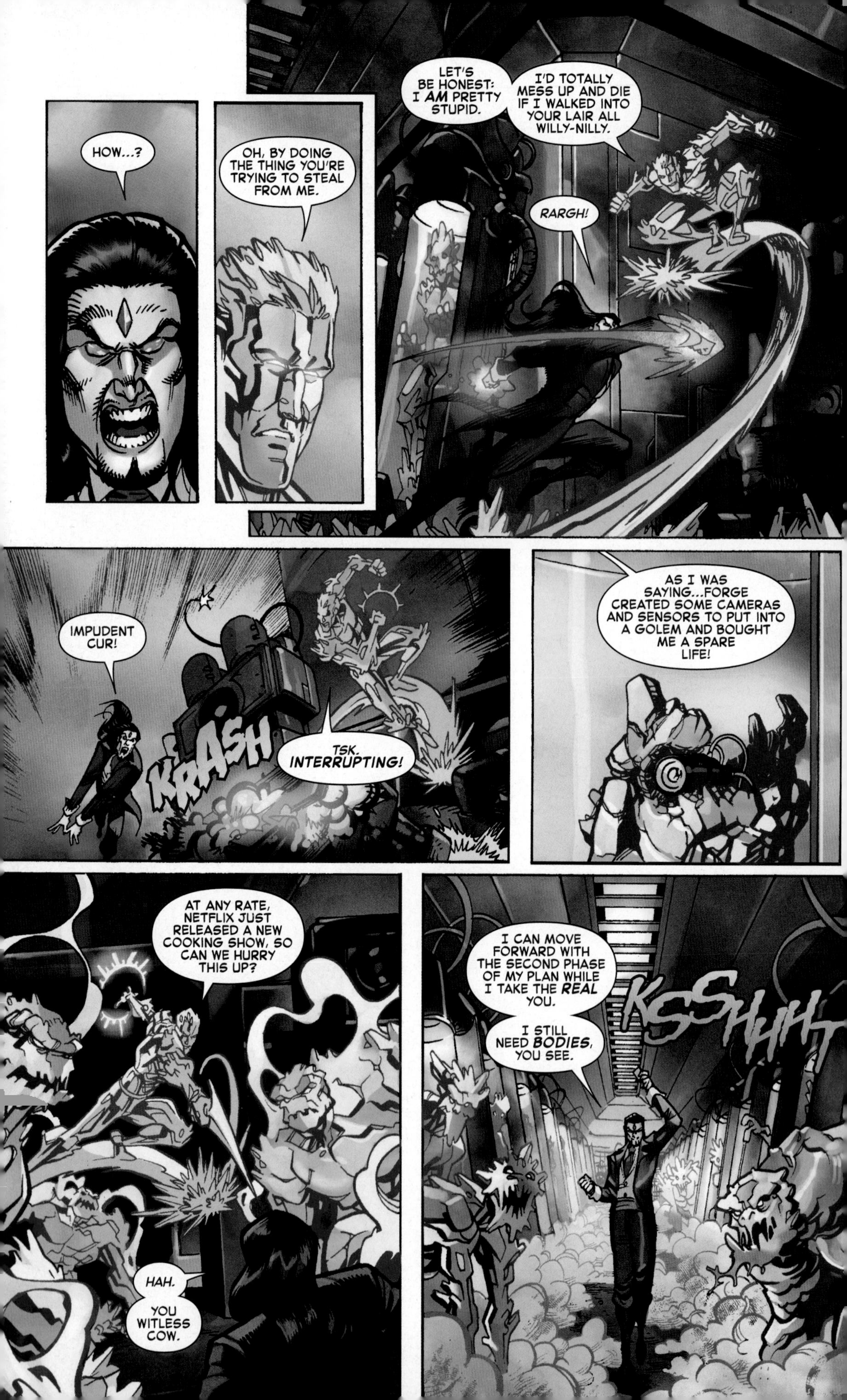
HOW...?
OH, BY DOING THE THING YOU'RE TRYING TO STEAL FROM ME.
LET'S BE HONEST: I AM PRETTY STUPID.
I'D TOTALLY MESS UP AND DIE IF I WALKED INTO YOUR LAIR ALL WILLY-NILLY.
RARGH!
IMPUDENT CUR!
KRASH
TSK. INTERRUPTING!
AS I WAS SAYING...FORGE CREATED SOME CAMERAS AND SENSORS TO PUT INTO A GOLEM AND BOUGHT ME A SPARE LIFE!
AT ANY RATE, NETFLIX JUST RELEASED A NEW COOKING SHOW, SO CAN WE HURRY THIS UP?
HAH.
YOU WITLESS COW.
I CAN MOVE FORWARD WITH THE SECOND PHASE OF MY PLAN WHILE I TAKE THE REAL YOU.
I STILL NEED BODIES, YOU SEE.
KSSHHH

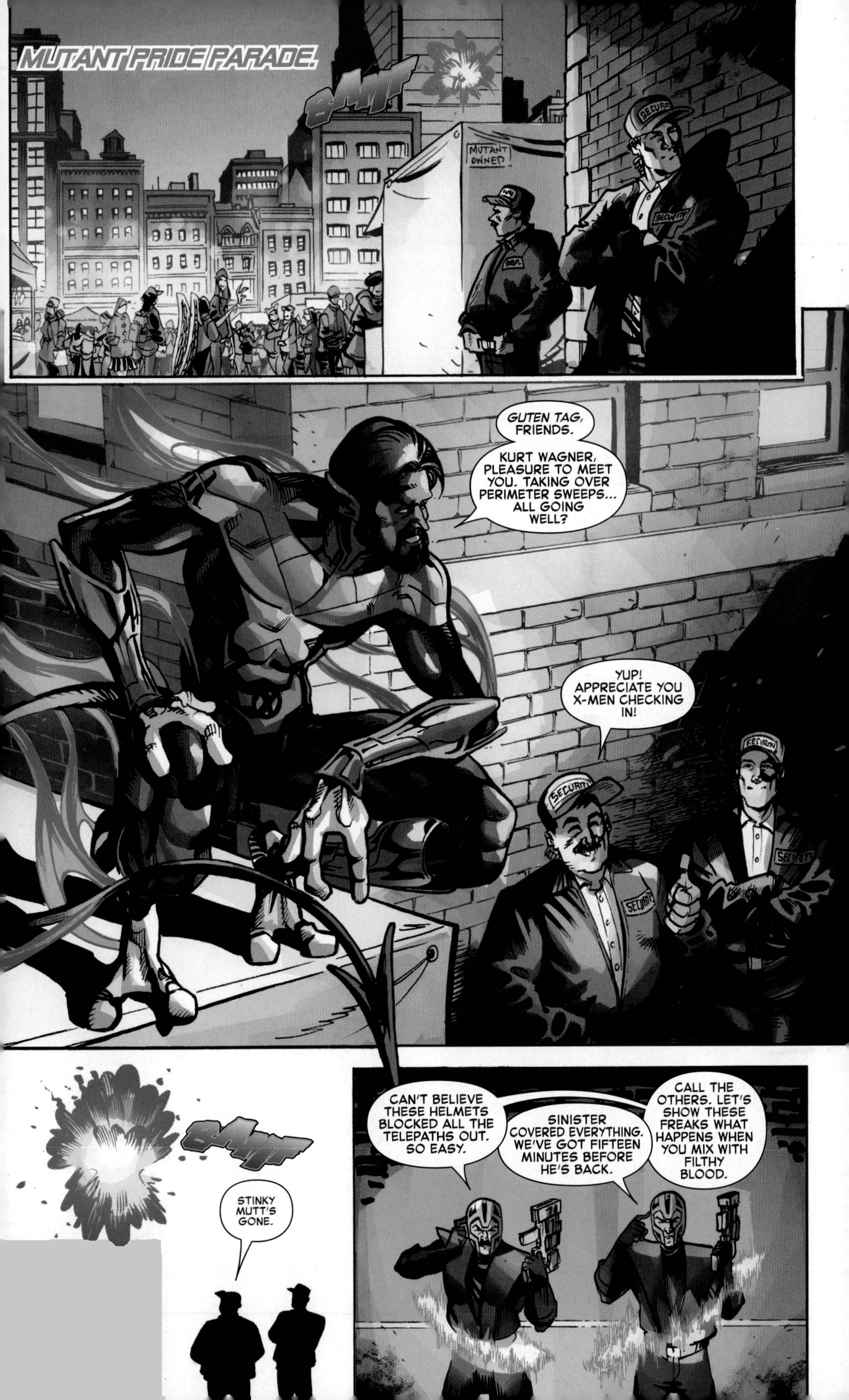
MUTANT PRIDE PARADE.
BAMF
MUTANT OWNED
GUTEN TAG, FRIENDS.
KURT WAGNER, PLEASURE TO MEET YOU. TAKING OVER PERIMETER SWEEPS... ALL GOING WELL?
YUP! APPRECIATE YOU X-MEN CHECKING IN!
BAMF
STINKY MUTT'S GONE.
CAN'T BELIEVE THESE HELMETS BLOCKED ALL THE TELEPATHS OUT. SO EASY.
SINISTER COVERED EVERYTHING. WE'VE GOT FIFTEEN MINUTES BEFORE HE'S BACK.
CALL THE OTHERS. LET'S SHOW THESE FREAKS WHAT HAPPENS WHEN YOU MIX WITH FILTHY BLOOD.

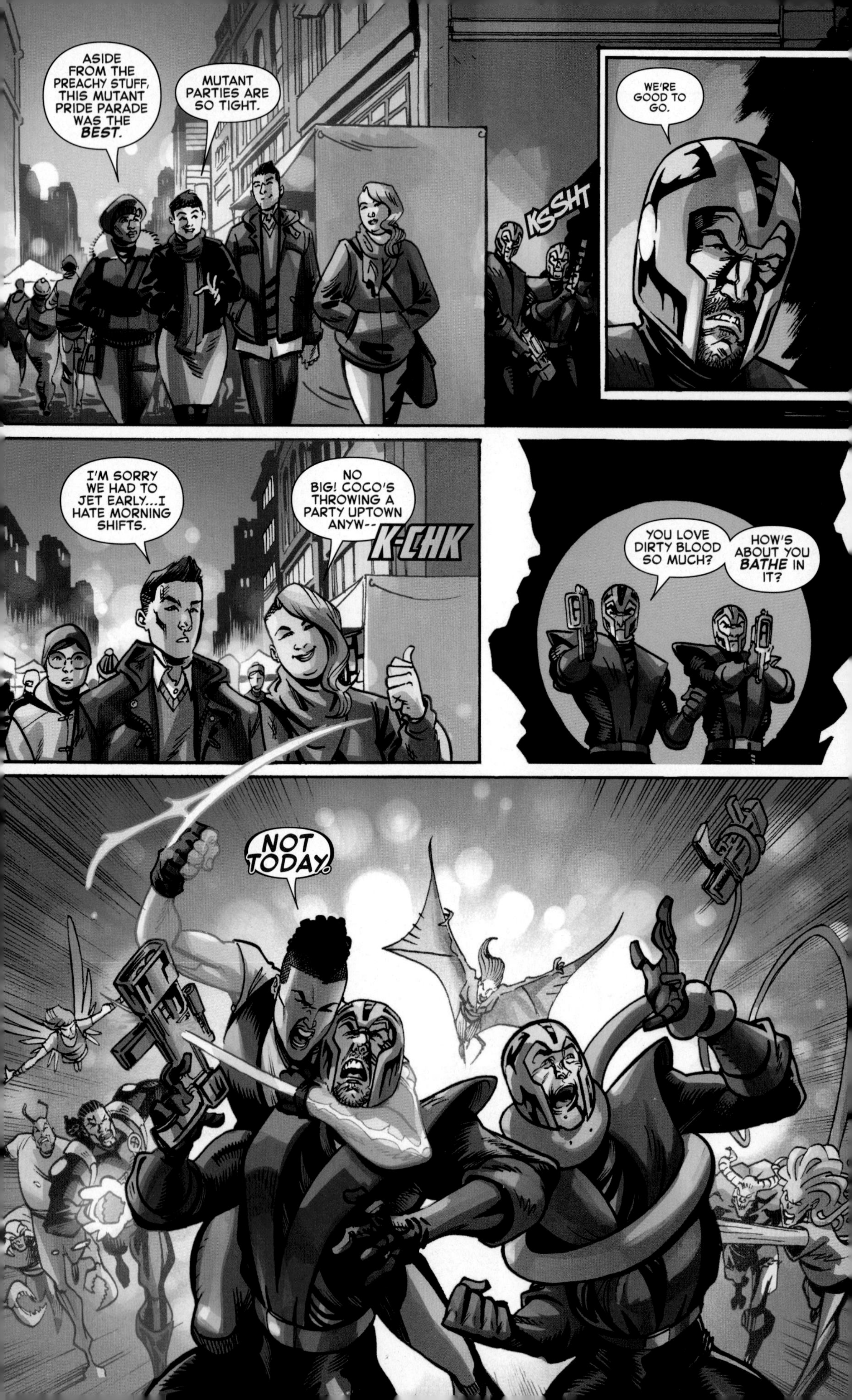

ASIDE FROM THE PREACHY STUFF, THIS MUTANT PRIDE PARADE WAS THE BEST.
MUTANT PARTIES ARE SO TIGHT.
KSSHT
WE'RE GOOD TO GO.
I'M SORRY WE HAD TO JET EARLY...I HATE MORNING SHIFTS.
NO BIG! COCO'S THROWING A PARTY UPTOWN ANYW--
K-CHK
YOU LOVE DIRTY BLOOD SO MUCH?
HOW'S ABOUT YOU BATHE IN IT?
NOT TODAY.

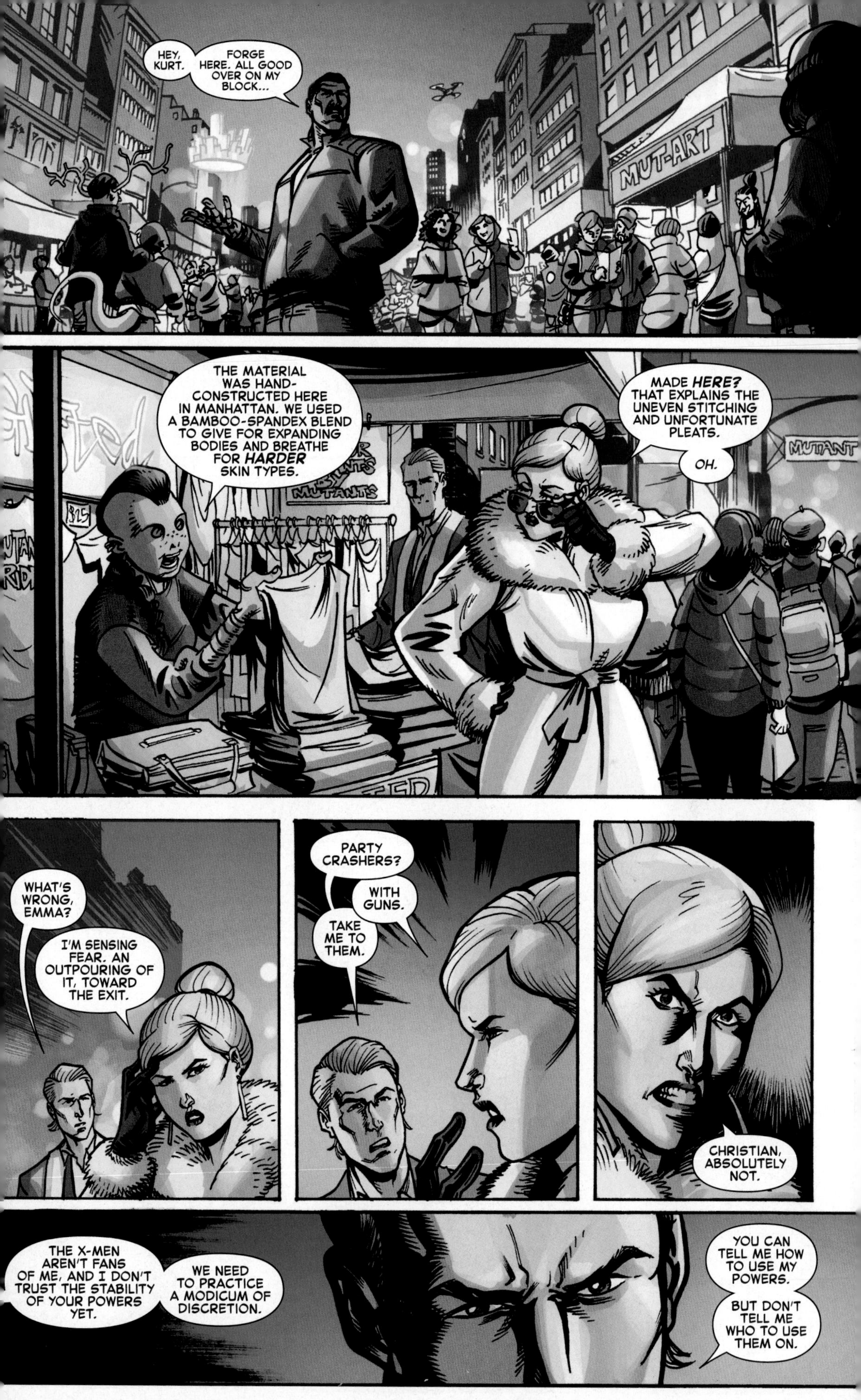
HEY, KURT.
FORGE HERE. ALL GOOD OVER ON MY BLOCK...
MUT-ART
THE MATERIAL WAS HAND-CONSTRUCTED HERE IN MANHATTAN. WE USED A BAMBOO-SPANDEX BLEND TO GIVE FOR EXPANDING BODIES AND BREATHE FOR HARDER SKIN TYPES.
MADE HERE? THAT EXPLAINS THE UNEVEN STITCHING AND UNFORTUNATE PLEATS.
OH.
MUTANT
WHAT'S WRONG, EMMA?
I'M SENSING FEAR. AN OUTPOURING OF IT, TOWARD THE EXIT.
PARTY CRASHERS?
WITH GUNS.
TAKE ME TO THEM.
CHRISTIAN, ABSOLUTELY NOT.
THE X-MEN AREN'T FANS OF ME, AND I DON'T TRUST THE STABILITY OF YOUR POWERS YET.
WE NEED TO PRACTICE A MODICUM OF DISCRETION.
YOU CAN TELL ME HOW TO USE MY POWERS.
BUT DON'T TELL ME WHO TO USE THEM ON.

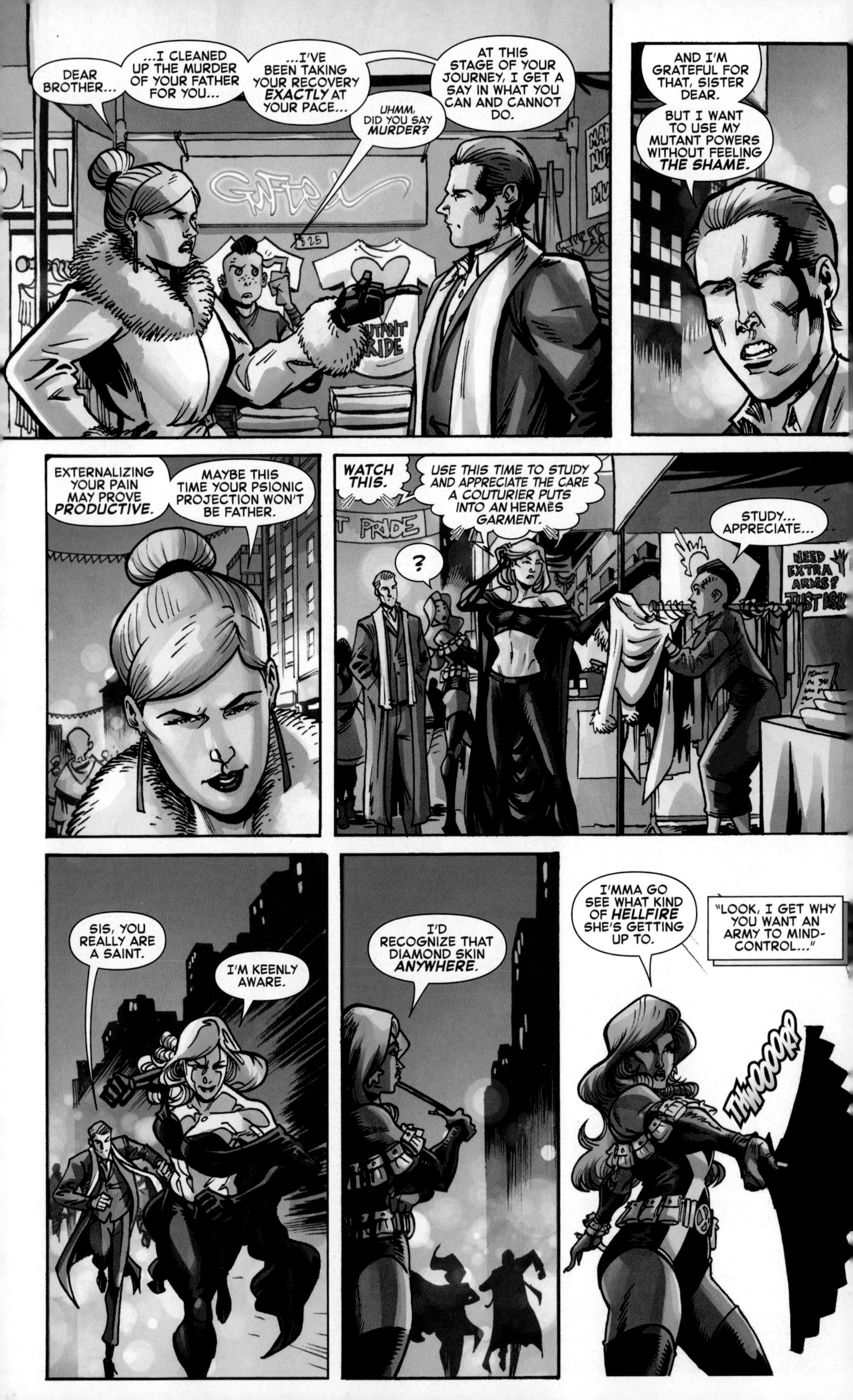
DEAR BROTHER...
...I CLEANED UP THE MURDER OF YOUR FATHER FOR YOU...
...I'VE BEEN TAKING YOUR RECOVERY EXACTLY AT YOUR PACE...
UHMM, DID YOU SAY MURDER?
AT THIS STAGE OF YOUR JOURNEY, I GET A SAY IN WHAT YOU CAN AND CANNOT DO.
AND I'M GRATEFUL FOR THAT, SISTER DEAR.
BUT I WANT TO USE MY MUTANT POWERS WITHOUT FEELING THE SHAME.
EXTERNALIZING YOUR PAIN MAY PROVE PRODUCTIVE.
MAYBE THIS TIME YOUR PSIONIC PROJECTION WON'T BE FATHER.
WATCH THIS.
USE THIS TIME TO STUDY AND APPRECIATE THE CARE A COUTURIER PUTS INTO AN HERMES GARMENT.
?
STUDY... APPRECIATE...
NEED EXTRA ARMS? JUST ASK
SIS, YOU REALLY ARE A SAINT.
I'M KEENLY AWARE.
I'D RECOGNIZE THAT DIAMOND SKIN ANYWHERE.
I'MMA GO SEE WHAT KIND OF HELLFIRE SHE'S GETTING UP TO.
"LOOK, I GET WHY YOU WANT AN ARMY TO MIND-CONTROL..."
THWOOORP

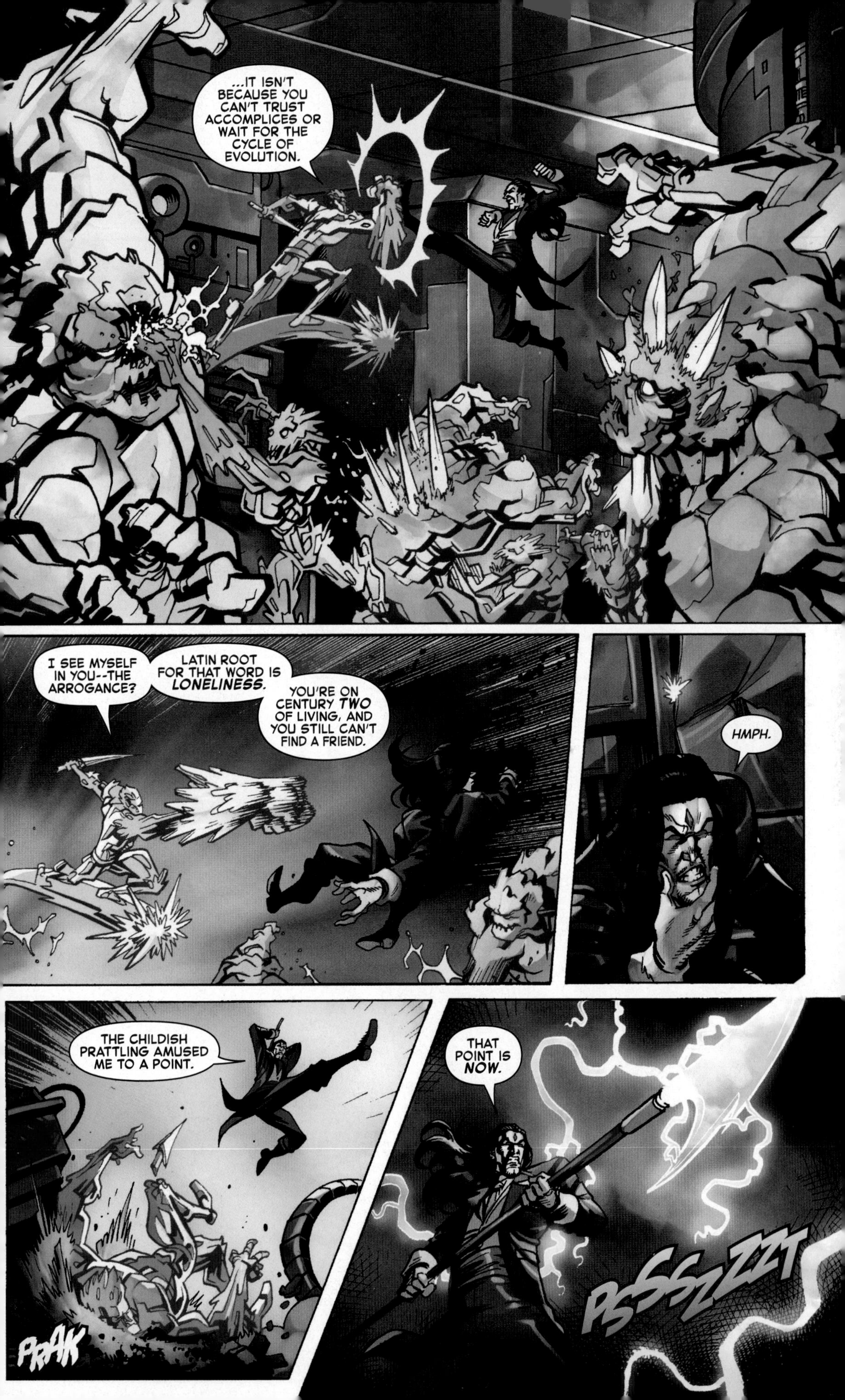
...IT ISN'T BECAUSE YOU CAN'T TRUST ACCOMPLICES OR WAIT FOR THE CYCLE OF EVOLUTION.
I SEE MYSELF IN YOU--THE ARROGANCE?
LATIN ROOT FOR THAT WORD IS LONELINESS.
YOU'RE ON CENTURY TWO OF LIVING, AND YOU STILL CAN'T FIND A FRIEND.
HMPH.
THE CHILDISH PRATTLING AMUSED ME TO A POINT.
PRAK
THAT POINT IS NOW.
PSSSZZZT

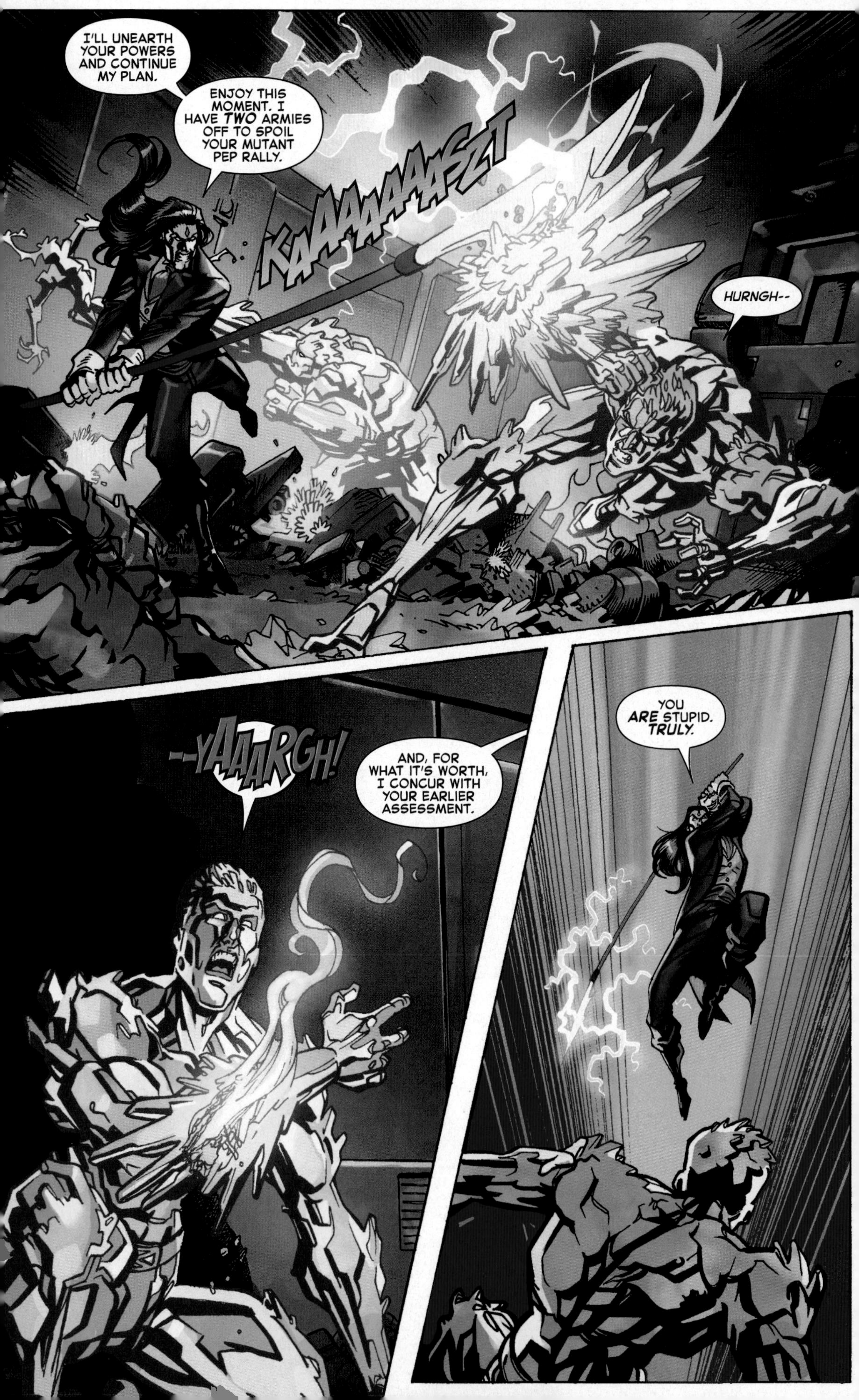
I'LL UNEARTH YOUR POWERS AND CONTINUE MY PLAN.
ENJOY THIS MOMENT. I HAVE **TWO** ARMIES OFF TO SPOIL YOUR MUTANT PEP RALLY.
KAAAAAAASZT
HURNGH--
--YAAARGH!
AND, FOR WHAT IT'S WORTH, I CONCUR WITH YOUR EARLIER ASSESSMENT.
YOU **ARE** STUPID. **TRULY.**

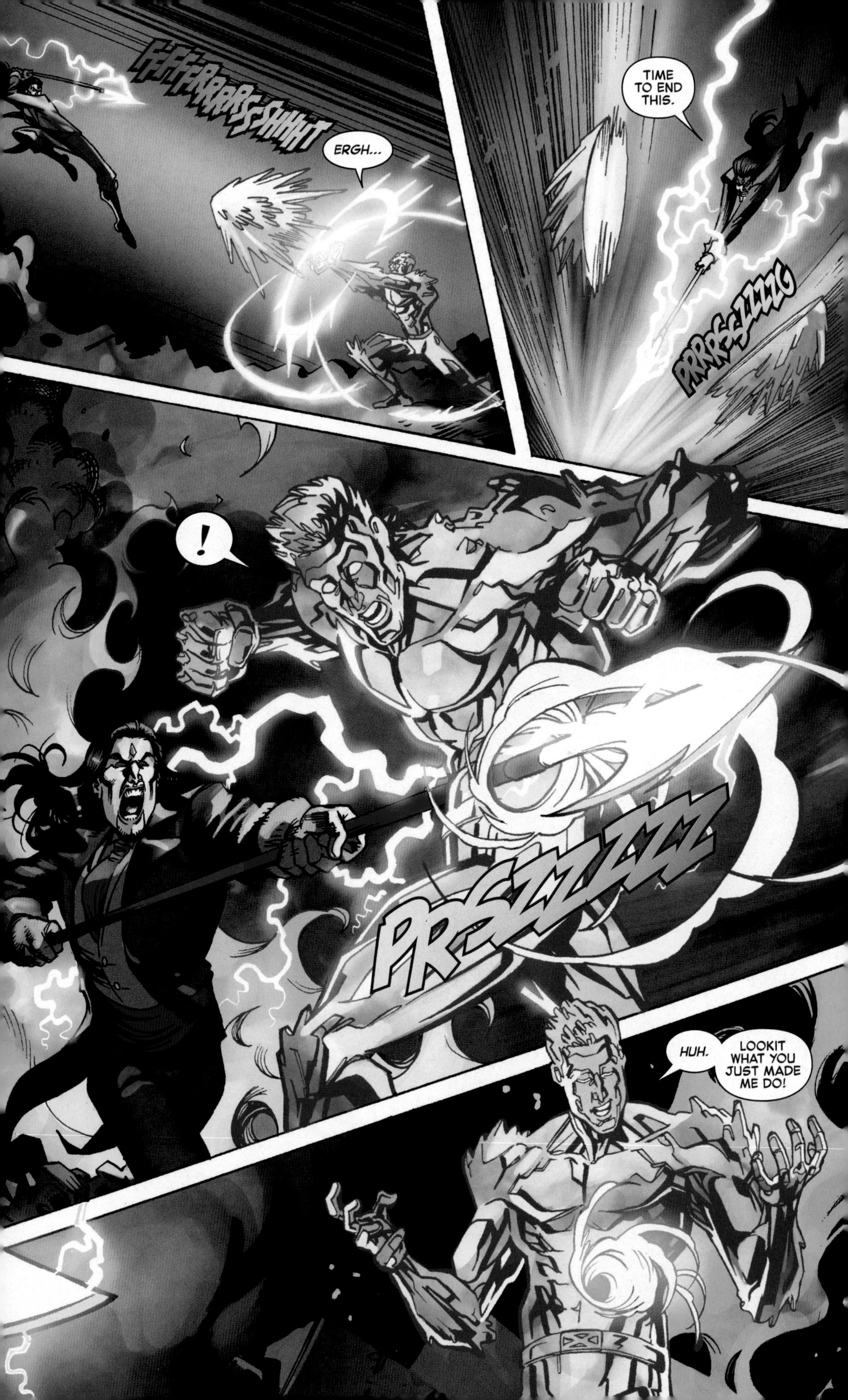

FFFFRRRRS-SHHHT
ERGH...
TIME TO END THIS.
PRRRS-ZZZZG
!
PRSZZZZZ
HUH.
LOOKIT WHAT YOU JUST MADE ME DO!

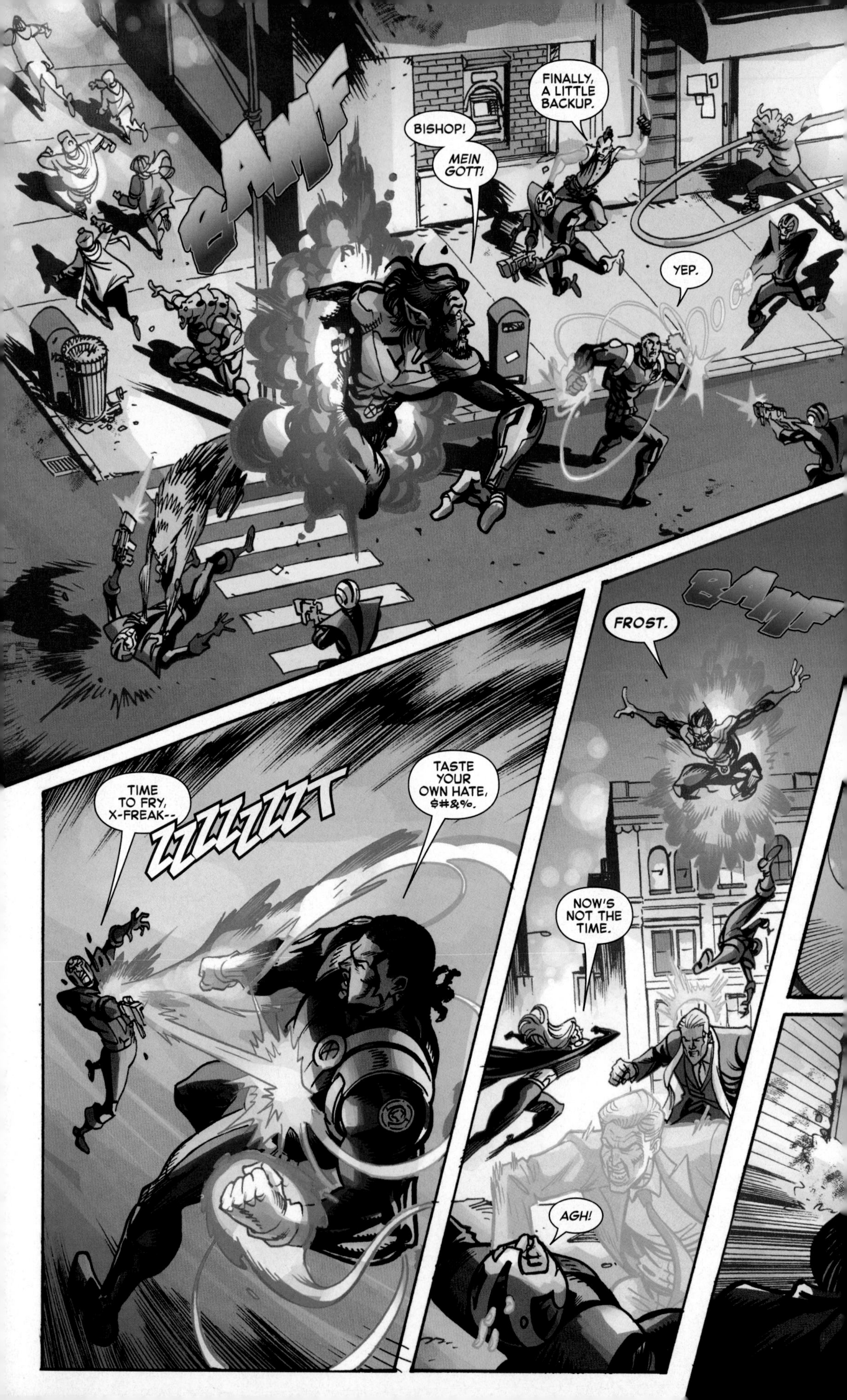
BAMF
BISHOP!
MEIN GOTT!
FINALLY, A LITTLE BACKUP.
YEP.
TIME TO FRY, X-FREAK--
ZZZZZZZT
TASTE YOUR OWN HATE, $#&%.
BAMF
FROST.
NOW'S NOT THE TIME.
AGH!

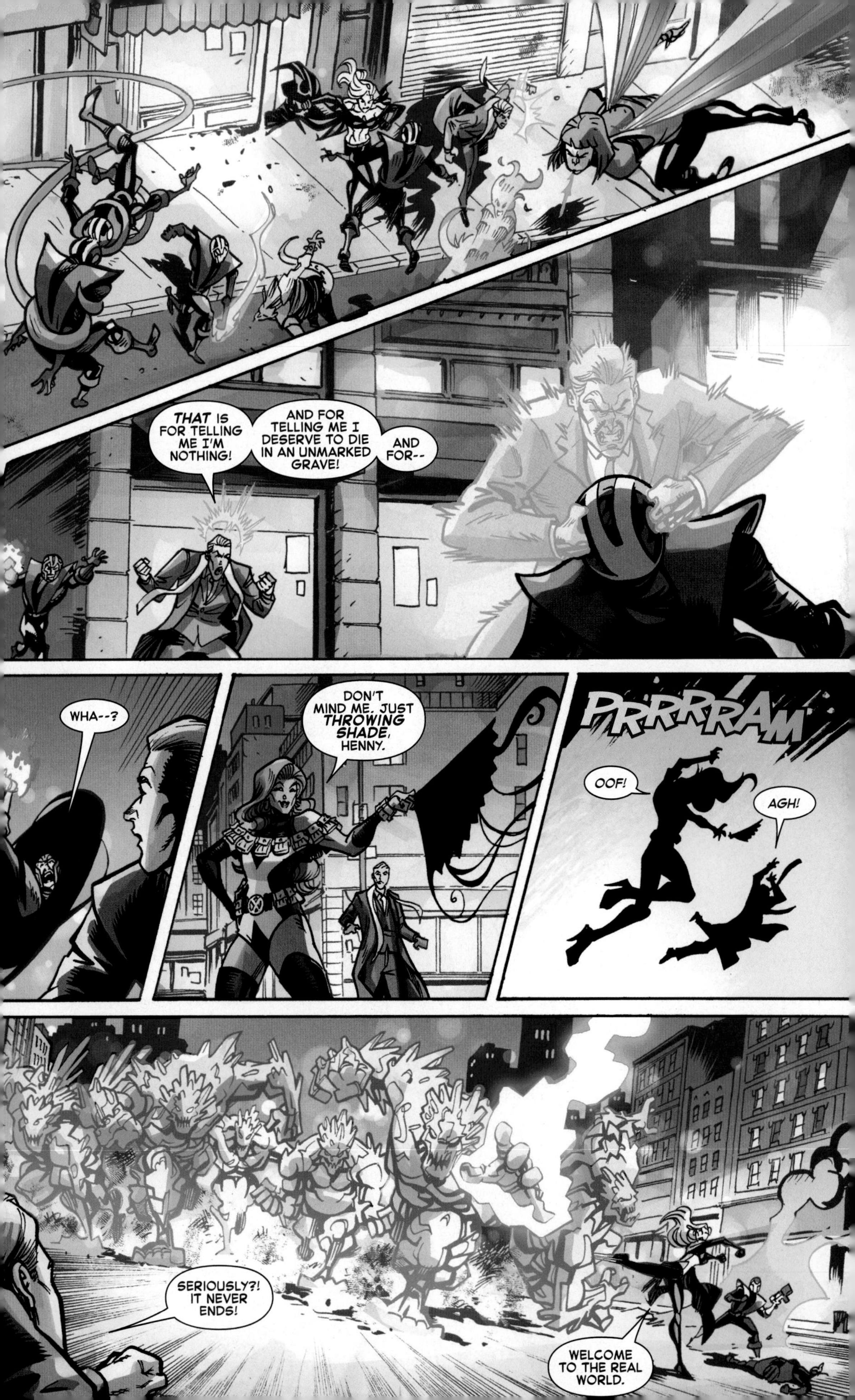
THAT IS FOR TELLING ME I'M NOTHING!
AND FOR TELLING ME I DESERVE TO DIE IN AN UNMARKED GRAVE!
AND FOR--
WHA--?
DON'T MIND ME. JUST THROWING SHADE, HENNY.
PRRRRAM
OOF!
AGH!
SERIOUSLY?! IT NEVER ENDS!
WELCOME TO THE REAL WORLD.

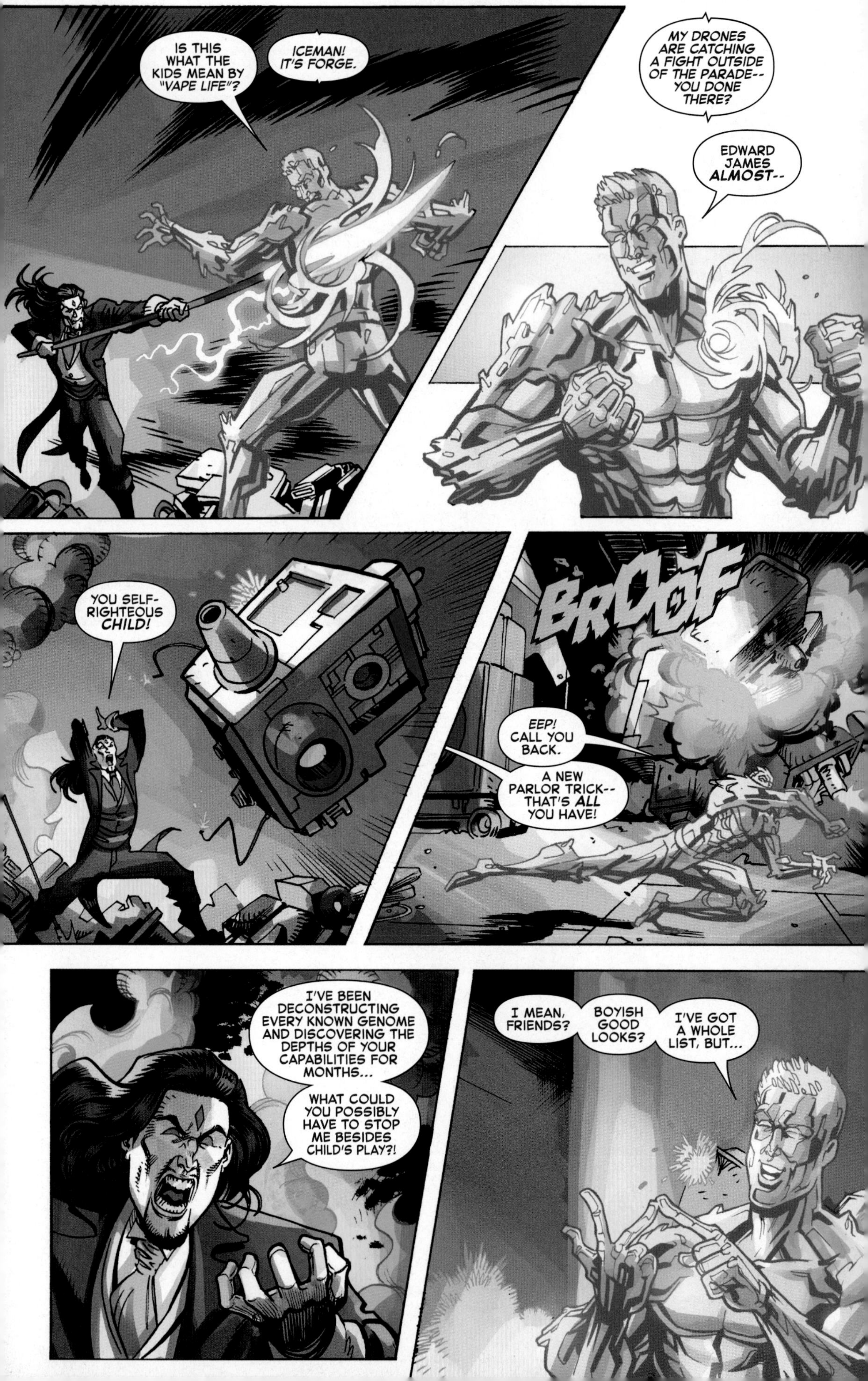

IS THIS WHAT THE KIDS MEAN BY "VAPE LIFE"?
ICEMAN! IT'S FORGE.
MY DRONES ARE CATCHING A FIGHT OUTSIDE OF THE PARADE-- YOU DONE THERE?
EDWARD JAMES ALMOST--
YOU SELF-RIGHTEOUS CHILD!
BROOF
EEP! CALL YOU BACK.
A NEW PARLOR TRICK-- THAT'S ALL YOU HAVE!
I'VE BEEN DECONSTRUCTING EVERY KNOWN GENOME AND DISCOVERING THE DEPTHS OF YOUR CAPABILITIES FOR MONTHS...
WHAT COULD YOU POSSIBLY HAVE TO STOP ME BESIDES CHILD'S PLAY?!
I MEAN, FRIENDS?
BOYISH GOOD LOOKS?
I'VE GOT A WHOLE LIST, BUT...

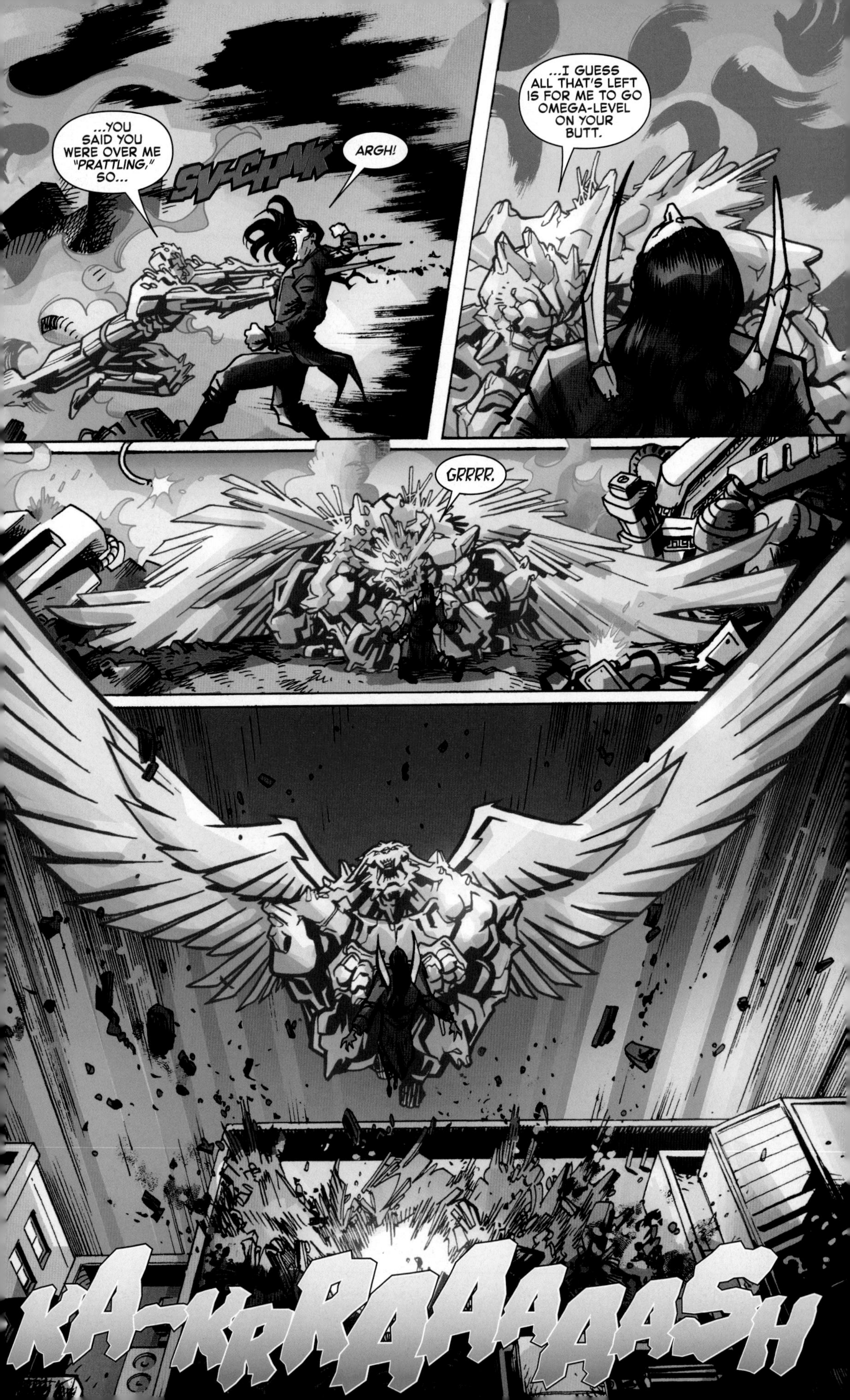
...YOU SAID YOU WERE OVER ME "PRATTLING," SO...
SV-CHNK
ARGH!
...I GUESS ALL THAT'S LEFT IS FOR ME TO GO OMEGA-LEVEL ON YOUR BUTT.
GRRRR.
KA-KRRAAAAASH

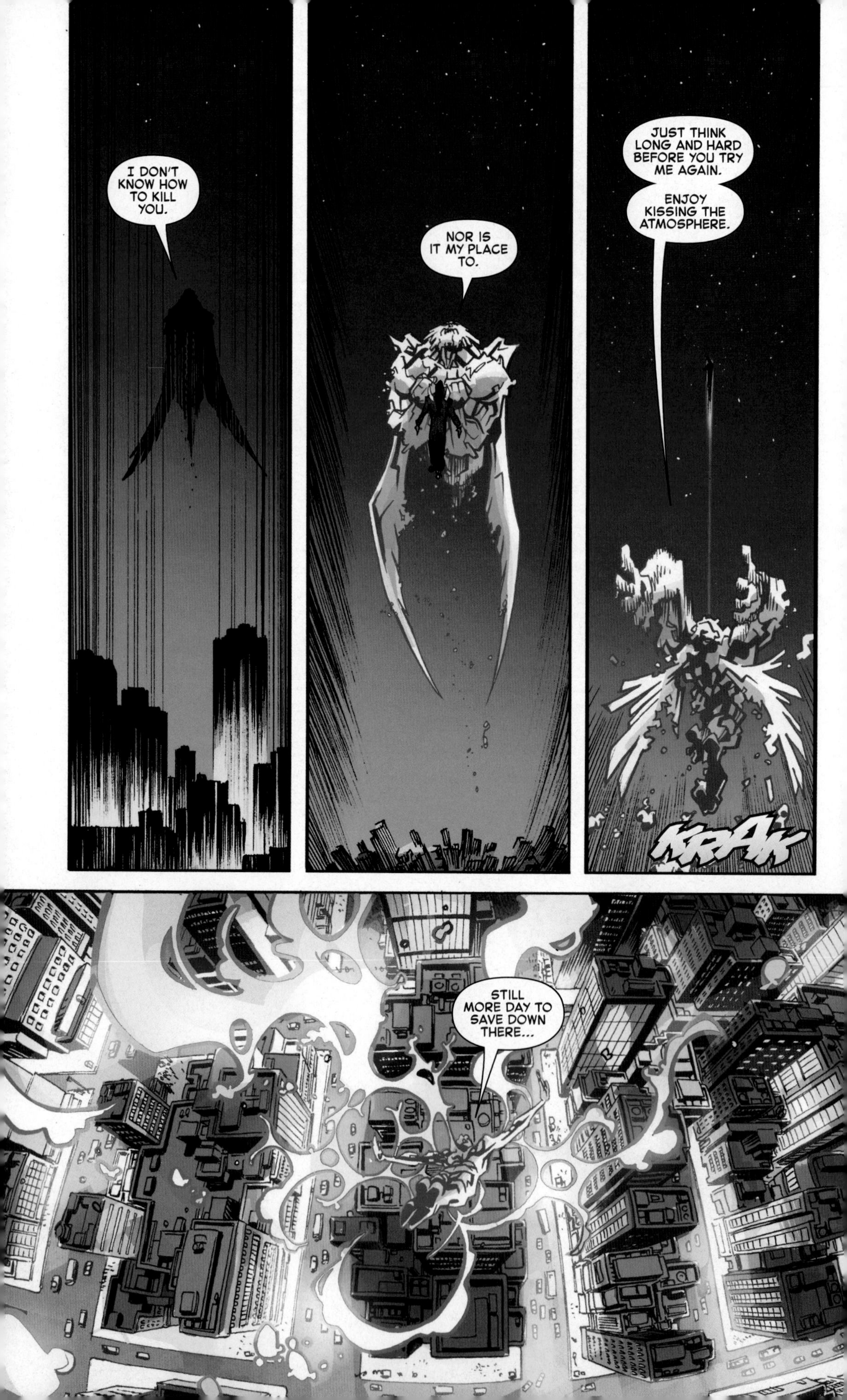
I DON'T KNOW HOW TO KILL YOU.
NOR IS IT MY PLACE TO.
JUST THINK LONG AND HARD BEFORE YOU TRY ME AGAIN.
ENJOY KISSING THE ATMOSPHERE.
KRAK
STILL MORE DAY TO SAVE DOWN THERE...

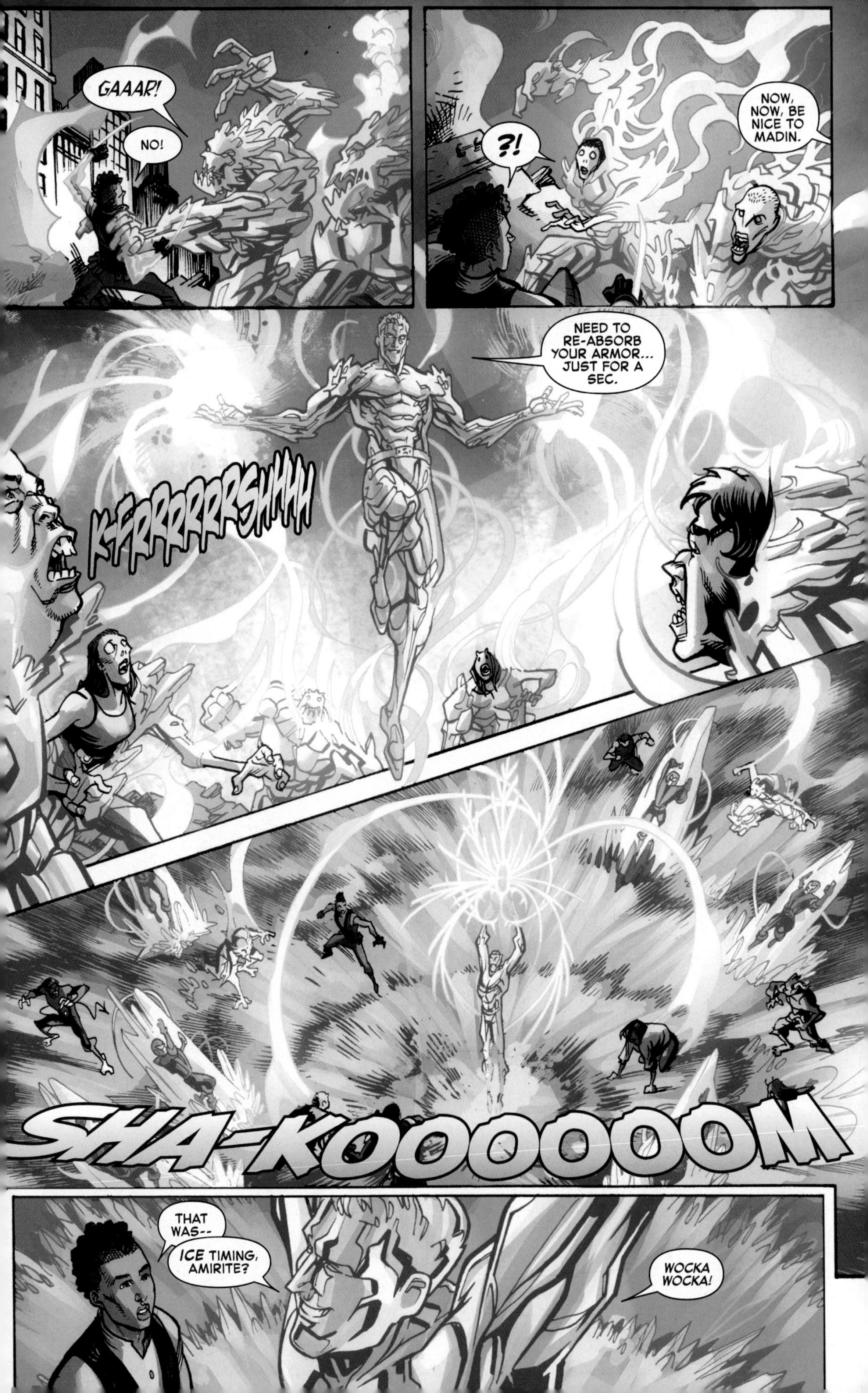
GAAAR!
NO!
?!
NOW, NOW, BE NICE TO MADIN.
NEED TO RE-ABSORB YOUR ARMOR... JUST FOR A SEC.
K-FRRRRRRSHHHH
SHA-KOOOOOOOM
THAT WAS--
ICE TIMING, AMIRITE?
WOCKA WOCKA!

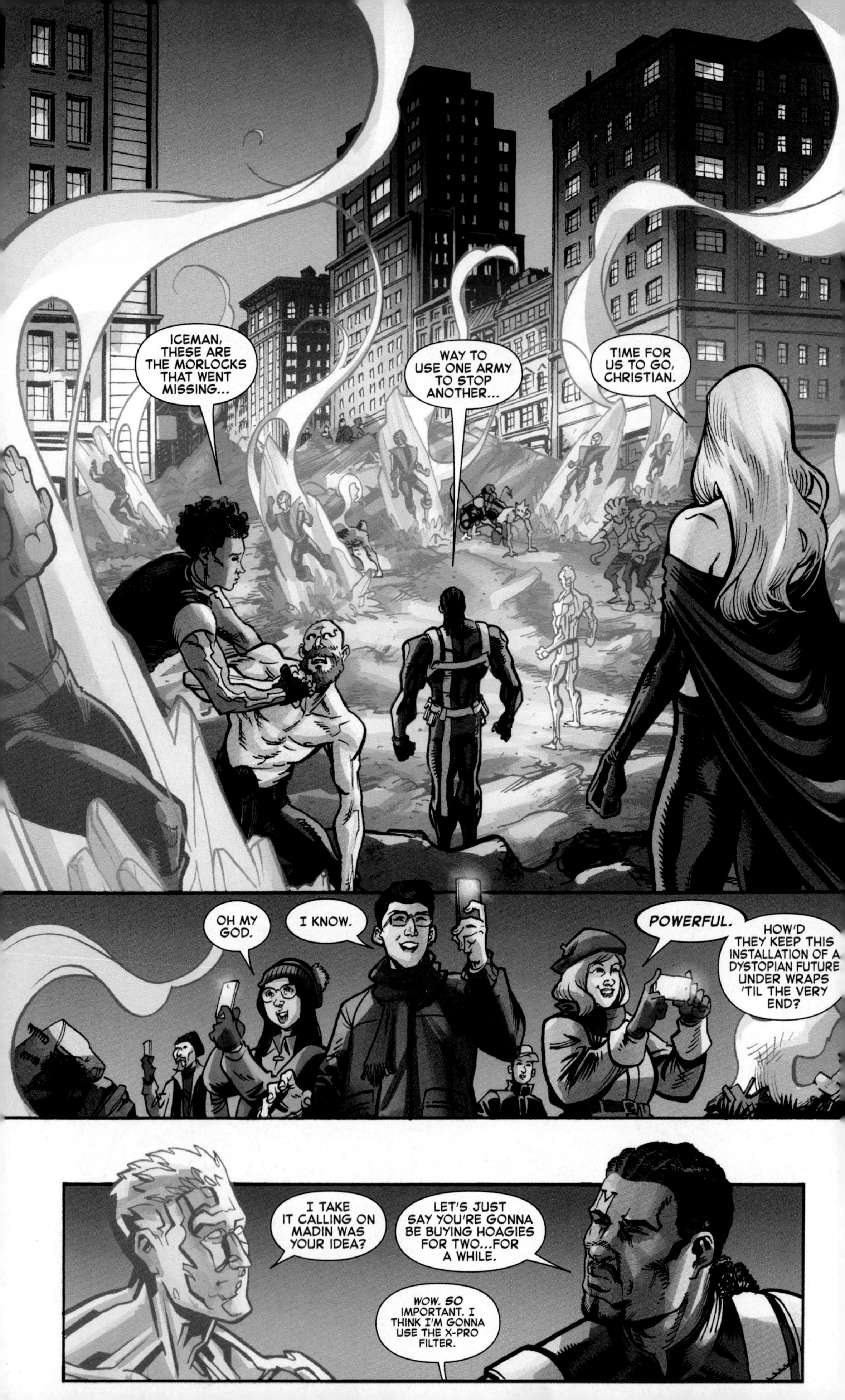
ICEMAN, THESE ARE THE MORLOCKS THAT WENT MISSING...
WAY TO USE ONE ARMY TO STOP ANOTHER...
TIME FOR US TO GO, CHRISTIAN.
OH MY GOD.
I KNOW.
POWERFUL.
HOW'D THEY KEEP THIS INSTALLATION OF A DYSTOPIAN FUTURE UNDER WRAPS 'TIL THE VERY END?
I TAKE IT CALLING ON MADIN WAS YOUR IDEA?
LET'S JUST SAY YOU'RE GONNA BE BUYING HOAGIES FOR TWO...FOR A WHILE.
WOW. SO IMPORTANT. I THINK I'M GONNA USE THE X-PRO FILTER.

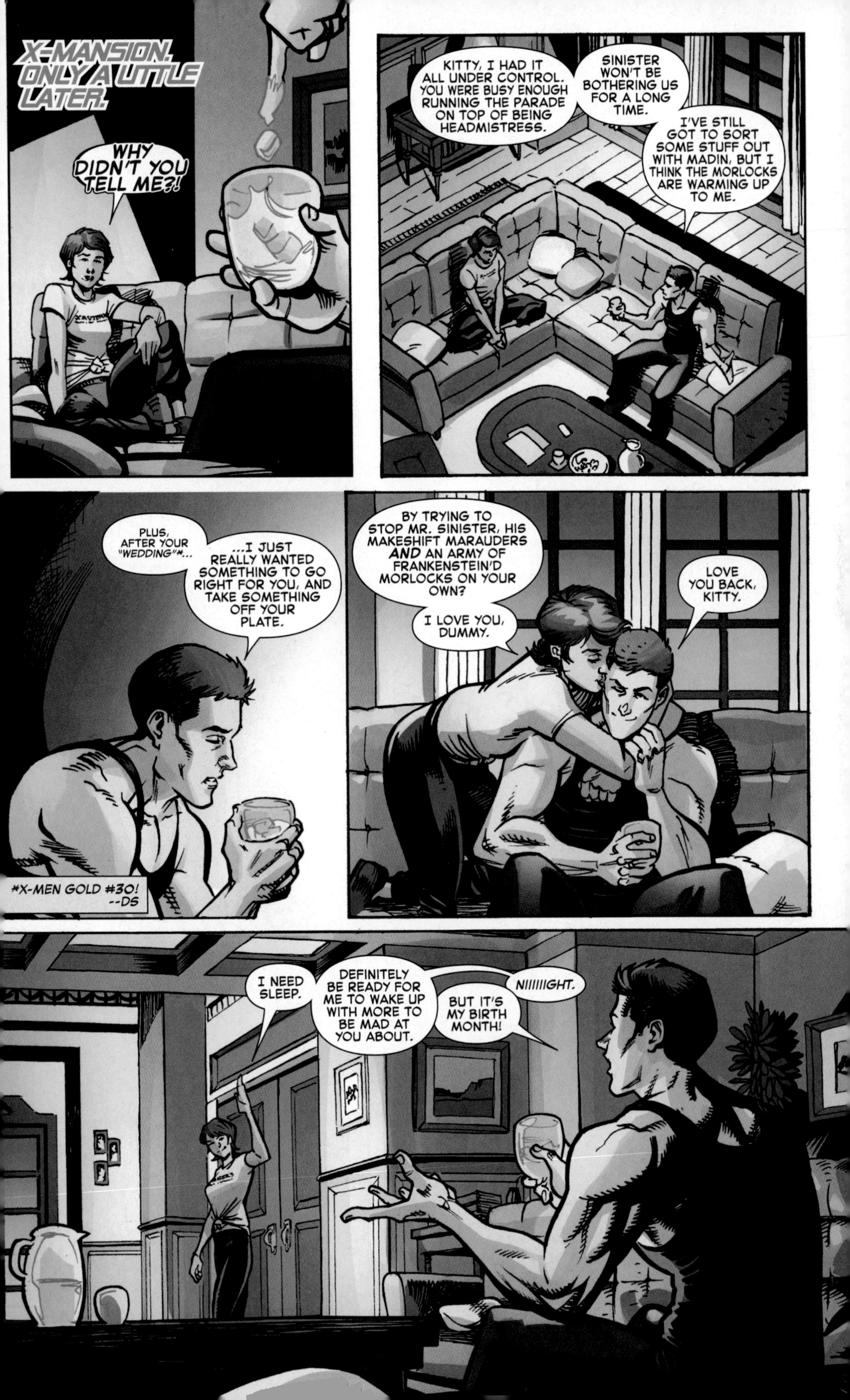
X-MANSION. ONLY A LITTLE LATER.
WHY DIDN'T YOU TELL ME?!
KITTY, I HAD IT ALL UNDER CONTROL. YOU WERE BUSY ENOUGH RUNNING THE PARADE ON TOP OF BEING HEADMISTRESS.
SINISTER WON'T BE BOTHERING US FOR A LONG TIME.
I'VE STILL GOT TO SORT SOME STUFF OUT WITH MADIN, BUT I THINK THE MORLOCKS ARE WARMING UP TO ME.
PLUS, AFTER YOUR "WEDDING"*...
...I JUST REALLY WANTED SOMETHING TO GO RIGHT FOR YOU, AND TAKE SOMETHING OFF YOUR PLATE.
*X-MEN GOLD #30! --DS
BY TRYING TO STOP MR. SINISTER, HIS MAKESHIFT MARAUDERS AND AN ARMY OF FRANKENSTEIN'D MORLOCKS ON YOUR OWN?
I LOVE YOU, DUMMY.
LOVE YOU BACK, KITTY.
I NEED SLEEP.
DEFINITELY BE READY FOR ME TO WAKE UP WITH MORE TO BE MAD AT YOU ABOUT.
BUT IT'S MY BIRTH MONTH!
NIIIIIIGHT.

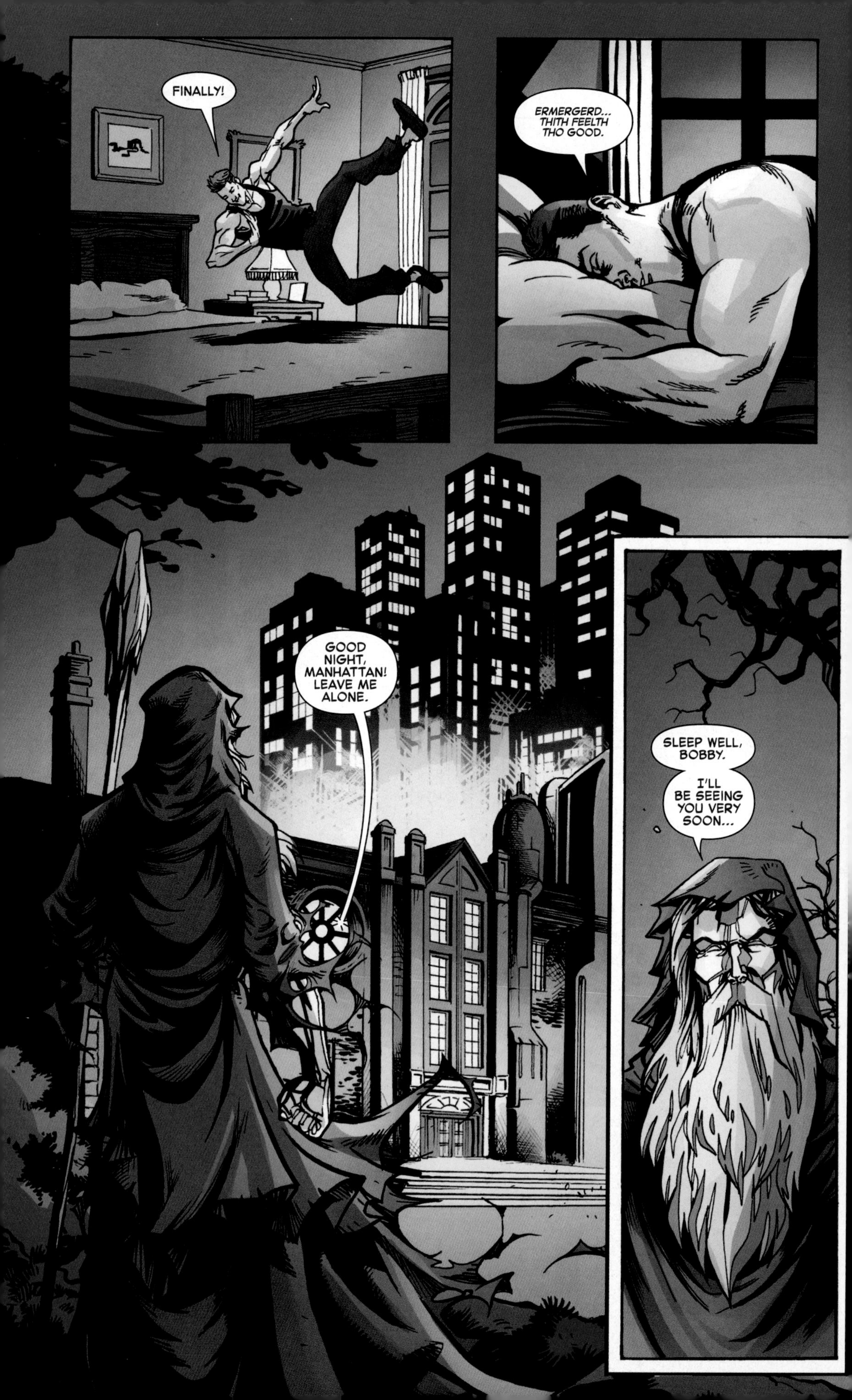
FINALLY!
ERMERGERD... THITH FEELTH THO GOOD.
GOOD NIGHT, MANHATTAN! LEAVE ME ALONE.
SLEEP WELL, BOBBY.
I'LL BE SEEING YOU VERY SOON...

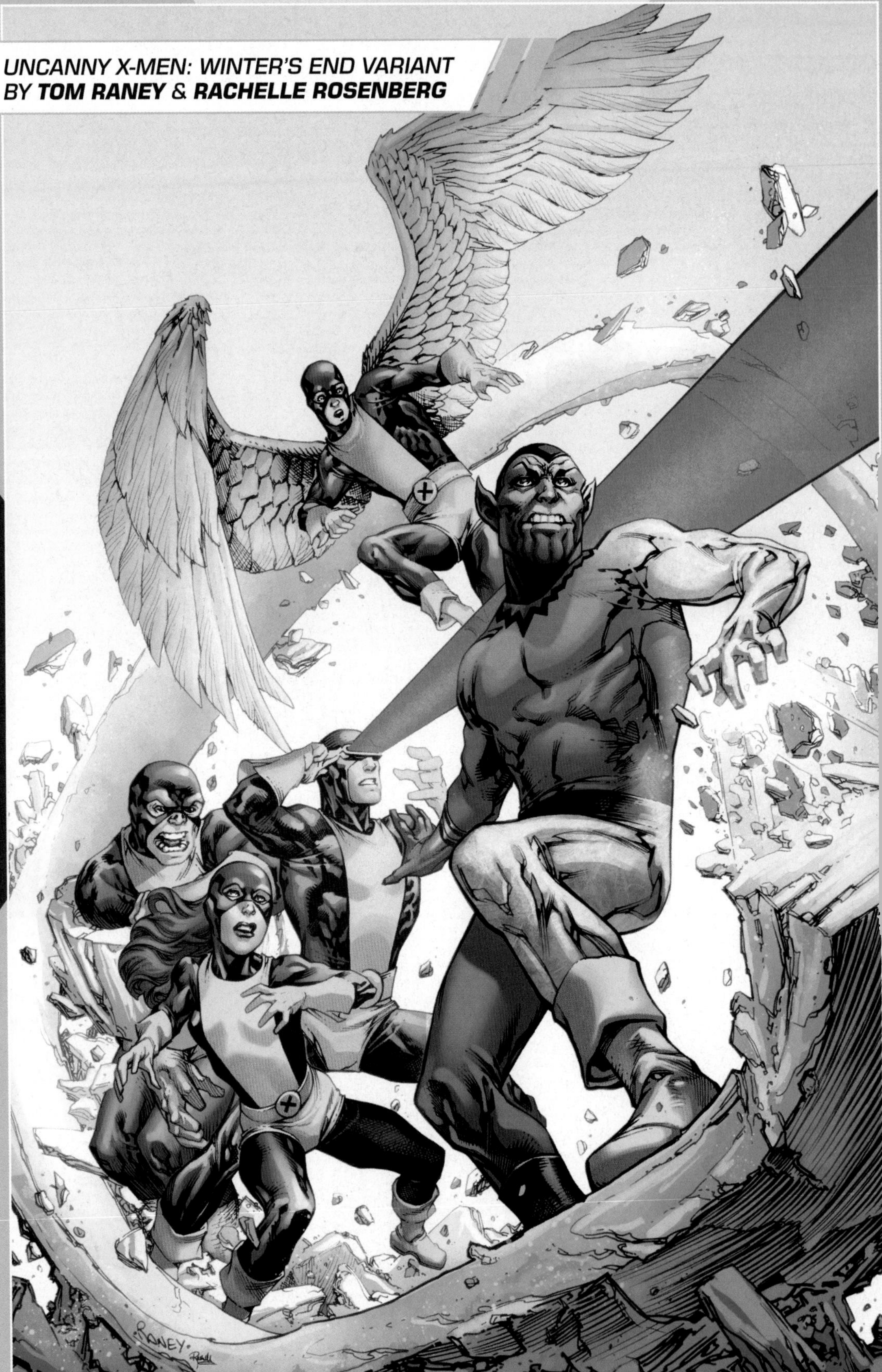

UNCANNY X-MEN: WINTER'S END VARIANT
BY ***TOM RANEY*** *&* ***RACHELLE ROSENBERG***

UNCANNY X-MEN: WINTER'S END

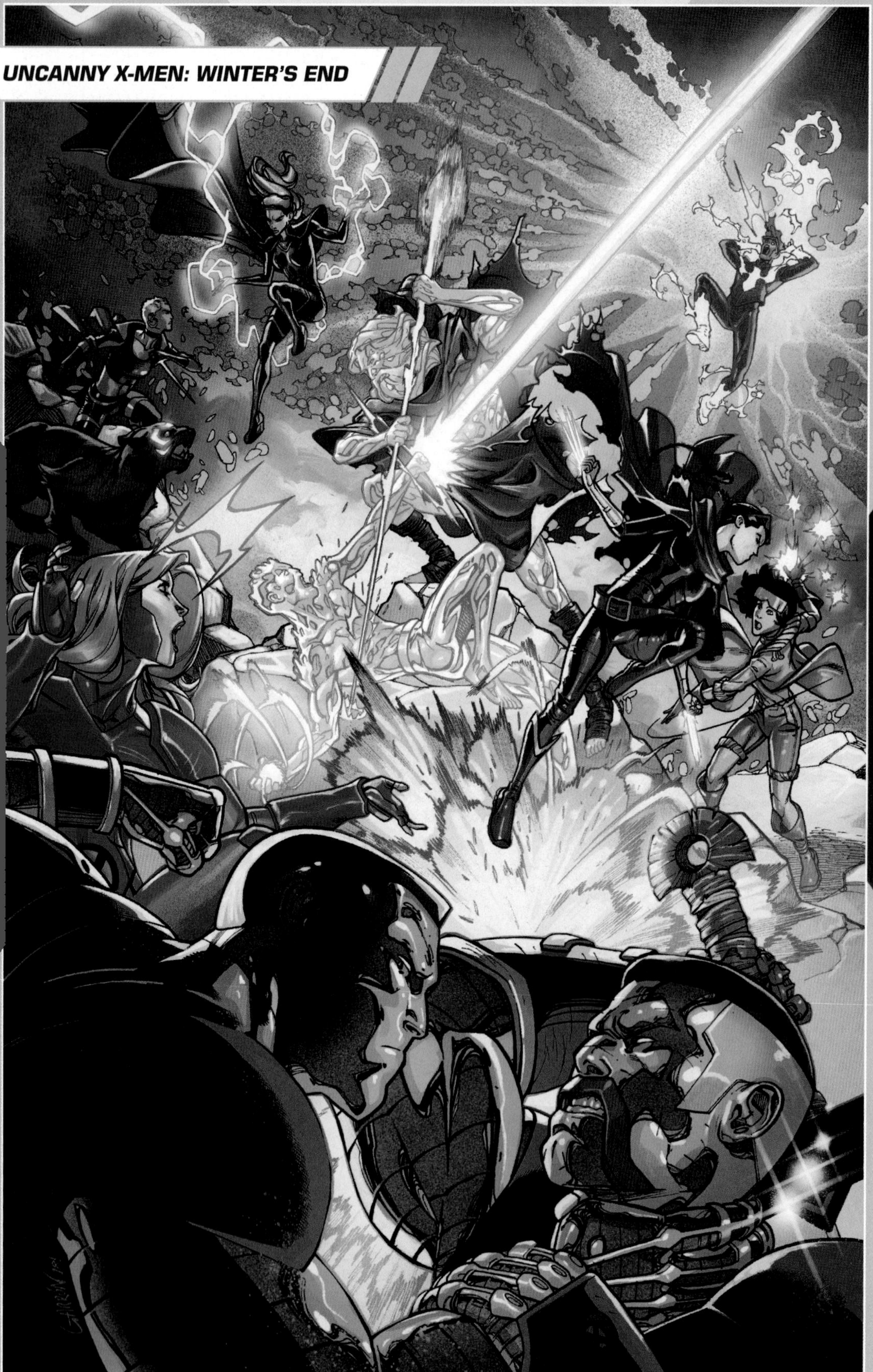

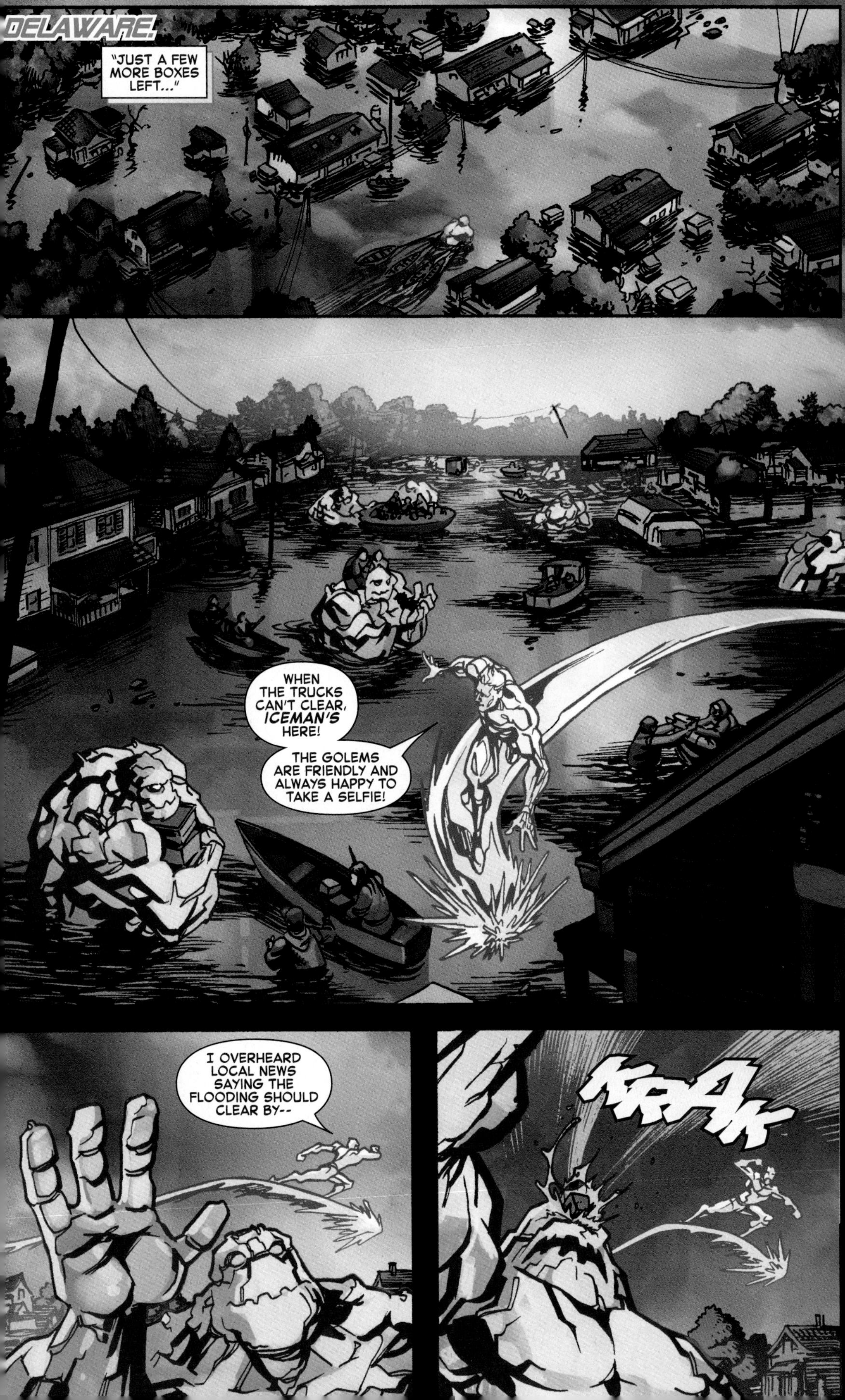
DELAWARE.
"JUST A FEW MORE BOXES LEFT..."
WHEN THE TRUCKS CAN'T CLEAR, ICEMAN'S HERE!
THE GOLEMS ARE FRIENDLY AND ALWAYS HAPPY TO TAKE A SELFIE!
I OVERHEARD LOCAL NEWS SAYING THE FLOODING SHOULD CLEAR BY--
KRAK

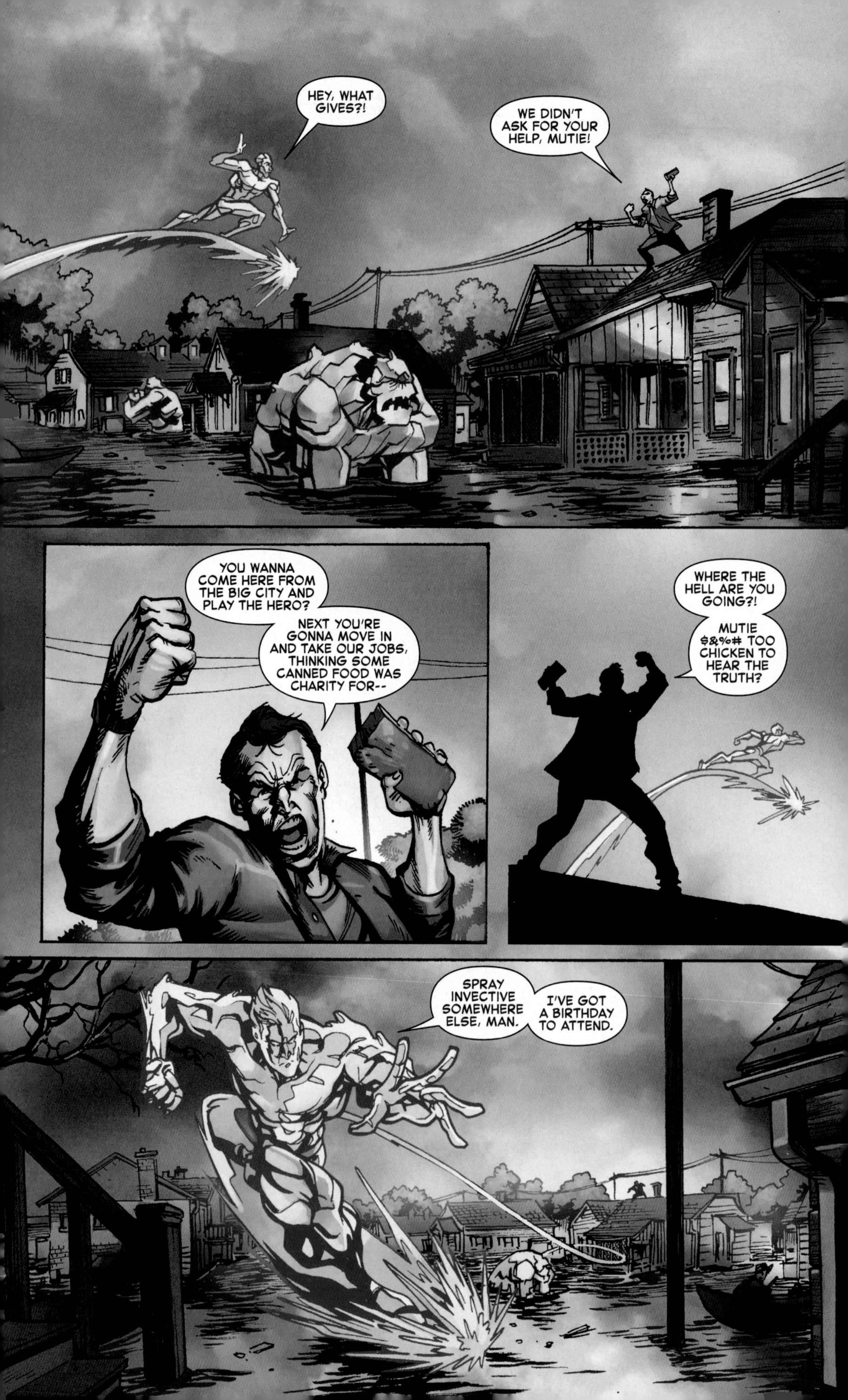
HEY, WHAT GIVES?!
WE DIDN'T ASK FOR YOUR HELP, MUTIE!
YOU WANNA COME HERE FROM THE BIG CITY AND PLAY THE HERO?
NEXT YOU'RE GONNA MOVE IN AND TAKE OUR JOBS, THINKING SOME CANNED FOOD WAS CHARITY FOR--
WHERE THE HELL ARE YOU GOING?!
MUTIE $&%# TOO CHICKEN TO HEAR THE TRUTH?
SPRAY INVECTIVE SOMEWHERE ELSE, MAN.
I'VE GOT A BIRTHDAY TO ATTEND.

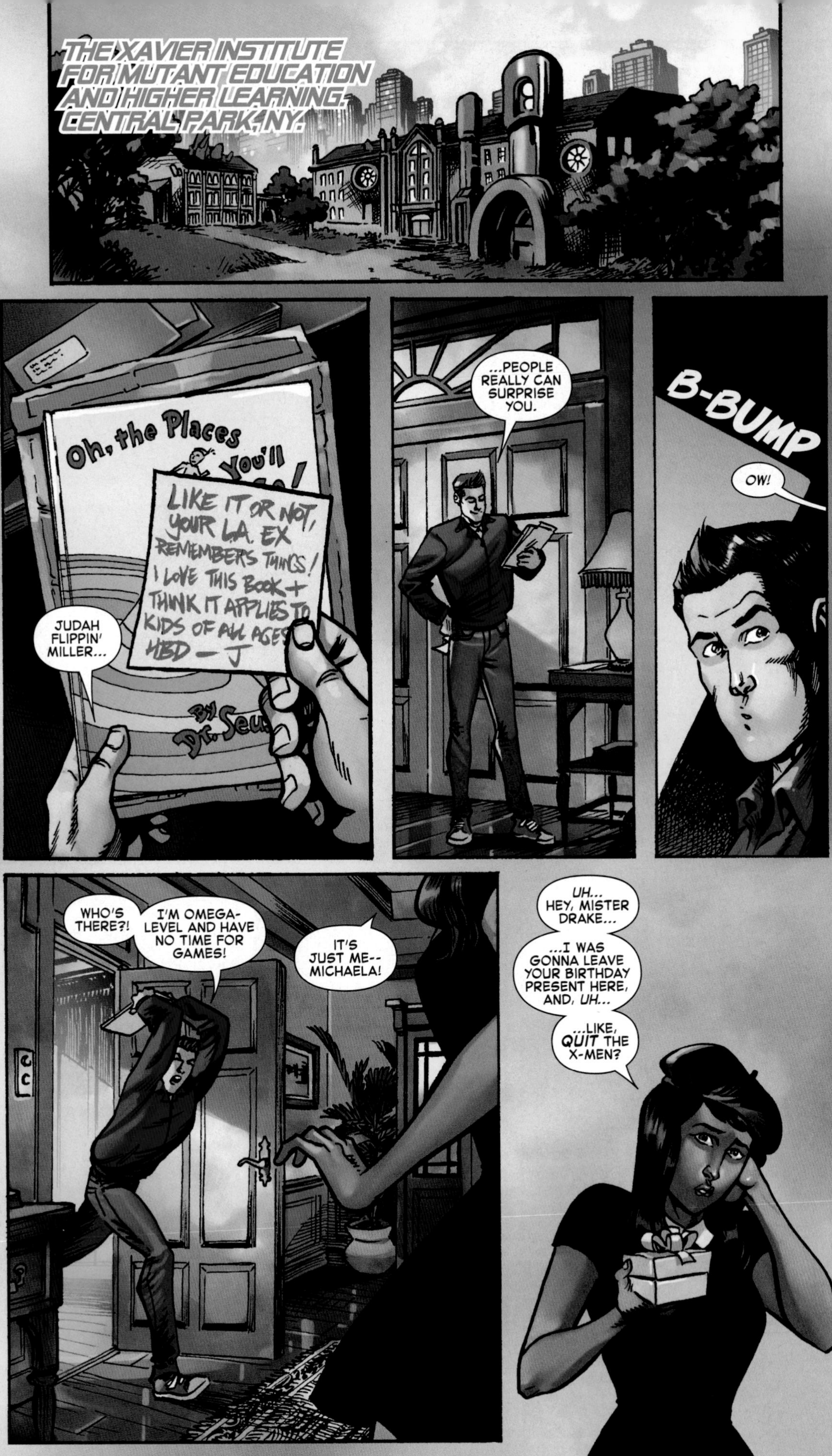
THE XAVIER INSTITUTE FOR MUTANT EDUCATION AND HIGHER LEARNING. CENTRAL PARK, NY.
Oh, the Places You'll
LIKE IT OR NOT, YOUR L.A. EX REMEMBERS THINGS! I LOVE THIS BOOK + THINK IT APPLIES TO KIDS OF ALL AGES HBD — J
By Dr. Seu
JUDAH FLIPPIN' MILLER...
...PEOPLE REALLY CAN SURPRISE YOU.
B-BUMP
OW!
WHO'S THERE?!
I'M OMEGA-LEVEL AND HAVE NO TIME FOR GAMES!
IT'S JUST ME--MICHAELA!
UH... HEY, MISTER DRAKE...
...I WAS GONNA LEAVE YOUR BIRTHDAY PRESENT HERE, AND, UH...
...LIKE, QUIT THE X-MEN?

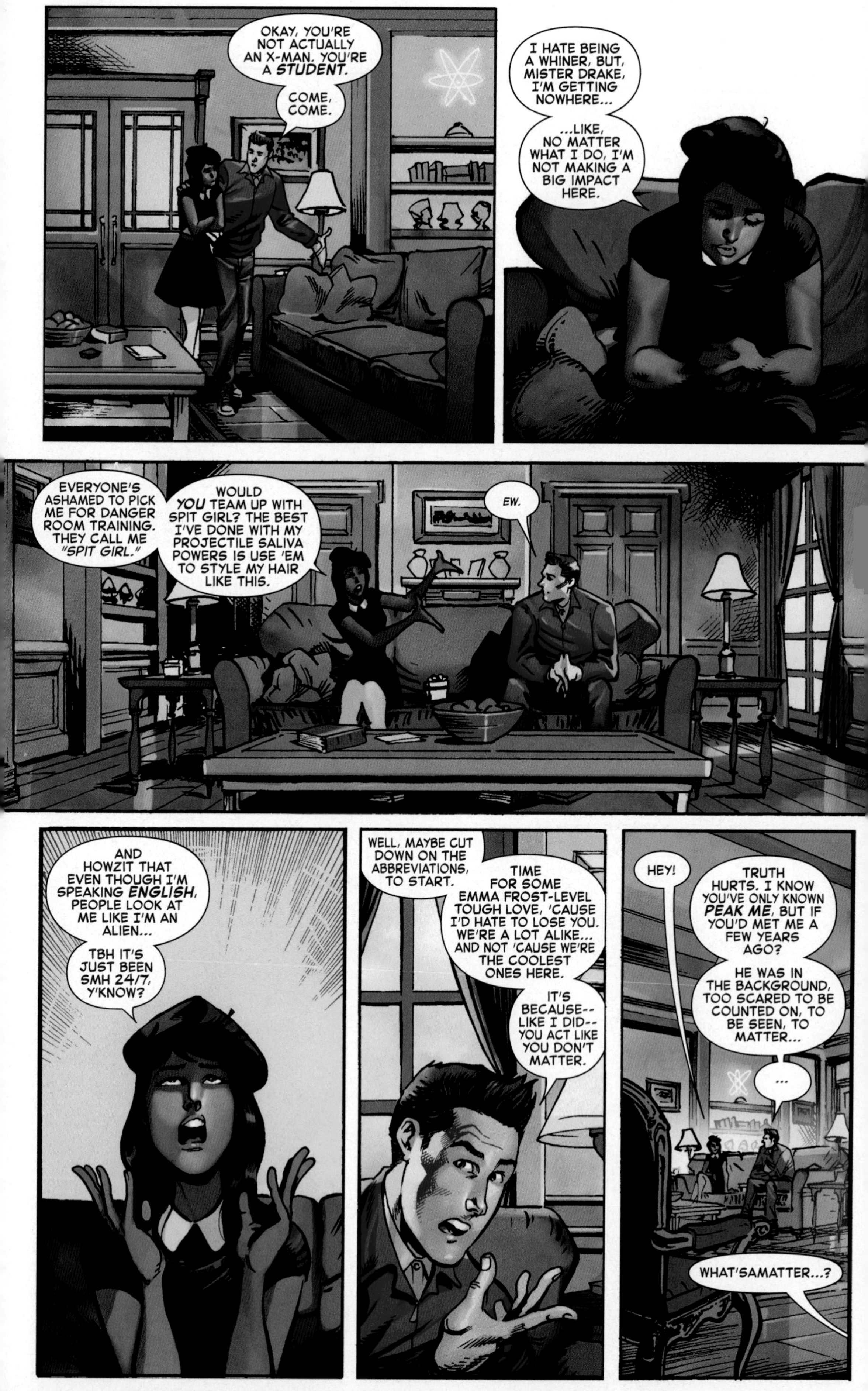
OKAY, YOU'RE NOT ACTUALLY AN X-MAN. YOU'RE A STUDENT.
COME, COME.
I HATE BEING A WHINER, BUT, MISTER DRAKE, I'M GETTING NOWHERE...
...LIKE, NO MATTER WHAT I DO, I'M NOT MAKING A BIG IMPACT HERE.
EVERYONE'S ASHAMED TO PICK ME FOR DANGER ROOM TRAINING. THEY CALL ME "SPIT GIRL."
WOULD YOU TEAM UP WITH SPIT GIRL? THE BEST I'VE DONE WITH MY PROJECTILE SALIVA POWERS IS USE 'EM TO STYLE MY HAIR LIKE THIS.
EW.
AND HOWZIT THAT EVEN THOUGH I'M SPEAKING ENGLISH, PEOPLE LOOK AT ME LIKE I'M AN ALIEN...
TBH IT'S JUST BEEN SMH 24/7, Y'KNOW?
WELL, MAYBE CUT DOWN ON THE ABBREVIATIONS, TO START.
TIME FOR SOME EMMA FROST-LEVEL TOUGH LOVE, 'CAUSE I'D HATE TO LOSE YOU. WE'RE A LOT ALIKE... AND NOT 'CAUSE WE'RE THE COOLEST ONES HERE.
IT'S BECAUSE-- LIKE I DID-- YOU ACT LIKE YOU DON'T MATTER.
HEY!
TRUTH HURTS. I KNOW YOU'VE ONLY KNOWN PEAK ME, BUT IF YOU'D MET ME A FEW YEARS AGO?
HE WAS IN THE BACKGROUND, TOO SCARED TO BE COUNTED ON, TO BE SEEN, TO MATTER...
...
WHAT'SAMATTER...?

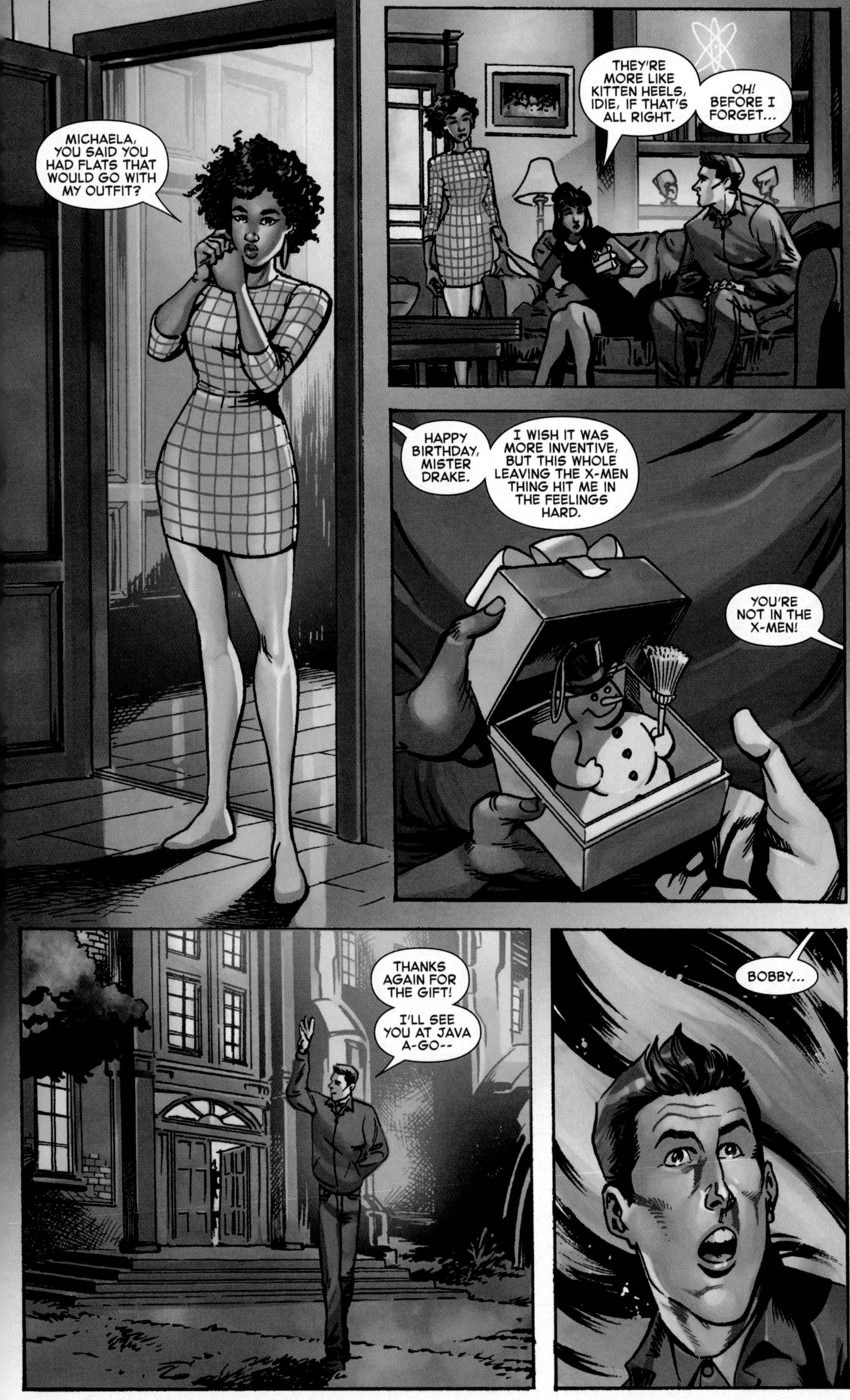
MICHAELA, YOU SAID YOU HAD FLATS THAT WOULD GO WITH MY OUTFIT?
THEY'RE MORE LIKE KITTEN HEELS, IDIE, IF THAT'S ALL RIGHT.
OH! BEFORE I FORGET...
HAPPY BIRTHDAY, MISTER DRAKE.
I WISH IT WAS MORE INVENTIVE, BUT THIS WHOLE LEAVING THE X-MEN THING HIT ME IN THE FEELINGS HARD.
YOU'RE NOT IN THE X-MEN!
THANKS AGAIN FOR THE GIFT!
I'LL SEE YOU AT JAVA A-GO--
BOBBY...

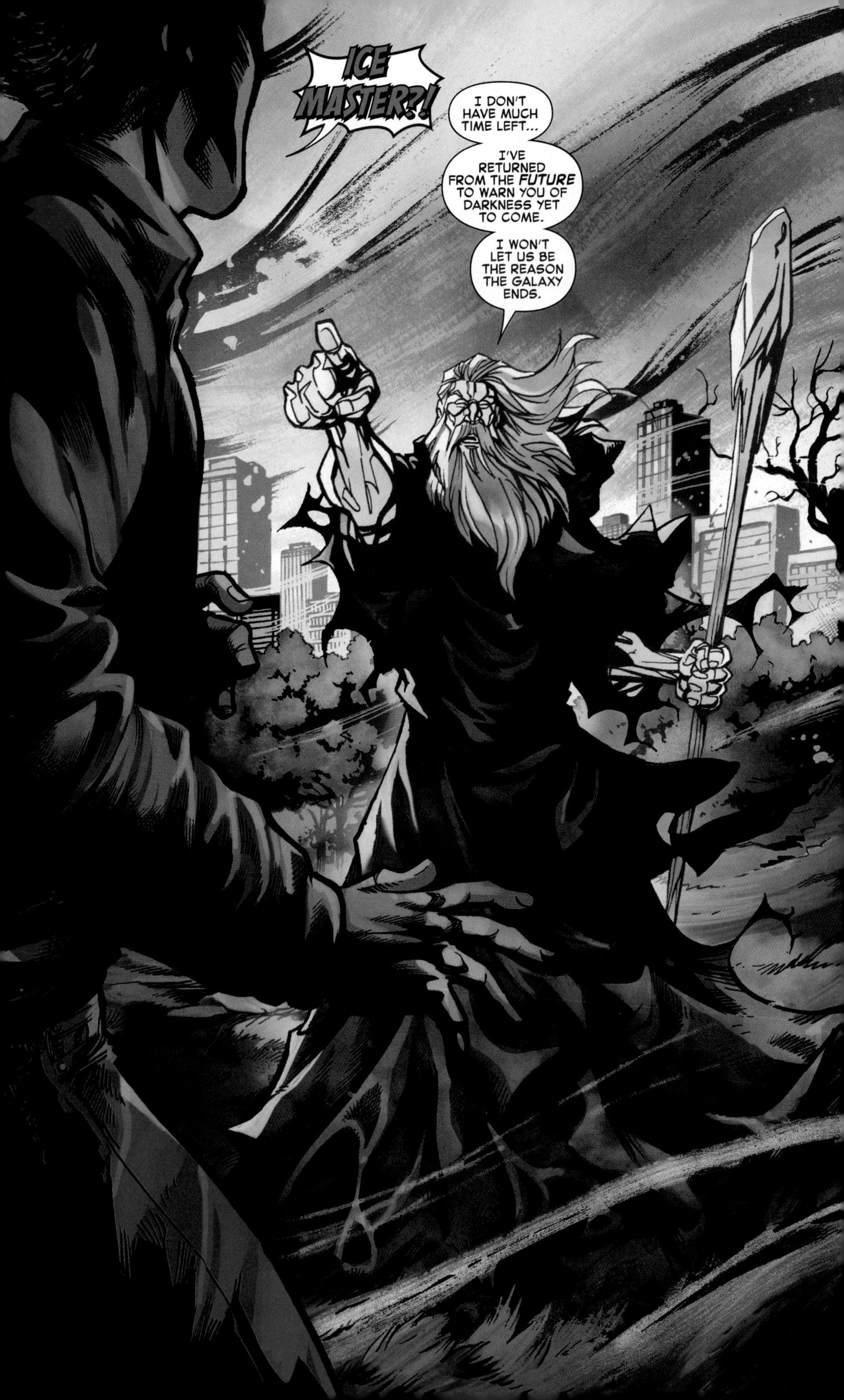
ICE MASTER?!
I DON'T HAVE MUCH TIME LEFT...
I'VE RETURNED FROM THE *FUTURE* TO WARN YOU OF DARKNESS YET TO COME.
I WON'T LET US BE THE REASON THE GALAXY ENDS.

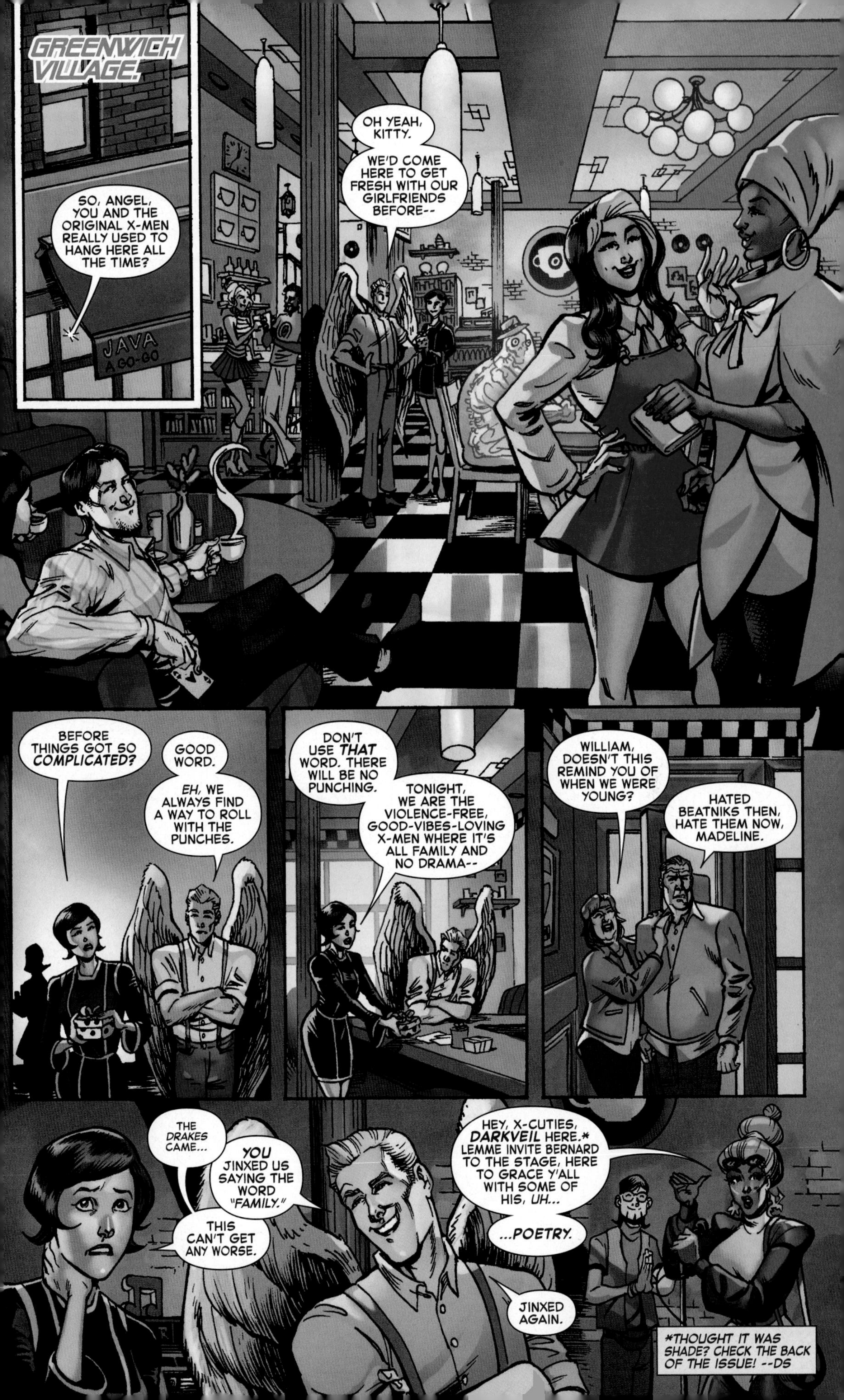
GREENWICH VILLAGE.
JAVA A GO-GO
SO, ANGEL, YOU AND THE ORIGINAL X-MEN REALLY USED TO HANG HERE ALL THE TIME?
OH YEAH, KITTY.
WE'D COME HERE TO GET FRESH WITH OUR GIRLFRIENDS BEFORE--
BEFORE THINGS GOT SO COMPLICATED?
GOOD WORD.
EH, WE ALWAYS FIND A WAY TO ROLL WITH THE PUNCHES.
DON'T USE THAT WORD. THERE WILL BE NO PUNCHING.
TONIGHT, WE ARE THE VIOLENCE-FREE, GOOD-VIBES-LOVING X-MEN WHERE IT'S ALL FAMILY AND NO DRAMA--
WILLIAM, DOESN'T THIS REMIND YOU OF WHEN WE WERE YOUNG?
HATED BEATNIKS THEN, HATE THEM NOW, MADELINE.
THE DRAKES CAME...
YOU JINXED US SAYING THE WORD "FAMILY."
THIS CAN'T GET ANY WORSE.
HEY, X-CUTIES, DARKVEIL HERE.* LEMME INVITE BERNARD TO THE STAGE, HERE TO GRACE Y'ALL WITH SOME OF HIS, UH...
...POETRY.
JINXED AGAIN.
*THOUGHT IT WAS SHADE? CHECK THE BACK OF THE ISSUE! --DS

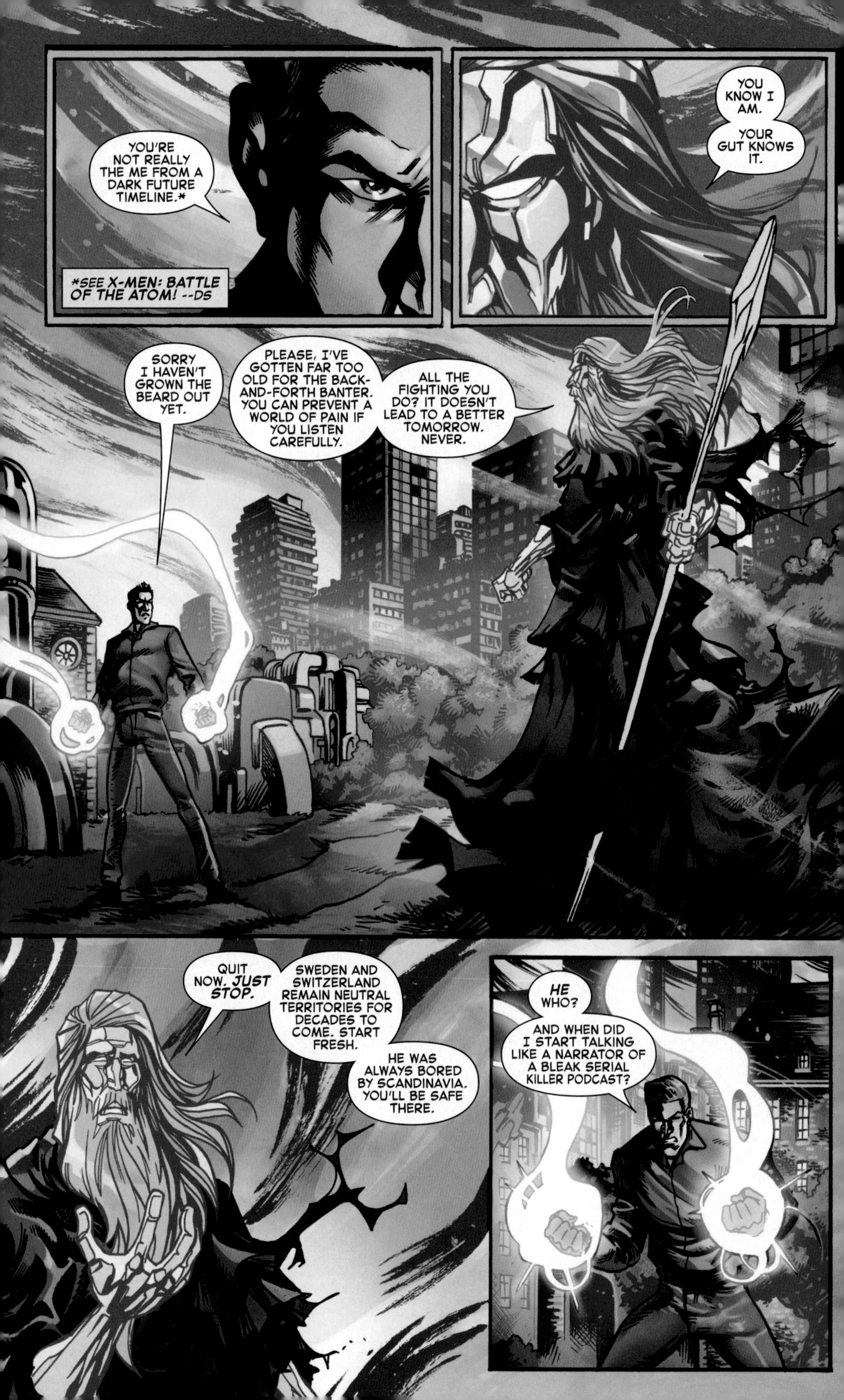

YOU'RE NOT REALLY THE ME FROM A DARK FUTURE TIMELINE.*
*SEE X-MEN: BATTLE OF THE ATOM! --DS
YOU KNOW I AM.
YOUR GUT KNOWS IT.
SORRY I HAVEN'T GROWN THE BEARD OUT YET.
PLEASE, I'VE GOTTEN FAR TOO OLD FOR THE BACK-AND-FORTH BANTER. YOU CAN PREVENT A WORLD OF PAIN IF YOU LISTEN CAREFULLY.
ALL THE FIGHTING YOU DO? IT DOESN'T LEAD TO A BETTER TOMORROW. NEVER.
QUIT NOW. JUST STOP.
SWEDEN AND SWITZERLAND REMAIN NEUTRAL TERRITORIES FOR DECADES TO COME. START FRESH.
HE WAS ALWAYS BORED BY SCANDINAVIA. YOU'LL BE SAFE THERE.
HE WHO?
AND WHEN DID I START TALKING LIKE A NARRATOR OF A BLEAK SERIAL KILLER PODCAST?

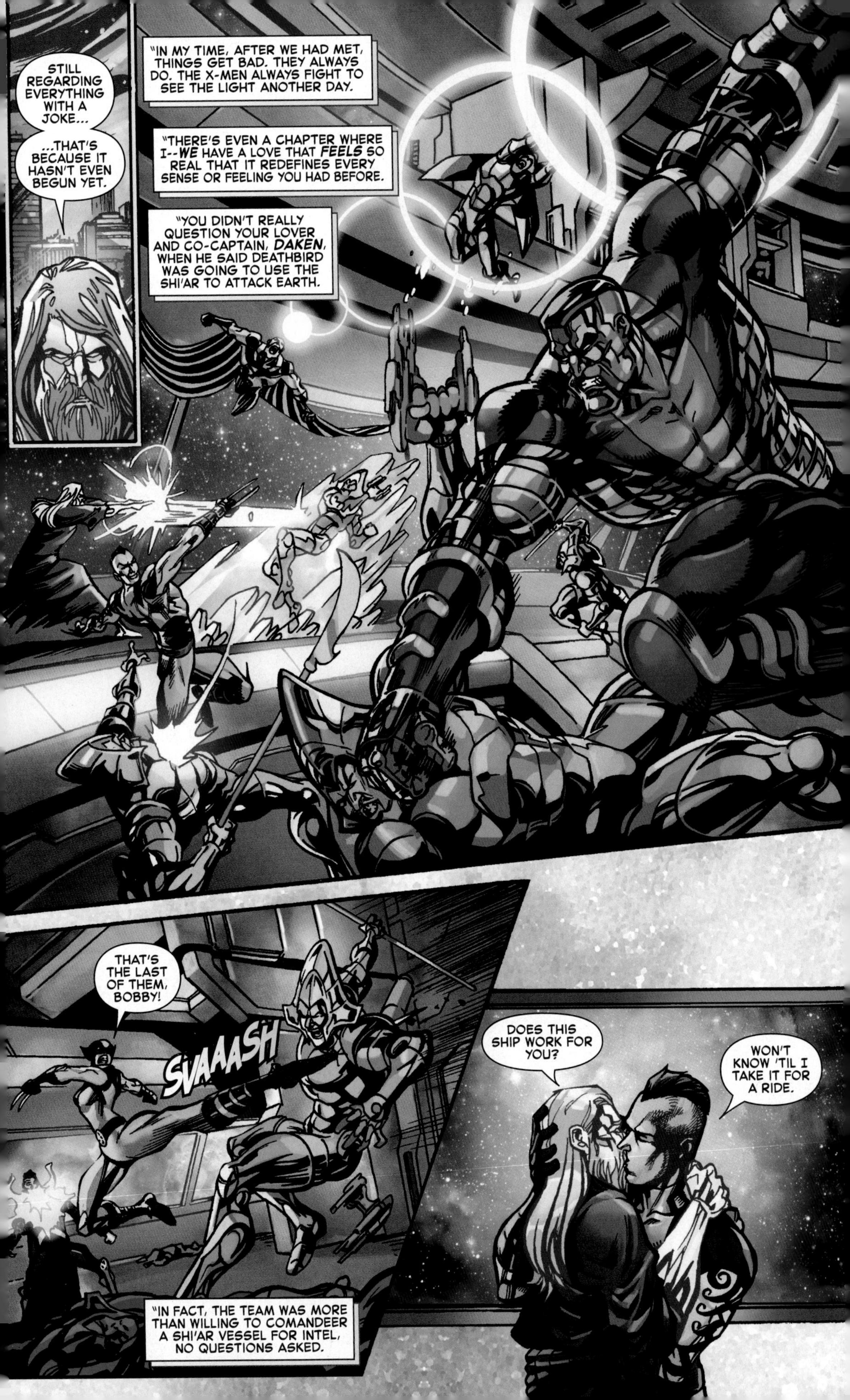
STILL REGARDING EVERYTHING WITH A JOKE...
...THAT'S BECAUSE IT HASN'T EVEN BEGUN YET.
"IN MY TIME, AFTER WE HAD MET, THINGS GET BAD. THEY ALWAYS DO. THE X-MEN ALWAYS FIGHT TO SEE THE LIGHT ANOTHER DAY.
"THERE'S EVEN A CHAPTER WHERE I--WE HAVE A LOVE THAT FEELS SO REAL THAT IT REDEFINES EVERY SENSE OR FEELING YOU HAD BEFORE.
"YOU DIDN'T REALLY QUESTION YOUR LOVER AND CO-CAPTAIN, DAKEN, WHEN HE SAID DEATHBIRD WAS GOING TO USE THE SHI'AR TO ATTACK EARTH.
THAT'S THE LAST OF THEM, BOBBY!
SVAAASH
"IN FACT, THE TEAM WAS MORE THAN WILLING TO COMANDEER A SHI'AR VESSEL FOR INTEL, NO QUESTIONS ASKED.
DOES THIS SHIP WORK FOR YOU?
WON'T KNOW 'TIL I TAKE IT FOR A RIDE.

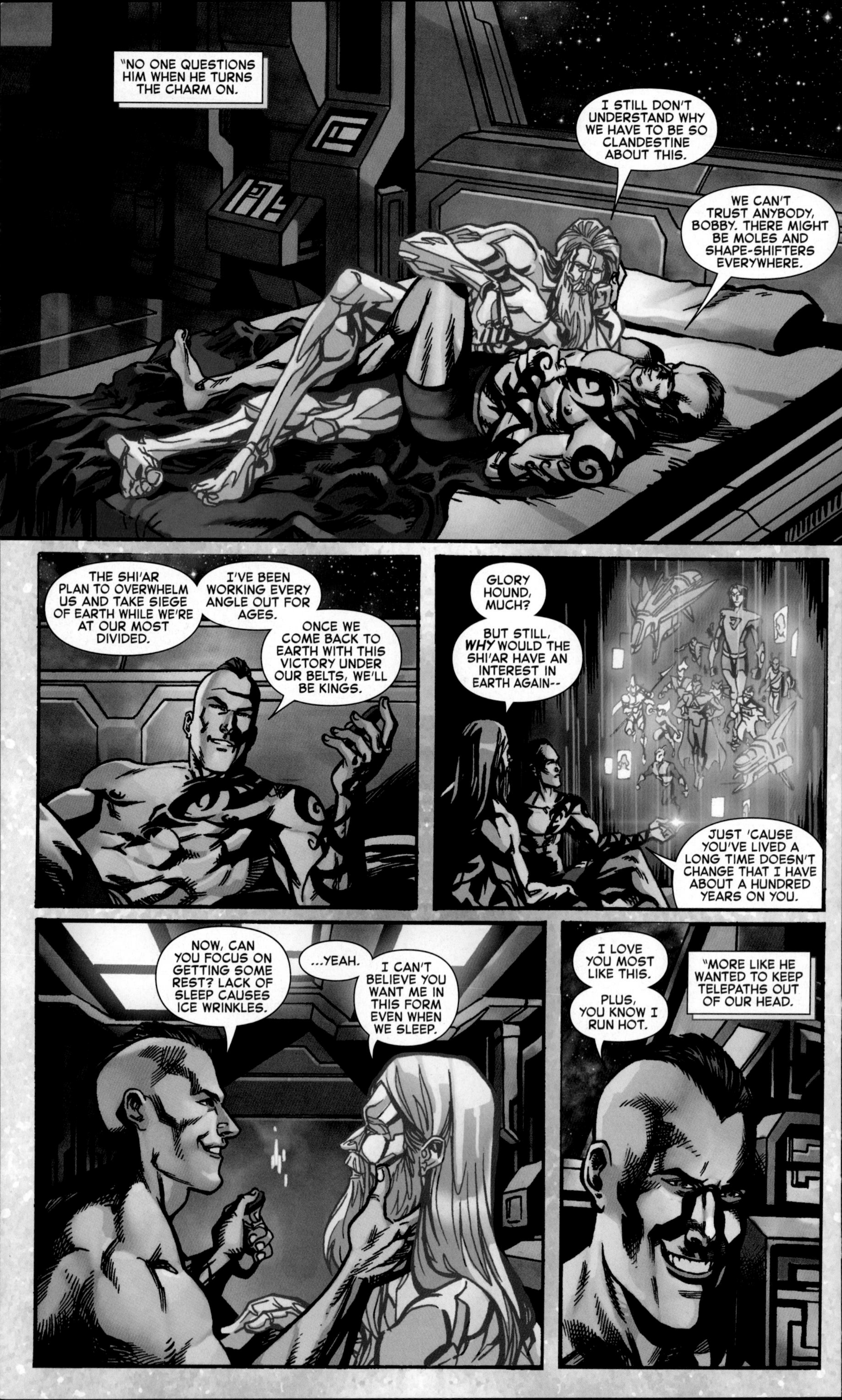
"NO ONE QUESTIONS HIM WHEN HE TURNS THE CHARM ON.
I STILL DON'T UNDERSTAND WHY WE HAVE TO BE SO CLANDESTINE ABOUT THIS.
WE CAN'T TRUST ANYBODY, BOBBY. THERE MIGHT BE MOLES AND SHAPE-SHIFTERS EVERYWHERE.
THE SHI'AR PLAN TO OVERWHELM US AND TAKE SIEGE OF EARTH WHILE WE'RE AT OUR MOST DIVIDED.
I'VE BEEN WORKING EVERY ANGLE OUT FOR AGES.
ONCE WE COME BACK TO EARTH WITH THIS VICTORY UNDER OUR BELTS, WE'LL BE KINGS.
GLORY HOUND, MUCH?
BUT STILL, WHY WOULD THE SHI'AR HAVE AN INTEREST IN EARTH AGAIN--
JUST 'CAUSE YOU'VE LIVED A LONG TIME DOESN'T CHANGE THAT I HAVE ABOUT A HUNDRED YEARS ON YOU.
NOW, CAN YOU FOCUS ON GETTING SOME REST? LACK OF SLEEP CAUSES ICE WRINKLES.
...YEAH.
I CAN'T BELIEVE YOU WANT ME IN THIS FORM EVEN WHEN WE SLEEP.
I LOVE YOU MOST LIKE THIS.
PLUS, YOU KNOW I RUN HOT.
"MORE LIKE HE WANTED TO KEEP TELEPATHS OUT OF OUR HEAD.

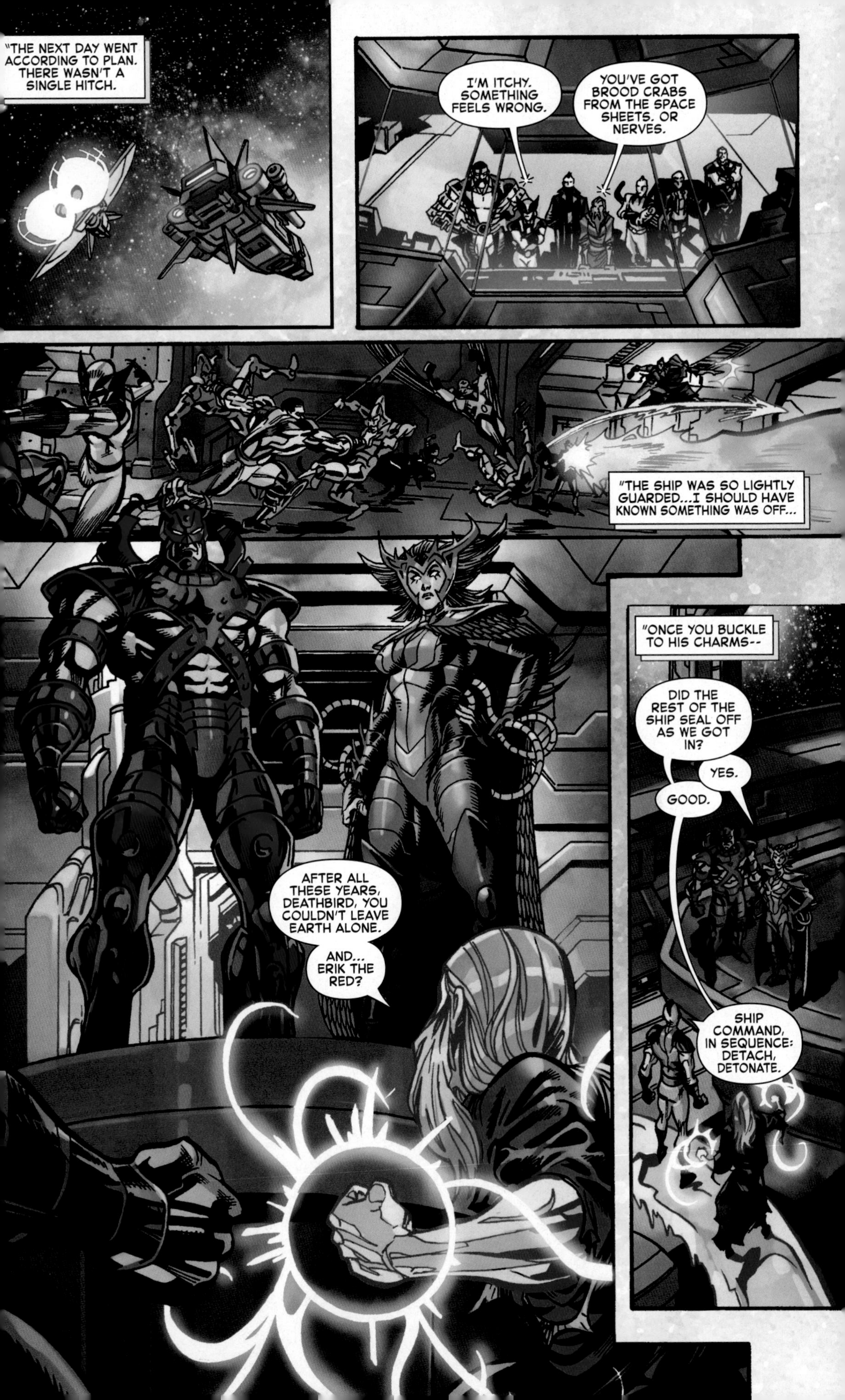
"THE NEXT DAY WENT ACCORDING TO PLAN. THERE WASN'T A SINGLE HITCH.
I'M ITCHY. SOMETHING FEELS WRONG.
YOU'VE GOT BROOD CRABS FROM THE SPACE SHEETS. OR NERVES.
"THE SHIP WAS SO LIGHTLY GUARDED...I SHOULD HAVE KNOWN SOMETHING WAS OFF...
AFTER ALL THESE YEARS, DEATHBIRD, YOU COULDN'T LEAVE EARTH ALONE.
AND... ERIK THE RED?
"ONCE YOU BUCKLE TO HIS CHARMS--
DID THE REST OF THE SHIP SEAL OFF AS WE GOT IN?
YES.
GOOD.
SHIP COMMAND, IN SEQUENCE: DETACH, DETONATE.

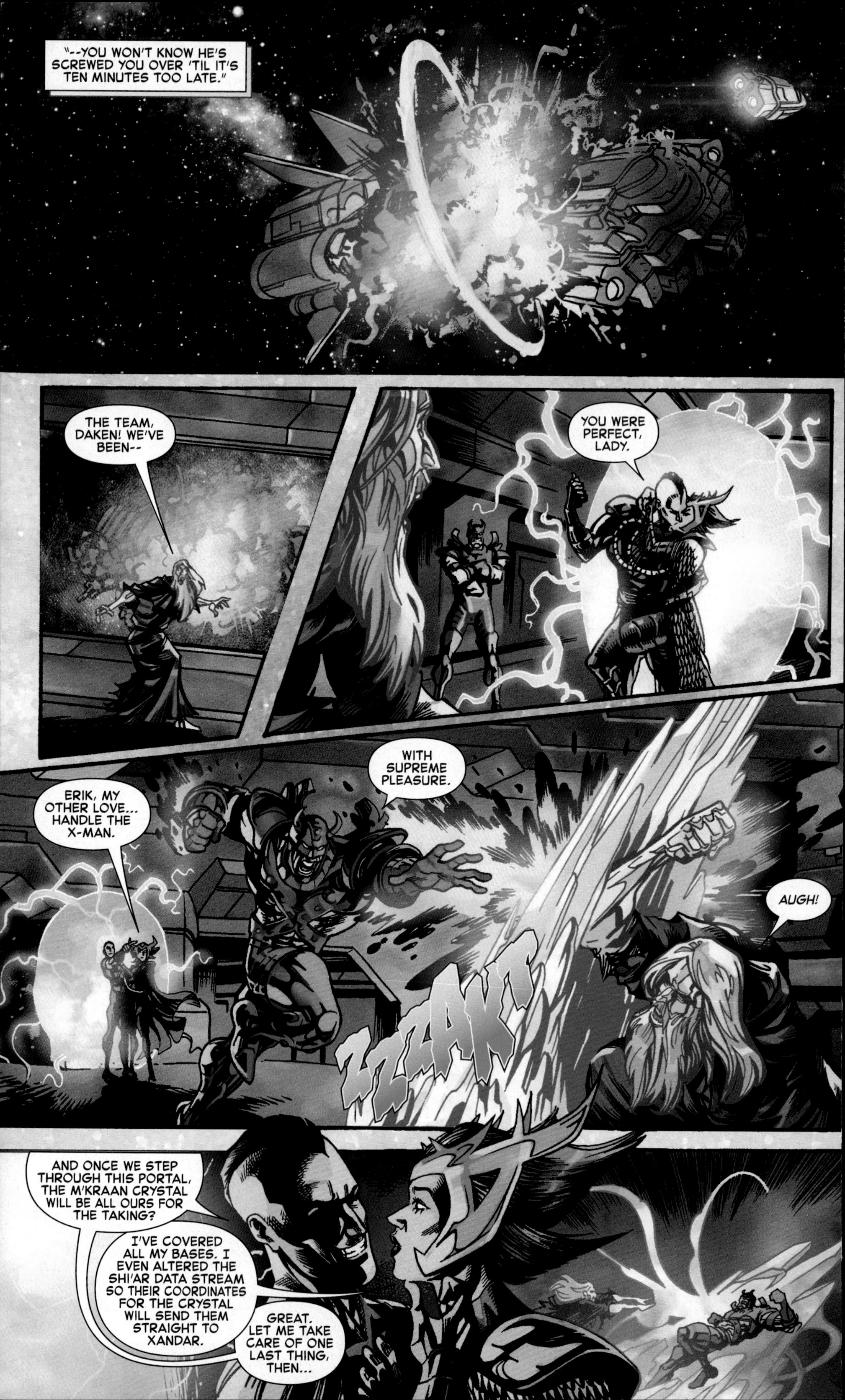
"--YOU WON'T KNOW HE'S SCREWED YOU OVER 'TIL IT'S TEN MINUTES TOO LATE."
THE TEAM, DAKEN! WE'VE BEEN--
YOU WERE PERFECT, LADY.
ERIK, MY OTHER LOVE... HANDLE THE X-MAN.
WITH SUPREME PLEASURE.
AUGH!
ZZZAKT
AND ONCE WE STEP THROUGH THIS PORTAL, THE M'KRAAN CRYSTAL WILL BE ALL OURS FOR THE TAKING?
I'VE COVERED ALL MY BASES. I EVEN ALTERED THE SHI'AR DATA STREAM SO THEIR COORDINATES FOR THE CRYSTAL WILL SEND THEM STRAIGHT TO XANDAR.
GREAT. LET ME TAKE CARE OF ONE LAST THING, THEN...

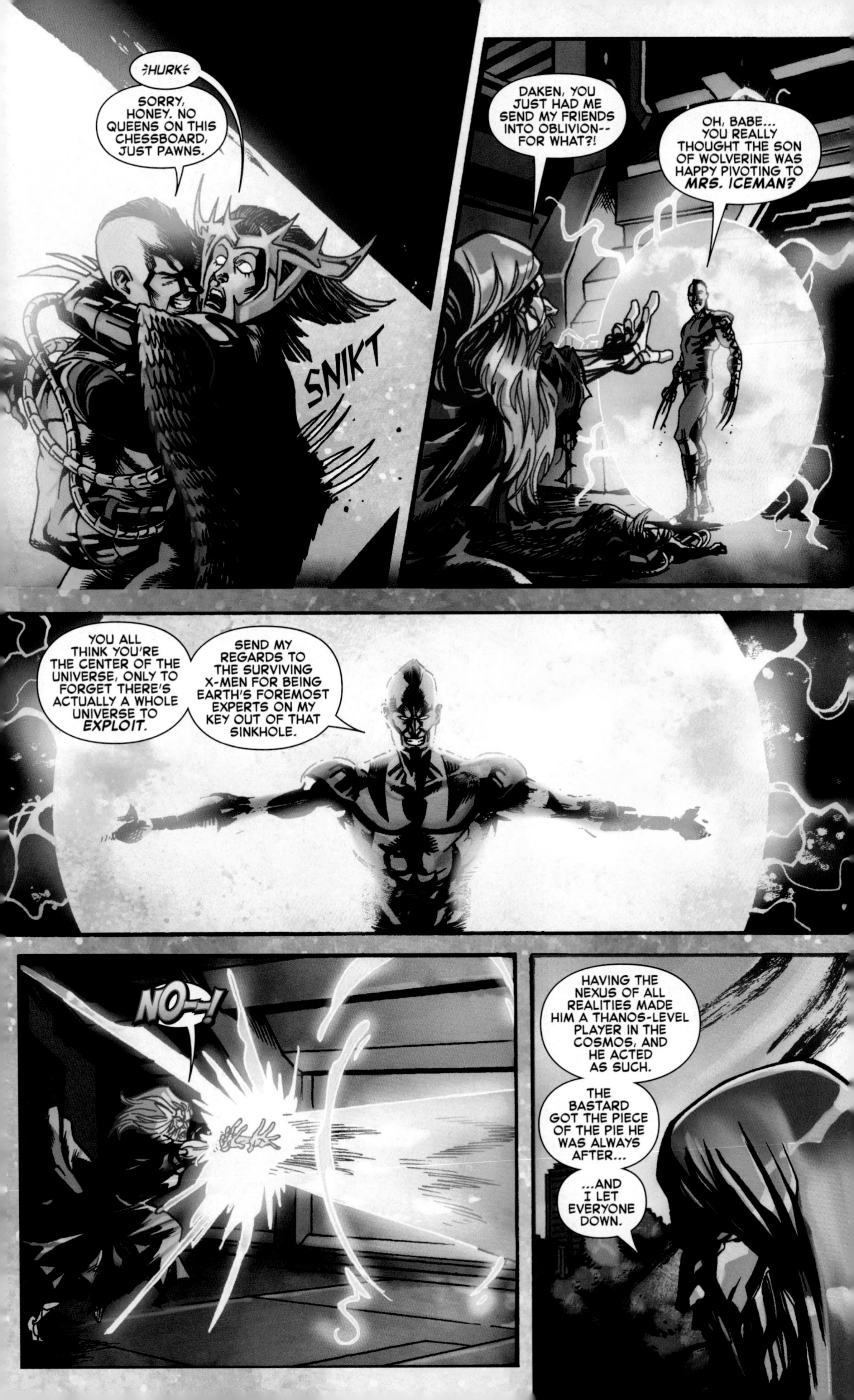

HURK
SORRY, HONEY. NO QUEENS ON THIS CHESSBOARD, JUST PAWNS.
SNIKT
DAKEN, YOU JUST HAD ME SEND MY FRIENDS INTO OBLIVION-- FOR WHAT?!
OH, BABE... YOU REALLY THOUGHT THE SON OF WOLVERINE WAS HAPPY PIVOTING TO MRS. ICEMAN?
YOU ALL THINK YOU'RE THE CENTER OF THE UNIVERSE, ONLY TO FORGET THERE'S ACTUALLY A WHOLE UNIVERSE TO EXPLOIT.
SEND MY REGARDS TO THE SURVIVING X-MEN FOR BEING EARTH'S FOREMOST EXPERTS ON MY KEY OUT OF THAT SINKHOLE.
NO--!
HAVING THE NEXUS OF ALL REALITIES MADE HIM A THANOS-LEVEL PLAYER IN THE COSMOS, AND HE ACTED AS SUCH.
THE BASTARD GOT THE PIECE OF THE PIE HE WAS ALWAYS AFTER...
...AND I LET EVERYONE DOWN.

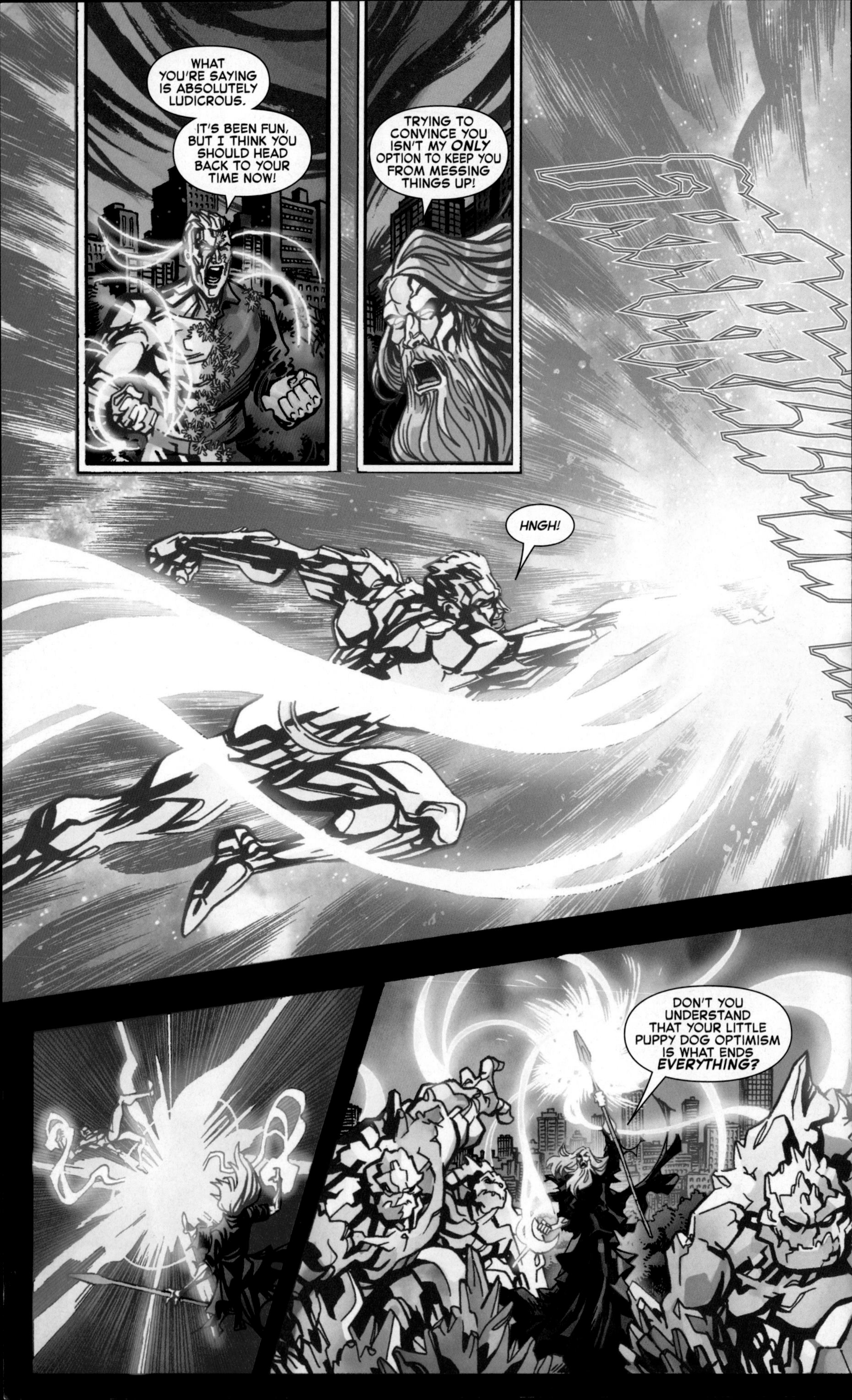
WHAT YOU'RE SAYING IS ABSOLUTELY LUDICROUS.
IT'S BEEN FUN, BUT I THINK YOU SHOULD HEAD BACK TO YOUR TIME NOW!
TRYING TO CONVINCE YOU ISN'T MY *ONLY* OPTION TO KEEP YOU FROM MESSING THINGS UP!
HNGH!
DON'T YOU UNDERSTAND THAT YOUR LITTLE PUPPY DOG OPTIMISM IS WHAT ENDS *EVERYTHING?*

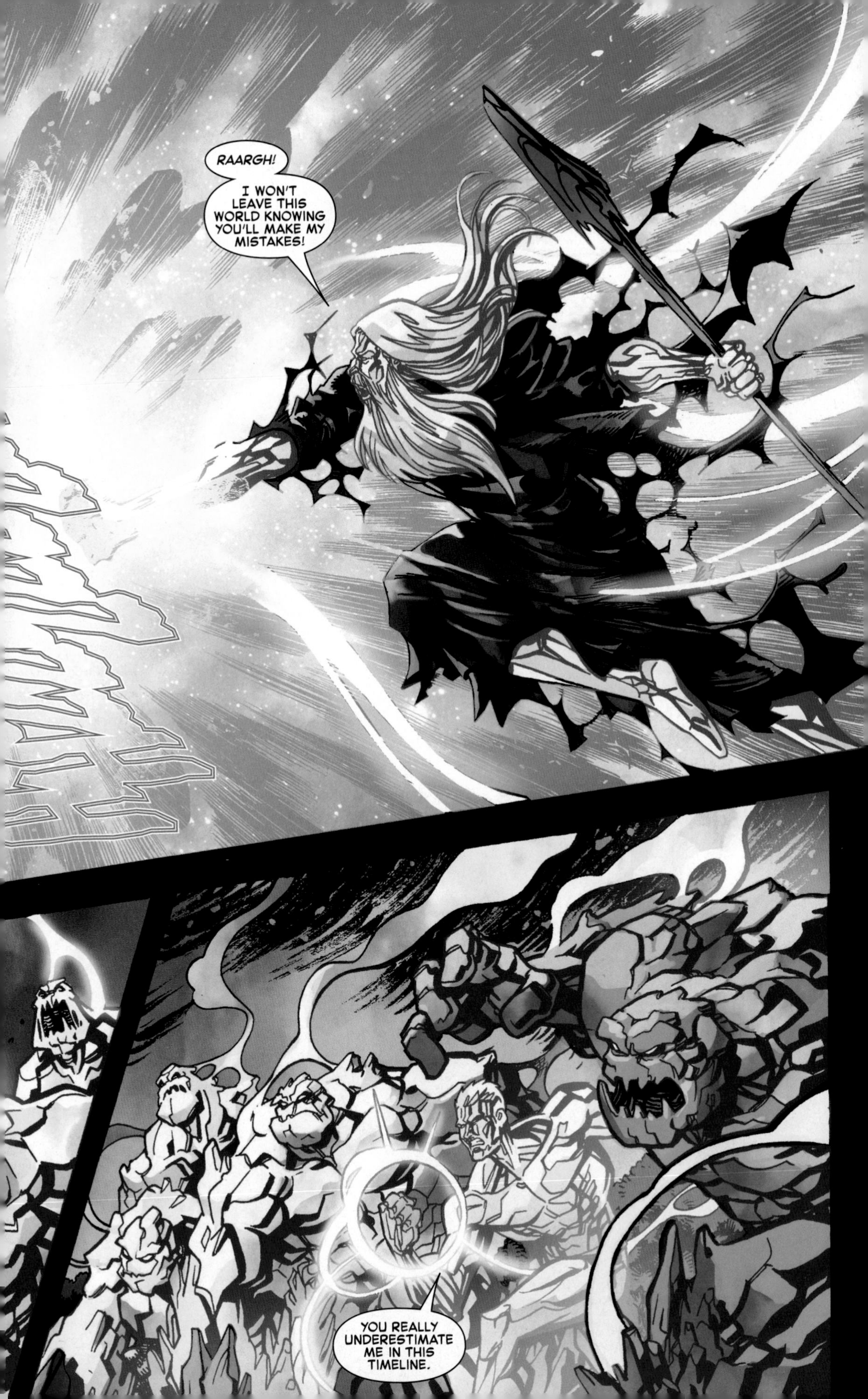
RAARGH!
I WON'T LEAVE THIS WORLD KNOWING YOU'LL MAKE MY MISTAKES!
YOU REALLY UNDERESTIMATE ME IN THIS TIMELINE.

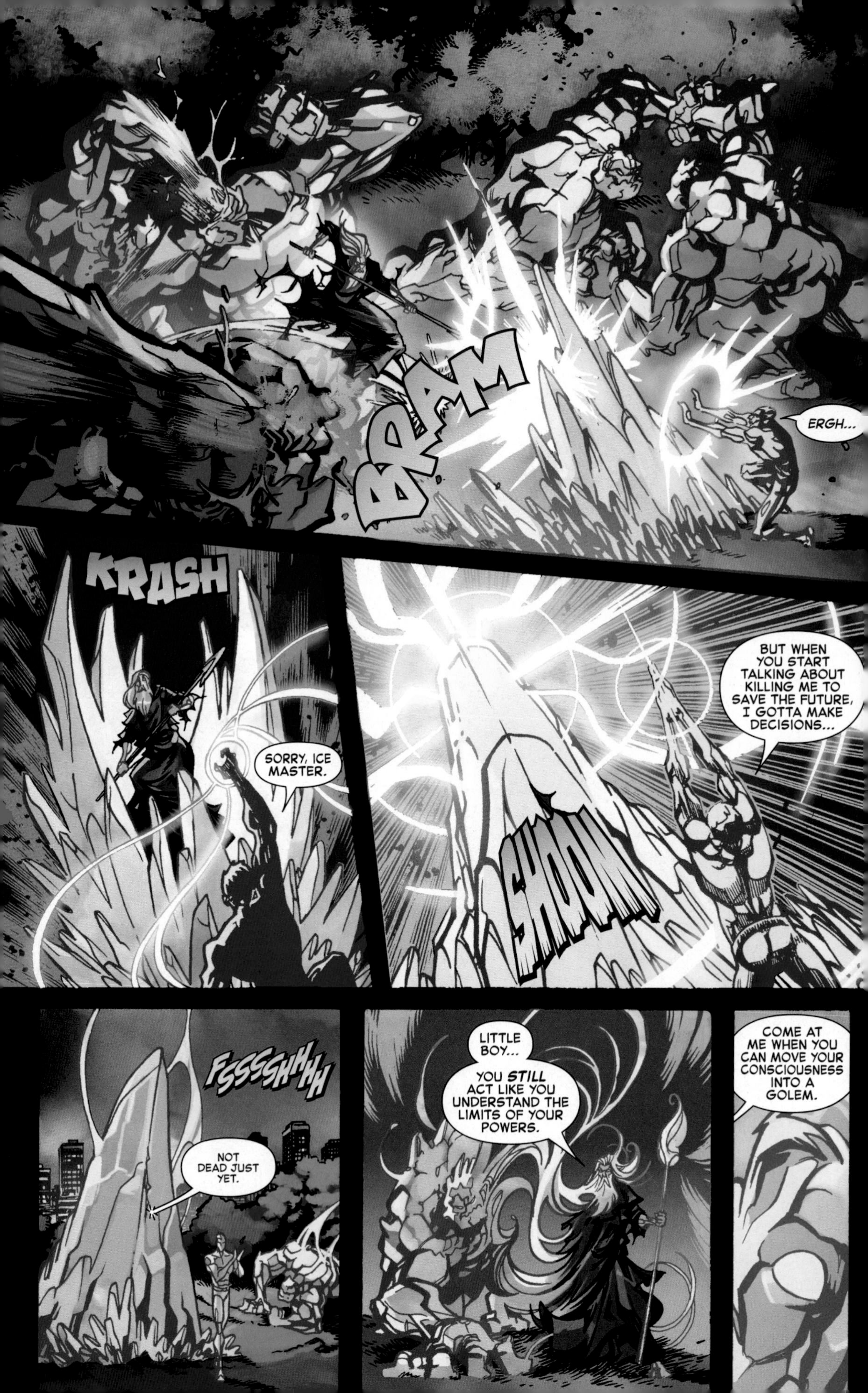
BRAM
ERGH...
KRASH
SORRY, ICE MASTER.
BUT WHEN YOU START TALKING ABOUT KILLING ME TO SAVE THE FUTURE, I GOTTA MAKE DECISIONS...
SHOOM
FSSSSHHHH
NOT DEAD JUST YET.
LITTLE BOY...
YOU STILL ACT LIKE YOU UNDERSTAND THE LIMITS OF YOUR POWERS.
COME AT ME WHEN YOU CAN MOVE YOUR CONSCIOUSNESS INTO A GOLEM.

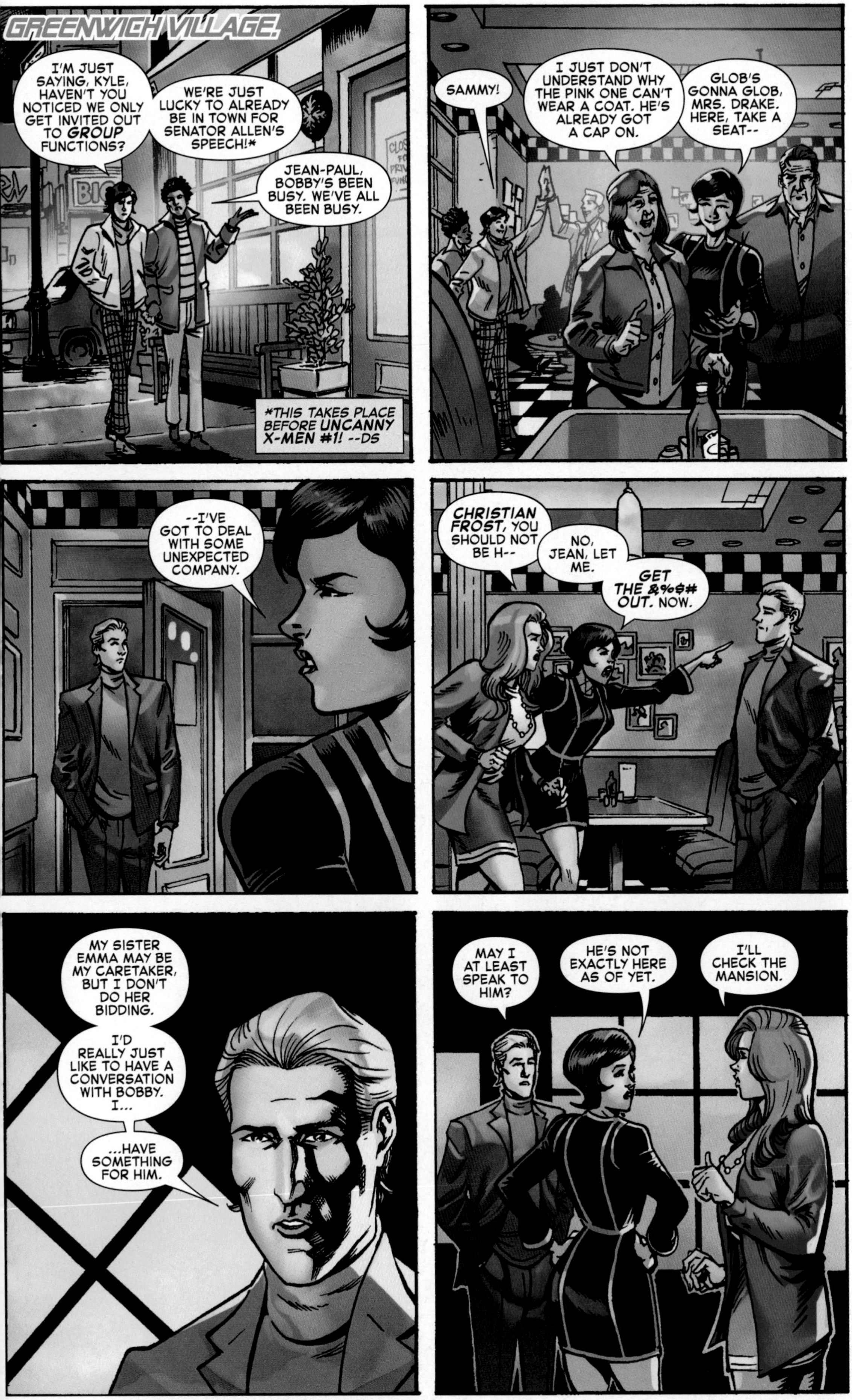
GREENWICH VILLAGE.
I'M JUST SAYING, KYLE, HAVEN'T YOU NOTICED WE ONLY GET INVITED OUT TO GROUP FUNCTIONS?
WE'RE JUST LUCKY TO ALREADY BE IN TOWN FOR SENATOR ALLEN'S SPEECH!*
JEAN-PAUL, BOBBY'S BEEN BUSY. WE'VE ALL BEEN BUSY.
*THIS TAKES PLACE BEFORE UNCANNY X-MEN #1! --DS
SAMMY!
I JUST DON'T UNDERSTAND WHY THE PINK ONE CAN'T WEAR A COAT. HE'S ALREADY GOT A CAP ON.
GLOB'S GONNA GLOB, MRS. DRAKE. HERE, TAKE A SEAT--
--I'VE GOT TO DEAL WITH SOME UNEXPECTED COMPANY.
CHRISTIAN FROST, YOU SHOULD NOT BE H--
NO, JEAN, LET ME.
GET THE &%$# OUT. NOW.
MY SISTER EMMA MAY BE MY CARETAKER, BUT I DON'T DO HER BIDDING.
I'D REALLY JUST LIKE TO HAVE A CONVERSATION WITH BOBBY. I...
...HAVE SOMETHING FOR HIM.
MAY I AT LEAST SPEAK TO HIM?
HE'S NOT EXACTLY HERE AS OF YET.
I'LL CHECK THE MANSION.

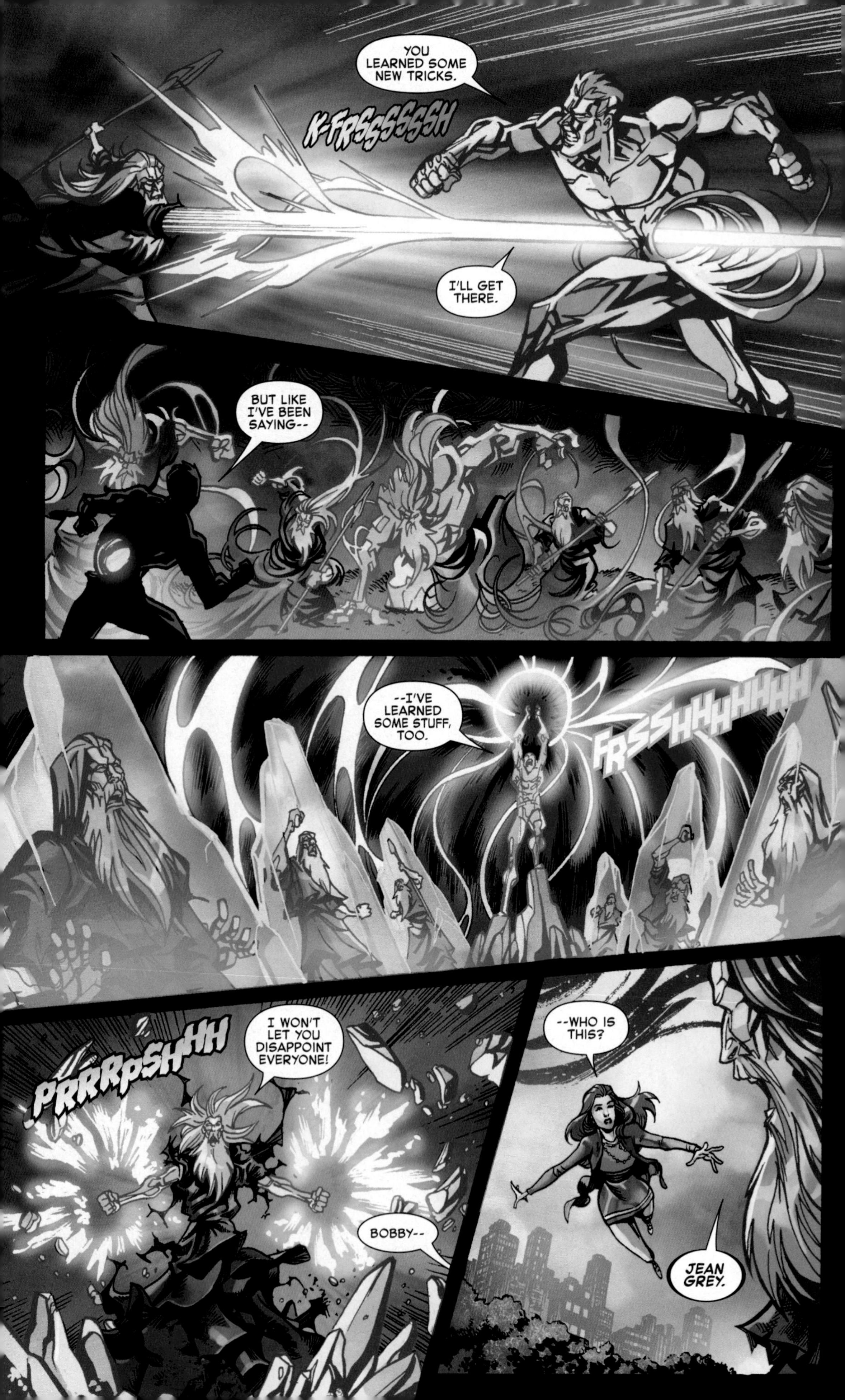
YOU LEARNED SOME NEW TRICKS.
K-FRSSSSSSH
I'LL GET THERE.
BUT LIKE I'VE BEEN SAYING--
--I'VE LEARNED SOME STUFF, TOO.
FRSSHHHHHHH
PRRRPSHHH
I WON'T LET YOU DISAPPOINT EVERYONE!
BOBBY--
--WHO IS THIS?
JEAN GREY.

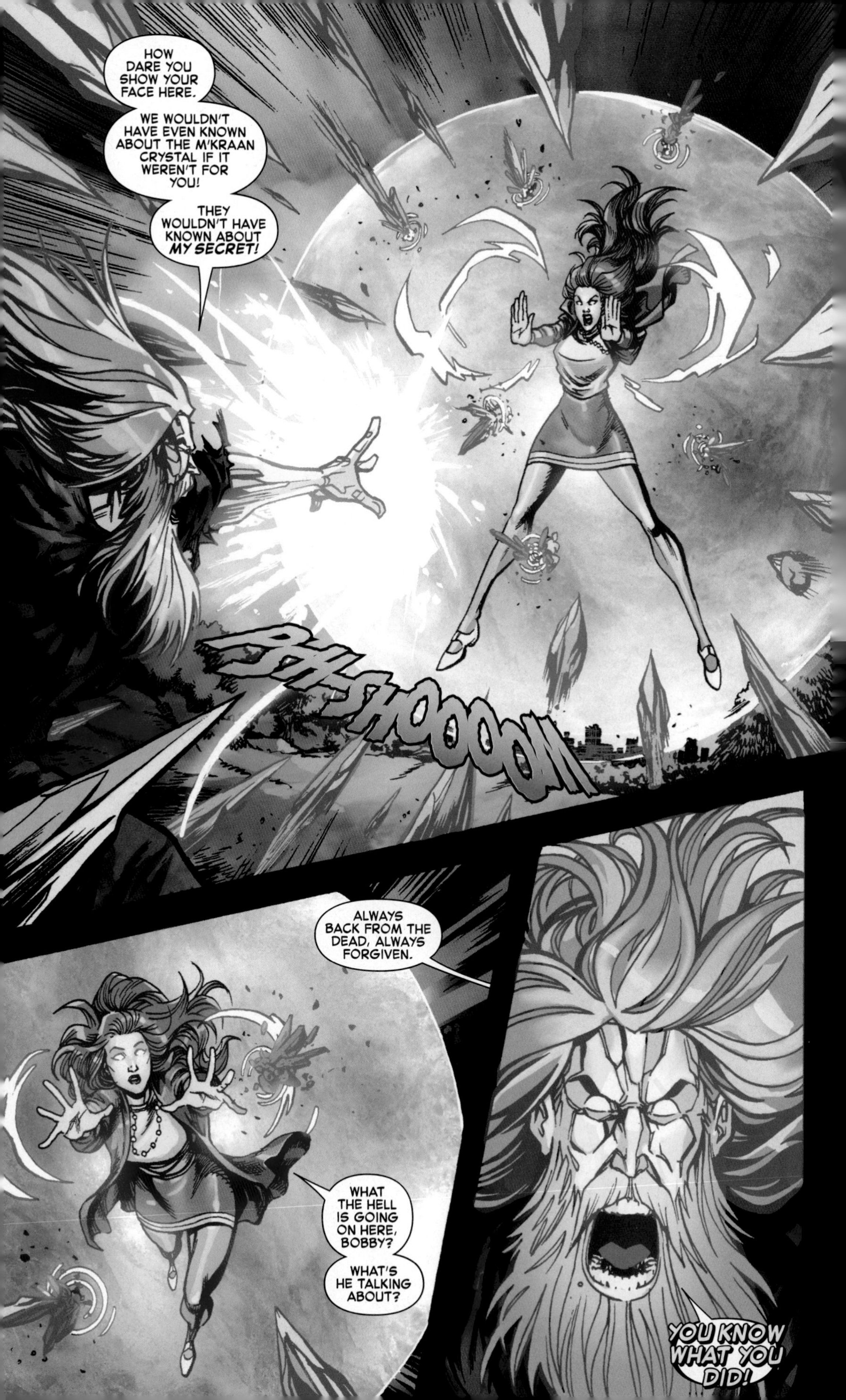
HOW DARE YOU SHOW YOUR FACE HERE.
WE WOULDN'T HAVE EVEN KNOWN ABOUT THE M'KRAAN CRYSTAL IF IT WEREN'T FOR YOU!
THEY WOULDN'T HAVE KNOWN ABOUT *MY SECRET!*
BSHSHOOOOM
ALWAYS BACK FROM THE DEAD, ALWAYS FORGIVEN.
WHAT THE HELL IS GOING ON HERE, BOBBY?
WHAT'S HE TALKING ABOUT?
YOU KNOW WHAT YOU DID!

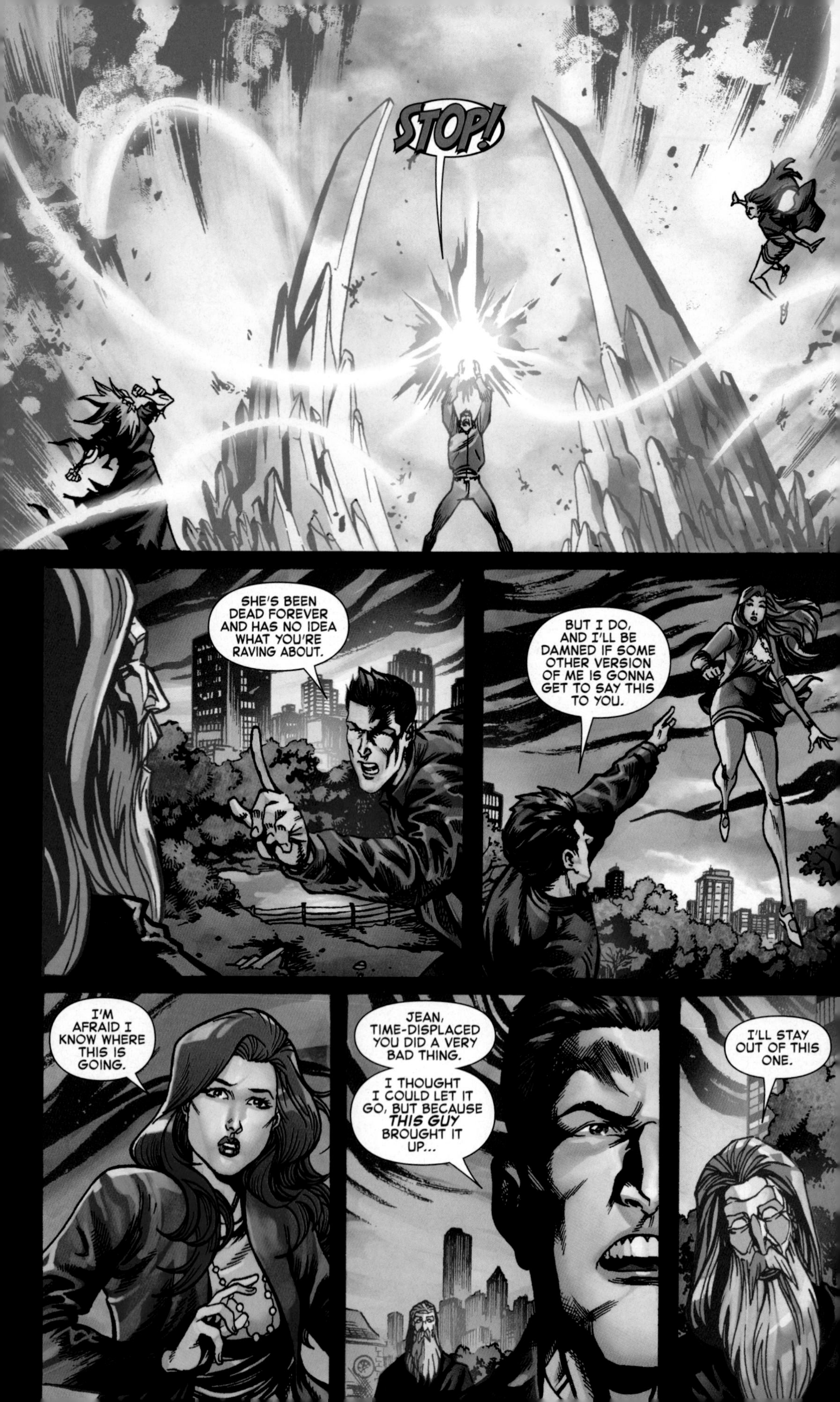
STOP!
SHE'S BEEN DEAD FOREVER AND HAS NO IDEA WHAT YOU'RE RAVING ABOUT.
BUT I DO, AND I'LL BE DAMNED IF SOME OTHER VERSION OF ME IS GONNA GET TO SAY THIS TO YOU.
I'M AFRAID I KNOW WHERE THIS IS GOING.
JEAN, TIME-DISPLACED YOU DID A VERY BAD THING.
I THOUGHT I COULD LET IT GO, BUT BECAUSE THIS GUY BROUGHT IT UP...
I'LL STAY OUT OF THIS ONE.

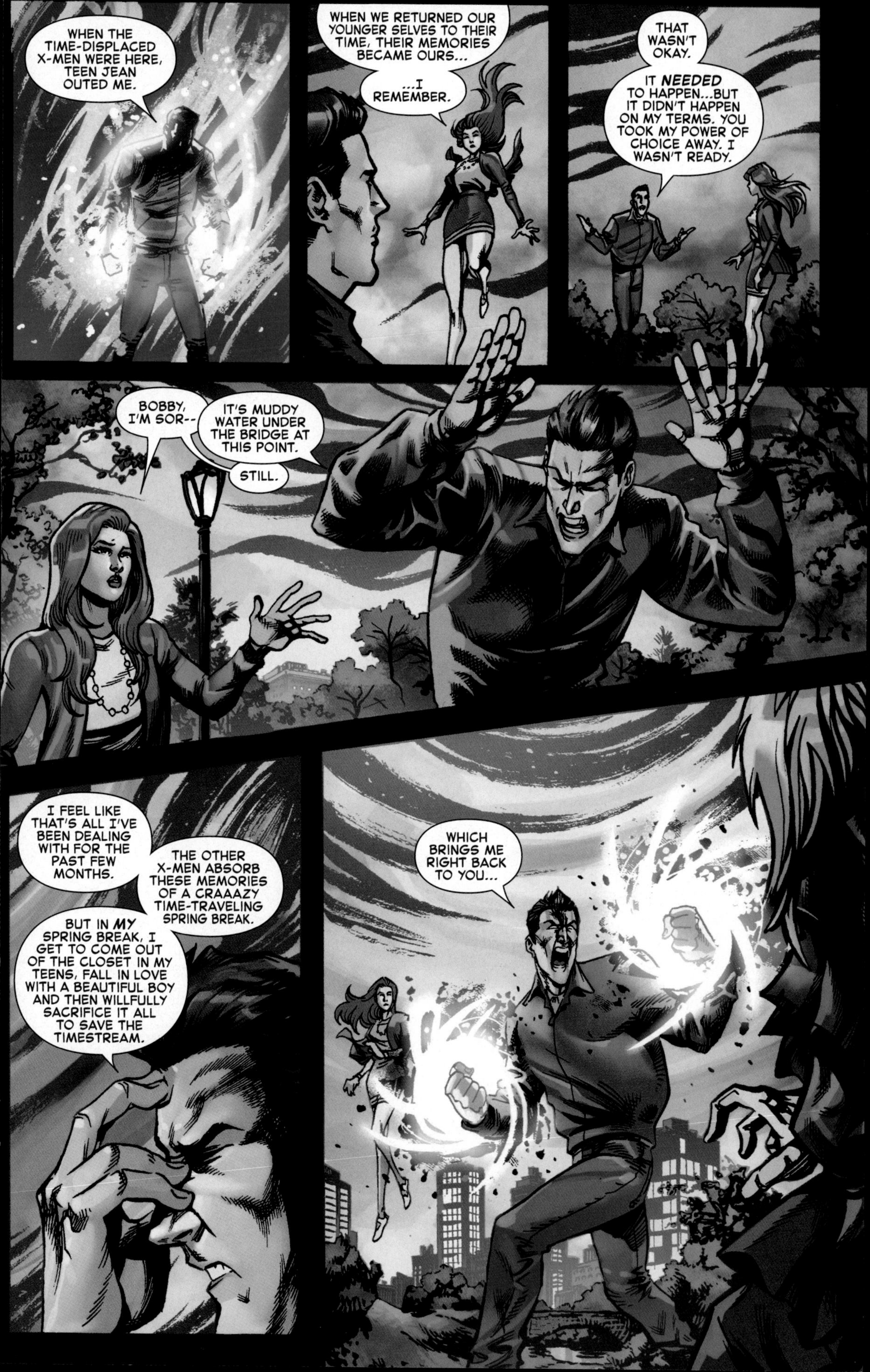
WHEN THE TIME-DISPLACED X-MEN WERE HERE, TEEN JEAN OUTED ME.
WHEN WE RETURNED OUR YOUNGER SELVES TO THEIR TIME, THEIR MEMORIES BECAME OURS...
...I REMEMBER.
THAT WASN'T OKAY.
IT NEEDED TO HAPPEN...BUT IT DIDN'T HAPPEN ON MY TERMS. YOU TOOK MY POWER OF CHOICE AWAY. I WASN'T READY.
BOBBY, I'M SOR--
IT'S MUDDY WATER UNDER THE BRIDGE AT THIS POINT.
STILL.
I FEEL LIKE THAT'S ALL I'VE BEEN DEALING WITH FOR THE PAST FEW MONTHS.
THE OTHER X-MEN ABSORB THESE MEMORIES OF A CRAAAZY TIME-TRAVELING SPRING BREAK.
BUT IN MY SPRING BREAK, I GET TO COME OUT OF THE CLOSET IN MY TEENS, FALL IN LOVE WITH A BEAUTIFUL BOY AND THEN WILLFULLY SACRIFICE IT ALL TO SAVE THE TIMESTREAM.
WHICH BRINGS ME RIGHT BACK TO YOU...

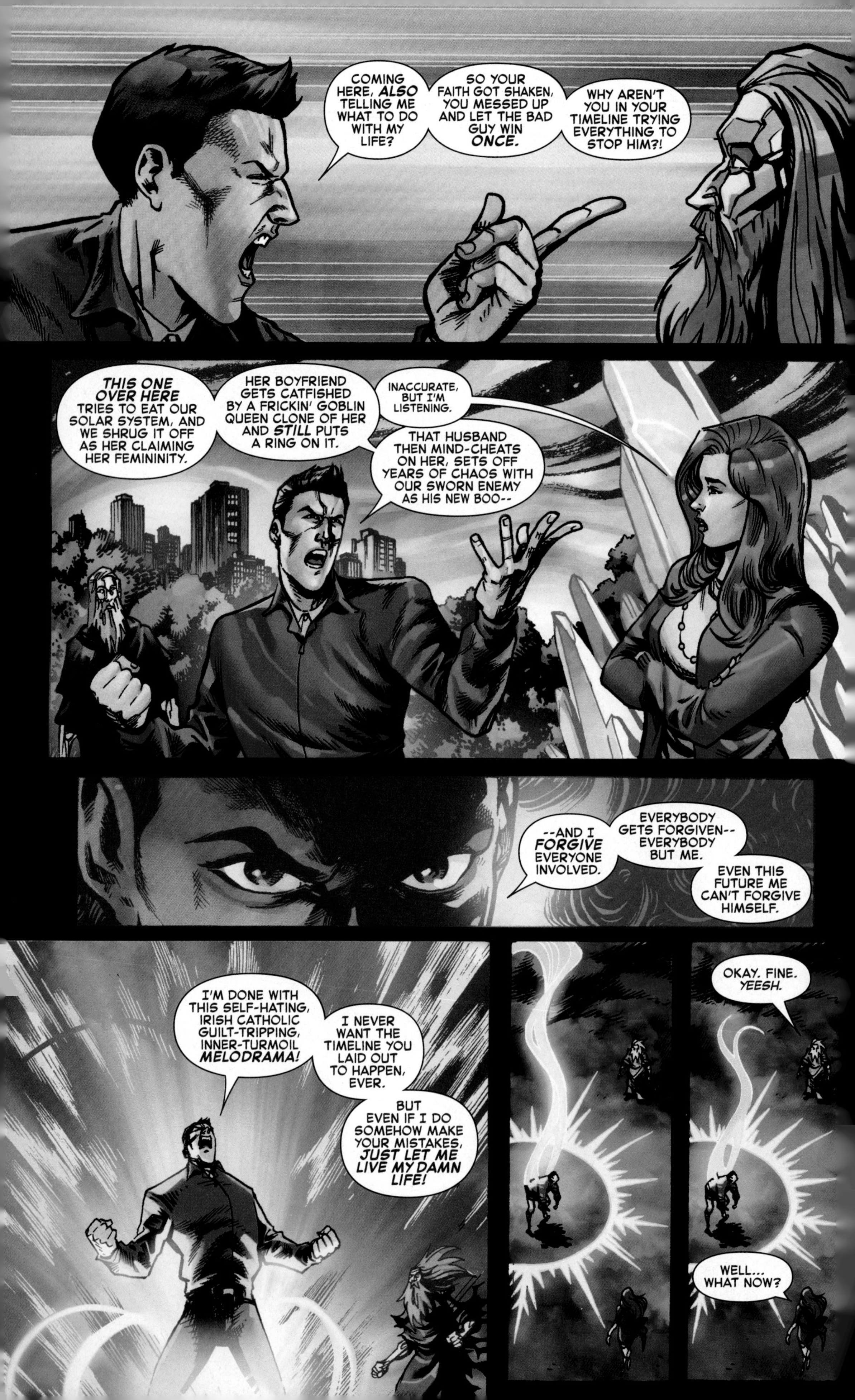

COMING HERE, ALSO TELLING ME WHAT TO DO WITH MY LIFE?
SO YOUR FAITH GOT SHAKEN, YOU MESSED UP AND LET THE BAD GUY WIN ONCE.
WHY AREN'T YOU IN YOUR TIMELINE TRYING EVERYTHING TO STOP HIM?!
THIS ONE OVER HERE TRIES TO EAT OUR SOLAR SYSTEM, AND WE SHRUG IT OFF AS HER CLAIMING HER FEMININITY.
HER BOYFRIEND GETS CATFISHED BY A FRICKIN' GOBLIN QUEEN CLONE OF HER AND STILL PUTS A RING ON IT.
INACCURATE, BUT I'M LISTENING.
THAT HUSBAND THEN MIND-CHEATS ON HER, SETS OFF YEARS OF CHAOS WITH OUR SWORN ENEMY AS HIS NEW BOO--
--AND I FORGIVE EVERYONE INVOLVED.
EVERYBODY GETS FORGIVEN-- EVERYBODY BUT ME.
EVEN THIS FUTURE ME CAN'T FORGIVE HIMSELF.
I'M DONE WITH THIS SELF-HATING, IRISH CATHOLIC GUILT-TRIPPING, INNER-TURMOIL MELODRAMA!
I NEVER WANT THE TIMELINE YOU LAID OUT TO HAPPEN, EVER.
BUT EVEN IF I DO SOMEHOW MAKE YOUR MISTAKES, JUST LET ME LIVE MY DAMN LIFE!
OKAY. FINE. YEESH.
WELL... WHAT NOW?

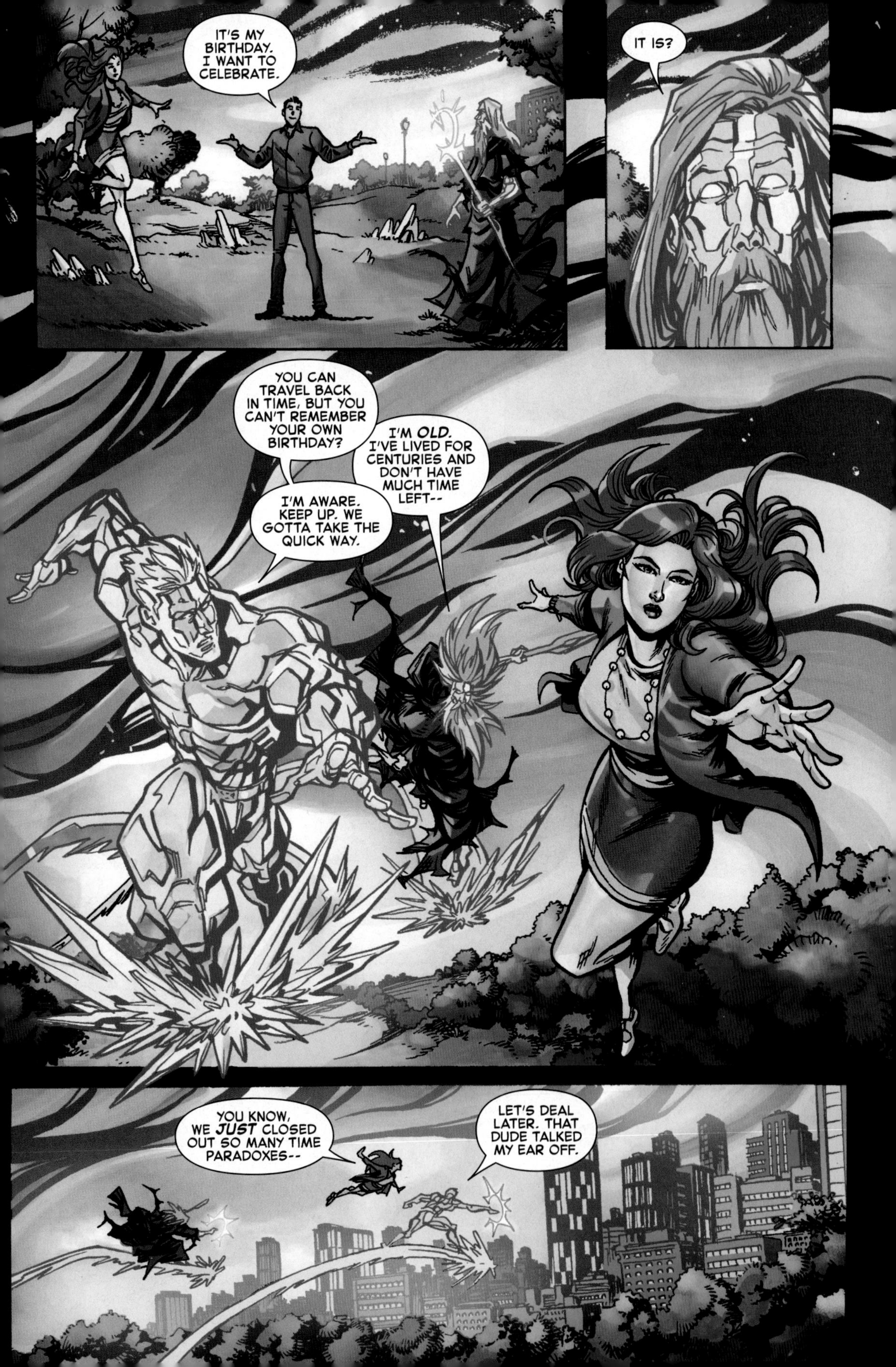
IT'S MY BIRTHDAY. I WANT TO CELEBRATE.
IT IS?
YOU CAN TRAVEL BACK IN TIME, BUT YOU CAN'T REMEMBER YOUR OWN BIRTHDAY?
I'M AWARE. KEEP UP. WE GOTTA TAKE THE QUICK WAY.
I'M OLD. I'VE LIVED FOR CENTURIES AND DON'T HAVE MUCH TIME LEFT--
YOU KNOW, WE JUST CLOSED OUT SO MANY TIME PARADOXES--
LET'S DEAL LATER. THAT DUDE TALKED MY EAR OFF.

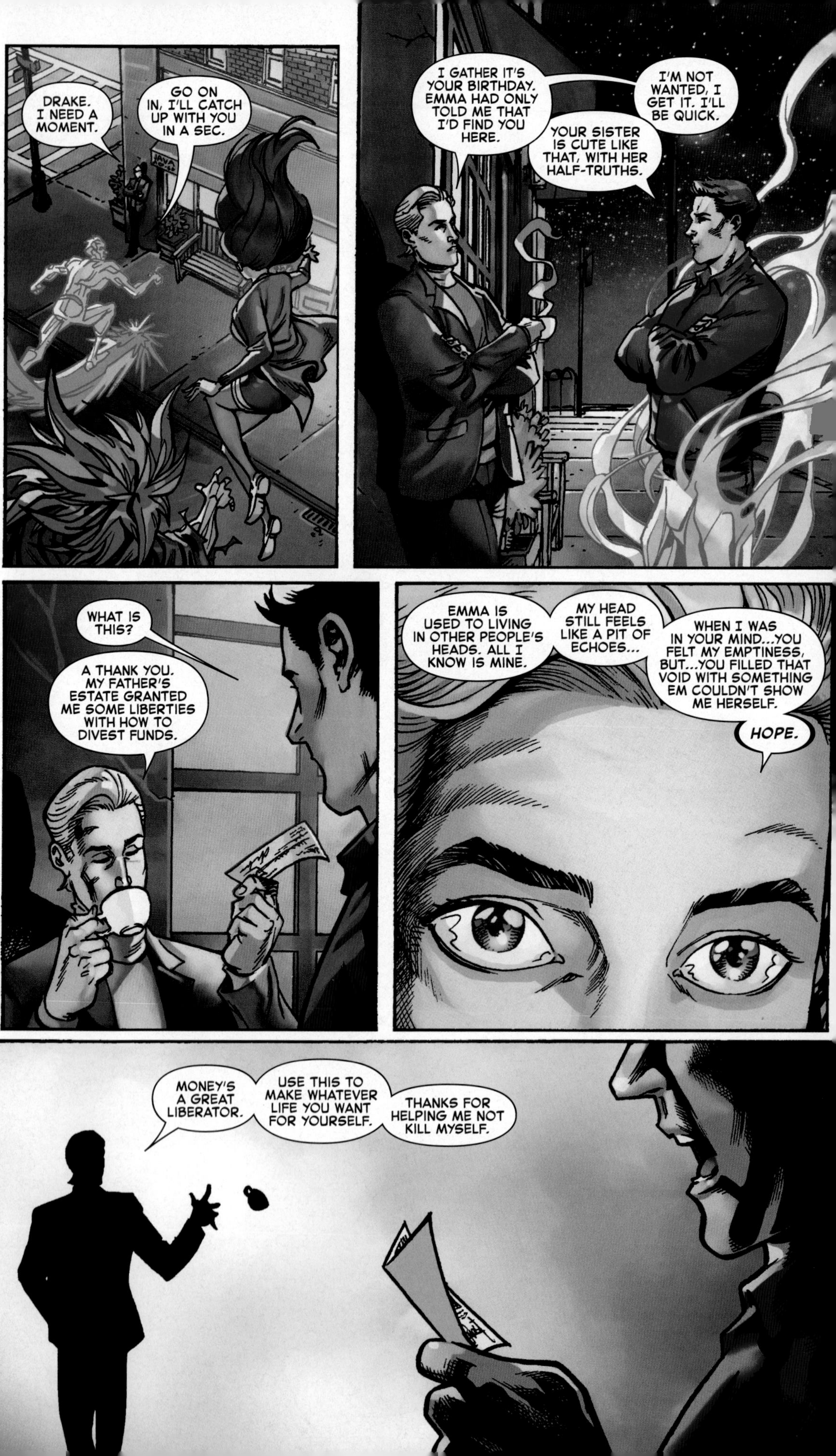
DRAKE. I NEED A MOMENT.
GO ON IN, I'LL CATCH UP WITH YOU IN A SEC.
JAVA
I GATHER IT'S YOUR BIRTHDAY. EMMA HAD ONLY TOLD ME THAT I'D FIND YOU HERE.
YOUR SISTER IS CUTE LIKE THAT, WITH HER HALF-TRUTHS.
I'M NOT WANTED, I GET IT. I'LL BE QUICK.
WHAT IS THIS?
A THANK YOU. MY FATHER'S ESTATE GRANTED ME SOME LIBERTIES WITH HOW TO DIVEST FUNDS.
EMMA IS USED TO LIVING IN OTHER PEOPLE'S HEADS. ALL I KNOW IS MINE.
MY HEAD STILL FEELS LIKE A PIT OF ECHOES...
WHEN I WAS IN YOUR MIND...YOU FELT MY EMPTINESS, BUT...YOU FILLED THAT VOID WITH SOMETHING EM COULDN'T SHOW ME HERSELF.
HOPE.
MONEY'S A GREAT LIBERATOR.
USE THIS TO MAKE WHATEVER LIFE YOU WANT FOR YOURSELF.
THANKS FOR HELPING ME NOT KILL MYSELF.

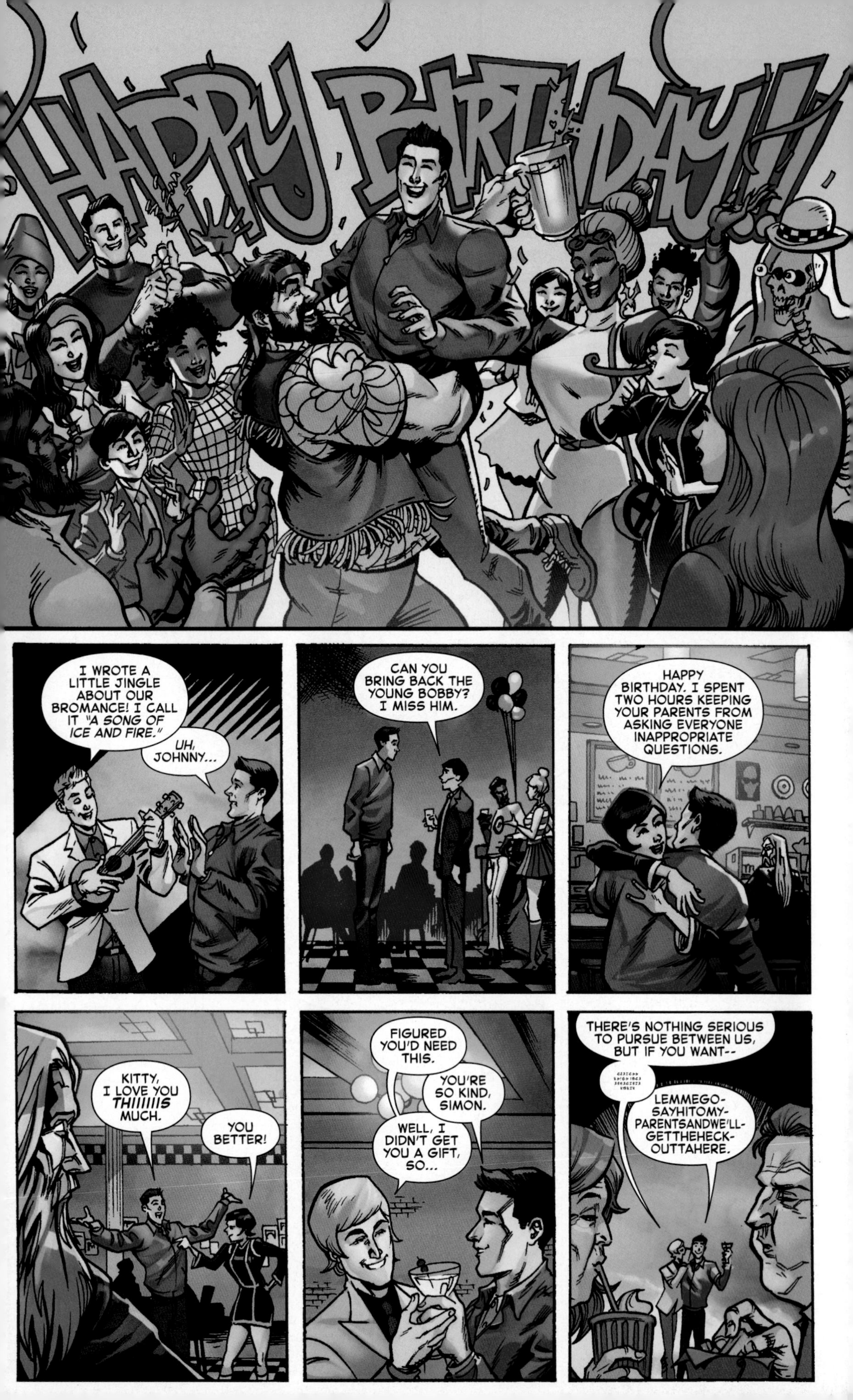
HAPPY BIRTHDAY!!
I WROTE A LITTLE JINGLE ABOUT OUR BROMANCE! I CALL IT "A SONG OF ICE AND FIRE."
UH, JOHNNY...
CAN YOU BRING BACK THE YOUNG BOBBY? I MISS HIM.
HAPPY BIRTHDAY. I SPENT TWO HOURS KEEPING YOUR PARENTS FROM ASKING EVERYONE INAPPROPRIATE QUESTIONS.
KITTY, I LOVE YOU THIIIIIIS MUCH.
YOU BETTER!
FIGURED YOU'D NEED THIS.
YOU'RE SO KIND, SIMON.
WELL, I DIDN'T GET YOU A GIFT, SO...
THERE'S NOTHING SERIOUS TO PURSUE BETWEEN US, BUT IF YOU WANT--
LEMMEGO-SAYHITOMY-PARENTSANDWE'LL-GETTHEHECK-OUTTAHERE.

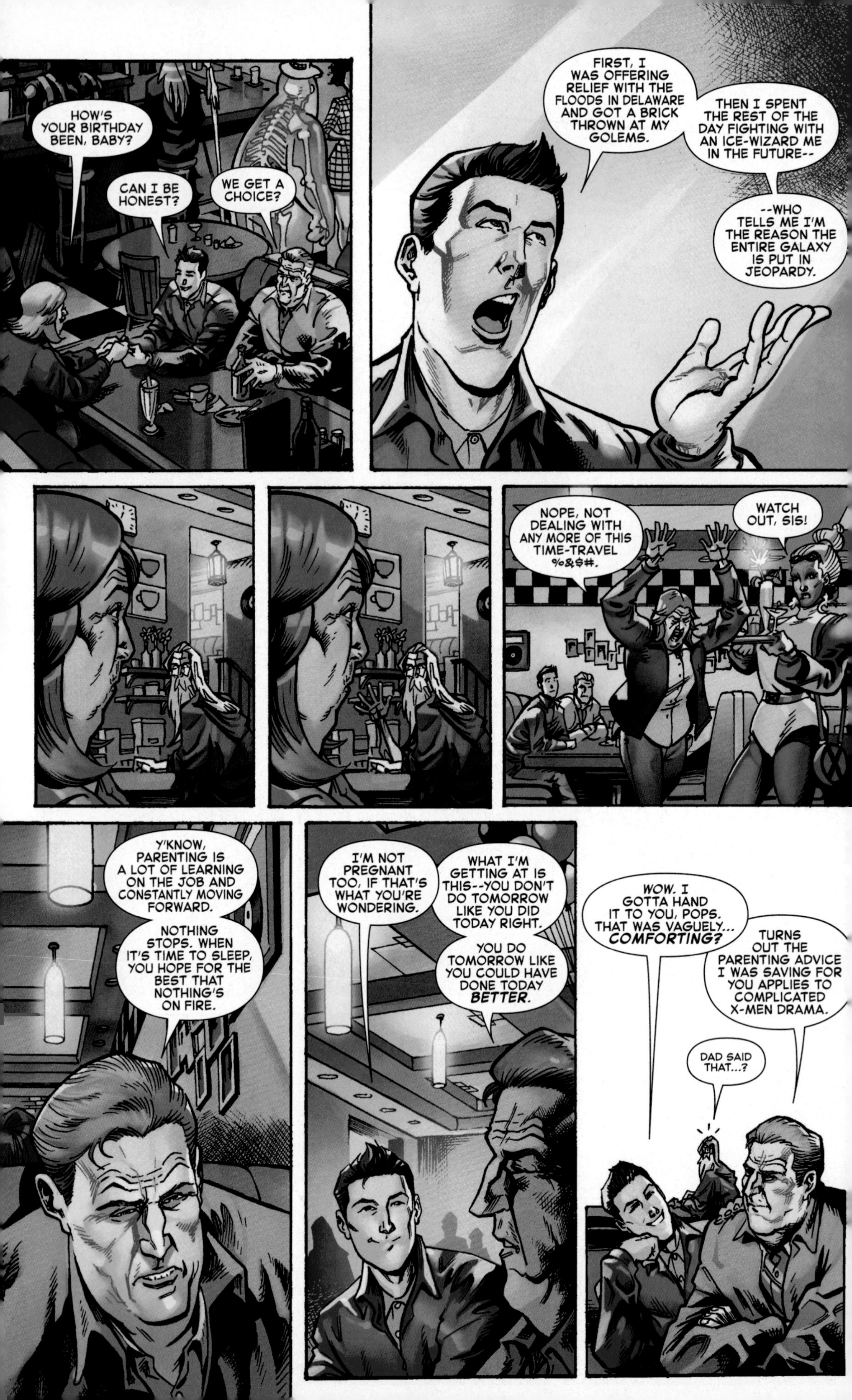
HOW'S YOUR BIRTHDAY BEEN, BABY?
CAN I BE HONEST?
WE GET A CHOICE?
FIRST, I WAS OFFERING RELIEF WITH THE FLOODS IN DELAWARE AND GOT A BRICK THROWN AT MY GOLEMS.
THEN I SPENT THE REST OF THE DAY FIGHTING WITH AN ICE-WIZARD ME IN THE FUTURE--
--WHO TELLS ME I'M THE REASON THE ENTIRE GALAXY IS PUT IN JEOPARDY.
NOPE, NOT DEALING WITH ANY MORE OF THIS TIME-TRAVEL %&$#.
WATCH OUT, SIS!
Y'KNOW, PARENTING IS A LOT OF LEARNING ON THE JOB AND CONSTANTLY MOVING FORWARD.
NOTHING STOPS. WHEN IT'S TIME TO SLEEP, YOU HOPE FOR THE BEST THAT NOTHING'S ON FIRE.
I'M NOT PREGNANT TOO, IF THAT'S WHAT YOU'RE WONDERING.
WHAT I'M GETTING AT IS THIS--YOU DON'T DO TOMORROW LIKE YOU DID TODAY RIGHT.
YOU DO TOMORROW LIKE YOU COULD HAVE DONE TODAY BETTER.
WOW. I GOTTA HAND IT TO YOU, POPS. THAT WAS VAGUELY... COMFORTING?
TURNS OUT THE PARENTING ADVICE I WAS SAVING FOR YOU APPLIES TO COMPLICATED X-MEN DRAMA.
DAD SAID THAT...?

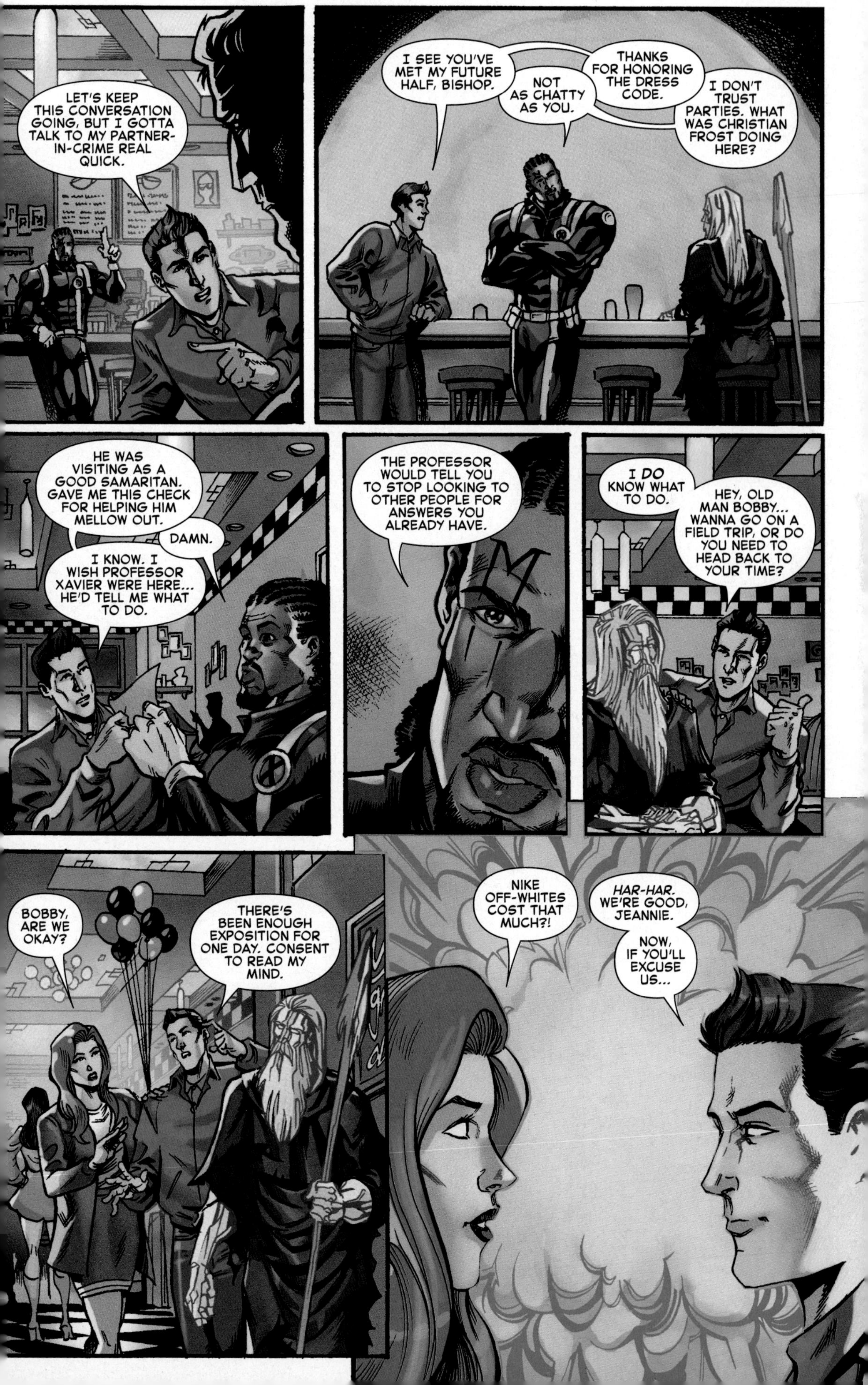

LET'S KEEP THIS CONVERSATION GOING, BUT I GOTTA TALK TO MY PARTNER-IN-CRIME REAL QUICK.
I SEE YOU'VE MET MY FUTURE HALF, BISHOP.
NOT AS CHATTY AS YOU.
THANKS FOR HONORING THE DRESS CODE.
I DON'T TRUST PARTIES. WHAT WAS CHRISTIAN FROST DOING HERE?
HE WAS VISITING AS A GOOD SAMARITAN. GAVE ME THIS CHECK FOR HELPING HIM MELLOW OUT.
DAMN.
I KNOW. I WISH PROFESSOR XAVIER WERE HERE... HE'D TELL ME WHAT TO DO.
THE PROFESSOR WOULD TELL YOU TO STOP LOOKING TO OTHER PEOPLE FOR ANSWERS YOU ALREADY HAVE.
I *DO* KNOW WHAT TO DO.
HEY, OLD MAN BOBBY... WANNA GO ON A FIELD TRIP, OR DO YOU NEED TO HEAD BACK TO YOUR TIME?
BOBBY, ARE WE OKAY?
THERE'S BEEN ENOUGH EXPOSITION FOR ONE DAY. CONSENT TO READ MY MIND.
NIKE OFF-WHITES COST THAT MUCH?!
HAR-HAR. WE'RE GOOD, JEANNIE.
NOW, IF YOU'LL EXCUSE US...

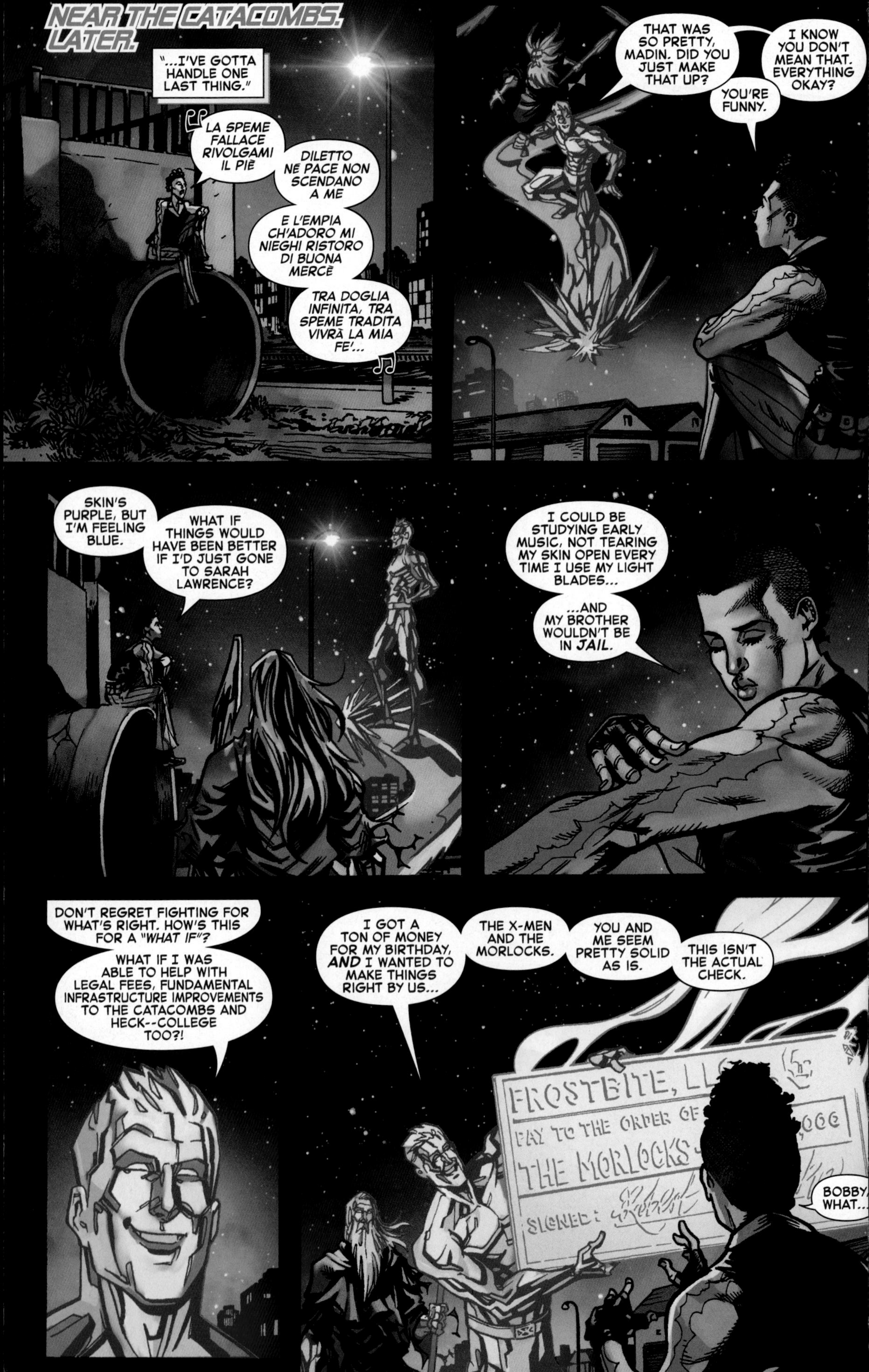
NEAR THE CATACOMBS. LATER.
"...I'VE GOTTA HANDLE ONE LAST THING."
LA SPEME FALLACE RIVOLGAMI IL PIÈ
DILETTO NÉ PACE NON SCENDANO A ME
E L'EMPIA CH'ADORO MI NIEGHI RISTORO DI BUONA MERCÈ
TRA DOGLIA INFINITA, TRA SPEME TRADITA VIVRÀ LA MIA FE'...
THAT WAS SO PRETTY, MADIN. DID YOU JUST MAKE THAT UP?
YOU'RE FUNNY.
I KNOW YOU DON'T MEAN THAT. EVERYTHING OKAY?
SKIN'S PURPLE, BUT I'M FEELING BLUE.
WHAT IF THINGS WOULD HAVE BEEN BETTER IF I'D JUST GONE TO SARAH LAWRENCE?
I COULD BE STUDYING EARLY MUSIC, NOT TEARING MY SKIN OPEN EVERY TIME I USE MY LIGHT BLADES...
...AND MY BROTHER WOULDN'T BE IN JAIL.
DON'T REGRET FIGHTING FOR WHAT'S RIGHT. HOW'S THIS FOR A "WHAT IF"?
WHAT IF I WAS ABLE TO HELP WITH LEGAL FEES, FUNDAMENTAL INFRASTRUCTURE IMPROVEMENTS TO THE CATACOMBS AND HECK--COLLEGE TOO?!
I GOT A TON OF MONEY FOR MY BIRTHDAY, AND I WANTED TO MAKE THINGS RIGHT BY US...
THE X-MEN AND THE MORLOCKS.
YOU AND ME SEEM PRETTY SOLID AS IS.
THIS ISN'T THE ACTUAL CHECK.
FROSTBITE, LL
PAY TO THE ORDER OF
THE MORLOCKS
SIGNED:
BOBBY, WHAT...

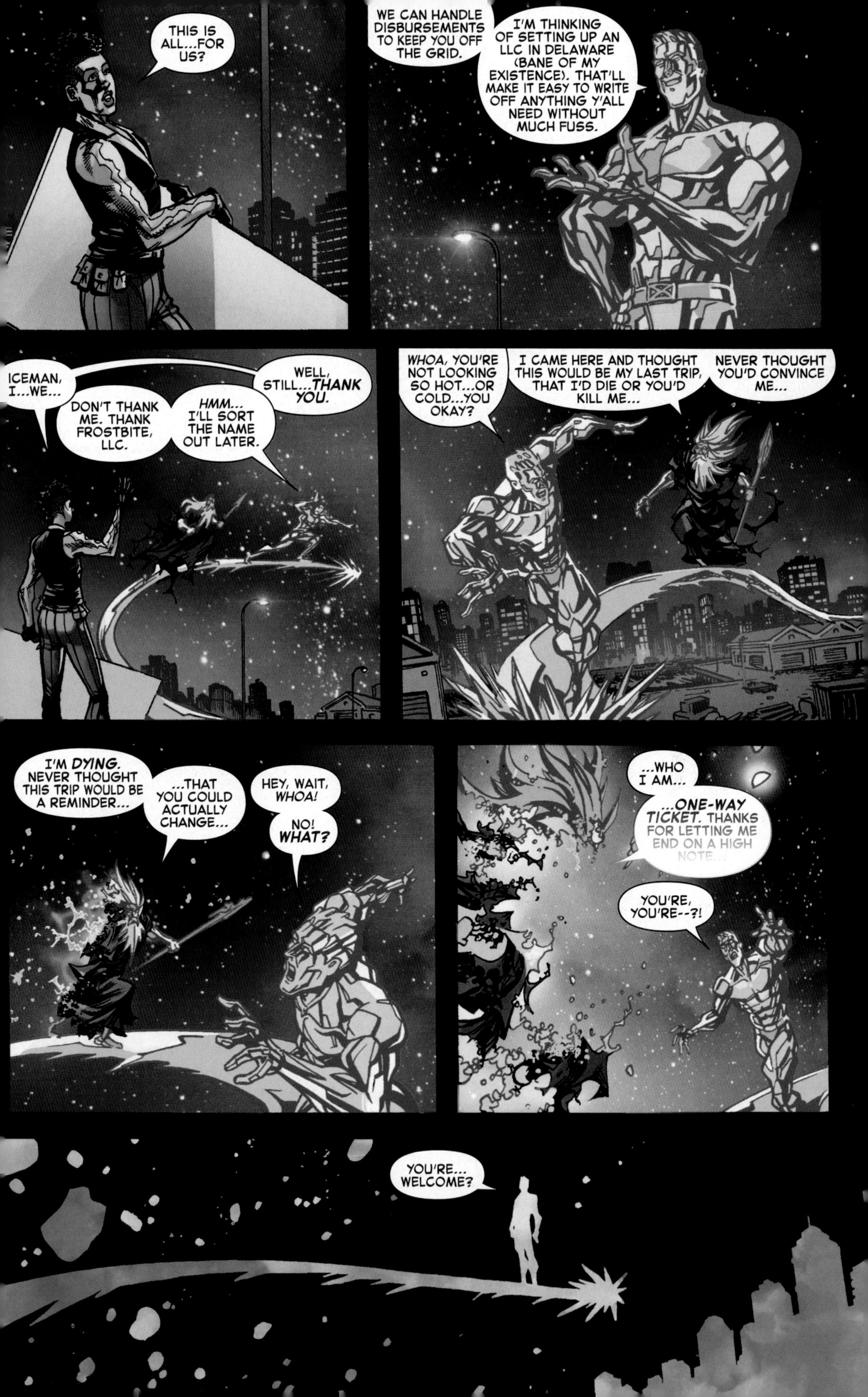
THIS IS ALL...FOR US?
WE CAN HANDLE DISBURSEMENTS TO KEEP YOU OFF THE GRID.
I'M THINKING OF SETTING UP AN LLC IN DELAWARE (BANE OF MY EXISTENCE). THAT'LL MAKE IT EASY TO WRITE OFF ANYTHING Y'ALL NEED WITHOUT MUCH FUSS.
ICEMAN, I...WE...
DON'T THANK ME. THANK FROSTBITE, LLC.
HMM... I'LL SORT THE NAME OUT LATER.
WELL, STILL...THANK YOU.
WHOA, YOU'RE NOT LOOKING SO HOT...OR COLD...YOU OKAY?
I CAME HERE AND THOUGHT THIS WOULD BE MY LAST TRIP, THAT I'D DIE OR YOU'D KILL ME...
NEVER THOUGHT YOU'D CONVINCE ME...
I'M DYING. NEVER THOUGHT THIS TRIP WOULD BE A REMINDER...
...THAT YOU COULD ACTUALLY CHANGE...
HEY, WAIT, WHOA!
NO! WHAT?
...WHO I AM...
...ONE-WAY TICKET. THANKS FOR LETTING ME END ON A HIGH NOTE...
YOU'RE, YOU'RE--?!
YOU'RE... WELCOME?

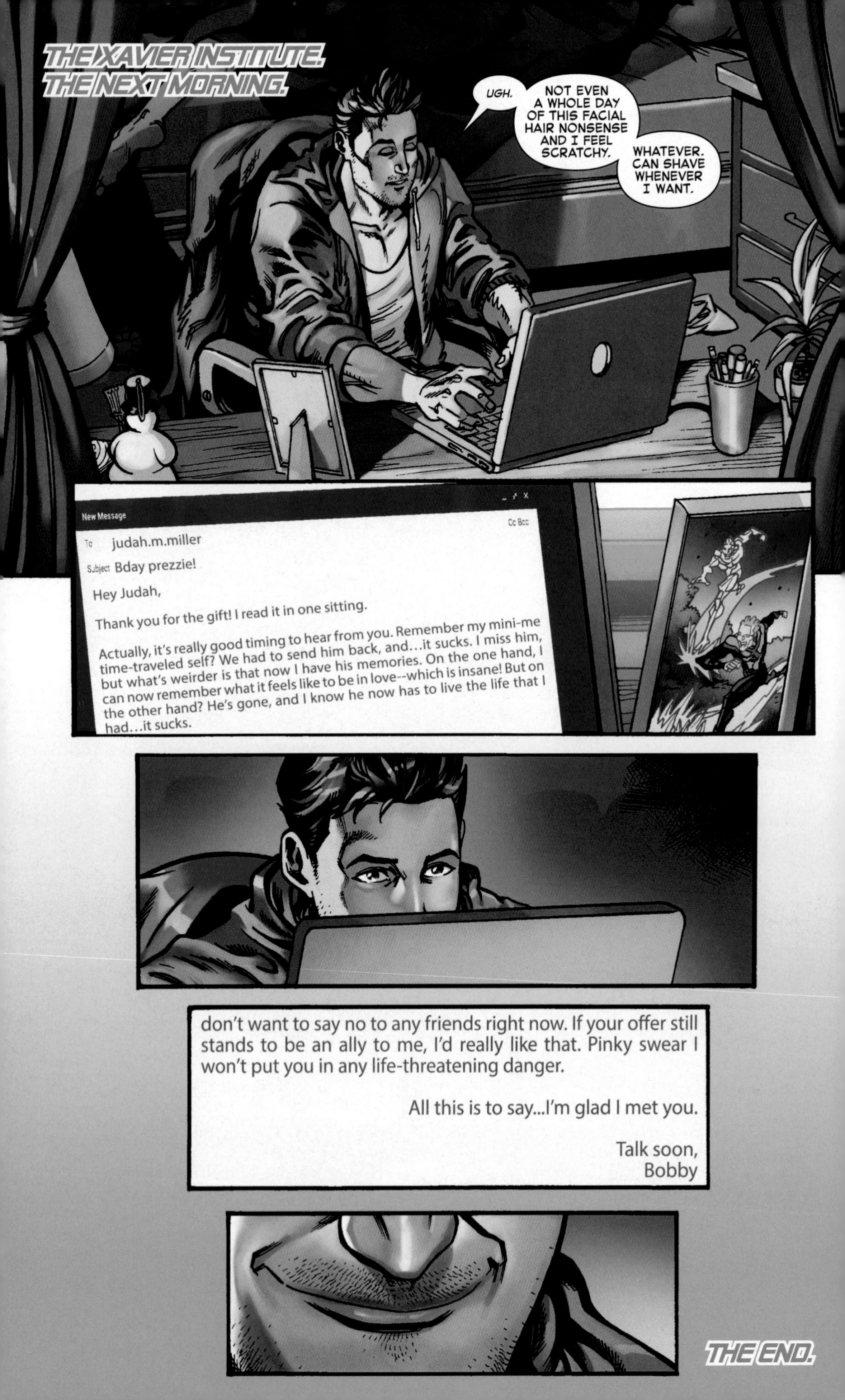
THE XAVIER INSTITUTE. THE NEXT MORNING.
UGH.
NOT EVEN A WHOLE DAY OF THIS FACIAL HAIR NONSENSE AND I FEEL SCRATCHY.
WHATEVER. CAN SHAVE WHENEVER I WANT.
New Message
Cc Bcc
To judah.m.miller
Subject Bday prezzie!
Hey Judah,
Thank you for the gift! I read it in one sitting.
Actually, it's really good timing to hear from you. Remember my mini-me time-traveled self? We had to send him back, and…it sucks. I miss him, but what's weirder is that now I have his memories. On the one hand, I can now remember what it feels like to be in love--which is insane! But on the other hand? He's gone, and I know he now has to live the life that I had…it sucks.
don't want to say no to any friends right now. If your offer still stands to be an ally to me, I'd really like that. Pinky swear I won't put you in any life-threatening danger.
All this is to say...I'm glad I met you.
Talk soon,
Bobby
THE END.

DARKVEIL

REAL NAME: Darnell Wade
OCCUPATION: Retail
IDENTITY: Secret-ish
LEGAL STATUS: American Citizen with no criminal record
FORMER ALIASES: Shade
PLACE OF BIRTH: Crown Heights, Brooklyn, New York
MARITAL STATUS: Single, but not without suitors
KNOWN RELATIVES: None (that we know of)
GROUP AFFILIATION: None
BASE OF OPERATIONS: Brooklyn, New York
FIRST APPEARANCE: ICEMAN (2018) #4

ORIGIN: While some kids saw their super heroes fighting the good fight on TV or on phones, Darnell Wade heard it on his rooftops, saw it out his windows and felt them everywhere in New York City. Passed around Brooklyn's foster care system, Darnell always knew there were heroes everywhere, but none close enough to help save him from a world of hard knocks.

Now an adult in his mid-20s, the never-on-time and always-broke Darnell barely makes ends meet working at a used clothing store while moonlighting as Shade, a drag queen inspired by New York's super heroes. She and BFF queen Spillin' Tea-yana Taylor run a lip-sync night in Astoria, hoping to get on a drag competition show. Tea gets picked without her partner and brings a reality crew to film her snubbing Shade while taking their duo show away from her. The rock hits bottom when Darnell comes home to find his electricity has been shut off.

Disconsolate, Darnell wishes he could just disappear...and that's when his mutant powers emerge. Darnell's fan becomes imbued with Darkforce, allowing him to create pocket voids. A "shopping spree" at a makeup store with a fellow queen goes awry when the cops come, and Darnell loses his friend while escaping through the Darkforce. From that point on, Darnell vows to never use the Darkforce unless he's bringing joy in drag as the newly minted and newly solo Darkveil. With a power so dark, he chooses to use it only as a means of creating light in the world. ■

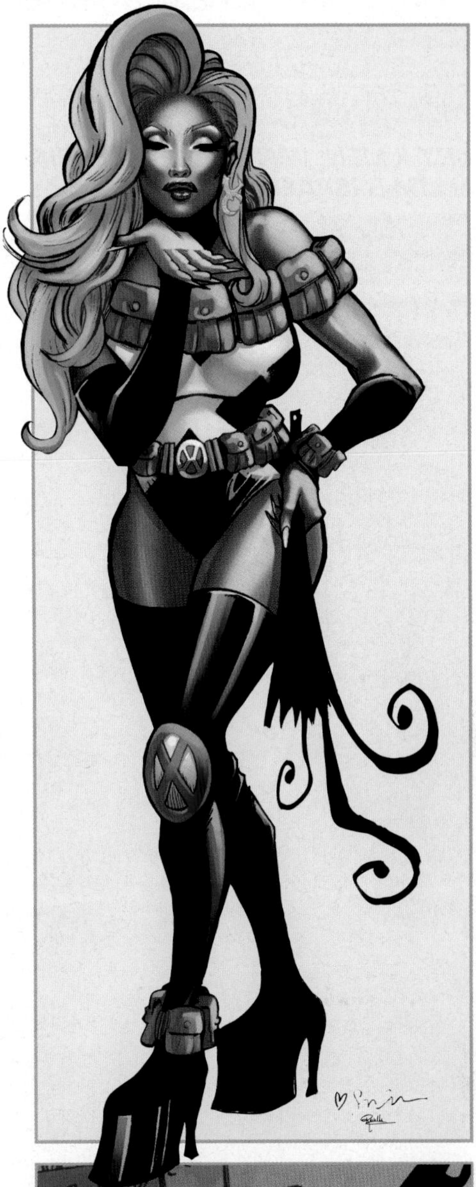

Text and Art by Sina Grace. Colors by Rachelle Rosenberg.

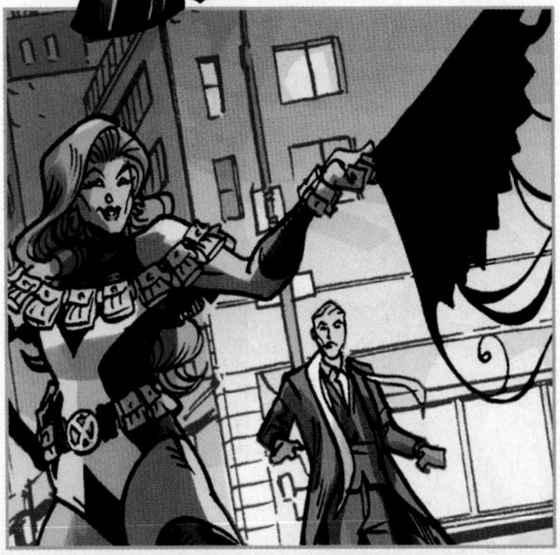

Art by Nathan Stockman. Colors by Federico Blee.

HEIGHT: 6' (6'7" in heels!)
WEIGHT: Never ask a lady!
EYES: Brown with purple contacts
EYESHADOW PALETTE: Pine blended with gold highlights
HAIR: Chartreuse
LIP COLOR: Amethyst, but she won't say no to a Royal Ruby

POWERS: Darkveil possesses the mutant ability to manipulate/control darkness and shadow, due to her connection to the Darkforce, a powerful extradimensional energy. This includes teleportation of self and others through this dimension.

She's also been graced with an impeccable wit and is a lip-sync assassin.

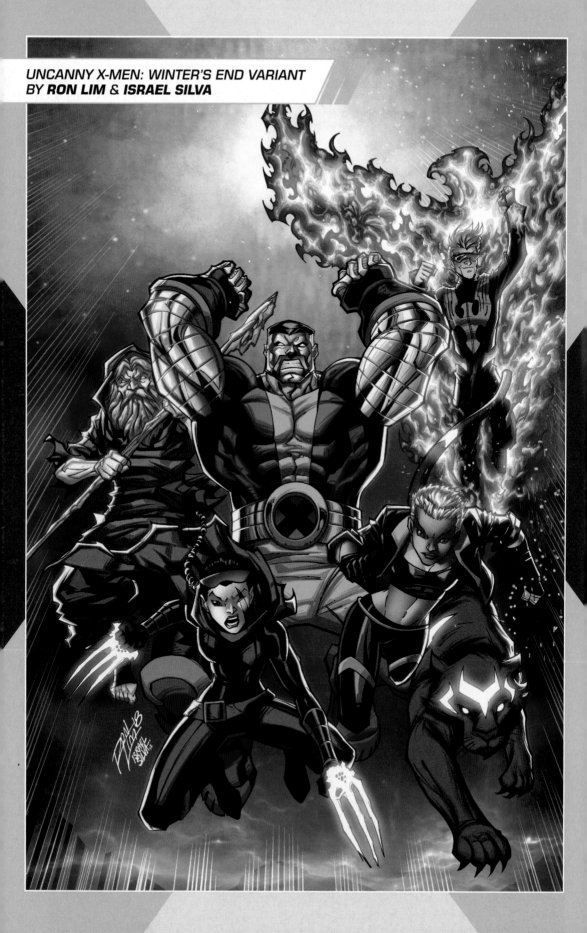

UNCANNY X-MEN: WINTER'S END VARIANT
BY **RON LIM** & **ISRAEL SILVA**